THE GOLDEN AGE OF BOXING ON RADIO AND TELEVISION

A BLOW-BY-BLOW HISTORY FROM 1921 TO 1964

FREDERICK V. ROMANO

CARREL BOOKS

Carrel Books may be purchased in bulk at special discounts for sales promotion, corporate gifts, fund-raising, or educational purposes. Special editions can also be created to specifications. For details, contact the Special Sales Department, Carrel Books, 307 West 36th Street, 11th Floor, New York, NY 10018 or sportspubbooks@skyhorsepublishing.com.

Carrel Books® is a registered trademark of Skyhorse Publishing, Inc.®, a Delaware corporation.

Visit our website at www.carrelbooks.com.

10 9 8 7 6 5 4 3 2 1

Library of Congress Cataloging-in-Publication Data is available on file.

Cover design by Tom Lau
Cover photo courtesy of AP Images

ISBN: 978-1-63144-074-8
Ebook ISBN: 978-1-63144-075-5

Printed in the United States of America

To my mother and father, Rosemarie and Fred Romano,
for their unwavering support and for always taking seriously
my love for the sweet-sickness that is boxing.

CONTENTS

ACKNOWLEDGMENTS

It is with sincere gratitude that I would like to thank the following: The New York Public Library and its staff at both the Science, Industry, and Business Library in Manhattan and the Bronx Library Center; professional boxing referee Vic de Wysocki, who provided numerous vintage television shows from his vast boxing video collection; Radio Yesteryear, whose radio catalog proved an indispensable resource; the many boxing writers who have come before me who have written boxing articles and books that I have relied upon; those who have contributed to the warehouse of information on the Internet, particularly those who have exponentially expanded the availability of boxing video; the people at ProQuest who have made the arduous task of researching significantly more palatable; and special thanks to my sister, Lisa Romano Licht, who served as my presubmission editor for this volume.

INTRODUCTION

While much has been written about boxing from the 1920s through the early-1960s, there has not been a comprehensive treatment of the era specifically and exclusively from the prisms of radio and television. Those media were as important to both the development and portrayal of the sport as they were to the reshaping of our culture.

The Golden Age of Boxing on Radio and Television explores the many roles that each medium played in both the development and depiction of the sport. Principal topics covered are the ever-changing role in technology during the period of more than four decades; how the media impacted the manner in which the sport was presented to its public audience; the exponential growth of those audiences; and the impact radio and television had on the financial aspects of the sport. The selective use of radio and television and the financial boom that they created are also examined.

Additionally, the book assays radio and boxing during the Second World War; the role of organized crime and the monopolistic practices during the television era; a comprehensive look at the announcers who brought the action to the listeners and viewers; the many appearances that boxers made on radio and television when not in the ring; and the media's portrayal of the sport in an array of dramatic, comedic, and other programming.

PART I
RADIO

RADIO PROLOGUE

A. The Newspaper Industry and Boxing

To place the story of radio and the sport of boxing in proper context, it is helpful to understand the relationship between boxing and the newspaper industry as well as radio's displacement of that industry.

Prior to the commercialization and proliferation of radio in the 1920s, the undisputed communicator of contemporaneous events and information was the newspaper industry. To appreciate the power of the printed press during the preradio era, one need only to consider the telling fact that both 1920 US Presidential nominees, Warren G. Harding and James M. Cox, were newspaper publishers.[1]

During this era, major cities offered multiple publications, and many printed more than one edition daily. Other than attending a boxing match in person, a newspaper was the only means to obtain information about the fight game in a timely way. Magazines filled an important niche but were limited in number and reached the newsstands as much as a month after events occurred. The daily newspaper, however, could give almost immediate fight results. For example, a fight on a Friday evening in New York City could be reported in a late edition hitting the newsstands that very same evening. If the fight didn't make the late edition, it could be reported in the early morning paper, to be consumed with breakfast.

At the beginning of the twentieth century, boxing was not a legalized sport in the state of New York. Gotham had yet to ascend to the prominent role it would maintain for fifty years as the epicenter of the boxing world. Therefore, many major bouts of the era were fought in California, and the sport was West Coast-centric.

New York State took its first step to establish its dominance of the fight game in 1911, when the passage of the Frawley Law legalized boxing.[2] Legalization came with a caveat: matches would be "boxing exhibitions," with a maximum of ten rounds. A "no decision" would be rendered at the end of the bout if it did not end earlier by knockout.[3] New York was not the only state to adopt no-decision rules during this era. Other significant fight locations such as Pennsylvania, New Jersey, and Illinois passed similar laws.

The no-decision clause was inserted into the Frawley Bill and other eastern states' laws primarily for two reasons. First, it served to placate a portion of the public that objected to boxing's brutality and preferred that the sport be made illegal. It was believed by some that no-decisions would remove a fighter's incentive to fight viciously, and consequently, the barbaric element of the sport would be curbed. In practice, this notion was ludicrous; the rule had just the opposite effect. The no-decision rule actually made the knockout the only definitive means of distinction between the two fighters and, consequently, a highly coveted commodity.

Second, it was believed that the no-decision clause would serve to hold in check a voracious betting public under the theory that a definitive decision was a prerequisite to wagering. This reasoning was also flawed. Bets could still be waged on a knockout result. As for bouts that went the distance, it was the newspapers that filled the void. Once the no-decision rule was put in place, gamblers agreed to rely on a given newspaper's writer, letting his unofficial, written opinion stand as the final arbitrator of the bet. More sophisticated bettors would create a pool of judges by polling a number of different newspapers, letting the majority decision rule.

The no-decision rule spawned a system that was ripe for abuse. The newspaper industry—in theory an objective news source—became complicit in delivering a distorted version of the sport. It was common knowledge that bribes were given to and accepted by some newspaper writers. Sometimes, an unscrupulous manager would sway an unequally savory writer onto his fighter's payroll to ensure repeated favorable results.[4] As the nearly exclusive reporter of boxing, newspapers had been charged with the great responsibility of accurately reporting the fight game, but too often they failed. Between the corrupt decisions and an occasional legitimate difference of opinion, "newspaper decisions" varied greatly.

The 1921 bantamweight championship between Johnny Buff and Jabez White, held in Jersey City, New Jersey, illustrates how newspaper reporters sometimes created boxing's own version of Kurosowa's *Rashamon.* The *New York Globe* reported: "When the smoke cleared away at the bout's close, Buff had another victory to his ever increasing collection. Buff outfought and outgeneraled his heavier opponent all the way."[5] At the *Sun,* another local New York paper, the reporter saw the fight as follows: "Johnny Buff and Jebez White staged a give-and-take fight for twelve rounds. Each boxer jabbed carefully during the bout, ready to cross with the right, but the fight ended in a draw."[6] In still another interpretation, the sportswriter at the *New York Evening Mail* wrote that "Jabez White demonstrated his superiority over Johnny Buff, bantam champion. White was credited with having seven out of the twelve sessions."[7] Such a disparity of opinion was not uncommon. When the no-decision rule ebbed and was finally erased from the sport in the latter part of the 1920s, the peculiar era of newspapermen serendipitously acting as judges came to a merciful end. The newspaper industry's entanglement in the no-decision debacle was a black mark on its record, obscured only by the public's reliance upon it for fight news.

Newspaper publication was still on the rise during the end of World War I. Despite the swift growth of radio, print maintained its dominant position as the overwhelming source of daily news, including boxing news, for most Americans throughout the 1920s. Newspapers had dominated daily communications for hundreds of years. In 1929, they were enjoying all-time high revenues, twenty times those of radio. Nevertheless, in the brief period of a decade, radio's exponential growth was evidence of its potential to present the newspaper industry with legitimate competition. Radio advertising revenues were exploding, increasing tenfold from $4 million in 1927 to $40 million in 1929.[8] Radio broadcasts of boxing matches were attracting tens of millions of listeners over newly established national networks with their own sponsors contributing to the financial boom.

The advent of commercial radio at the beginning of the 1920s immediately raised the suspicions of newspaper publishers.[9] As the radio industry would invest in television a generation later, fortuitous publishers started radio stations of their own although initially believing that radio would primarily service their newspaper enterprises.

The *Detroit News, Chicago Tribune, Los Angeles Times, Atlanta Journal,* and *Chicago Daily News* all promptly established radio stations. Industry giant William Randolph Hearst went on to develop a series of radio stations under the banner of Hearst Radio, Inc.[10]

The newspaper industry displayed soothsayer-like abilities in its early awareness of the threat of slow-forming competitive storms. However, it possessed only a limited ability to avert the dire consequences. The influence of the newspaper industry would be permanently degraded at the hands of radio, exploding during the Depression and pushing publishers into rapid decline by the eve of World War II. During that era, boxing broadcasts overtook newspapers as the most significant communicator of the sport to the public. Newspapers still performed the important but secondary function of providing the buildup for boxing events, as well as postfight summations and analysis. Ironically, one short generation later, television would undo the significance of radio in a similar fashion—minimizing that industry and its role in the boxing world even more rapidly.

B. The Relationship Between "Fight Films" and Radio

During the same period in which the newspaper and radio industries competed for dominance, the medium of film provided a complementary method of reporting boxing news. Filmed boxing matches and other activities related to the bout, such as the weigh-in, were commonly referred to as "fight films."

The term *fight film* has a number of connotations. During the golden age of radio, it usually described a motion picture of a boxing match captured on film stock for later playback at a movie theater or similar forum. Similar boxing content of a shorter duration was also made available in theaters in the form of feature stories or brief vignettes and news items. This filmed material was part of a longer, multisubject program commonly referred to as newsreel.

Fight films were commercially important for a number of reasons. A compelling match on radio was certain to cultivate a large viewing audience eager to see what they had listened to. Additionally, if an important or entertaining bout was not presented on radio, and only ticket holders saw the event, an even greater audience was provided. Typically, these bouts were shown during the ensuing week while interest was still keen. When Max Schmeling shocked Joe Louis and the world in their first match on June 19, 1936, the film was rushed into movie theaters within a few days. These boxing films often played as part of a double bill with a movie, as was the case with Louis-Schmeling I. They were also subject to film critiques: "Strictly on performance basis, Joe Louis and Max Schmeling are giving a better account of themselves on the Rialto's screen these days than John Howard, Frances Farmer, Grant Withers and the other lads engaged in a melodramatic trifle called *Border Flight,*" one newspaper reviewer noted.[1]

Due to the expense, filming was reserved for championship contests and other high-profile matches with a high probability of drawing theater audiences. This economic factor defined the role of the fight film in boxing—a specialized commodity that carried a disproportionate significance.

Sometimes a fight of great interest would extend its stay, just like a successful Broadway play. When Ernie Schaaf died at the hands of Primo Carnera from injuries sustained at Madison Square Garden during a Depression-era contest, the film of the tragic affair played to large audiences and was "held over" at the Mayfair in New York.[2]

Because of the racial violence precipitated by the national viewing of the 1910 Jack Johnson-James J. Jeffries bout, a law was passed two years later prohibiting the movement of fight films in interstate commerce. Practically speaking, this meant that it was illegal to transfer boxing films over state lines. For example, films of a match contested in New York City could not be viewed in Newark, New Jersey, just a few miles away. In effect, the viewing of these films was reduced to parochial affairs. Since many of the fights filmed were held in New York or other large cities like Chicago, they were still capable of drawing large local audiences. However, these gatherings paled in comparison to the lost potential national viewership.

The law, which remained in effect until 1940, was regularly enforced. Promoter George "Tex" Rickard was fined $7,000 for a violation in connection with Dempsey-Carpentier fight films. At the time, indictments were also pending for a similar offense: transportation of films of the Rickard-promoted Dempsey-Firpo bout from New York to New Jersey.[3]

The logic of "state lines" determining who could view a bout was suspect at best. Perhaps more incredible was another notion that the showing of these films in the state where they were filmed could also be banned under existing censorship laws. The issue was credible enough for the State Motion Picture Commission to make inquiry with the New York Attorney General in connection with the 1926 Paul Berlenbach-Young Stribling bout. Fortunately for fight fans in New York, it was ruled that such pictures constituted permissible current events or pictorial news within the censorship law.[4]

Years later, when early television broadcasting arrived, the issue of whether telecasts transmitted over state lines would be in violation of the interstate commerce law was raised.[5] However, by the time the question arrived, it had become moot. The fight film law was patently antiquated, if not inherently illogical, and in 1940 it was repealed.

Undoubtedly, the fight film law increased the value of a radio broadcast. Radio was the only option outside the live arena to truly experience the fight unless you were local to the fight and could view a theatrical release. Before television, fight films and radio broadcasting coexisted as complementary media offering a combined audio and visual accounting of the sport. However, it was a fragmented presentation, an imperfection that was eventually resolved by television.

Another disadvantage of fight films that TV ameliorated was their lack of immediacy. As soon as big-time boxing made it to television with the first Baer-Nova bout in 1939, this glaring deficiency was immediately confirmed: "This seeing by radio is far more exciting than watching a belated and cut newsreel of such warfare, because here the result is in suspense, it may be revealed at any moment on the screen," noted one viewer.[6]

From a historical perspective, the great value of the fight film is the visual record of the sport created prior to 1947 and the advent of kinescope—the preservationist of boxing on early television. Without these films, a visual ring record of Jack Johnson, Jack Dempsey, Gene Tunney, Mickey Walker, or Joe Louis in his prime would not exist. Likewise, the skills of the great little men such as Benny Leonard, Kid Chocolate, Tony Canzoneri, Barney Ross, and Jimmy McLarnin would have been lost forever. Indeed, before radio recordings circa 1930, almost the entire period of gloved fighting up to that time is preserved only on film.

Even for the period after kinescope arrived in the late 1940s, these fight films maintain a significant value due to their superior visual quality to those of televised recordings. Additionally, only a small number of television kinescopes remain, often leaving the fight film as the only surviving recording. Today, these fight films are frequently featured in boxing historical retrospectives, documentary films, and news items, reflecting their equal role with radio and television in the preservation of boxing history.

PREFACE

The golden age of boxing on radio spans two milestones of the sport. It began just after Jack Dempsey's ascension to the heavyweight crown in 1919 and lasted into the twilight of Joe Louis's heavyweight reign and his retirement in 1949. The Dempsey era of the Roaring Twenties was spearheaded by promoter Tex Rickard. The Louis period from the late Depression through World War II and its immediate aftermath was orchestrated by Rickard protégé Mike Jacobs.

In between Rickard and Jacobs, a stagnant period of five or six years featured neither a star heavyweight champion nor a memorable promoter. This faceless epoch can appropriately be labeled the "Madison Square Garden Era" for that corporation's promotional dominance.

Because of the enormous popularity of Dempsey and Louis, press coverage of their fights was disproportionate to that of other boxers, even fellow champions of the period. Therefore, the historical record is slanted in favor of the pair.

More specifically, the broadcast of Dempsey and Louis fights, as well as other information relating to those broadcasts, were much more widely memorialized in newspapers and other print media than the vast majority of the other fights aired on the radio during the same period. Consequently, the broadcast of radio, from both a technical and anecdotal standpoint, was fairly well preserved for those fighters and their fights. Conversely, specific information about radio broadcasts of fighters in other divisions, even those other ring greats, exists in a much more limited breadth and scope.

That is not to say that radio did not cover these other fighters and fights. In fact, many of the boxing radio broadcasts from 1930 to 1950 featured championship contests. Other broadcasts were comprised of nonchampionship bouts featuring contenders, former contenders, rising prospects, journeymen, and a host of amateur boxers. At the height of these broadcasts, these fighters were collectively heard several times weekly.

Unfortunately, not as much about these broadcasts is known: the machinations of how the broadcasts were realized by the promoters; the technical triumphs and gaffes of putting the events on the air; the events' social context from who listened to the fights to where they gathered to listen, to why the fights were important to them. For many broadcasts, only a fragmented view of the past can be parceled together from an incomplete record.

The history of boxing on the radio during the 1920s is preserved exclusively in the records of print media because virtually no audio broadcasts have survived. During most of this decade, although there were many fewer broadcasts, a focus on the social and technological significance of those broadcasts was often highlighted in print coverage.

Conversely, the record of boxing radio during the 1930s and '40s is almost diametrically opposed. By the end of the twenties, radio as an event had become passé. Print media during the subsequent decades often took a passive role with regard to radio. Often the routine mention of the time and station of a broadcast and the percentages of radio receipts the fighters received were the only "radio perspective" deemed worthy of coverage. As a result, the historical record of boxing on radio during the Depression, war years, and beyond is disproportionately reflected in whatever has survived of the actual broadcasts themselves.

This volume is a reflection of the historical record. Great fighters such as Harry Greb, Harry Wills, Tony Canzoneri, Henry Armstrong, Barney Ross, Tony Zale, Sugar Ray Robinson, and Beau Jack figured prominently in the broadcast of the sport. Any broader coverage in these pages of fighters such as Dempsey or Louis is merely a reflection of that record.

Chapter 1

FROM FANCY TO PHENOMENON: THE SEMINAL BOXING BROADCASTS

While the rise of radio may never be associated with the simultaneous three-division boxing champion Henry Armstrong, he nevertheless shares the birth date of December 12 with the medium. On that date in 1901, Italian inventor Guglielmo Marconi took a major step in revolutionizing communications. Marconi ran a box kite up a group of thin wires that acted as an antenna. This resulted in the transmission of a simple three-dot Morse code message representing the letter "S."[1]

Unlike Samuel B. Morse's revolutionary code transmission in 1835 that traveled via wire, Marconi's signal carried through the air without a conduit. It journeyed over 2,000 nautical miles from St. John's, New Foundland, across the Atlantic Ocean to its final destination in England. The faint sound created by the keying of the dot-dot-dot message in North America was received by Marconi in Cornwall.[2] Within the next fifteen years, Marconi's "wireless" went from transmitting simple dot-dash Morse code signals to music and voice transmissions. The foundation for modern radio had been laid.[3]

Several years later, in 1920, commercial radio launched its first regular broadcast from Westinghouse Electric and Manufacturing Companies station KDKA, Pittsburgh. The following year, a few other radio stations joined the airwaves.[4] Radio quickly developed a number of nicknames including "the wireless." Radio transmissions were also called "telephony," broadcasting by "radio telephone," "talking through the ether," or other technically descriptive terminology.

While early radio was perceived by the public as a technological marvel, its practical applications and permanent nature were initially overlooked. Radio was considered to be the latest fad, a novelty that provided whimsical amusement carrying "word pictures" on its "invisible wings." One advertisement for a radio company featured the picture of a little girl marveling before the Radiola. A caption explained her belief that the invention "brings to her the voice of the Man in the Moon—from up in the sky."[5] A songwriter was inspired to write the fanciful ballet *Kiss Me by Wireless* after hearing the voice of actress Norma Shearer over the "radio phone."[6] Audacious couples took their wedding vows on the air, and it was reported that they were "married by radio." "It's the latest thing," the public was informed.[7]

Ironically, a form of entertainment—sports—with boxing at its forefront would play a major role in the development of radio. The broadcast of boxing was a seminal contributor to the establishment of radio's financial viability, as well as an early mirror of changing social norms.

The relationship between boxing and early radio was a natural fit. Since boxing matches are scheduled well in advance, problems relating to equipment setup was minimal. A stationary ring also eliminated the necessity for any movement of equipment once the initial hookup was completed. While today's technology has made such logistics moot, they were critical to early broadcasting. Additionally, with the somewhat repetitive actions of only two participants, the listening audience could clearly visualize the ring action in their mind's eye.

The first boxing match broadcast on radio occurred on April 11, 1921, with KDKA's transmission of a bout between Johnny Ray and

Johnny Dundee from Pittsburgh's Duquesne Garden.[8] Boxing's first broadcaster was Harold W. Arlin, a KDKA announcer who was also the first person to be employed as a full-time radio announcer and the first to broadcast a major league baseball game.[9, 10, 11] The experimental broadcast of the Ray-Dundee match has long been forgotten by all except a few radio historians. Even boxing historians tend to omit it from boxing's "firsts," often citing the O'Gatty-McFarland fight on the Dempsey-Carpentier undercard as the first boxing broadcast.[12]

Due to the significance of the match and the scope of the broadcast attempted, the Jack Dempsey-Georges Carpentier heavyweight championship bout, a Tex Rickard–chaperoned event a few months later, would serve as the true courting stage for the marriage of technology and sport. Rickard's adventurous partner in this grand-scale experiment was communication prodigy David Sarnoff, a former Marconi employee. While working for Marconi in 1912 as a wireless operator stationed in Nantucket Island, Massachusetts, Sarnoff was one of the few who received distress signals from the sinking Titanic.[13] Now employed by RCA, he was looking for a high-profile event to catapult RCA into broadcasting. He found it in Dempsey-Carpentier.[14]

Some claim that Sarnoff's role in orchestrating the broadcast was embellished over time, a rewriting of history that squeezed several key players out of the story.[15] Reports contemporaneous with the event indicate that the idea to broadcast the bout originated with Julius Hopp, manager of concerts at Madison Square Garden. Hopp received support for his idea from Garden promoter Rickard and other decision makers at the Garden. A few months prior, they had promoted the Benny Leonard-Richie Mitchell fight with certain proceeds of the affair going to the American Committee for Devastated France. This event would be structured along similar lines, with a charitable component.[16]

Rickard charged Hopp with the responsibility of obtaining a transmitter and overseeing the various theaters, halls, and auditoriums where the broadcast would be received. Hopp would also engage amateur radio enthusiasts who possessed the knowledge to set up the radio receiving equipment. Since few individuals at the time owned their own radio receivers, this was the only way to reach a substantial audience.

To find the technical experts needed, Hopp garnered the support of Major J. Andrew White, acting president of the National Amateur Wireless Association. White then went to Sarnoff at RCA. Unlike some of his colleagues, Sarnoff took an interest in the project.[17] One element of the Sarnoff tale not in dispute is that he provided the $1,500 seed money for the venture and loaned out several RCA engineers.

J. Owen Smith, one of the RCA engineers, was granted permission to borrow the world's largest portable transmitter, a General Electric apparatus made for the US Navy. Franklin Delano Roosevelt, then Undersecretary of the Navy, facilitated the loan.[18] White made arrangements to have the transmitter delivered by tug from General Electric's plant in Schenectady, New York. Roosevelt was the president of the Navy Club at the time, and the club was added as a second charitable beneficiary of the broadcast.[19]

A temporary transmitter authorization was received with the call sign WJY. WJY in Newark, New Jersey, would deliver the historic broadcast. Additionally, KDKA in Pittsburgh also carried the bout by relaying WJY's announcements.[20]

The transmitter was positioned two and one-half miles from the arena. An antenna was strung between two railroad towers on the property of the Delaware, Lackawana and Western Railway terminal in Hoboken. The radio equipment was set up in a galvanized hut used by Pullman porters to change their uniforms. When the porters objected to their displacement, Smith was forced to sleep in the hut to guard the equipment.[21]

At Jack Dempsey's training camp several days before the fight, Major White tuned in a "radio music box," while Dempsey wore a headset attached to a receiver. The champion experienced a sample of the technology that would shortly deliver his historic bout to the largest audience in boxing history.[22] In one version of the historic

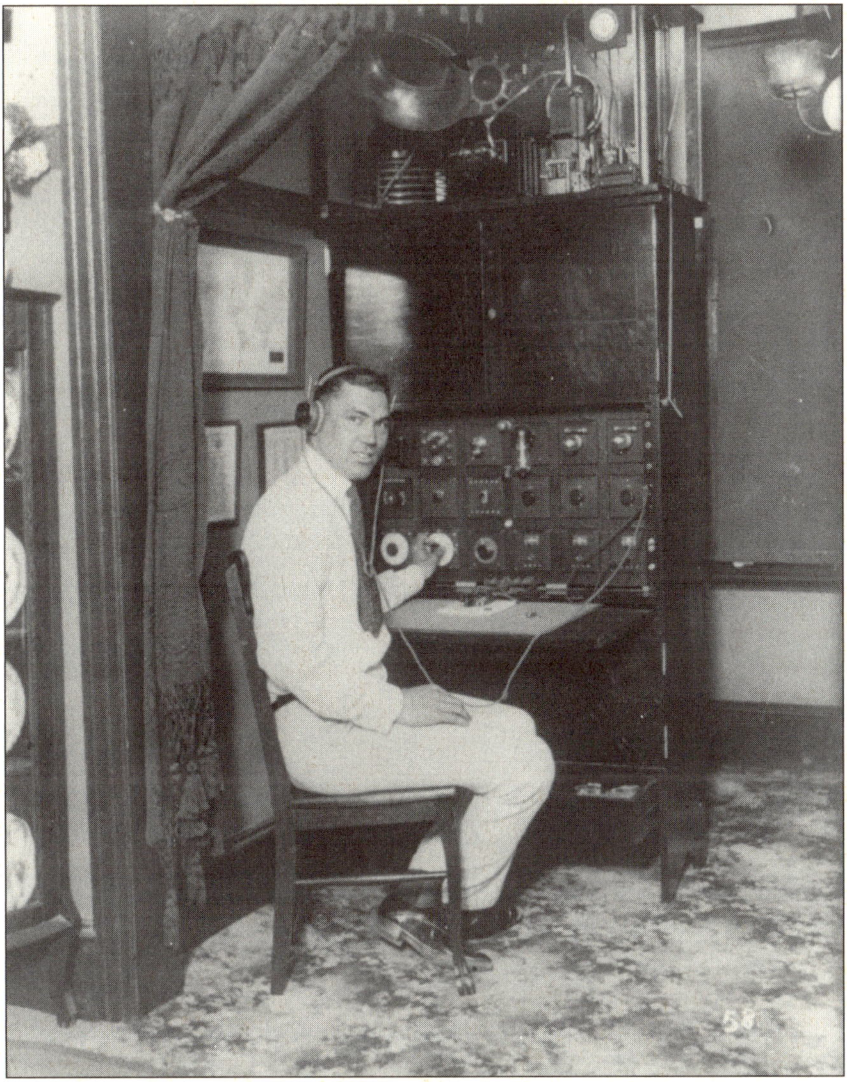

Heavyweight champion Jack Dempsey tests the equipment that will deliver the historic broadcast of his bout with Georges Carpentier. Dempsey retained the title by KO in the fourth round. *Photo courtesy of the Library of Congress.*

broadcast, Sarnoff sat ringside next to Major White, editor of *The Wireless Age*, who delivered the first blow-by-blow description of a championship boxing contest. However, White's voice was not broadcast over the airwaves. J. O. Smith received White's description in the porter's hut, and then Smith repeated White's words into the broadcast microphone for the relay to reach the public via radio station WJY.[23] A relay was required because AT&T refused to allow White's ringside telephone wire to be directly connected to the transmitter.[24, 25]

A more compelling argument has been made that Sarnoff was not at ringside. Photographs prove that an individual named Harry Welker sat next to White. Written accounts also support the theory Welker was White's assistant for the broadcast.[26] Early accounts of the broadcast confirm Smith on the air. White spoke into a telephone line, and a high-speed telegrapher created a verbatim, typed bulletin of his words, which were then repeated by Smith in the hut and sent out over the air.[27] However, many years later, White explained how Smith circumvented the AT&T restriction so it was actually White's voice transmitted to the public: "Smith put a five-inch diaphragm into the receiving telephone and hooked another telephone with a big diaphragm to the radio transmitter," so that White's voice would be picked up and transmitted directly over WJY."[28]

While it will probably never be known for sure whether it was Smith or White heard by radio audiences that day, the broadcast was a technological success, reaching an unprecedented radio audience. Thirty halls and theaters, each operated by the two charities, carried the fight. Ten were located in New York. Another twenty stretched as far north as Springfield, Massachusetts, westward to Bethlehem, Pennsylvania, and as far south as Wilmington, Delaware. Other enthusiastic radio amateurs organized their own operations, which contributed to the broadcast.

The single largest single audience was comprised of 1,200 people attending the Lowe's New York Roof Theater. Typical public audiences included the Yonkers, New York, Elks Club with an audience of 100, and 140 people gathered at the Springfield,

Massachusetts, Plaza Theater. One creative radio amateur reported that he "was able to perfect reception in a roller chair on the Asbury Park, Boardwalk." Individual radio amateurs tuning in on their crystal radio sets at home received the signal as far north as Maine and west to Ohio.[29] J. Andrew White described his historic ringside experience as the toughest of his reporting career: "Jammed up against the ring in a little coop, without elbow room, and with the hot sun beating down, and bedlam breaking loose on every side . . . it's a wonder it even sounded intelligible. The men punched quicker than could be noted by speech. Their speed baffled the tongue; even the eye was strained. I could give only the 'highlight' punches—the ones that did some damage."[30]

The ring announcer that memorable day was Joe Humphries, the dean of his profession. His vocals were a part of the fight game from the days of Jefferies until the dawn of the Louis era. Up until Dempsey-Carpentier, announcers had to rely exclusively upon the natural strength and range of their voices. It was the only way to reach the seemingly endless rows of fans stretched out before them. Humphries bristled when he learned that Rickard's engineers wanted him to use a new electronic gadget—a Magnavox—to make his introductions of the fighters. Although he took the request as a personal condemnation and a slight against his craft, he ultimately acquiesced. Humphries greeted the audience by speaking into "a square black jigger about the size of a strawberry box with a trailing wire running down to the batteries under the scaffold" of the ring. He lauded Carpentier as "the idol of France and the hero of the war to end war." A taken-aback Dempsey perceived this introduction as carrying an implied message magnifying his well-known reputation as a draft dodger.[31]

An estimated 300,000 people are believed to have heard the broadcast. Reuters, the British news agency, called the Dempsey-Carpentier fight "the world's first real broadcast."[32] *The Wireless Age* recognized a seismic shift in the communications paradigm: "While the eyes of the world were awaiting the issuance of the time-honored descriptive printed word to tell the story—radio told it by voice!"[33]

After Dempsey knocked out the French war hero in four rounds in the main event, and 88,000 fans filed out of the massive wooden arena, a tally of the gross gate receipts hit a staggering $1,789,238, the highest in boxing history.[34]

Since the fight itself was of enormous public interest, its broadcast on radio was somewhat tangential. However, it heralded in the new age of boxing on radio and all its potentialities. It was also an opportunity not lost upon the ultraambitious and ingenious duo of entrepreneurs Rickard and Sarnoff.[35]

They continued their new partnership, arranging for radio sets and loudspeakers to be set up in theaters, lodge halls, and barns throughout the eastern US, utilizing promotion of a sponsorship committee headed by Roosevelt. FDR, along with Rickard and Georges Carpentier, advanced their efforts by signing certificates for amateur wireless groups whose expertise was used to set up the radio equipment at the selected locations.[36] Radio's potential for influence and power was quickly recognized by a number of other interests, as well. This awareness was reflected in the dramatic increase in the number of commercial radio licenses issued in 1922, exceeding 500. In 1923, broadcasting licenses were obtained by seventy-two universities, colleges, and schools; sixty-nine newspapers; twenty-nine department stores; twelve religious organizations; and a few automobile dealers, theaters, and banks.[37] The public tuned into these stations on an ever-growing number of radio receivers from only 50,000 in 1921 to as many as 600,000 in 1922.[38]

The proven technological success of the Dempsey-Carpentier affair from Boyle's Thirty Acres arena was a formula that would be repeated the following summer on three occasions. Radio's second broadcast of a championship boxing match was the fistic idol Benny Leonard's attempt to wrestle the welterweight title away from Jack Britton. The match was contested on June 26, 1922, in the open-air, 30,000-seat Velodrome in New York City, and broadcast from station WJZ in Newark, New Jersey. Unlike the Dempsey-Carpentier bout, which might have been telephoned by wire from ringside and then broadcast over the radio by a second person elsewhere, it was reported that "for the first time in the history of general radiophone broadcasting, every detail of the championship battle will be transmitted direct from ringside."

This was achieved through "a special telephone connection" made between ringside and the transmitting station at WJZ. Major J. Andrew White spoke into an ordinary telephone transmitter. His voice was then carried over telephone lines to Newark, transferred into a special microphone, amplified, and then broadcast by WJZ. In a showing of radio solidarity, other metropolitan radio stations in close proximity to WJZ's operation at 360 meters agreed to suspend their broadcasts at fight time to ensure no reception interference.[39]

Many radio shops rigged speakers outside their establishments so New Yorkers could hear the broadcast. They hoped that curious listeners would become their next consumers. Stores with small speaker amplifiers had only a brief range. If those gathered were beyond the radio's reach, others passed along snippets of the fight as it happened. However, at most shops, such as one at 94th Street and Broadway, the broadcast was loud and "the streets were blocked from sidewalk to sidewalk with a listening mob." In several instances, precinct police had to be called to clear overflowing foot traffic. At 23rd Street, police lines were formed to hold the crowd in check. In Times Square, a broadcast reached all the way to the Claridge Hotel, 250 yards away. To reduce the swelling crowd, the radio shop manager was forced to turn down the volume and limit the radio's range.

Over 250,000 listeners within a radius of 800 miles heard Major White's call of the bout, with audiences as far west as Ohio and Indiana and as far north as Nova Scotia. F. R. Krupp of Scranton, Pennsylvania, was one of many listeners who wrote WJZ complimentary letters regarding the broadcast: "We could hear all of the details," including "the uproar of the crowd because of the foul." A. P. Clark of Bridgeton, Maine, told friends, "he heard every word of the announcer perfectly and he could catch the noise of the crowd and the ringing of the gong clearly."[40]

A month later, Leonard laid his lightweight title on the line against Lew Tendler. A description in a newspaper's radio listing of the bout highlights how the most fundamental aspects of sound recreation were noteworthy during the infancy of radio: "Sensitive pick-up microphones will be installed at the ringside at Boyle's Thirty Acres in Jersey City, New Jersey with direct connection to the radio transmitting apparatus of WJZ. A blow description of the fight will be given and even the timekeeper's whistle and the clang of the gong at the beginning and end of each round as well as the cheers and comments of the spectators will be broadcast by the radiophone."[41]

Like the Britton fight, the Tendler match brought about similar gatherings in the streets of New York, including a throng of people at 125th Street and Seventh Avenue in Harlem. A more comfortable setting for listening was provided at the Hotel Alpin, where an audience including several women adorned with necklaces sat in cushion-seated chairs around the radio. It was reported that "among the listeners were many of the fair sex," including Olga Steck, prima donna of the Broadway musical comedy *Sue Dear*, who listened to the bout on her Aeriola Senior set in her dressing room.[42]

The technical aspects of the broadcast were uniformly appreciated by listening audiences. Even a fan who received reception interference from a station broadcasting a children's program with a speaker who "insisted upon reciting portions of bedtime verses" was otherwise complimentary. Another fan from Jersey City, New Jersey, summed up the average home listener's experience: "It was better than being at the fight, as I had a big, comfortable easy chair, a box of cigars, a cold glass (no, not of what we used to have) and all the comforts of home, yet I 'saw' the bout."[43] A writer for *The Wireless Age* concluded that "this bout clinched radio as a successful means of transmitting sporting results. In the future, no sport event of major importance will be complete without it."[44, 45]

By the end of 1922, radio was gaining recognition as a practical invention: "Radio in the Home—and in the office, on board ship, everywhere. There is hardly a place of business in which radio cannot fit, cannot be used for pleasure or profit or both."[46] As radio was developing its universality, live blow-by-blow boxing broadcasts were still a rarity. With national and international coverage still nonexistent, creative use of available technologies was sometimes implemented to speedily deliver fight results to distant fans.

Such was the case of the Johnny Kilbane-Eugène Criqui bout in 1923. French fans still stinging from Carpentier's shortfall against Dempsey anxiously awaited the opportunity for Criqui to bring a world championship back to France. A twofold plan was devised to accommodate these fans. The Department of Telegraphs in the French Ministry would expedite the results from New York via telegraph and then make a radio transmission from the Eiffel Tower. The broadcast provided the results to thousands of Parisians who were lucky enough to own private radio sets provided they kept "their receivers tuned up to the proper wave length."[47]

A few years later, WBZ in Boston, KDKA in Pittsburgh, CKAC in Montreal, and *La Nacion* in Buenos Aires, Argentina, hatched a multipart relay scheme that seemed disproportionate in effort to its broadcast of a radio description of international amateur boxing.

In one relay, a direct-line connection would bring bouts from Boston to Pittsburgh, where the strong signal of KDKA would broadcast a detailed account of the bouts. The final leg of the first relay was based on a wing and a prayer whereby "the Buenos Aires station can try to detect the waves and re-radiate them." The Canadians would receive the blow-by-blow account from nearby WBZ in Boston and then rebroadcast the matches over the Montreal airwaves, completing the second relay.[48]

The strategy proved successful. The ringside report from Boston via Pittsburgh was "plainly audible at the receiving end" in Buenos Aires 6,000 miles away. From Buenos Aires, a rebroadcast all over South America was made. Still, a relay transmission was not direct or "live" in the manner of today. A representative of *La Nacion* was sending the ringside report from Boston to Pittsburgh, where it was translated and then rebroadcast from the US to South America. Europe had yet to become connected with American broadcasts, and the Associated Press cabled the story of the fights to Europe while it was broadcast.[49]

During the 1920s, radio broadcasts were also supplemented in imaginative, even bizarre ways. The Lafayette Billiard Emporium in

New York City planned to make special arrangements for "receiving the returns," "by radio and news telegraph service" of the Harry Wills-Charlie Weinert, Harry Greb-Mickey Walker doubleheader. A billiard table was to be converted into a small ring where two individuals would "demonstrate every blow and by whom delivered as they occur in the ring at the big fight."[50]

On other occasions, if radio did not exist, interested parties would build the "radio apparatus" for the sole purpose of promoting and/or broadcasting the fight. When Rickard staged the Dempsey-Gibbons affair on July 4, 1923, with the Chamber of Commerce of Shelby, Montana, he built a broadcasting station with a purported range of 3,000 square miles. Nearby Great Falls already had a radio station and would accommodate "short talks" by Dempsey on evenings as the fight approached, with Gibbons doing the same from the new station in Shelby. "This will be another innovation and will make the bout from this standpoint the most modern in the history of the ring," it was proudly reported.[51]

The fight was broadcast back east over station WGY, Schenectady, New York, with the blow-by-blow provided by famed sportswriter Hype Igoe. One writer suggested that the new luxury of the portable radio be taken advantage of: "Go to the seashore or the mountains or on that automobile trip and take your radio set with you . . . draw up along the roadside at an attractive spot shaded by trees with a prospect of rugged mountain or sloping hills or purling brook before you, rig up your aerial and ground and listen in to the fight as your wife spreads the picnic meal."[52]

A few short months later, Dempsey was back in the ring against Luis "Angel" Firpo, the "Wild Bull of the Pampas." The morning of the fight, Dempsey and Firpo weighed in at the boxing commission's office in Manhattan's Flatiron building. The bout would produce the four wildest minutes in heavyweight history with Firpo down nine times and Dempsey downed twice, including being knocked out of the ring.[53]

Major White called the bout from the Polo Grounds. Grantland Rice described the radio broadcast as having "reproduced by electrical magic a roar of profanity, a yell of 100,000 throats."[54] The fight was carried to a burgeoning radio audience: "Scarce a hamlet in the eastern half of the United States had but one or more loud speakers set up to the street with a crowd listening and cheering and going wild as at the ringside."[55] The audience also reflected a surprising new demographic for the sport: "Gentle, home-living women who thought they could never be interested in a prize-fight found themselves standing on chairs during the excitement of the Dempsey-Firpo match."[56]

In Argentina, it was reported that "European affairs" and "the situation in Spain" were "subordinated to the comments on the probable results of the Firpo-Dempsey match." All of the sporting clubs were outfitted with radios. When returns were received by radio and results known, colored rockets were to be sent into the sky to notify the public.[57] Current shortwave technology did not permit White's voice to reach South America. White's English language broadcast from New York was transcribed into "dot-dash" language and then transmitted to Buenos Aires. The signal was then translated into the Spanish language and broadcast to Argentina, Chile, Paraguay, and Uruguay.[58]

Although some commercial broadcast transmitters were emitting signals with considerable range, home radios during the early 1920s were limited in their ability to clearly tune into a broadcast. To assist in hearing transmissions, receivers could be equipped with one or more headsets. Wearing headsets was referred to as "putting the cans on." One manufacturer's ad boasted that "A Brandes Wireless Headset can be worn as comfortably as an old soft hat."[59] When famed radio broadcaster Don Dunphy was a child, he listened to Major White's broadcast of the Dempsey-Firpo bout using this equipment. Dunphy tuned White's blow-by-blow into his headset and then relayed White's call to the rest of the family, who huddled around in eager anticipation.[60]

It was financially prudent for radio to follow the world's heavyweight champion wherever he might fight, and it was no surprise that fans were willing to work a little to tune in elusive radio signals that carried his escapades. However, regional broadcasts of boxing's lesser main events were also becoming regular fare during the mid- and late-1920s. WSB in Atlanta, for instance, featured the ringside broadcast of the Young Stribling-Billy Shade contest in 1924. Local flavor was provided by the southern headliner Stribling to listeners in that region. Depending on the atmospheric conditions, northeasterners might have also been able to tune in the bout.[61]

Other local headliners were regularly featured on major radio stations in the boxer's home base city such as WNAC's coverage of Red Chapman in Boston.[62] Additionally, the broadcast of local club fights from locales such as Ridgewood Grove in New York were also popular.[63] During this era, even the most parochial of fisticuffs found their way onto the airwaves. WPAB, State College, Pennsylvania—283.5—broadcast ringside reports of collegiate boxing matches;[64] and AT-9, the Army broadcasting station at Fort Bragg, North Carolina, provided descriptions of Army contests.[65] Catholic Big Sisters charity bouts were aired from New York City.[66]

Madison Square Garden became a regular contributor to boxing programming on the radio from its beginning, providing radio coverage for championship matches it hosted from 1921 to 1924.[67] MSG even helped promote the radio industry with a weeklong radio fair in 1924, attracting 165,000 patrons to its exhibits.

At this time, radio was emerging as a standard industry, becoming as ubiquitous as the automobile. For the first time, a radio stock had been listed on the New York Stock Exchange.[68] Guglielmo Marconi found the medium that he helped create to have no limitations: "Is it too much to suggest that at no distant date a doctor will be able to diagnose by wireless?" he posited.[69]

However, from the start, effects of radio on the sport of boxing were viewed as a double-edged sword. Radio provided enormous publicity for the product, but its contribution to the promoter's bottom line was suspect. Ironically, at the same time that the Garden was touting the industry with the Radio Fair, it was moving away from broadcasting its championship bouts. The Garden's promoter, Tex Rickard, pulled the plug on radio broadcasts on November 25, 1924.

Garden officials cited radio listeners' satisfaction with the blow-by-blow descriptions as the cause for reduced "live" attendance and a decline in his financial return.[70, 71] The very same day, it was reported that the famed Garden, an architectural gem designed by Stanford White in 1890, was scheduled for demolition. The previous June, Rickard, who was also president of the new Madison Square Garden, had purchased the Car Barns on the west side of Eighth Avenue from 49th to 50th Streets, with plans to develop the spot into "the largest place of amusement in the world."[72]

Boxing fans had become accustomed to listening to boxing on the radio for free. When deprived of this privilege, they were expectedly disappointed. The night before the 1925 Tunney-Gibbons bout, contested for the right to meet Jack Dempsey for the title, it was announced that there would be no radio broadcast of the fight and its undercard. Fans were sometimes subjected to these last-minute broadcasting decisions. Radio coverage of the bout depended upon the strength of advance ticket sales. When sales did not meet the promoter's expectations, fans had no choice but to pay at least the price of a general admission ticket ($2.40 for Tunney-Gibbons) for the privilege of enjoying the bout.[73]

Several years after Rickard's Garden vision became a reality, radio would return to the Garden. In January, 1926, shortly after the new arena opened, it was reported that Rickard had purchased station WWGL. The station planned to broadcast Garden fights from its location on top of the arena. When asked if he had changed his attitude regarding boxing broadcasting, Rickard refused to make a statement. However, he apparently had a greater comfort zone with radio when he had more direct control over its use.[74]

Rickard would move forward with radio, changing the station's name to WMSG. The station would broadcast various events, including boxing, from the Garden. For example, in 1927, WMSG broadcast the holiday boxing carnival from the New York Navy Yard, which entertained personnel of the ships docked at the yard for the Christmas season. Rickard and light-heavyweight champion Tommy Loughran served as two of the bout's judges.

However, Rickard did not always utilize WMSG for his blockbuster boxing matches. Some aired over other major stations such as WEAF in New York and various stations on the NBC and CBS radio networks.[75] By the spring of 1927, Rickard was publicly supporting the idea of boxing on the radio without qualification. "Radio is a great aid to boxing," he explained. "It serves two purposes. It is steadily breaking down the idea which many persons still hold that boxing is a brutal game. In addition it is attracting a higher-type of fan to the bouts." On the issue of its financial repercussions, Rickard, at least temporarily, made his metamorphosis when he stated, "I think broadcasting a show makes new customers."[76] At this time, the Garden and NBC's Blue Network struck a new radio deal opening with the broadcast of the Jack Sharkey-Jack Delaney bout in 1928 with Major J. Andrew White at the microphone.[77] Rickard's liberal radio stance continued the following year, with WMSG and WPCH broadcasting all of the Garden's fights, including championship bouts.[78]

A national survey conducted by station WJZ at the time indicated that sports fans favored baseball and then football as radio sports, with boxing ranked third ahead of horse racing and other sports.[79] Statistics, however, may not have appropriately reflected the level of popularity of boxing in the eastern US. The July 1926 light-heavyweight championship bout between Jack Delaney and Paul Berlenbach, for example, was broadcast by three local radio stations: WNYC, WFBH, and WMCA.[80] For another card from the Polo Grounds, two different radio stations broadcast opposite ends of a boxing doubleheader: WGBS covered the Dave Shade-Jimmy Slattery bout and WHN broadcast the Harry Wills-Charlie Weinert match.[81]

Broadcasts from Rickard's new Garden in the years that followed played a substantial role in increasing boxing's popularity on the radio and helping the Garden become synonymous with boxing. During this same period, legal restrictions on boxing matches in Chicago were lifted. A brand new arena, the Chicago Stadium, was erected, and radio would cover the opening of the new arena with the broadcast of Tommy Loughran's split-decision victory over Mickey Walker. This broadcast would mark the beginning of Chicago Stadium's ascension as "The Madison Square Garden of the Midwest." For decades to follow, the Stadium would periodically host radio coverage of bouts of regional and national importance.[82]

Chapter 2

DEMPSEY, TUNNEY, AND THE FORMATION OF RADIO NETWORKS

Tex Rickard not only held sway at the Garden as its president, but also as promoter of the jewel of the sport—heavyweight champion Jack Dempsey. After a three-year hiatus from the ring, Dempsey was ready for his return against the heavyweight division's premier challenger, Gene Tunney. Dempsey's dispute with the New York State Athletic Commission would keep the first Tunney match out of New York and Garden-controlled arenas, but the bout was still within the purview of Rickard and the Garden's influence. Rickard also controlled the radio aspects of the promotion. These were made in conjunction with the Sesquicentennial officials who provided a new, oversize stadium in Philadelphia for the bout.

Under the banner of Rickard, Colonel John S. Hammond, vice president of the Garden Corporation, sold broadcasting rights of the bout to George Edward Smith, president of the Royal Typewriter Company of New York. The broadcast would be implemented by a consortium of radio giants of the day, including the WJZ network of the Radio Corporation of America, the WEAF chain and at least twenty-five of its most powerful stations, and the high-powered

Tex Rickard was not only boxing's foremost promoter of the 1920s, but also the first to grapple with the financial implications of radio's influence on the sport. *By Bain News Service via Wikimedia Commons.*

stations of General Electric and the Westinghouse Electric and Manufacturing Company. The stations of Rickard's giant radio network would cover two-thirds of the land area of the US and would "carry a word picture to the largest audience of fight fans ever assembled in boxing history."[1]

A precursor to closed-circuit video broadcasts in arenas from the 1950s through the 1980s, an audio hookup would allow MSG attendees to hear Major White's blow-by-blow from ringside at Philly's Sesquicentennial Stadium. The trick was accomplished with a special telephone wire running from Philadelphia into the "large public addressograph" suspended in the Garden. The price to listen to the radio broadcast with thousands of other enthusiasts in the arena was fifty cents or a dollar, with all preliminaries included.[2]

If the broadcast of the Dempsey-Carpentier bout marked a historic occurrence in boxing radio history, then the first Dempsey-Tunney encounter was its watershed moment of maturity. With the heavyweight championship dormant for three years, the public was starved for a title contest. Interest in the bout between the draft dodger and the former Marine was acute. Utilizing a shortwave radio relay, the fight was broadcast through a network of radio stations throughout the United States. Numerous stations in the Northeast and Midwest would carry the bout. The action could also be heard across America from Philadelphia to Pittsburgh, Cincinnati to St. Louis, and Kansas City to Denver to Oakland.[3]

Once a scientific curiosity, radio was now a necessity. Industrial-looking crystal sets with exposed tubes and wires had been replaced by handcrafted furniture worthy of the parlor in any respectable home. Some of the names of the manufacturers still resonate: Philco, Zenith, and RCA. Others have been long forgotten: Stromberg Carlson, Sparton Equasonne, and Federal Orthosonic.[4]

Fifteen million listeners would gather around their radios for the fight. Announcing chores were assigned to the sport's premier men of the day—Major J. Andrew White and Graham McNamee. They set the scene of the epic encounter for the radio audience. McNamee: "Gene is standing in the corner of the ring now. He has got probably the most up-to-date covering in the bathrobe line that has ever been seen in the history of the prize ring. On the back he has a gigantic emblem of the marines. It is not a bathrobe. It is a dressing gown with a red back. . . . If you hear a buzzing roar in this besides our voices, you will know it is the local announcer, who is handling the large speaker, which has a battery screened about thirty feet above our heads. . . . They are both rubbing the resin into their shoes now and they are ready for the gong. (Bell rings). There it goes, the heavyweight championship. This battle is on!"[5]

McNamee between rounds two and three: "This fight shows what happens to a fighter that doesn't fight. . . . Three or four times Dempsey has looked groggy in these two rounds. . . . Gene Tunney leads by a long margin at the end of the second round. He looks fresh as a daisy and Jack looks a little tired." Major White during round five: "You see Dempsey crowding and pushing, but he does not show the whirling, rushing attack that has been so characteristic of his fighting and which made him champion." White at the conclusion of the fight: "There is the bell and unquestionably we have a new champion . . . the crowd is going wild and is beginning to climb over our heads."[6]

In a move that today could only be considered a gross breach of protocol, if not professional suicide, McNamee stood in the ring and announced to the crowd of 120,000 and fifteen million radio listeners: "Ladies and gentleman, the decision has not been made yet, but undoubtedly Gene Tunney is the new heavyweight champion of the world." McNamee had jumped the gun, but fortunately, the judges were in agreement. Tunney then summed up his experience for the radio audience: "I have realized all my ambition, and I will try to defend the title that I have worked so hard for six years, and I am going to try to defend it as becomes a marine."[7]

While there is no known surviving recording of the bout, the blow-by-blow description was captured by three expert shorthand writers of the State Law Reporting Company at the *New York Times* office. Therefore, a written record of the broadcast has survived—possibly the first big news event to be reported verbatim in a newspaper.[8]

In England, a few lucky listeners were able to distinctly hear the broadcast from ringside by "listening in on the wireless." Hundreds of individuals watched the "tickers" in clubs and newspaper offices for the returns. Still hundreds more "walked the streets all night to await late editions of the newspapers giving results."[9] In South Africa, radio amateurs attempted to pick up American shortwave station 2XAF direct, and others listened in on crystal sets to the broadcast of station "JB," which was rebroadcasting the American shortwave signal.[10]

Sometime later, Tunney revealed his innermost thoughts on the title win to a WEAF radio audience: "I knew that I was just as physically fit, had a knowledge of the game accumulated over seven years of actual experience, knew that my resistance was good as any man's, knew that my recuperative powers must be as good as any man's and know that there are no supermen. So that, in spite of what the consensus of opinion was, I was not going to permit anything to rob my consciousness of this knowledge."[11]

The first Tunney-Dempsey fight had propelled the marriage of boxing and radio into high gear, and boxing content on radio continued to diversify. Chicago's WGN began a series of historical boxing recreations, *Famous Fights of All Time*, featuring classic ring battles. The radio series opened with the 1882 Sullivan-Paddy Ryan bare-knuckle tussle in Mississippi. Other memorable bouts featured were Gans-McGovern (1900), the St. Patrick's day clash between Battling Siki-Mike McTigue, Johnson-Ketchel, and Pancho Villa's defeat of Jimmy Wilde for the flyweight title. Apparently the Windy City, only recently reinstating boxing after a twenty-five-year prohibition following the Gans-McGovern fiasco of a fixed fight, was still hungry for tales of the fight game.[12]

The popularity of radio led to a proliferation of stations nationally. With a limited number of wavelengths for broadcasting, the inevitable problem arose of two or more stations with the same or adjacent wavelength causing reception interference for one another. The problem was serious enough for Radio Commissioner O. H. Caldwell to come to New York in May, 1927, to address the need for the national reallocation of wavelengths.[13] While commercial radio worked out its growing pains, it continued to evolve. Just two weeks later, it was reported that testing proved that the KDKA transmitter could put out as much as 50,000 watts, with audiences in New England, Michigan, and New York reporting a stronger and sharper signal.[14]

Commensurate with these technical improvements, radio seemed to offer a milestone of sorts with each succeeding major broadcast. After Dempsey lost his title to Tunney, he sought to reinsert himself into the heavyweight championship picture. In the summer of 1927, he was matched with the "Boston Gob," Jack Sharkey. The bout was broadcast over a national network to an estimated fifty million listeners—a staggering figure far exceeding the fifteen million of the Tunney match only a year before. It was believed to be the largest radio audience in history.[15] Radio would bring the bout to every corner of American society. Even the Ladies' Aid Society of St. Mary's Church in Corning, New York, listened to the bout as part of their ice cream social.[16]

The transcontinental network also boasted fifty-one stations, more than the record fifty stations that had recently broadcast Charles Lindbergh's historic transcontinental flight and the post-flight reception held in Washington, DC.[17] Like the first Tunney bout, the writers of the State Law Reporting Company recorded the fight in shorthand as described by announcers Graham McNamee and Phillips Carlin at ringside at Yankee Stadium. It remains the only surviving blow-by-blow description of the match:

McNamee: The crowd is giving Jack Dempsey . . . as great an ovation as any man ever received on any occasion. . . . He really looks like the old Dempsey. . . . Jack Sharkey in the other corner took his bathrobe off, and now they have wrapped it around him to keep the cool winds off . . . Dempsey . . . with black and red tights, and Sharkey with the purple tights . . . The bell! They immediately rush in."

The historic seventh round: "Sharkey is down from a left to the side of the body. Sharkey is down! Dempsey has returned to his corner. They are counting over Sharkey, and he is out. Sharkey, knocked cold by Jack Dempsey, is carried to his corner by Dempsey and the referee. Sharkey is knocked cold! . . . I am sorry I just stopped for a moment. Time, forty-five seconds, Joe Humphries just told me—a left hook to the jaw. . . . Jack, Jack, Jack! Just say 'Hello,' Jack." A jubilant Dempsey then addressed the radio audience: "Hello everybody! I am tickled to death to be here. Thank you very much."[18]

The Dempsey-Sharkey broadcast was a tremendous hit for NBC. A wire to the company's president, M. H. Aylesworth, delivered the following message: "Broadcasting of the Dempsey-Sharkey fight on the Pacific coast was a great success. Estimated audience equal to either Lindberg broadcast. City and country clubs, auditoriums and public gathering places were equipped with radio sets. Everybody today is talking about and praising the broadcast."[19] The Dempsey-Sharkey fight would begin in earnest a long and historic relationship between NBC and the sport of boxing.

In Mexico, numerous fans listened to direct transmissions delivered by American stations from ringside. Others listened on local stations including the retransmission to station CYJ. Some gathered around the twenty-five loudspeakers installed at important locations throughout Mexico City. In Australia, successful reception of American shortwave station 2XAF was reported, and station 2FC in Sydney provided the rebroadcast.[20]

Large national network broadcasts of bouts such as Dempsey's with Tunney and Sharkey would soon become standard fare. The typical network hookup operated similarly to that for the Dempsey-Sharkey encounter. For that broadcast, essentially a wire network was used where all participating stations had a "Morse line" connecting with the "mother ship," WEAF in New York. In order for all stations to be on the air at the same time, all stations' chronometers were synchronized in advance. Tone frequencies were tested to ensure each station had the same broadcast volume. Repeaters and amplifiers were subsequently used to maintain proper volume levels.

Five minutes before the main event was aired, the Morse operator in New York signaled the telegraph operators at the other fifty-one stations: "We will want your carrier in five minutes." Then, two minutes before, New York would send out the "QRX" or standby signal.

Finally, an NW or "now" signal was flashed from New York to all stations. At that moment, the local stations immediately switched the local microphone circuit to the incoming line from New York.[21]

Technical achievements notwithstanding, the NBC production came under the scrutiny of fans for the announcers' failure to report a crucial low blow delivered by Dempsey in the seventh round. In response, the NBC representative stated that McNamee, who was on transit to Toronto and unavailable for comment, did not see a foul blow. Even if he did, the announcer could not call a foul on the radio. According to the rules of the state boxing commission, an announcer cannot make an editorial comment. Only when a referee calls a foul can the announcer characterize a blow as such. Major J. Andrew White reported that from his ringside position he did not see a foul blow struck. He also appeared on radio station WOR and reiterated his position after the fight.[22]

Several weeks later, White's position was disproven. The film of the bout clearly showed that Dempsey had delivered a low blow as the set-up punch to the knockout shot he landed just as Sharkey was appealing to the referee. Of course, Sharkey was complicit in his moment of doom by failing to follow one of boxing's most sacred commandments, "Protect yourself at all times."

Undaunted by the backlash created by the unreported low blow on the fight broadcast, New York State Athletic Commissioner William Muldoon added an additional shackle to radio announcers the next day. In future broadcasts, announcers would be prohibited from giving personal opinions or descriptions of a fighter's physical appearance during the fight. That information was deemed irrelevant. "The public," said the commissioners in justification of their position, "is not interested in the announcer's opinion. What they want to know is how the fight progresses, what blows are struck and by whom."[23] "Furthermore," Muldoon stated, "if descriptions of bloody fights reach children or other sensitive persons, it will reflect on the sport and perhaps bring forth condemnation of boxing as brutal."[24]

A few days later, a letter to the editor appeared in *The New York Times* lambasting the new radio rule: "heaven help us—more prohibition." The letter exposed the rule's illogical nature: "What kind of ingenuous explanation would the announcer be obliged to give of a battle such as was recently fought in which Mike McTigue . . . was obliged to abandon the contest because of a flow of blood that could not be checked immediately?"[25]

Muldoon's call for silence was just one example of the New York commission's testing the limits of their authority over radio. In the fall of 1926, capitalizing on the laissez-faire approach of the Federal Radio Commission, the New York State Athletic Commission had passed a regulation requiring its approval of radio announcers before a broadcast would be sanctioned. The fundamental effect of this ruling on the industry resulted in prejudice against the smaller broadcasting interests. NBC had no problem receiving approval for the use of announcers such as Major White, but smaller broadcasting stations received consistent disapprovals.[26] The commission's approval requirement also had the concomitant effect of dictating whether certain broadcasts would reach the air at all. In one instance, they rejected former bantam and featherweight champion Terry McGovern as the announcer for the Dundee-Latzo bout at the Polo Grounds. No reason was given for their decision. WGL was forced to cancel the broadcast rather than be dictated to by the commission.[27] The commission wielded its self-delegated authority inconsiderately. For Sharkey-Maloney, it waited until fifteen minutes before the start of the bout to advise WMSG who the announcer would be, leaving no time for coordination between the station and its announcer.[28]

An additional part of the regulation set the announcer's fee. Besides the general control these rules afforded, they also allowed the commissioner to provide work to members of their referee/judge cadre who might otherwise sit idle. The commission's instructions to WMSG one evening were typical: "Referee Arthur Donovan assigned to broadcast bouts at Garden to-night. Broadcasters are to receive $25 to-night."[29] These assignments of commission officials led to a rash of poor announcing. One critic of boxing Judge Harold Barnes, who took the microphone for the Sharkey-Maloney bout, lamented how he "leaned against the uninformative props of repetition and extraneous information whenever the action grew strenuous."[30] The commissioner's appointed announcers were met with great disapproval of the radio audience. Radio stations such as WMSG began investigating the commission's legal authority. Mercifully, the era of the commission-appointed announcers was merely symptomatic of the growing pains of the industry that would soon give way to radio's legal autonomy.[31]

Shortly after the Dempsey-Tunney bout in Philadelphia, NBC announced plans to form NBC, Inc., "a solution [to] the problem of establishing national and permanent radio broadcasting." WEAT, formerly of AT&T, would serve as the nucleus of a national broadcasting service. The goal was "to conserve and make permanent existing facilities, rather than to add anything to the growing contention for wavelengths . . . so that every event of national importance may be broadcast widely throughout the United States."[32]

While radio networks were a new phenomenon at the time, it was not long before network wars were underway. NBC had broadcast the Dempsey-Sharkey fight and claimed exclusive rights to the Dempsey-Tunney rematch through their contractual relationship with Rickard. Nevertheless, CBS, "in the interest of widening the scope of its service," and ostensibly for "competition offered . . . for excellence only," instructed AT&T to supply wire facilities to allow CBS to broadcast a ringside description of the bout. It was an intrusive maneuver by CBS, which Rickard squashed.[33, 34]

A Dempsey-Tunney rematch would be a fait accompli the moment Tunney's hand was raised in victory. The legendary "Battle of the Long Count" between Dempsey and Tunney has been recounted and retold during many intellectual debates, heated arguments, and bar fights for almost a century. Motion pictures of the knockdown dramatically captured the famous seventh round on film and have since become a part of boxing lore. However, the blow-by-blow description that millions across the country heard live is an obscurity.

Unlike Dempsey's other title bouts, the actual broadcast of the fight survived. Graham McNamee described the most famous knockdown in boxing history as follows: "Tunney shot a hard left to Dempsey's face which he follows up with two lefts, and as the left was into Dempsey's face, he lands a right, and Dempsey comes back and Tunney is down! Tunney is down from a barrage of lefts and rights to the face; something is going on; Tunney is down and Dempsey is on the other side . . . eight . . . nine . . . and Tunney is up! And now they're at it again, Tunney, Tunney is backing away and Dempsey is following."[35]

The match contested at Chicago's Soldiers Field was not only an event of great importance to broadcasters, but of unprecedented national interest. It was also one of the earliest sporting events with worldwide appeal.

In such distant and exotic places as Shanghai, China, Rio de Janeiro, Brazil, and Guayaquil, Ecuador, throngs of people anxiously gathered outside newspaper and telegraph offices, clubs, and hotels to receive news bulletins, wireless reports, and press flashes of the bout's outcome. While not live radio, to receive such contemporaneous information from as far as halfway around the world was still cutting edge at the time.[36]

The rights to broadcast the fight in the US were hotly contested and still unresolved two weeks prior to the bout. Previously, Tex Rickard had sold the radio rights to Tunney's first defense to NBC in New York. It was a right that the network desired to keep exclusive.

The fight was to be held in Chicago, and the rental of Soldiers Field needed to be secured. In a moment of municipal solidarity that the fractious city of Chicago had rarely seen, their South Park Board stood behind the local radio contingency. The $100,000 rental agreement for the cavernous stadium was not finalized until local radio privileges were granted to WGN, the *Chicago Tribune*'s radio station, and several other Chicago newspaper-owned stations.[37]

To capitalize on its coup of radio rights, WGN quickly moved into publicity mode. As Dempsey put the final touches on his training, each Saturday night Don Maxwell, Sporting Editor of the *Tribune*, would cover some aspect of the fight on his sports summary.[38] WGN also created a new radio program, a three-part serial called *The Fighting Life of Jack Dempsey*. WGN's Frank Dahm wrote the script, with music composed by Alfred G. Wathall. Bill Hay provided the narrative, and Quin Ryan recreated Dempsey's battles. The serial chronicled Dempsey's ring career from his victory over Fred Fulton up through his recent triumph over Jack Sharkey.[39]

WGN broadcast the famous fight from its studios in the Drake Hotel. The ringside blow-by-blow description and color commentary was made by Quin Ryan and Bill Hay, sent to the Drake's control room and then on to Elgin, Illinois, where it went over the airwaves.

A special musical program was created to air after the bout. Accounts of the fight prepared by *Chicago Tribune* writers for the paper periodically interrupted the music as soon as they were pulled from their typewriters.[40]

NBC's national broadcast was carried by a network of fifty-eight stations led by WEAF and WJZ in New York. The strong signal of shortwave radio station 2XAF from Schenectady, New York, was picked up by some as far off as England. In Puerto Rico, fans received a powerful signal so clear that some listeners claimed to hear the shuffling of the boxers' feet.[41] Some fifteen hundred miles from Chicago, hundreds of passengers of the *Berengaria* thrilled to the fight received on a Radiola Twenty while the ship was at sea.[42]

Back in the United States, prison wardens unexpectedly became radio censors deciding which inmates would be entitled the privilege of listening to the radio broadcast. In the New Jersey State Prison in Trenton, the warden permitted all five hundred prisoners to hear the bout, except four who were on death row—apparently deeming them unworthy. At Sing Sing prison in New York, a more liberal approach was followed, and all male inmates were allowed to listen, including fifteen on death row. At least one exception was made for the female prisoners. Ruth Snyder, a death row inmate scheduled for execution for murder in a crime of national notoriety, heard Graham McNamee's historic broadcast through an open door between the men's and women's cells.[43]

So intense was the bout that upwards of ten deaths were attributed to it, five coming during the seventh-round knockdown.[44] After listening to the radio broadcast, a Seattle man describing another bout he had seen in Chicago years earlier was stricken with a fatal heart attack.[45]

Dempsey's retirement from the ring following "The Battle of the Long Count" left Rickard with the highly competent but less compelling Gene Tunney as his main attraction. For Tunney's first title defense, Rickard choose New Zealander Tom Heeney from a lot of fair-to-middling contenders.

On a rain-soaked day two weeks before Heeney met Tunney at Yankee Stadium, ten-year-old John Merton ran away from his home in Elizabeth, New Jersey. It was the start of a forty-mile journey on foot to his hero Tom Heeney's training camp. John's fifteen-year-old brother Donald followed. Incredibly, Donald completed the trip, receiving dry clothes and coffee from a surprised Heeney.[46] This was the kind of fanatical interest in the New Zealander that Rickard was banking on when he matched "The Hard Rock From Down Under" against the champion.

Rickard knew the fight had its financial risks; chief among them was Heeney's lack of exposure. After the Dempsey-Tunney rematch, Rickard also had concerns that the radio broadcast had hurt the gate and feared a repeat occurrence. Only 104,000 people had filled the approximate 160,000 seats, leaving many of the cheap seats empty, including the bargain five-dollar seats. Rickard directly blamed the radio industry. Chicago area dealers had sold radios with a down payment for as low as the price of a Dempsey-Tunney II ticket. They slyly advertised that purchasers could both listen to the fight and own a radio.[47] State taxes, which accounted for $9.20 on a $40.00 ticket, also made the fight so expensive it prompted some to have "wandered around looking for friends with radio sets."[48] In what proved to be Tunney's swan song, he dispatched his game but overmatched challenger in the eleventh round before a disappointing crowd of 50,000. Rickard was peeved. He lamented that he only received $15,000 from NBC for the radio rights and ultimately lost $150,000 on the promotion. He publically asserted that everyone else made money on his promotion including the radio manufacturing companies, radio dealers, and radio servicemen who "made millions from the fight broadcast."[49]

If Rickard felt that a Tunney-Heeney conspiracy was afoot, he had the anecdotal evidence to support his sentiment. In at least one instance, a local movie house interrupted its motion picture to pipe in the radio broadcast of the bout as a free bonus to patrons.[50] To remedy the problem, Rickard played his favorite card. He declared a ban on further radio broadcasts of his promotions until the radio industry provided him with an economic solution.[51]

One fan, the radio director of WCAP, apparently had enough of Rickard's bellyaching. Having opted to listen to the fight over the radio rather than buy a ticket, he sent seven dollars to the promoter as a fee. In all likelihood Rickard was furious. However, he diplomatically returned the money and expressed interest in the continued broadcast of his boxing matches over the station.[52]

The Tunney-Heeney affair would prove to be the last battle of Rickard's decade-long love-hate relationship with the medium. Whether or not the poor gate was actually attributable to radio's drawing power or due to Heeney's lack thereof, international radio audiences were smitten. Standard US commercial broadcast radio stations, even those that emitted the most far-reaching signals such as WEAF, had no possibility of reaching Europe, to say nothing of the listening audience of Heeney's countrymen in New Zealand. However, alternative radio transmissions utilizing shortwave were getting close to reaching audiences halfway around the world.

Just a year earlier, C. R. Runyon Jr., a Yonkers, New York, amateur radio operator, received Jack Philbin's blow-by-blow description of the Heeney-Uzcudun fight from WMSG in New York and "transmitted by telegraph on 40.9 meters to John Grinan at station NJ2PZ in Jamaica, British West Indies, 1,500 miles away." At the end of the fight, the Jamaica station transmitted a similar "dot-and-dash" report of the match to amateur station OZ2AC in New Zealand on 21 meters. This allowed the following afternoon's newspapers to include a report of the fight.[53]

While the signal on 40.9 meters sent by Runyon was unable to reach New Zealand directly, superior transmitters would soon remedy that problem. For the Tunney-Heeney bout, WEAF was linked directly to the powerful shortwave radio station 2XAF, the 31.4-meter broadcaster of the General Electric Company at South Schenectady, New York. This allowed New Zealanders in such places as Palmerston North to listen to a blow-by-blow description of the fight. Halfway around the world in Sweden, similar setups would give Scandinavian fight fans the same opportunity.[54] Others in the world audience included Rome, where "atmospheric conditions occasionally blotted out the announcer's voice," and Copenhagen, where the broadcast and Tunney's short speech after the fight were clearly heard.[55]

The excitement of plucking a radio broadcast out of the air from a distant land was a thrill that might be hard to appreciate from today's perspective. However, at the time, it was an adventurous, sometimes exhilarating pastime, particularly for a live event that offered only one opportunity. It was like catching lightning in a bottle.

A radio enthusiast known as "Yoedeller" had such an experience while tuning in the Tunney-Heeney broadcast from New York. Sitting in his chalet in the Swiss Alps during the wee hours of the night, he began his search: "At 2 A.M. I switched on my four valver, somewhat dubiously, and tuned into Daventry, but heard nothing. Then changing down to the lower wavelengths I searched round [*sic*] to see if any of the German stations might be attempting to relay the Tunney-Heeney contest, but again there was nothing doing. Resolved to give Daventry one more trial, I tuned it in, and lo and behold! there came to me the sound of American voices in the distance, and I knew that I was in Yankee Stadium, New York. . . . A wonderful fight and a wonderful relay by the American shortwave and the English longwave transmitters," the satisfied listener beamed.[56]

A shortwave radio station in Massachusetts was also able to deliver a postfight message from Heeney to his home in Gisborne, New Zealand, twelve thousand miles away: "I am very sorry, but you folks at home know I did my best. I have been defeated but not hurt. Tom." A touching reply followed: "We are not disappointed. We heard broadcast of fight. Love from all. Father and Mother."[57]

Although carried on the airwaves, such messages were considered to be personal in nature. The Federal Communications Commission warned listeners against divulging the contents of these communiqués and requested that radio salesmen educate the consumer on the broadcasting rules. They also advocated for the creation of a maximum fine of up to $10,000, two years' imprisonment, or both, to be assessed to violators. However, in this instance it is doubtful that listeners feared consequences for divulging the fact that Heeney was loved by his Dad and Mom.[58]

Chapter 3

THE POST-RICKARD ERA AND MADISON SQUARE GARDEN

Shortly after the Heeney bout, Tunney would announce his retirement. The sudden death of Tex Rickard after appendicitis surgery followed in January, 1929. Rickard would lie in repose at his Madison Square Garden in a $15,000 coffin with "a cluster of radio amplifiers suspended above the bier." [1] It was a symbolic reminder of his love-hate relationship with the medium, even in death.

The sport now lacked a champion in its flagship division and was without one of its all-time great promoters. The corporate machine at Madison Square Garden quickly moved to redress both issues. The first order of business was to proceed with Rickard's promotion of the Sharkey-Stribling bout in Miami. This served as the initial step in a series of fights leading to a successor to Tunney's crown. For the time being, William Carey, vice president of Madison Square Garden, serves as their new promotional front man in Rickard's place. Originally, no radio coverage of the fight was scheduled, but the fight was ultimately broadcast.[2]

Boxing on the radio under Carey's watch proved to be similar to Rickard's in its Jekyll-and-Hyde approach. Several weeks after

Rickard's passing, WMSG aired Jack Sharkey's triumph over K. O. Christener as a warm-up to its broadcast of the Stribling fight the following month.[3]

However, as the search for Tunney's successor continued during the 1929 outdoor season, major elimination matches were conspicuously kept off the airwaves. These included Max Schmeling-Paulino Uzcudun and Tommy Loughran's light-heavyweight title defense against Jimmy Braddock, both contested at Yankee Stadium. The Garden's broadcasting trepidation was hardly unique. That same summer, promoters at Chicago Stadium offered no radio coverage for the highly anticipated Sammy Mandell-Tony Canzoneri lightweight title match, citing that radio would hurt the gate.[4] Keeping the match off the air was part of Stadium boss Paddy Harmon's general ban on radio.[5] The promoters in large cities were not the only ones who believed that radio was hurting the live gate. In Portland, Oregon, the local boxing commission compared receipts of radio and nonradio fights and determined that radio reduced live attendance. Radio broadcasts were subsequently banned, and the succeeding five shows showed more favorable receipts.[6]

In the fall of 1929, with the indoor season underway, Carey articulated the reasoning behind the Garden's radio ban and its guidelines. At that time, the ban only allowed broadcasting of bouts from the Garden itself, but not from outside arenas. Citing differences in financial factors, Carey explained how events at his own venue were less expensive because there was no rental fee for the facility, and the cost for preliminary bouts were usually substantially less. Additionally, the local clientele's superior accessibility to the Garden versus outdoor events contributed to a more reliable gate without fear of radio's encroachment.

"For the sake of cripples and bedridden people who might like to listen in over the radio I am very sorry," Carey said in a halfhearted apology for the nonbroadcast of bouts from outside arenas. It followed his explanation of the pressing obligation owed to the Garden Corporation and its stockholders. Grasping for a long-term solution,

Carey floated a suggestion to radio manufacturers to sponsor big fights outside of the Garden.[7]

In all fairness, it might not be accurate to characterize Carey's concerns for his infirm audience as disingenuous, but at least two promoters took action in this regard where Carey did not. Several years later, when the new fistic sensation Joe Louis burst on the scene, radio was eschewed for the sake of the gate, but promoter Foley carved out an exception. When Louis had his first major bout against "Kingfish" Levinsky, a special line was set up to the Hines Memorial Hospital. This allowed an account of the fight to be delivered to 1,700 bedridden World War I veterans who heard Louis depose the King.[8]

When John Henry Lewis met Max Marek at Chicago's Comiskey Park, in an elimination bout for James J. Braddock's title, similar accommodations were made by promoter Fred Irvin. In a bout for the Edward Hines Memorial Hospital Fund, hospital residents listened in on the fight with welterweight champion Barney Ross participating in the broadcast. Approximately 200 disabled veterans were also seated ringside, courtesy of the promoter.[9]

Acts of compassion aside, a permanent fix to the radio broadcast conundrum was elusive. With Jack Sharkey honing in on a shot for the vacant title, his match against Englishman "Fainting Phil" Scott in February, 1930, was passed over by radio. The radio audience was cheated out of another dramatic performance by Scott, who repeated his frequently exhibited "foul claim" histrionics.[10]

With the first decade of commercial radio at its close, it was clear that radio was now a permanent fixture of American life. Owen D. Young, president of the Radio Advisory Council of NBC, reported on the influence of radio and its effect upon all aspects of society, noting its role in politics, industry, religion, science, the arts, social service work, sports, and entertainment.[11] Yet, even as radio was gaining ground, its chief competitor had already appeared on the horizon. Just one month after Mr. Young's promising status report heralding radio's unlimited possibilities, Dr. A. N. Goldsmith, vice president of RCA, conducted a private demonstration of a new sort of "radio vision" called television.

For more than an hour, a small audience in Dr. Goldsmith's home watched the actions of men in a "distant studio" (three miles away) on a five-inch screen. It was reported that "the moving pictures were as distinct and clear as pictures reproduced in a newspaper, except when static splashes and interference marred the clarity."[12]

Dr. Goldsmith proudly reported that the equipment used for the experiment was already obsolete since a picture of fifteen to eighteen inches could already be reproduced. According to Goldsmith, "It is now entirely possible . . . to take this television 'eye' to a properly staged boxing match and project the contest in a fairly satisfactory manner."[13] Despite this optimistic assessment, boxing broadcasting on commercial television would not arrive for another dozen years.

After Tunney's retirement, the heavyweight championship lay dormant for two years. Jack Sharkey and Max Schmeling emerged as the leading contenders for the crown. With boxing's greatest prize at stake, their match was too crucial to keep off the airwaves. Carey, now president of the Garden, announced that the card, one of the "milk fund bouts," would be broadcast over a network of NBC.[14, 15, 16]

A novel approach to the broadcast included the addition of a "woman radio observer" to the announcing team who would "give a description of the spectacle from the feminine viewpoint."[17] The surviving, verbatim written transcript of Graham McNamee's radio call documented the only time in heavyweight history the title changed hands on a foul: "[Max] goes down, claiming a foul. Max is down, claiming a foul. Jack swung a long left to the mid-section and Max walked over to his corner and is sitting down. At the same instant the blow was struck the bell ended the round. It looks as though the blow was in the pit of the stomach. . . . They are making an examination to see whether or not it is a low blow. . . . Max seems unable to rise. Max for the first time is able to take a little drink of water, but his face is still writhing in pain. Jack almost fainted. We don't know why yet. Yes, Max wins on a foul."[18]

The internationally flavored heavyweight championship match was received on shortwave radio in Cape Town and other parts of the South African Union. "Perfect" radio reception was reported from Rio de

Janeiro.[19] Back in the United States, the "Red Special" was engaged in a 10,000-mile trip featuring the most ambitious "continuous practical demonstration of centralized radio on a moving train." It was reported that "an important high spot from the passengers' standpoint . . . [was] the reception of the Sharkey-Schmeling fight broadcast."[20]

The Sharkey-Schemling bout seemed to be an aberration in the nonbroadcasting edict of major outdoor bouts. Later that summer, the highly anticipated Jack "Kid" Berg and "Kid Chocolate" lightweight contest was a "no radio" Garden promotion at the open-air Polo Grounds in New York.[21]

The controversial match between the "Boston Gob" and "Herr Max" led to the inevitable rematch the following summer. Despite a deepening Depression and the broadcast of the fight on radio, 70,000 journeyed to Yankee Stadium to see Sharkey win the title. The bout produced one of boxing's great catchphrases, when Schmeling's irate manager Joe Jacobs declared somewhat justifiably, "We Wuz Robbed!"

The bout was broadcast by NBC to millions of fans through a large network of sixty-nine stations in the US and Canada and carried locally in New York on WJZ and WEAF. Graham McNamee called the fight, assisted by Charles Coe. In a novel approach, they alternated every three rounds until the thirteenth, where they switched duties each round, with Coe concluding.[22] To accommodate the German-speaking fans, Harry Sperber gave an account in German over shortwave radio. Spanish-speaking fans in South America heard a summarized version of McNamee's account in Spanish over shortwave station W2XAD.[23]

Schmeling's mother, Amanda, sat by her radio in Germany, listening to the shortwave broadcast. "He is such a good dear fellow, and deserves his successes," she told the press shortly before the match. "My boy is sure to win and remain the world champion,"[24] she predicted, unaware of the sleight of hand that was soon to follow.[25]

While William Carey and his promotional cohorts at the Long Island City Bowl (also known as the Madison Square Garden Bowl) would let the public hear the bout on the radio gratis, no one was going to view it for free. To discourage residents of Queensboro, who had taken to a neighboring rooftop to eavesdrop on the fight, promoters pointed two huge searchlights in their direction, effectively blinding their view of the ring.[26]

Joe Jacobs's voracious attack regarding the judges' decision against his charge, aired over NBC, again placed radio amidst a boxing controversy. Just a few weeks after the bout, the New York State Athletic Commission adopted a resolution limiting broadcast comments to the assigned announcers only. This change eschewed the established tradition that fighters and their handlers address the radio audience immediately following the bout.[27]

Jacobs had crossed the line, and his suspension was warranted. One of the immediate effects was that radio fans were deprived of hearing the upcoming intriguing match between Mickey Walker and Schmeling.[27] However, the postfight interview ban lasted only temporarily. The dramatic value of those sessions far exceeded the occasional collateral damage caused by a malcontent boxer or his manager.[28]

The commission's alienation of Joe Jacobs's rights would pale in comparison to what was around the corner. In 1933, Nazi Germany would ban all Jews from the participation in the sport of boxing.[29, 30] The Nazis, however, had a clear understanding of the machinations of boxing and pragmatically made the exception of allowing Jacobs to handle Schmeling in bouts contested outside Germany's borders. Hitler wanted the heavyweight champion to again be of German blood at any cost.

The leading contenders for Sharkey's title were Schmeling; the enigmatic Californian, Max Baer; and the giant Italian, Primo Carnera. Schmeling and Carnera were promoted by Carey and his group at the Garden, which included vice president Jimmy Johnston.[31] Baer was guided by former heavyweight champion Jack Dempsey. The "Manassa Mauler" had entered the serious promotional ranks when he served as front man for Rickard's final inspiration, the Sharkey-Stribling bout in Miami. Dempsey was making a gambit by challenging the Garden as the top promoter in the game. He was promoting bouts with Tim Mara and held the rights to certain dates at the Polo

Grounds and Yankee Stadium.[32, 33] Baer, the most talented heavyweight in the world, was Dempsey's ace in the hole.

Final pieces of the heavyweight puzzle were put into place with Carnera fighting for Sharkey's crown and Baer battling Schmeling for the next shot at the title. Unfortunately, neither fight was broadcast live on the radio. Carnera-Sharkey later received some airplay. After Carnera knocked out Sharkey in the sixth, Graham McNamee's spirited blow-by-blow account was played over the air—the excitement in his voice arriving deflated at the ears of those who already learned of the result.[34] Disappointingly, the other high-profile match of the year, Mara's Ross-Canzoneri, was also a "no radio" affair.[35]

Baer disposed of Schmeling with a spectacular knockout three weeks before Carnera won the title. Dempsey sought to gain leasing privileges to the Garden's two most coveted locations, the Long Island City Bowl and the Garden itself. The Garden balked at Dempsey's further attempts to make inroads into their promotional empire.[36] However, it would soon prove academic. The following summer, Dempsey's charge pummeled Carnera and annexed the title. "Carnera has fallen, Carnera has fallen again, but he is up instantly," Graham McNamee told a radio audience moments before the "Ambling Alp" was knocked out. "The man won't stay down, he'll fight till he's dead, that man," McNamee praised Carnera, who endured eleven knockdowns at the hands of Baer.[37]

By the end of 1934, Dempsey was once again on top of the fistic world, this time as the promoter of the heavyweight champion. In what seemed at the time to be a flight of whimsy, Dempsey purchased a Manhattan office building with plans to open a restaurant on the ground floor. During the Christmas season, the cornerstone was laid by mayor Fiorello LaGuardia, launching "Dempsey's Café." Unbeknownst to Jack, his promotional conquests would be short-lived, while his career as a restaurateur would keep his name in the press and in lights on Broadway for half a century.[38]

Nineteen thirty-five would prove to be a pivotal year for boxing. It would set the course for the heavyweight championship, the promotion of the sport, and, consequently, the destiny of the fight game on radio for the next fifteen years.

In retrospect, Jack Dempsey's recent promotional assault on Madison Square Garden proved minor in comparison to the real coup that former Rickard ticket scalper Mike Jacobs was staging. Unwittingly, Dempsey was for Jacobs what George Patton would later be for Dwight Eisenhower at D-Day—the perfect diversion. Jacobs, under the auspices of his newly formed Twentieth Century Sporting Club, was charging at the Garden's rear, wielding a titanic new weapon by the name of Joe Louis. Directing the Louis-led assault along with Jacobs from his newly established high ground at the Hippodrome was Garden turncoat William Carey. Carey switched his allegiance from the Garden to Jacobs, becoming the president of Twentieth Century.

Under the Twentieth Century banner, the Louis gun was unleashed against the gigantic target of Primo Carnera. Louis blasted Carnera out of the heavyweight picture. There was no radio coverage of the June 25 fight; this was of little concern to Jacobs, who scored a financial success with the promotion.

Two weeks before, James J. Braddock pulled a monumental upset of the champion Baer in a Garden-promoted event at its Long Island City Bowl. From a financial standpoint, Braddock had not been a particularly attractive opponent for Baer. Radio played a significant role in bringing about the fight—and Baer's defeat. The Braddock deal included revenue from *Taxi*, a radio serial starring Baer, the renewal of that program if Baer was victorious, and a movie option to make the serial into a motion picture. Had the deal not included these incentives, Baer would not have signed for the fight.[39] While his manager, Ancil Hoffman, had favorably negotiated the fight's radio rights, the title loss turned the affair into a long-term financial setback for Baer.[40]

Braddock's shocking upset against Baer was carried by radio to an audience of millions. One of the broadcast's many memorable moments was a radio tribute given to perennial ring announcer Joe Humphries. In a role reversal of sorts, the ailing ring announcer, who was as familiar to the radio audience as any personality in the sport, listened on his receiver to the tribute given by his replacement, Al Frazin.[41]

Dempsey's big gun Baer had misfired against Braddock, and Jack's promotional flank was now exposed. Sensing the changing winds of fortune, he made a last-ditch effort to get back in the fight by pitting his charge against Twentieth Century's Louis.

The Garden's two largest adversaries, Twentieth Century and Dempsey, had combined forces. In a meeting held by the Madison Square Garden Corporation, panic was evident. Addressing two hundred of the Garden's biggest stockholders, Chairman of the Board Colonel John S. Hammond attacked Carey's replacement, Garden President John Reed Kilpatrick, and his boxing director, Jimmy Johnston.[42] Just a few months prior, Kilpatrick and Johnston were taking bows as the masterminds of Baer-Braddock. Now they were both on the hot seat.[43]

Referring to the Louis-Baer encounter, which, not coincidently, was to occur that night, Hammond railed that the fight "which promises to be the most profitable boxing event in many years" is one "in which the stockholders of this corporation have not the slightest financial interest." In a house on fire, charges of corruption were also laid at Kilpatrick's feet, which he denied.[44]

Radio gave the fans the Brown Bomber's precision-punching dismantlement of the erstwhile heavyweight champion Baer. Louis was not only proving to be a titan in the ring, but a financial one, as well. Radio had absolutely no effect on the live gate, which for the first time since Dempsey-Sharkey exceeded a million dollars in a nontitle bout.

The arrival of Mike Jacobs completely changed how radio rights were handled in the fight game. Until that time, the rights were sold or bid on an individual basis and were not directly tied to other financial arrangements for the fight. For example, in a typical Max Baer bout, several sponsors would bid for the privilege of broadcasting the match. This competition ensured that Baer would receive the best financial deal possible.

Transactions were negotiated by the fighter's manager. Sometimes a specialist called a "radio manager" was used. Money earned from the broadcast was usually divided pursuant to the terms of the boxers' original fight contract. The sponsorship of a major bout could change fight to fight. Baer-Carnera was sponsored by B.F. Goodrich Co., Baer-Louis by General Motors, and so on.

For his own benefit, Jacobs favored a package deal. When he signed a promotional contract or otherwise made an arrangement with a fighter, the radio (and later television) broadcast rights were part of that overall transaction and compensation for a fighter. A fighter would typically receive a specific percentage of the "radio rights." The control of radio rights became promoter-centric. Jacobs could sell the radio rights to a sponsor of his

Promoter Mike Jacobs changed the way radio rights were handled, leading to an era of a more promoter-centric model with long-term sponsors. Pictured is Jacobs (far left), joined by Madison Square Garden promoter Jimmy Johnston and manager Joe Jacobs, greeting Max Schmeling as he arrives from Germany on the Zeppelin Hindenberg in 1936. *AP Photo.*

choosing. The deal Jacobs made with a sponsor would assuredly be the best for "Uncle Mike's" interests, but not necessarily for that of the fighter.[45]

While Braddock enjoyed the accolades for his unexpected upset of Max Baer, Louis was matched with Max Schmeling, the third ex-heavyweight champion he would face. The Brown Bomber's confidence was brimming. His biggest concern the day before the bout was his handlers' refusal to allow him to play a round of golf. Joe confidently predicted an early victory but would not tell the radio audience the round the fight would end.[46]

Foreshadowing serious social and political matters that would come to the fore at the time of their rematch two years later, a week before the match, radio station WEVD in New York broadcast the program "Three and a Half Million Jews in Poland Facing Extinction."[47] However, at the time most radio listeners were preoccupied with the upcoming fight, which was to be carried by NBC Radio by national hookup on ninety-seven stations from Maine to Honolulu. Shortwave also planned to carry the fight to Spain, Germany, and other foreign countries.[48]

The bouts scheduled for June 18 were postponed due to rain. Rudy Vallee, the host of radio's *The Fleischmann's Yeast Hour*, had already stacked his program that evening with guests related to the fight. Sparring partners for Louis and Schmeling appeared, and each advocated a victory by their employer. Bill Corum, sports editor of the *New York Evening Journal* and soon to become a fixture on boxing radio broadcasts, served as an impartial prognosticator. Corum, as did most of the experts, found Louis a prohibitive favorite, telling Vallee and the radio audience: "You can't possibly expect Schmeling to go more than three rounds."[49]

The following evening, the skies cleared and the fight proceeded. Schmeling's right hand stunned Louis in the fourth round, knocking him down. The Brown Bomber never fully recovered. Clem McCarthy described Louis's demise in the twelfth round, also brought about by the Schmeling right hand, to an incredulous radio audience: "Louis is down, Louis is down, hanging through the ropes, hurting badly, he is a very tired fighter, he is blinking his eyes, shaking his head, the count is nine, the fight is over! The fight is over!"[50]

Schmeling's wife, actress Anny Ondra, had an aversion to watching her husband box in person. She instead listened to the bout over shortwave radio in Germany with the country's Reich Minister of Propaganda, Dr. Joseph Goebbels. After the bout, Goebbels cabled Schmeling: "To your wonderful victory, my best congratulations. I know you fought for Germany; that it's a German victory. We are proud of you. Heil Hitler. Regards."[51]

Germany's Crown Prince Frederick Wilhelm, a former amateur boxer, also listened on shortwave radio and cabled Schmeling a congratulatory cable. Interest in Schmeling's victory in Germany was so acute that wax impressions were made of the match's radio recording of the match, to replay at a more convenient listening time the next evening.[52]

To describe the fight's results as shocking is not an overstatement. Twelve deaths were attributed to the bout, eleven coming from listeners of the radio broadcast in the US and Canada. One African American woman was stricken with a heart attack when Louis was knocked out.[53]

Schmeling's decisive victory made him the rightful challenger for Braddock's crown. At the time, the Garden was promoting Braddock. Braddock-Schmeling for the championship, promoted by Madison Square Garden, should have been a fait accompli. However, Mike Jacobs's attorneys had found a loophole in Braddock's contract with the Garden. Jacobs then persuaded Braddock to come aboard the Twentieth Century promotional express. Braddock was promised 10 percent of Louis's total earnings for the next ten years if he gave Louis the next crack at the title. Louis also acquiesced to the terms as a condition to "Uncle Mike" giving him a title shot.[54]

Jacobs's contract for a Louis-Braddock fight was signed in February, 1937, despite the fact that Braddock had already committed to a June 3 match against Schmeling at the Garden. Braddock's manager, Joe Gould, mockingly referred to the Garden contract as "a scrap of paper," stoking the controversy with incendiary remarks such as

"Hey, be sure that Kilpatrick and Jimmy Johnston get a picture of this signing right away."[55]

To protect their various interests, Schmeling, Garden president John Reed Kilpatrick, and even Nazi Germany scrambled to prevent the Louis bout. Schmeling made an offer of $250,000 to Braddock to fight in Berlin, with the Nazi regime's full support, but it was rejected.[56] The Nazis railed against NBC radio for canceling a Schmeling broadcast meant for him to make a case for his right to fight for the title.[57]

In a moment as bizarre as any in heavyweight history, Schmeling defiantly donned his boxing trunks and weighed in at the New York State Athletic Commission's office for his phantom match with Braddock. Schmeling scaled at 186 pounds and was declared ready, willing, and able to fight.

Braddock and Gould, both no-shows, were fined $1,000 each and suspended in New York State. Significantly, Braddock was not stripped of his title. Equally relevant was the Illinois State Boxing Commission's failure to honor the New York suspension. In effect, Illinois gave the green light for Braddock-Louis in their state. Attempts by the Garden's legal wizards to prevent the match were made in vain, with the bout ultimately taking place at Comiskey Park in Chicago.[58]

The significance of these events cannot be emphasized enough. Jacobs and the Twentieth Century Sporting Club had not only wrested the heavyweight championship away from Madison Square Garden, but with it, the control of radio. Radio (and later television) revenue would increasingly become a more lucrative part of the sport's operation. The Madison Square Garden Corporation was no longer king of this domain. Reduced to a feudal landlord, it would not share in these profits. It would need to subsist on the rental fees for its properties—the Garden and other facilities it controlled. The need for its services would be subject to the whims of Mike Jacobs, the new ruler of boxing.

Just as he had against Baer, Braddock would make a spirited attempt against Louis. He would even floor Joe in the first round before succumbing to inevitable defeat in the eighth round. By the time Louis ascended to the heavyweight throne, the broadcast of boxing on radio, with national hookups and international shortwave broadcasts, had become standard practice.

Chapter 4

LOUIS AND THE WAR: A MIKE JACOBS RADIO PRESENTATION

As heavyweight champion, Joe Louis would amass a record-setting twenty-five title defenses from 1937 to 1949. Domestic broadcasts of these events became perfunctory and were handled by the ever-growing national radio networks operated by NBC and the Mutual Network. They were often accompanied by international coverage via shortwave radio.

Louis's first title defense at Yankee Stadium against the scrappy Welshman Tommy Farr was broadcast through a coast-to-coast hookup via NBC and by shortwave to Great Britain, Argentina, Canada, and Mexico.[1] Farr made Louis work for a unanimous decision. Following the fight, Louis admitted to the radio audience that Farr had hurt him twice. Vanquished but still proud, Farr told radio listeners: "I've got plenty of guts—that's old Tommy Farr, you know, I'm a Welshman."[2] In his next bout, Louis easily disposed of Harry Thomas by knockout. Meanwhile, Schmeling waited in the wings—still the logical contender for the title due to his earlier KO of Louis.

Radio listeners in Germany were closely following their hero's road back to the heavyweight championship. In December, 1937, they listened to the shortwave broadcast of the Schmeling-Harry Thomas affair coming from New York. When the bout was over, they exploded onto the streets of Berlin to celebrate his eighth-round knockout.[3] The following month, Schmeling won a decision over Ben Foord in Hamburg, with his countrymen listening to the German radio broadcast. New York audiences would hear the rebroadcast on WOR the following morning at the odd hour of 11:30 A.M.[4] Not to be outdone by Schmeling, Louis also knocked out Harry Thomas in his final tune-up, paving the way for their historic June 22, 1938, rematch.

The whole world had an opinion on Schmeling-Louis II, boxing's biggest fight since the "Battle of the Long Count." Boxing broadcasters Ted Husing and Bill Stern picked Louis, with Stern specifying a knockout victory. Graham McNamee picked Max by decision "because Schmeling is a better fighter and a smarter man." Radio comedian Edgar Bergen picked Louis. "I pick Schmeling because Bergen says Louis," his wooden companion Charlie McCarthy countered.[5]

Against the orders of Mike Jacobs, Schmeling flew from Schenectady, New York, to Newark Airport on the day of the fight. Schmeling, an aviator himself, was so relaxed that he even took the controls for part of the flight.

The fight was heralded as the greatest sports broadcast in radio history. NBC carried the bout over both its Blue and Red Networks on 146 stations. The contest was broadcast in multiple languages including Spanish, German, and Portuguese and was carried via shortwave to Canada, Mexico, South America, Great Britain, and Germany.[6]

The conclusion of the most famous round in boxing history was called by Clem McCarthy as follows: "A left to the head, a left to the jaw, a right to the head and [referee Arthur] Donovan is watching carefully. Louis measures him. Right to the body, a left hook to the jaw, and Schmeling is down. The count is five, six, seven, eight—the men are in the ring. The fight is over on a technical knockout. Max Schmeling is beaten in one round."[7]

Schmeling suffered a longitudinal fracture through the third lumbar vertebrae. While an unusual injury for a boxer, it was not a

After Joe Louis defeated Max Schmeling in their rematch in one round, African American radio listeners in Washington, DC, jam the streets in celebration. *AP Photo.*

long-term or serious condition. However, rumors regarding the injury were rampant. Telephone inquiries to radio studios, *The New York Times* switchboard, and the Polyclinic Hospital where Schmeling was taken quickly reached into the thousands. The hospital was so besieged by calls that it was compelled to ask radio officials to make an announcement on the airwaves denying Schmeling's death and requesting that further inquiries cease.[8]

With the loss to Schmeling reversed and five ex-heavyweight champions vanquished, Jacobs set a course for Louis to mop up the rest of the heavyweight division. In the next three years, Louis would defend his title an incredible fifteen times.

In 1939, a national radio hookup, courtesy of NBC, delivered Louis's raucous defense against the human beer barrel, "Two Ton" Tony Galento.[9] Galento was proprietor of a bar in Orange, New Jersey. A crowd of 1,000 of Galento's friends and fans packed his tiny tavern to listen to Tony and Joe swap bombs at Yankee Stadium via radio. The tavern reached a moment of euphoria when Galento floored the champion with his big left hook. Shortly after that, Galento was battered into submission. His bar emptied. The crowd silently dispersed into the Jersey summer evening. But they had not abandoned their charge. Two hours later they returned in full force to greet their defeated hero.[10]

That same year, Joe Louis tracked down the fleet-footed Bob Pastor in eleven rounds in a surprisingly entertaining bout, also broadcast nationally by NBC.[11] Just three weeks earlier, Germany had invaded Poland, and World War II began in Europe. However, the war had no immediate effect on boxing in America.

In 1940, the high point of Louis's defenses was his first bout against Arturo Godoy. The Chilean with the crab-like defense surprised the Brown Bomber, lasting the full fifteen rounds. The contest was broadcast nationally over the NBC Network and on WJZ in New York.[12]

Chileans heard the bout over shortwave radio. In Santiago, crowds gathered in the main plaza to listen to the fight over loud speakers. The throng grew more intense with each passing round. Men were seen slapping each other on the back in a congratulatory manner as Godoy made it through another session with Louis, sometimes with apparent success. When the unfavorable decision was announced, Godoy's countrymen were crestfallen but calm. In a true expression of the "good-neighbor policy," Godoy's Chilean promoter explained, "I think the decision was well made, and if it is ever claimed in Chile that Godoy was robbed of a triumph it will be because of over-enthusiasm of the loudspeaker accounts . . . Chileans may be proud that Godoy fought the best fight any Chilean boxer ever made."[13] Godoy's newfound fame immediately brought him several offers to appear on radio in South America.[14]

Louis's next significant bout was his June 1941 defense against former light-heavyweight champion Billy Conn, who had vacated his throne to compete as a heavyweight. The announcing team of Don Dunphy and Bill Corum made their partnership debut for the call of the fight. Dunphy, with between-round embellishment from Corum, thrillingly described how Conn, lighter by 25 pounds, outsped and outboxed the champ until the fateful thirteenth round, when Louis scored a convincing knockout.

Tallying a record-setting twenty title defenses in four short years as heavyweight champion, Louis had solidified his position as one of America's greatest sports heroes. For a generation of Americans, particularly those of African descent, listening to a Joe Louis fight on the radio was a genuinely meaningful, sometimes exhilarating experience. Throughout the cities of America, people from all walks of life retreated indoors and huddled around their radios with heightened anticipation and rapt attentiveness before a Louis bout. Streets and stoops were left eerily vacant. The poor and others in rural areas without a radio would set off on a "holy quest" to find the nearest receiver.

Radio could elicit powerful emotions and create enduring memories. Motown musical impresario Berry Gordy remembers the second Louis-Schmeling fight: "We were crowded around the radio. It was like a magical something that was happening in our house and I still feel it today."[15]

And former President Jimmy Carter: "I was fourteen years old and our family had the only radio in the area. Some of our African American neighbors came and asked my father if they could come and listen to the fight. So, daddy thought there would be three or four of them but when the time for the fight came, I would guess about forty showed up. It was very interesting because the customs of the South then prevailed and there was not a sound out of the Black listeners. Nothing, just absolute quiet, after Louis won. And then they walked across the railroad, a couple hundred yards away, and all hell broke loose. They celebrated all night long to early, almost daylight."

Radio required that the listener have a high degree of engagement in the process. Consequently, it possessed a wondrous power for the creation of vivid visual images in the minds of its participants. Famed poet and activist Maya Angelou recalls that everyone listened quietly to the Louis blow-by-blow descriptions on the radio, and how a sudden "explosion of sound" would follow at the end of each round. "Did you see that—and it was never hear—it was always did you *see* Joe Louis." And then at the start of the next round, she explains, "the radio would be turned up . . . silence."[16]

One newspaper account described the radio broadcast of the Louis-Schmeling rematch in Harlem, New York, and its aftermath as follows: "For a few seconds over two minutes Harlem here was as silent as a tomb with the exception of the rapid-fire account of the goings-on in Yankee Stadium as relayed to millions through radio loud speakers. Then suddenly bedlam broke loose. Thousands of overjoyed persons poured from apartment houses and private homes, stores, halls and other meeting places, shouting deliriously, shaking hands, hugging each other. Joe Louis had won."[17] While Louis's radio broadcasts could hold entire communities spellbound, they also forged intense bonds on the personal level. Mrs. Mary Gillepsie of Youngstown, Ohio, age 103 and originally from Eutaw, Alabama, spent the first twenty years of her life in slavery. Unable to read, she used radio as her prime source of entertainment. Listening to a Louis fight was her pride and joy. She was said to never have missed one. "When is he going to fight again?" she would anxiously ask her granddaughter while Louis was inactive during the war years.[18]

As the war raged on in Europe during the summer of 1941, American sports moved along jauntily . . . almost blindly. Joe DiMaggio was building his fifty-six-game hitting streak, Ted Williams was flirting with a .400 batting average, and Joe Louis had defended his title six times in just six months. Then on December 7, 1941, the Japanese bombed Pearl Harbor, and the United States entered the war. Like so many aspects of domestic American life, the boxing landscape would undergo a complete overhaul.

During the next four years, fighters turned in their jabs, hooks, and crosses for weapons of a more destructive nature. Almost every American boxing champion wore a military uniform. After a stint at Fort Dix, New Jersey, heavyweight champion Joe Louis traveled the world. First as a private and later as a sergeant in the US Army, he held boxing exhibitions before countless United States servicemen.

Middleweight champion Tony Zale joined the Navy and served as a boxing instructor at the Great Lakes Naval Station. Another middleweight claimant and former Zale opponent, Al Hostak, served in the Army. The Naval reserve augmented its ranks with welterweight champion Freddie "Red" Cochrane, who taught boxing at the Newport, Rhode Island, station. The Coast Guard was provided boxing instruction from light-heavyweight champion Gus Lesnevich. Contenders also ranked among the enlisted. Billy Conn and Melio Bettina joined the Army, as did middleweights Billy Soose and Georgie Abrams.[19] In all, more than 4,500 boxers served in the United States military during World War II.

Mike Jacobs had anticipated the mass exodus of boxing talent and the expiration of Louis, his meal ticket. Before Louis would embark on a world tour in which he would box a staggering ninety-six exhibitions during the war, Jacobs would squeeze two more promotions out of his heavyweight charge.

However, from this point forward, the sport would be administered through the prism of the war effort. In an immediate patriotic gesture just a month after Pearl Harbor, Jacobs had Louis in the ring in the first of two charity promotions.

The first pitted Joe in a rematch against Buddy Baer at Madison Square Garden. The bout was staged for the benefit of the Navy Relief Society, a charity for families of servicemen recently killed in action. Louis and Baer donated their entire purses to the fund while Jacobs contributed the entire gate proceeds. Madison Square Garden also reduced its rental fee, effectively increasing Jacobs's donation.

Baer had knocked Louis through the ropes in their first encounter, and there was keen interest in the return bout. The fight was broadcast over the radio by the Mutual Broadcasting System and its 190 stations across the US and Canada.[20] Wendell Willkie, the recently defeated Republican presidential candidate, addressed a national radio audience prior to the bout, praising both fighters for their generosity.[21] Louis dispatched Baer in a single canto, but the galvanizing event was only anticlimactic from an athletic standpoint.

The next day, Louis volunteered for service in the US Army.[22] Two months later, the heavily-favored champion would reenter the ring as "Private Joe Louis" against the gigantic Abe Simon. Simon had shown durability in their first match before succumbing to Joe in the thirteenth round in Detroit. Equitable in his support of the military's various branches, this time the "Brown Bomber" donated his entire purse to the Army Relief Fund. The match was carried in North America over 201 stations of the Mutual Broadcasting System with Dunphy and Corum at the microphone. Their efforts were complemented by international coverage via shortwave.[23]

Before the bout, Under Secretary of War Robert F. Patterson spoke to thousands of servicemen listening over the radio: "It is an army of champions. It is engaged in a championship fight and it is going to win. We pay a special tribute to Private Joseph Louis Barrow. He is truly a great champion. He is a credit to the ring and a credit to the Army."[24] US servicemen overseas in England, Ireland, and Iceland listened to the bout the following morning during a 9:30 A.M. rebroadcast.[25]

Almost overnight, boxing broadcasts had taken on a patriotic hue. During the call of the bout, Don Dunphy noted the "real American gameness in both boys," and that "Louis keeps moving in all the time, the American way." Dunphy concluded the broadcast of Louis's victory via a sixth-round TKO by reminding the audience, "We won't stop punching, just as Joe does, till we win."[26] With Joe in the Army, the championship would be frozen. Louis would not defend his heavyweight laurels for the next four years.

Louis had appeared at the Garden a few weeks earlier as a guest of Wendell Willkie for the Navy Relief Society's combination dinner and show program. Wearing his military uniform, he took the stage to address those gathered at the event.[27] The moment was brought to a national audience over the Red Network of NBC.[28] With a few simple words, Louis captured the hearts and minds of his countrymen: "We gon do our part, and we will win, because we are on God's side."[29] The line would become one of the most memorable of the war. Virtually overnight, Louis metamorphosed into a symbol of America's fighting spirit and physical prowess and a representation of the country's ideals of hard work, dedication, and fair play. Over the next several years, radio broadcasts featuring news coverage of Louis's military career echoed these ideas, solidifying them in the American consciousness.[30]

When NBC Radio broadcast the opening ceremonies of "I Am Proud to be an American Day," from New York's Central Park, Louis stood shoulder-to-shoulder with a million-and-a-quarter other patriotic Americans. The mere mention of his presence to the radio audience could deliver the desired effect.[31]

Just as Joe Louis became a soldier and symbol for the United States, Max Schmeling assumed a similar role for Germany. And as with Louis, radio would now follow the exploits of Schmeling, not from ringside, but from the front lines.

Germany was at war for almost two years by the summer of 1941, when Louis was still defending his title. At that time, German radio proudly reported that Schmeling was one of the first parachutists to land as part of Germany's invasion of the strategic Greek island of Crete.[32] A much more sober, subsequent radio report claimed Schmeling was seriously injured and would never box again.[33] British and New Zealand sources even reported that Schmeling had been killed in action. However, he was alive in a German hospital.[34] The following year, the *London Daily Sketch* reported that a Nazi-controlled Paris radio station had broadcast that Schmeling was seriously injured and captured by the Russians.[35] German radio, however, confirmed that Schmeling was in Berlin still recovering from wounds he received in the Battle of Crete.[36]

To accompany Schmeling's newfound militaristic bravery, Joseph Goebbels and the German Ministry of Propaganda refitted "Herr Max" with an equally impressive boxing résumé. Nazi shortwave broadcasts would now cast Schmeling as a victim of a Louis foul in the fabled rematch.[37]

Schmeling was eventually released from active military duty. Hamburg radio reported that he was sentenced for a three-month

World War II elevated heavyweight champion Joe Louis to the status of patriotic symbol, reflected in both his boxing and nonboxing radio appearances. Louis is shown sewing on sergeant stripes after his promotion. *By US Office of War Information via Wikimedia Commons.*

prison term by a British military tribunal for building a house in defiance of postwar occupation authorities.[38] He eventually retreated to his farm in Cologne amid speculation that he was to box a Nazi paratrooper in Rome. He recovered sufficiently to appear in five professional bouts between September 1947 and October 1948 after an eight-year hiatus from the ring.[39]

Louis would fare better at the conclusion of the war. A national radio audience listened to *The Army Hour* to hear Sergeant Joe Louis receive the Legion of Merit at a ceremony conducted at Fort Hamilton. The award was bestowed on Louis for boxing ninety-six exhibitions before more than two million soldiers. He achieved this as a member of an Army group that toured the US as well as European, Mediterranean, North African, and Italian theaters.

The citation explained that Louis had taken considerable risk regarding his future as heavyweight champion but boxed for the servicemen nevertheless. Louis was lauded as "a model soldier in training and an inspiration to soldiers everywhere. . . . You have made one of the greatest contributions to the reconditioning program of soldiers overseas."[40] When reminded of the earnings he might have made in civilian life for the many bouts he staged for the troops, Louis responded, "Heck, lots of soldiers have give up a lot more than Joe Louis have."[41]

On December 7, 1945, Louis appeared on the *Bill Stern Sports Reel* radio program in New York and spoke from Seattle via a live radio feed: "I suppose tonight I am expected to talk about Billy Conn and the fight for my title next June. But I'd rather talk about a bigger fight. Today is December the seventh. Four years ago, America was attacked at Pearl Harbor. Over four thousand boxers joined the service. Some of those are not coming back. I thought I knew something about fighting, but the Army taught me a lot more. Mainly, that a great champion get off the floor to win. America was on the floor four years ago today. Our chance didn't look so good, but we won. Thanks to a lot of American youngsters who refused to be beaten. I hope I beat Billy Conn, but whether I do or not, I have the satisfaction of knowing at least, I have played on one All-American team that will never be licked, the United States Army."[42]

Louis's contributions to the war effort exceeded that of all others in the boxing community. The heavyweight champion's services were unique in that his value as American propaganda far exceeded the participation of a single combat soldier. However, most boxers including some champions and former champions actively fought in the conflict, making extraordinary contributions. The most notable was former lightweight and welterweight champion Barney Ross, who served with unsurpassed distinction at Guadalcanal in the Pacific.

Guadalcanal was host to some of the fiercest fighting and most severe casualties of the war. In the brief respites from the daily horror, diversions were necessary. A radio station, dubbed "the mosquito network," was constructed on the island by army engineers and signalmen under the supervision of the Armed Forces Radio Service. The station broadcast a blow-by-blow description of the prizefights held on the island for the benefit of those unable to attend in person.[43] In one match at Guadalcanal, Ross faced a 215-pound Samoan, the champion of the island. He credited his scientific boxing and the $2,000 his marine buddies waged on him for spurring him on to victory.

In combat, Ross was credited with killing countless Japanese soldiers "while guarding wounded marine comrades in a shell hole at an advanced post on Guadalcanal." He was recommended for the Navy Cross. A wounded Ross returned home and appeared on the Leatherneck's Halls of Montezuma broadcast from the US Marine Corps base. He addressed a nationwide radio audience, updating the country on the efforts of America's fighting youth: "The boys on Guadalcanal had been more worried about the folks back home than they were about themselves."[44] Several months later, at the naval hospital in St. Albans, Long Island, Marine Sergeant Ross received the Silver Star Medal. Ross's recognition was part of the NBC Blue Network's Independence Day radio program honoring American fighting men. The accompanying citation read: "For conspicuous gallantry and intrepidity in action against the enemy while serving with a Marine battalion on Guadalcanal, British Solomon Island, November18–20, 1942."[45] Ross was a frequent supporter of the war effort and participated in other events including speaking at the Red Cross War Fund from Madison Square Garden.[46]

As boxers like Ross and Louis helped define the role of the boxer in the war, the value of the sport itself was capitalized upon by the United States military. Boxing was not only a natural subject for instructional training and recreation for servicemen, but also a form of entertainment carried abroad via radio.

In July of 1943, a modest group of transmitters began broadcasting to American soldiers overseas. These stations were collectively called American Forces Network. The network quickly incorporated boxing into its programming. American bouts could be heard through commercial radio broadcasts that were recorded and then shipped abroad. Local fights such as those staged by the American Red Cross were also broadcast, sometimes live and sometimes recorded.[47]

From the war's outset, it was also recognized that boxing on the home front proved a valuable form of entertainment for the ever-growing wartime population. On the heels of Pearl Harbor, a party was staged at the Infantry Armory in Patterson, New Jersey, for local defense workers. The event, broadcast over radio station WPAT, featured boxing as a primary part of the entertainment. The price of admission for local soldiers from a nearby Army camp was a package of cigarettes.[48]

The boxing community and radio would also join forces to raise money for the war effort through a multitude of charitable endeavors. In Los Angeles, two War Bond rallies were scheduled in connection with the Los Angeles Golden Gloves. The opening bouts were broadcast over KMPC in Los Angeles, and the station purchased first-row, ringside seats to distribute to purchasers of $2,500 bonds.[49] Frank Sinatra formed a singing group with Los Angeles sports figures called the "Bond Selling Quartet" to spearhead the efforts at the radio station during a half-hour broadcast.[50]

Boxing and radio would remain patriotic bedfellows until the conclusion of the war. In 1946, when the sporting world renewed its robust place in American society, boxing on radio continued to be a major component. However, in a few short years, radio's position as the sport's premier medium would be challenged by television. The golden age of radio's broadcast of boxing was drawing to its close. By the early-1950s, television would displace radio as the primary conduit for the sport.

After the war, radio did continue for more than a decade as an alternative choice to television. In practical terms, this option was preferable only when a television set was unavailable or if a match was "blacked out" on TV. Ironically, while radio was in its decline, its broadcasts featured some of the sport's greatest figures. Radio broadcasts of bouts featuring Rocky Graziano, Kid Gavilan, Sugar Ray Robinson, Rocky Marciano, Ezzard Charles, Carmen Basilio, and Gene Fullmer all created vivid, memorable experiences. Different from those created by television broadcasts, but no less compelling.

By the dawn of the 1960s, the idea of listening to an event such as a prizefight had become antiquated. With the exception of a few championship matches, boxing on the radio had passed into history.

Chapter 5

INVENTING AN INDUSTRY: THE RADIO ANNOUNCERS, PART 1

Every industry has its founding father. Boxing and radio broadcasting claimed J. Andrew White. White began as a public director for the Marconi Company of America during a time when people were amused with "a rumor . . . that you could send a human voice around the world." In 1913, he founded *The Wireless Age,* radio's first magazine. Years later, White would reflect that "the radio business was . . . a plaything for a group of stock manipulators."[1]

White used his position as the vice president and manager of *Wireless Press, Inc.* to advance the industry by making radio programs popular. He launched boxing broadcasting on radio by announcing its first four title matches: Dempsey-Carpentier, Britton-Leonard, Leonard-Tendler, and Britton-Walker. Throughout the Roaring Twenties, White remained a premier announcer for the sport. Notwithstanding his historic and legendary ringside broadcasts, White's greatest contribution to boxing was incorporating radio into the mainstream. He helped the medium earn a modicum of respectability when it had none. His positioning of radio also allowed for its successful alliance with the fight game.[2]

While White may have been radio's first boxing advocate and seminal announcer, his sometime partner Graham McNamee rivaled him as boxing's premier radio voice. McNamee was behind the microphone for many of the great boxing broadcasts of the 1920s and the Depression era. He covered such high-profile matches as Dempsey-Tunney II and Baer-Carnera.

McNamee and White stood above others in their profession. When they were not broadcasting partners, they were sometimes competitors. They even went head-to-head in broadcasting the 1924 Democratic Convention from Madison Square Garden. McNamee went on air for WEAF, while Major White handled coverage for rival station WJZ.[3]

McNamee began his radio announcing career in the early 1920s, capitalizing on a voice cultivated as a church baritone and concert singer of some repute. His radio reporting ran the gamut from philharmonic concerts and national political conventions to World Series games and championship boxing matches.[4]

His first opportunity in boxing came with live coverage for WEAF at the training camps of Johnny Wilson and Harry Greb. The pair was preparing for their August 1923 championship bout at the Polo Grounds. His call of Greb winning the title brought him critical acclaim. "I tried to give my thousands of hearers the impressions that I might have given a man sitting beside me who could not see," he explained.[5]

In just two years, McNamee reached the pinnacle of his trade. He won the honor of most popular announcer according to a national survey conducted by *The Radio Digest* and was presented with its gold cup at the 1925 Radio Show.[6]

McNamee participated in many seminal moments of radio's golden age. In an NBC program, 20 million listeners tuned in to a unique broadcast of the making of a motion picture. The filming of four scenes from Paramount's *Knockout Reilly* starring Richard Dix was described by McNamee. Several prominent boxing figures were in the ring during the filming including Joe Humphries, Jimmy DeForest, and Billy McPartland. Radio fans were taken "into the

Graham McNamee (pictured), along with J. Andrew White, was a premier broadcaster of boxing on radio during the 1920s. He was at the microphone for the iconic "Battle of the Long Count." *By National Photo Company Collection (Library of Congress) via Wikimedia Commons.*

studio for the first time" to hear "the voices of the actors, the megaphone instructions of the director, the shouts of the extras, the crackle of the klieg lights and the orchestra accompaniment to dramatic scenes."[7]

McNamee offered an interesting announcing style in that he operated in two distinctive gears. Speaking quickly, he would churn out the text of a radio commercial or a blow-by-blow description quite rapidly.

At other moments, you would swear he would seem drifting or entering into a moment of great repose. In a slow, clipped manner: "The judges for tonight . . . are . . . Tommy . . . Shortell . . . and Charlie Lynch." And then with even more deliberation: "Tommy . . . Shortell . . . and . . . Charlie . . . Lynch."[8] McNamee found his stride when he struck the proper balance between the two approaches. One early critic noted that "his immediate grasp of the psychology of the auditor, who sometimes waited breathless for a word or a sentence, brought him acclaim throughout the country."[9]

McNamee's casual manner with the audience had a certain appeal: "Boy, that man Carnera is big, Carnera is so big that your mind some way refuses to accept what you saw the last time you saw him and you get that same sense of surprise the next time you see him."[10] Proponents of McNamee would describe his blow-by-blow descriptions as including "much news, considerable color, just enough humor and no undue quantity of irrelevant chatter."[11] Despite all of McNamee's acclaim, there were detractors. Joe Jacobs, Max Schmeling's manager, claimed that his call of the first Sharkey-Schmeling fight was prejudicial to his fighter. Jacobs would convince NBC to remove McNamee from the microphone for the upcoming Stribling-Schmeling match in favor of Sam Taub. Graham's role was limited to between-round color commentary.[12]

One fair criticism of McNamee was his lack of smoothness. On occasion, he lapsed into halting delivery or momentary loss for words. However, these deficiencies were often superseded by a genuine enthusiasm and anxiousness that made his calls compelling.

However, broadcasting was in its infancy, and McNamee had no predecessors to study or emulate. Therefore, he invented his own approach and created standards. He admirably stands as an early primate, so to speak, on boxing's evolutionary announcing chart.

During the 1920s, the radio microphone attracted a diverse group of successful boxing participants like Harold W. Arlin, Phillips Carlin, Jim McDonald, and George Moore. Others found the experience fleeting or flawed. Boxing columnist and well-known writer Paul Gallico had a brief spell calling significant bouts. One involving Georges Carpentier was broadcast on WMSG. Another featuring André Routis vs. Eddie Anderson from the Polo Grounds aired over WNYC.[13]

Nat Fleischer, editor of *The Ring,* also had a dalliance with the microphone, calling the Sammy Baker-Larry Estridge bout over WMSG. He was paired with Walter Nehf, who provided the in-between round analysis. Boxing columnist Stuart Hawkins described the broadcast as "the most woefully inadequate, utterly colorless and consistently exasperating broadcast that has ever disappointed eastern listeners."[14] In a letter published a few days later, the fiery Fleischer provided his sarcastic response to Hawkins's column: "I have been watching the fights for only twenty-three years and therefore may not be acquainted with the sport and its terminology."[15]

While the brunt of Hawkins's criticism was aimed at Fleischer, Nehf was made sport of for his careless plugging of the sponsor's product. Nehf noted that its cigarettes were liberally consumed by those in attendance. He then added that "smoking is not allowed in the Garden on a fight night."[16]

Since early radio broadcasting covered an array of topics, typically a small cadre of experienced announcers under contract with a station or network received diverse assignments. While today it would seem incongruous for Jim Lampley to cover politics and Brian Williams to report on boxing, during the late twenties and early thirties, the voices of politics and boxing were often one and the same. The generalist was the soup du jour.

Ted Husing, for example, served double duty for William Paley's newly formed Columbia Broadcasting System (CBS). He not only acted as anchorman at both the Democratic and Republican presidential conventions in 1932, he also took the mike at the Schmeling-Sharkey heavyweight championship rematch at the Madison Square Garden Bowl.[17]

Boxing announcers of the period were assigned to all types of major news events. Graham McNamee broadcast the arrival of Charles A. Lindbergh in Washington, DC, after his historic trans-Atlantic flight. Several months later, he announced the second Dempsey-Tunney fight via the largest network of stations ever to carry a radio program to date.[18]

In 1930, Major J. Andrew White retired from announcing boxing with a desire to settle down and play polo. He had done it all—parlaying his position as editor of *The Wireless Age* and run as a radio sports announcer into a tenure as president of CBS. White's exit from announcing marked the decline of the initial era of boxing broadcasting.[19] A fundamental change would soon take place with the generalist giving ground to the boxing specialist. That same year, in sync with the ever-growing sophistication and specialization in the industry, a member of NBC took to the lectern at City College in New York to teach the first college course in broadcasting.[20]

During this time, Ted Husing began his rise and would eventually supplant Graham McNamee as the sport's premier broadcaster. As early as 1927, Husing was competing favorably with McNamee and his colleague Phillips Carlin in the calling of football games. He was credited with giving "more complete information . . . and more acute observations as to plays, possibilities and potentialities of the teams and individual players on the field." Husing would carry this superior attention to detail and analysis to his ringside broadcasts.[21]

While other boxing announcers of the Depression era were sometimes criticized by the black press for bias against black fighters, Husing received rare praise. An article in the African American newspaper, *New York Amsterdam News,* called his WABC radio program *Sportslants* "one of the boldest, most courageous" attempts at taking a stance against racial prejudice. Not only did the program feature black heavyweight George Godfrey as a guest, but Husing permitted the public airing of the position shared by Godfrey and others that there was discrimination against the fighter. Godfrey's absence from the championship bout being contested for Tunney's vacated title, it was argued, cast doubts as to the credibility of the upcoming Schmeling-Sharkey match.[22, 23]

Husing's voice had a touch of the patrician. It possessed a notably different tone and texture from that of his major contemporaries, particularly Clem McCarthy and Sam Taub. It is understandable why he was a successful announcer not only of boxing matches, but important news stories and events, as well.

James Dolan, sports director of CBS Radio Network, summarized the Husing style: "He was always in control of his voice. . . . He could bring you to the edge of your chair without screaming. He had a sense of pacing and an ability to transfer what he said very accurately. He loved language—the sound of it and the flow of it."[24]

Whether he was serving as the blow-by-blow announcer or acting as the between-round color commentator, Husing had the ability to entertain his audience without loss of technical analysis or detail. The Joe Louis-Jack Sharkey fight broadcast on CBS: "Sharkey, beginning the round, was forcing Louis to slow down, to fight the fight that Sharkey wanted. He was a sort of sneering, domineering Sharkey. He had Louie worried because Joe Louis was forcing the fighting, but Sharkey in return and in retaliation was light in those blows. Suddenly from nowhere at all, as Sharkey spun around, we noticed his left eye was cut. Light drops of blood were pouring down—and then before you could say Jack Robinson—that right ripped out, caught him high on the chin and dropped him right down here in front of the microphone for a nine count."[25]

Husing's color commentary for the Louis-Sharkey bout helped propel him to the top echelon of the sport. As late as 1951, he still attracted top-notch assignments such as Don Dunphy's color commentator for the radio broadcast of the Robinson-La Motta middleweight championship bout. He remained a force in boxing radio broadcasting for more than twenty years, eventually sidelined in 1954 due to health issues.

Husing's broadcast partner for the Louis-Sharkey fight, the ex-Navy welterweight Charles "Socker" Coe, was another popular boxing voice during the 1930s. Coe represented a certain brand of media man unique to his era but ubiquitous for his times—he had one foot in the newspaper world, and the other in the domain of radio. After providing his blow-by-blow description of the Louis-Sharkey tiff, he put down his microphone, remained seated at ringside, and typed his report of Louis's quick knockout of Sharkey. The article appeared in the *World Telegram* and other Scripps-Howard papers the next morning.[26]

Coe had a higher-pitched voice than most of his colleagues, somewhat reminiscent of Mickey Rooney. It was out of sync with his otherwise robust persona, which included his actions as an outspoken critic of the underworld.[27] While not as high-profile as some of his contemporaries, Coe was a very competent broadcaster of both professional and amateur boxing during radio's heyday during the Depression.

If Hollywood were casting the stereotypical blow-by-blow radio announcer, they need look no further than Clem McCarthy. McCarthy was a Pathé newspaper columnist who also worked as an NBC sports announcer.

The gravel-voiced McCarthy possessed boundless energy. He delivered his unabated ring descriptions through a stream of consciousness. This approach made listeners feel as though they never missed a blow. As the ring action intensified, McCarthy's voice deepened and became coarser. Imagine a junior version of Jimmy Durante's voice, and you hear Clem during his greatest moments of intensity.

Boxing announcers like McCarthy, unlike those on TV who succeeded them, had the distinct advantage of an audience blind to the action described. This led to the dramatization, if not the outright exaggeration, of many fight broadcasts. Potentially, even the most pedestrian encounter could be elevated to sound like a pitched battle.

The announcer, as a reporter, had an obligation to relay the facts. Yet, he was employed by a sponsor who demanded entertainment and ratings, a slippery slope indeed. Exactly how well McCarthy treaded the thin ridge between objectivity and showmanship is debatable, but his notoriety as a boxing announcer was once sufficient to make him the subject of a satirical skit.

In the bit, performed at the Lambs Club in New York, two fighters are boxing in a ring above the announcer—"McCarthy"—who is frantically describing the action. The call of the fight is so exciting that the two boxers, resting comfortably in a clinch, look around to see if another bout is taking place. The announcer continues his dramatic call as the two fighters lean over the ropes listening in admiration to his hyperbolic narrative.[28]

While McCarthy may have taken certain liberties in his approach, they were rooted in a broadcasting philosophy that stressed entertainment value. One critic claimed his description of Tommy Farr's efforts in the Louis fight went beyond embellishment, amounting to a prejudicial account. McCarthy flatly denied the characterization and justified his approach, explaining that "every fight broadcast must have its drama."[29]

McCarthy is best remembered for his memorable broadcasts of the "Carnival of Champions" from the Polo Grounds in 1937, which featured four world champion matches and his historic call of the Schmeling-Louis rematch the following year.[30]

If McCarthy represents the stereotypical radio boxing announcer with its heightened tone and frantic pace of delivery, then his NBC colleague John B. Kennedy stands as a caricature of the between-rounds fight reporter that we now refer to as the color man.

Kennedy was the king of the improvised analogy and the master of syrupy description. In retrospect, his sometimes forced, on-the-spot comments might seem a bit unusual, but some are flat-out entertaining. Kennedy handled the prefight coverage as Clem McCarthy's partner on the Joe Louis-Al Ettore broadcast in September

1936. His opening commentary described the sport as "the art of exterior decorating, known politely as a boxing contest."[31] A few moments later he informed his audience: "incidentally the ring is principally infected with mosquitoes, many of them large enough to wear numbers on their backs." He also reported that "both fighters are attired in the trimmest apparel . . . I suspect they might be two pairs of Mahatma Gandhi's Sunday suit."[32]

At one point in the broadcast, color commentator George Hicks misidentified a ringsider as Gene Tunney, and Kennedy announced him as the ex-champion. Upon realizing the error, Kennedy blurted out, "Pardon me, I got the wrong steer." Later, in a reference to the preliminary bouts: "the knockdown timekeeper [has] been very busy because heavyweights were dropping around us like bombs on a Spanish loyalist town."[33]

When Kennedy was on, he could deliver some gems: "galaxies of floodlights mocking what's left of a September moon," "the crowd holding back to let its lungs loose as Louis comes into the ring," "batteries of motion picture cameras aching to get into action."[34]

Some of Kennedy's lines were written in advance, or at least sketched out ready and waiting for the right moment. Unlike the unpredictability of the live blow-by-blow call of a fight, introductions and other segments of color commentary could be fashioned away from the frenzy and immediacy of the broadcast. There was opportunity to wax poetic. In these moments, radio writers painted vivid pictures for the boxing listening audience, albeit at times they were a bit overly colorful. For instance, the opening of the first Louis-Schmeling bout as described by Edwin C. Hill at ringside:

"The Buick people have asked me to set the stage for you . . . to see it all with a kindling eye of imagination. The huge crowd, the shifting, ever-changing scene, waking pin points of light from fifty thousand cigars and cigarettes, for all the world like fireflies in the blue-black night, wave on wave of sound rising and falling, the great stadium, the vast swell of darkness, walling in one brilliant square of light, set in the center of this vast throng. Reaching back, back, back, until the last rows lost in black obscurity, in the very center, the ring, blazing out under the hot glare of the floodlights, like an enormous square diamond on black velvet, the crowd makes you catch your breath, it stretches out endlessly, the first forty or fifty rows of panoramic white mask-like faces, the rest disappearing in the gloom of night. More than seventy thousand people who paid all the way up to forty dollars to see the dark boy from Detroit fight the German Max."[35]

While radio's boxing announcers in the United States were developing a style that one might describe as dramatic, tense, even emotional, across the sea in Great Britain, their English counterparts were creating an approach of their own. Not surprisingly, it was distinctly British.

Proper and unflappable, British announcers delivered their blow-by-blow descriptions deliberately and without fanfare—maintaining what one writer described as "a calm during a fistic storm." Consistent with the decorum of the call of the fight, the announcers' frenzied rush of the ring for a postfight interview was also not the norm in English broadcasts.

Despite this conservative approach, their colorful use of language created a wonderful picture for the radio listener: "Baer is grinning, although it is difficult to tell what he is grinning about, as Farr definitely has the edge. The American seems to be doing most of the leading with his nose. Farr is as keen as mustard, and full of initiative and courage. Baer's eye is closing, his face is bleeding. There were four beautiful punches by Farr, flicker, flicker, flicker. . . . Baer's got his back to me like a great barn door. . . . Baer is still handsome and truculent, but seems the least bit pensive. You can hear the crowd, like an ocean wave, every time Farr hits him."[36]

And when it was all over, 14,000 Farr fans at the Harringay Arena were heard cheering in the background. Nevertheless, the announcer gave a typically British clinical wrap-up to the broadcast, stating that "every Englishman must be proud of him, for it was an exhibition of pure English boxing."[37]

Years later, when Al Phillips of London fought Cliff Anderson of British Guyana for the featherweight championship of the British

Empire, all the cordiality of an English radio broadcast was again on display. Fighters were addressed as "Mister" and the boxers referred to as "pugilists." The colorful blow-by-blow was no less apparent: "Phillips is wobbling very badly, indeed. He's, shall we say, a bit woozy? Yes, a bit woozy. Ah, the bell goes. . . . Oh his footwork is lovely, Oh, I say, Anderson sneaked out a lovely right just there. . . . O-o-o-h, three lovely rights by Phillips, I'll wager Anderson's head is singing. . . . They're both swinging now. You know it's rather like they're both playing a big drum. Yes, a big drum, just beating away."[38]

Chapter 6

LOOK SHARP, FEEL SHARP: THE RADIO ANNOUNCERS, PART 2

Boxing broadcasting during the 1920s and 1930s, like any work in progress, underwent a series of incremental changes. Announcers sharpened their prose, technology continued to improve, and productions increasingly took on new levels of sophistication. Radio's blow-by-blow announcer and color commentator now stepped in concert with the ring announcer, referee, timekeeper, and other ring officials. Like a pit crew at the Indianapolis 500, they moved events along rapidly and smoothly. The introductions from the Max Baer-Primo Carnera bout:

Radio announcer McNamee: "Primo Carnera is wearing a blue robe with red trimming." At the request of ring announcer Joe Humphries, the timekeeper sounds the bell. The ringing of the bell was McNamee's cue to immediately turn affairs over to Humphries.

McNamee (cutting himself short): "Here's Joe Humphries, just a moment, listen to Humphries." And then, seamlessly: "Quiet please, quiet . . . quiet please," Humphries began, instructing the audience to settle down.[1]

Then away from the ring announcers' microphone (but serendipitously picked up faintly by the radio broadcast), Humphries urgently slips in a private message: "Graham, Graham, its Arthur Donovan," providing his colleague the referee's name. Immediately after that, on the air: "Arthur Donovan will referee," McNamee says, providing a missing piece of information to the radio audience.[2] Again, faultlessly, Humphries continues his presentation to fans in attendance and in the radio audience: "[the] main event, fifteen rounds for the world's heavyweight championship."[3]

Back and forth, McNamee and Humphries worked in split-second synchronization like two men pumping the opposite ends of a railroad cart handle. Humphries: "Presenting the present holder of the title—the Goliath of fistiana and a son of sunny Italy, Primo Carnera." And then McNamee, impeccable with his interjection: "And with that, Carnera took a bow amid a tremendous cheer from about fifty-five thousand people."[4]

As boxing broadcasting grew with consistent coverage on network radio, in the late 1930s its announcers settled into long-term, two-man broadcasting teams. Listening audiences soon associated these announcing tandems with a broadcast network and its specific sponsor. While these men might have other duties, they were principally viewed as boxing announcers.

The first and most notable was Sam Taub, who paired with Angelo Palange for NBC broadcasts sponsored by Adam Hats. These fights originated from the Hippodrome, Madison Square Garden, and other fight clubs around New York City, including bouts from Dexter Park, Long Island. Palange would later be replaced by Bill Stern.[5]

"Your Adam Hats Sports Parade is on the air" soon became a familiar introduction to NBC boxing broadcasts. After the NBC studio announcer completed his brief introduction, he would prepare the audience for the upcoming event: "Now that we are all comfortably gathered around our loudspeakers, let's go to the ringside [pause], come in Bill Stern."[6]

"Thank you and good evening ladies and gentlemen," the color commentator would begin, "this is Bill Stern speaking from ringside at Madison Square Garden, [courtesy of] Adam Hats, the world's largest retailer of men's hats. Say hello to Sam Taub and myself as we get ready for another world's championship boxing match. One of the many in the Adam Hats Sports Parade."[7, 8]

After completing the prefight show, the ring microphone was patched to the NBC broadcast, allowing the radio audience to hear the referee's prefight instructions. Stern then turned the broadcast back to Taub. "Thank you and good evening, friends," Taub would begin in his unmistakable New York accent.[9]

After Taub gave the blow-by-blow for each round, Stern provided a brief synopsis of each round. Of course, there was the obligatory advertisement from the sponsor: "As I walked through the main entrance of the Garden this evening, I noticed quite a crowd assembled before the windows of our Adam Hats store in Madison [Square] Garden. I was pleased to note the interest which was created by our display of the newest Adam Hats creations." And in another scripted pitch: "The Adam Hats style parade is in full bloom. Everywhere you go one sees Adam Hats, all colors, all styles, made for you, fitted for your taste, as well as your pocketbook. Remember $2.95, none higher."[10]

While it was announcer Taub's responsibility to paint a picture of the fight, Stern was charged with enabling the listeners to feel as though they were present at the event. Stern added color and texture to the broadcast through his keen powers of observation and bulldog-like tenacity with detail. The following excerpts from the second Fred Apostoli-Billy Conn fight are illustrative of Stern's contributions:

Ring announcer Harry Balogh: "Ladies and gentlemen, permit me to present to you at this time, the former lightweight and welterweight champion Barney Ross, come up Barney Ross."

Bill Stern: "Everybody is waiting to see Barney Ross, he hasn't put in his appearance yet. Imagine if you will, a jam-packed Madison Square Garden, New York City, well, he doesn't look like he is coming up,

Balogh goes back to the microphone, Here comes Barney, coming up on the opposite side of Billy Conn's corner, right into Apostoli's corner, behind him, in a moment he might step into the ring, here he comes, resplendent in a green suit—Barney Ross!"

Balogh: "Another former champion of the heavyweight division, James J. Braddock."

Stern: "And again, the usual craning of the necks, as you might see at a tennis match, everybody is looking in all directions, to find out where Jimmy Braddock is gonna come from. . . . Get in here and take a bow, he is a very popular man, undoubtedly he will get a splendid hand when he comes . . . and here comes Jimmy Braddock, coming up, Jimmy Braddock will be coming up in just a second, he shakes hands with the gentleman, now goes up the stairs, again in Apostoli's corner, here he is, former heavyweight champion of the world James J. Braddock."[11]

Stern was particularly good with detail as color commentator, illustrated in his coverage between rounds one and two of the Conn-Apostoli rematch: "In the ring at the [*sic*] time are two boys cleaning up the glass from the popped flash light bulb which went off in the middle of that round, which Sam called for you, as it happened. They're in there, down on their hands and knees picking up those bits of glass so these fighters will not become cut should anyone fall."[12]

Several rounds later when Conn went down in his corner on his own accord, Stern provided a detailed clarification: "They naturally give these boys a drink of water occasionally; sometimes they squirt water down the back of their necks or down their chest or over the top of their head, and when they do that a great deal of this water trickles down to the canvas floor underneath the stool so that when the stool is pulled away that part of the canvas sometimes remains slippery and wet. Oftentimes they throw rosin on it to dry it up; apparently in that last incident they did not throw rosin down"[13]

Stern's color commentary might be viewed as the program's anchor of Taub's simmering broadcast tempest. There was an underlying sense of urgency in Taub's blow-by-blow call. When the action picked up, the pitch of his voice rose commensurately. His description accelerated into a rapid-fire delivery—the rising roar of the crowd accompanying it like synchronized background music: "Apostoli moves in there, Conn seems to be cool just like an iceberg. . . . Here's a left hook to the body and a left to the jaw landed by Billy Conn! Conn then hooks a left to the jaw of Apostoli, another left hook on the chin by Billy Conn, and Apostoli works a right uppercut on the jaw; here's Apostoli jabbing a left on the nose, crowding Conn into the ropes and again Apostoli jabs a light left into the face, and Conn came back with a left into the body and Apostoli a right into the ribs, here's Apostoli taking a hard left to the body at the bell."[14]

If time permitted before the next round, when Stern turned the microphone back to Taub, Sam would squeeze in a bit of color of his own: "As we tried to tell you at the start, there is no love lost between the two managers, Johnny Ray, the manager of Billy Conn, and Larry White, who handles Apostoli." And a few rounds later: "OK Bill, boy they're going fast again Bill, like a couple of railroad trains running in each other's direction."[15]

During the reign of Taub and Stern, boxing broadcasting grew to new heights. The first paid radio sponsorship for a series of boxing matches occurred in 1937, with an eighteen-week contract between Hippodrome promoter Mike Jacobs and Adam Hats. Taub delivered the blow-by-blow for these fights over WHN, New York.[16] Stern, in his capacity as NBC sports director, would bring the bouts to the NBC Blue Network and garner national recognition.[17] Although Taub was the premier voice of boxing on the radio during the late 1930s, his dominance would end abruptly with his replacement by Don Dunphy.

Don Dunphy's debut as a radio announcer came in 1933, handling wrestling and hockey for WBXN. After a brief stint at WHOM, he landed at WINS, a small New York radio station where he served as sports director and sportscaster.[18] Dunphy was unable to break into the circle of top boxing announcers until 1941. That was the year Mutual Broadcasting drew the Madison Square Garden fights away from NBC's Blue Network. The Gillette Safety Razor Company would also replace Adam Hats as the Garden's new sponsor.[19]

Taub and Stern were too closely associated with Adam Hats for the new advertiser's tastes, so a search for fresh broadcast talent was launched. For the blow-by-blow position, Dunphy bested twenty competitors. These included Mel Allen, who went on to become an all-time great baseball announcer, and Paul Douglas, who forged a successful career as a film actor.[20]

Bill Corum replaced Stern as color commentator. Corum served as an officer of the 101st infantry regiment in France. He won three Silver Stars, the Purple Heart, and attained the rank of Major.[21] Another ex-newspaperman, he started his reporting career in the sports department of the *New York Times.* His talents were recognized by Hearst writer Arthur Brisbane, who hired him away from the *Times.* Corum became the top sports columnist for Hearst's *Journal-American,* the flagship newspaper in New York at that time.[22]

Corum had a common voice unmarked by any overtly distinguishing characteristics. It was the voice of an older man; a voice of resigned weariness mixed with a hint of wisdom. His appeal was that he came across as being comfortable in his own skin. One never felt that he was working at his profession; he was just conversing matter-of-factly.

The Dunphy-Corum team was destined for success. Their maiden voyage on the air was the classic match between Joe Louis and Billy Conn at the Polo Grounds on June 18, 1941. The broadcast drew the third largest ratings in American history and catapulted the duo into the big time.

Stern's "Your Adam Hats Sports Parade is on the air" was soon replaced with Corum's "Cavalcade of Sports is on the air." Mutual's studio announcer initiated each broadcast by informing the audience that "Your radio host is the Gillette Safety Razor Company, which broadcasts the World Series, Kentucky Derby, football bowl games, and other important sporting events, including all major boxing contests for your enjoyment month after month. . . . and now we switch you to Bill Corum of the *New York Journal-American* sports staff at ringside in Madison Square Garden." "Good evening, folks, this is Bill Corum, with Don Dunphy, your blow-by-blow reporter, here at ringside at Madison Square Garden," the new color commentator would typically begin.[23]

As Stern acted as a pitchman for Adam Hats, Corum served as an equally enthusiastic peddler of razor blades despite the sometimes less-than-stimulating advertisements: "Without the technical knowledge, skilled craftsmanship, and specialized equipment employed by Gillette, it is impossible to duplicate today's Blue Blade. That's just simple logic. Now let me point out that the precision machines and

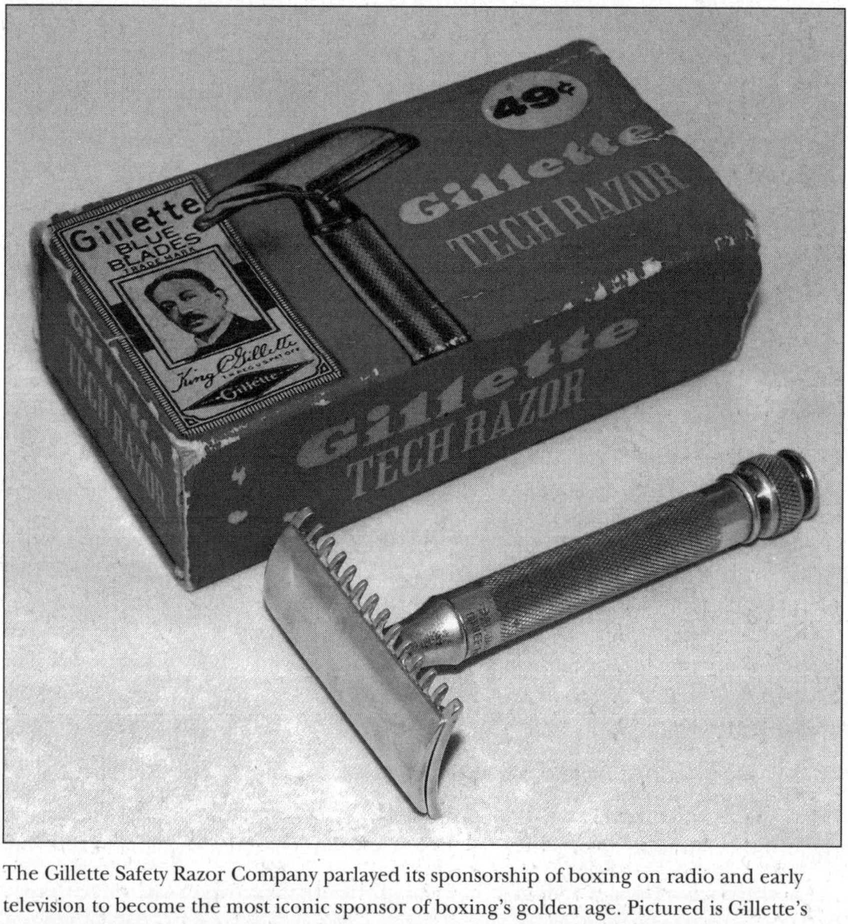

The Gillette Safety Razor Company parlayed its sponsorship of boxing on radio and early television to become the most iconic sponsor of boxing's golden age. Pictured is Gillette's popular "Blue Blades," circa 1940s. *By Joe Haupt from USA via Wikimedia Commons.*

scientific instruments developed by our technicians for the manufacture and testing of this blade are exclusive with Gillette . . . No other blade is as sharp, easy shaving, or long-lasting."[24]

Unlike today's broadcasts that feature several sponsors, for many years a boxing program on radio was the exclusive domain of a single sponsor. As with the broadcasting of any sports or entertainment program at the time, the sponsor may not have been the star of the show, but it was the undisputed puppet master.

Broadcasts were carefully scripted and peppered with commercial spots of various durations. Even during the seemingly nonusable period of time during the fast-paced blow-by-blow description, sponsors engineered a way to work in a pitch. Anytime the fighters would move toward the announcer, the announcer would throw in a plug. Dunphy would regularly remind the audience that the action was taking place "right above our Gillette microphone." Likewise, Russ Hodges used the "Pabst microphone" as broadcasting ground zero. On other occasions, the announcer compared the action in the ring to the sponsor's product, once again bringing an ad in through the back door. The advertisements were patently intrusive but basically innocuous.

Don Dunphy had paid his dues behind the microphone before gaining national prominence as the voice of Gillette. He handled everything from baseball to amateur Irish boxing matches, not to mention the ire of discontented wrestlers. On one occasion, during a WBMX broadcast, a wrestler chased a microphone-wielding Dunphy up one of the aisles at the Bronx Coliseum.

Dunphy gained his career-making opportunity by participating in an unusual competition. WOR-Mutual Radio set up two microphones at the Anton Christoforidis-Gus Lesnevich bout at Madison Square Garden. They then let prospective candidates take turn behind the mike and recorded them.[25] "The other guys tripped on the second names, but I just called them Gus and Anton," Dunphy said, explaining his winning approach.[26]

Dunphy's success was due not only to his intelligence, but also his dedication. When Don attended sporting events at which he was not announcing, he would often engage in what he called "whisper practice." He would quietly call the event to himself to keep his vocabulary and observations sharp.[27]

Perhaps because he took his craft so seriously, Dunphy adopted a style that strictly adhered to the facts. However, his delivery was peppered with genuine excitement and expectation. He created just the right dose of drama to make the bouts exciting, but not falsely so. As he would explain many years later, "Sometimes I would hear criticism that I was faking it on the broadcasts, but I never did. Not all the fights are epics; in fact most are not. But if punches weren't being thrown, I'd describe the body movements, the footwork, and that seemed to create excitement for the listeners. . . . The big thing is knowing when to talk, but you never really know. You start a sentence and a guy gets hit—you're hung up. So you watch your spots."[28]

Dunphy was equally proficient with postfight interviews. He was also aware of the potential difficulties brought about by their unpredictability. After Joe Louis knocked out Tami Mauriello in one round at Yankee Stadium, Dunphy asked Tami, who had rocked Joe early in the round, what had happened. "I got too blankety-blank careless!" the distraught Bronxite explained to a coast-to-coast radio audience. Dunphy said, "I was so startled I gulped, 'Thank you, Tami,' and handed the mike over to Bill Corum." Even many years later, the incident remained a cautionary tale for Dunphy—be prepared for anything.[29]

Dunphy's illustrious career included the broadcast of more than two thousand fights on radio and television. In 1985, at the end of his career, he was asked if putting fights back on radio would help the sport. Dunphy, true to his pedigree, avoided romanticizing the moment: "It might, if they would do fights which were not telecast. Most of them are telecast and it would be most unusual for the people to turn on the radio and not watch the television if they could."[30]

Dunphy served as the flagbearer for radio announcing throughout the 1940s, spearheading boxing's greatest bouts broadcast over NBC and the Mutual Network. In the 1950s, he was joined on the airwaves by several others, most notably Steve Ellis and Russ Hodges.

Ellis handed the color commentary duties as a set-up man and in-between rounds reporter for blow-by-blow announcer Russ Hodges for the Pabst Blue Ribbon broadcasts during the 1950s. Ellis's strength was his ability to pack the one-minute rest period with useful information through his concise commentary. When you consider that commercial spots might also run in that time, a good "color man" needed to be economical in his summations. Ellis could paint a picture or assess the situation in just a couple of words: "In round one we saw Archie Moore, smart and clever, use his arms and elbows as a defense. He covers the head . . . he blocks the swings . . . he rolls." And between rounds five and six, shortly before Rocky Marciano drops Moore twice with punches to the head: "He's been concentrating mainly on the body—It's a body fight—so he can bring the guard of Moore down."[31]

Hodges and Ellis were one of the top tandems of the era. The duo would even share responsibilities, divvying up the blow-by-blow chores as they did with the Marciano-Moore bout. Ellis brought a great deal of enthusiasm to his call. On occasion, he would stretch the pronunciation of a single word for emphasis with great effect. When the action was good, Ellis seemed to really enjoy the fight like any other fan. He gave the sense that he was thinking, "Wow, can you believe this round?"

Unlike some of his more reserved and measured announcing on television during the same period, Russ Hodges's radio blow-by-blow could be quite animated. Typically, his voice held a steady rhythm marked by its control. However, as the action would intensify, there was a rise in its octaves. The increasing excitability was palatable. Hodges was no longer describing what he was seeing, he was barking it out exuberantly.

Hodges and his Pabst colleague, Ellis, along with Don Dunphy dominated the radio landscape during the 1950s. However, during that period, many other broadcasters shared the boxing airwaves. Men such as Lester Bromberg, Les Keiter, Stew McPherson, Win Elliot, and Howard Cosell helped complete an engaging roster that comprised boxing's radio voice—the last representatives of a brief but compelling era in sports broadcasting.

Chapter 7

THE FIGHTERS TAKE TO THE MICROPHONE

While radio's major contribution to the sport of boxing was the live broadcast of matches and their pre- and postfight drama, the medium also provided an array of complementary boxing content for its listening audiences.

Early programming often focused on general commentary or was instructional in nature. For example, in 1923 on WOR, Newark, 450, Sam Taub, boxing scribe for the *New York Morning Telegraph,* could be heard during a ten-minute program simply called *Boxing.*[1] On another day, he was afforded a fifteen-minute window for a show with the timeless name *The Boxing Situation.*[2] That same year, Jimmy DeForest, trainer of Jack Dempsey and Mickey Walker, gave a radio talk on physical culture for the boxing fan and other athletic-minded listeners.[3] The following year, WJZ, one of the earliest broadcasters of boxing in the New York City area, offered ten minutes of *Boxing Lessons* by C.R. Temple.[4] In 1925, WHN, New York, aired a lengthy forty-five-minute program, *Boxing Period,*[5] and fans in Boston tuned in WHOO to listen to *Shadow Boxing.*[6] During that same year, James A. Farley, Sr. of the New York State Athletic Commission made his contribution with the program *Clean Boxing,* broadcast over WNYC in New York.[7]

Considering the limitations of radio as a nonvisual medium, some of this programming was probably a bit arduous on the listener. By the mid-1920s, these somewhat misplaced "how to" boxing programs were deemphasized. They were succeeded by interviews, discussions, and retrospectives of prominent fighters and other relevant members of the boxing community.

One episode of the thirty-minute program *Boxing Celebrities* featured former champion Terry McGovern.[8] Similar programming airing on WTAG in Worcester examined the career of former heavyweight contender Peter Mayer and his bout with Tom Sharkey.[9]

Other radio stations, including several in Los Angeles, focused on more contemporaneous talent. Mickey Walker appeared on KFI radio to chronicle his career. Fidel La Barba was interviewed on KHJ, and manager "Pop" Foster discussed his charge Jimmy McLarnin.[10] This type of programming would become commonplace in the '30s and '40s, when champions like Bob Montgomery regularly appeared with boxing broadcasters such as Bill Stern and Jimmy Powers.[11]

During the golden age of sport, the boxing community regularly mixed with the prevailing politicos of the day. High-ranking politicians were frequent guests at high-profile boxing events, and these gatherings were worthy of live radio coverage.

WHN began 1926 with a broadcast of a testimonial dinner from the Hotel Commodore to honor James A. Farley Sr. The event was attended by Governor Alfred E. Smith, Mayor James J. Walker, and Reverend Francis P. Duffy of the famed "Fighting 69th."[12] Boxing testimonials and the Hotel Commodore seemed to be common bedfellows. Gene Tunney was toasted there by the American Legion in an event broadcast by WNYC shortly after he won the heavyweight title. Mayor Walker and former president Theodore Roosevelt were among those attending.[13]

Of all those in the boxing community, radio favored the heavyweight champions such as Tunney. Both past and present champions of that division proved newsworthy commodities that warranted repeated live coverage.

After retiring as undefeated heavyweight champion, the erudite Tunney became a successful entrepreneur and public advocate. He often appeared on the radio or utilized other forums to comment on the sport. When Tunney assumed the position of Chairman of the Board for the American Distilling Company, in a counterintuitive move, he advocated to keep liquor advertisements off the airwaves. "There should be no disposition on part of the distiller to encourage spirits consumption by the youth of the country," Tunney explained.[14]

As an idol of American youth, Tunney was passionate about their development. He led a delegation of young Republicans, Democrats, and members of the Junior Chamber of Commerce in a bid for membership in The American Youth Congress. It was rejected. Tunney claimed the Congress was "communist controlled" and counterpunched with the formation of the National Foundation for American Youth. As its temporary chairman, he quickly called for action including the establishment of a radio program to help his group advocate its position.[15]

As an ex-Marine, patriotism was also at the forefront of Tunney's agenda. Shortly after World War II, the irrepressible Tunney found himself at odds with another contemporary American hero, Charles Lindbergh. In an address made to the Associated Industries of Massachusetts, Tunney explained his shock at the "impertinence" of Lindbergh regarding statements made by the aviator on a recent radio broadcast. Citing certain Lindbergh actions as an abandonment of England, Tunney also claimed the flyer made a "grave mistake" when accepting a medal from German Chancellor Adolph Hitler and "those gangsters."[16]

Tunney, like other boxers who achieved notable celebrity status, used radio to help support philanthropic causes. On WJZ, he advocated for the United Hospital Fund of New York. He urged a listening audience just coming to grips with effects of the Depression for their continued "support, interest, and goodwill," in fundraising efforts to raise a million dollars to aid local medical institutions. The hospital is "the last hope of the destitute," he explained.[17]

Tunney's thoughts and opinions on all major topics were considered newsworthy. In a memorial eulogy to Notre Dame football coach Knute Rockne aired to nearly fifteen million listeners, Tunney spoke in person while other titans of the day such as Admiral Richard Evelyn Byrd and Charles Lindbergh wrote letters that were read to the audience.[18] Tunney praised Rockne for his principles, noting that his team always gave "a fine exhibition of coordination of eleven men as a unit." Rockne's name, Tunney concluded, was "an inspiration to all those interested in clean sport."[19]

When Tunney was not advancing his diverse agenda on the airwaves, he would share the microphone with several other heavyweight champions. James J. Corbett was already a bankable stage actor and silent-screen performer by the time radio arrived. Although twenty years removed from the ring, he could still draw an audience with the most mundane material.

In 1923, Corbett made the first public reading of the new "Roosevelt Boxing Rules" in a broadcast by WOR, Newark, to "boxing fans of the eastern states." The former champion, who was one of the architects of the proposed rules, was something of a reactionary. He advocated the elimination of the use of two judges and a referee scoring a bout in favor of the referee as sole arbitrator. Several boxing experts were at the ready to express their own opinions over the "wireless" immediately following the broadcast. No doubt, some found this recommended change unfavorable. It was never adopted in New York State.[20]

When network radio arrived, Corbett was given his own weekly radio series on CBS. In the initial program, he waxed poetic on his "early boyhood scraps," including his first meeting with Joe Choyinski.[21] Choyinski was always a favorite subject of "Gentleman Jim." A few years later at an Advertising Club's weekly luncheon, Corbett entertained a live radio audience and other attendees including Babe Ruth by recanting his famous battle with Choyinski on a San Francisco barge. The radio appearance was something of a swan song for Corbett, who was seriously ill and died several months later. He admitted he probably should not have attended the luncheon but explained, "I'm glad I did. . . . Just to sit here and watch a big fellow like Babe Ruth eat so much food makes me feel better."[22]

Former heavyweight champion James J. Jeffries, two-time Corbett opponent, appeared on the radio as a guest star on the musical-variety program *Shell Chateau* hosted by Al Jolson. Jeffries told the radio audience about his two toughest opponents: Sailor Tom Sharkey—"He's like a bunch of tigers, he never quits," and Bob Fitzsimmons, who early in the second bout, "hit me so hard . . . that I felt needles in my feet."[23]

The controversial Jack Johnson brought his larger-than-life personality to radio long after he left the ring's center stage, finding work in more collegial atmospheres. Some two decades after Johnson fought a no-decision bout with Victor McLaglen in Vancouver, British Columbia, McLaglen, now a film star, interviewed his former opponent on the air.[24] Johnson also appeared as a guest star on the weekly *Hall of Sport* quiz program aired over WBBM in Chicago. He was teamed with the program's regular panel of experts in a trivia battle against "sports-quizzers."[25]

Johnson was as eclectic as he was controversial. After his boxing career, he dabbled in wrestling, majored in professional orchestras, and was a café owner. In 1936, he landed a leading role in the grand opera *Aida,* which found its way to radio. One journalist cautioned his readers to tune into the broadcast of the operatic performance with pacified expectations to "hear a very fine child-like voice yelping from Mike Jacobs's New York Hippodrome that you may or may not like."[26]

Jack Dempsey, the biggest name in boxing during the Roaring Twenties, remained immensely popular with the American public for decades to follow. He was a sought-after guest for boxing shows and general sports programs, alike. Typical was his appearance on Ted Husing's *Sports Slants,* which was broadcast locally in Baltimore over WMAL. On the program, the "Manassa Mauler" answered questions about himself and discussed the present-day boxing scene.[27] After Dempsey retired from the ring, he became a relevant boxing promoter. He used the radio to advance his own promotions

The diversity of Jack Johnson's talents was displayed during the radio broadcast of his 1936 performance in the opera *Aida*. Pictured is younger Johnson during his boxing days. *Photographer Unknown via Wikimedia Commons.*

including that of the Jackie Fields-Vince Dundee nontitle welterweight bout at the Chicago Coliseum. On this particular occasion, Dempsey took to the microphone and participated in the actual broadcast of the fight.[28]

When famed humorist Will Rogers passed away, there were a number of radio tributes. WHN eulogized Rogers with a memorial broadcast from the Friars Club in New York featuring remarks from Dempsey and Rogers's colleague Bill Robinson.[29]

Dempsey appeared as a special guest with his old nemesis Gene Tunney on the *Lux Radio Theater* during a respite of the 1938 presentation of *Kid Galahad,* broadcast over CBS. It was one of many public appearances the pair would make together over the course of the half-century following their two historic battles. Over time, the duo would become close friends. Reading from a prepared script, Dempsey's words to Tunney, if not already genuine, would one day become so: "I'm glad I lost to a straight-shooter like you and that's from the heart."[30]

Dempsey was arguably the most enduring media personality of all of the former boxers. More than forty years after his title-winning effort against Jess Willard, he was still front and center, using the latest medium of television to perpetuate his brand.

Radio required a comfort level with public speaking that not all heavyweight champions possessed. After defeating Paulino Uzcudun, Max Schmeling arrived at Tempelhof flying field in Berlin and showed distaste for broadcasting, telling a radio audience: "I'd rather box another fifteen rounds with Paulino than speak into this microphone."[31]

Schmeling's contemporary Max Baer was the complete opposite of the German, and like Dempsey, he was a radio natural. While his good looks did not translate on the airwaves, his larger-than-life personality did. Even before Baer became world heavyweight champion, his reputation as a playboy had been established. He was unapologetic about his lifestyle. "The first time I hit New York I was twenty-one," Baer once explained. "The town was loaded with theaters, night clubs, blondes, brunettes, and red-heads and I had $10,000 in my pocket. What would you have done in my place?"[32]

The affable and gregarious Max Baer had the perfect personality for radio. He was signed to star in a weekly radio serial, *Taxi*, before he won the heavyweight title in June 1934. *Courtesy of Bill Pollock / Champions of the Ring.*

Although only a contender at the time, his public appeal was strong enough to warrant his own coast-to-coast radio program. Maxie's antics would be delivered in a vehicle called *Taxi.* The serial's premise was simple: Baer's character had a "penchant for blondes," and they conveniently turned up at his cab company. Comic situations and opportunities for Maxie to act heroic abounded. To accommodate Baer's schedule, a portable studio to broadcast the program was set up at his training camp. The marketing value of radio to promote the sport of boxing was taken to another level with the serial. It was primarily a publicity piece that was tied into the upcoming broadcast of Baer's title fight against champion Primo Carnera.

After Baer steamrolled Carnera for the title, he was cast in his second coast-to-coast serial, NBC's *Lucky Smith.* Baer starred in the title role as a private detective "with a punch" who "preferred action to theory." The famed playwright and director, Garson Kanin, an actor at the time, played Max's sidekick in both programs. Boxing announcer Graham McNamee also appeared in *Taxi.*[33]

On Baer's first day of training for his title defense against James J. Braddock, he left his camp to squeeze in a radio rehearsal for *Lucky Smith* at the tiny studio set up at the Berkeley Carteret Hotel in Asbury Park, New Jersey. During the rehearsal of one scene, he joked that the sound effect of his gun was not loud enough. Baer then examined the revolver and accidently discharged it. The .32 caliber cartridge and the paper wad used to cap the powder struck him in the chest directly above his heart, creating a burn six inches in diameter.

Baer was rushed seven miles to the Hazard Hospital in Long Branch by his manager Ancil Hoffman and camp manager Jerry Casale. The fighter was not seriously hurt. At the hospital, the ever-jovial Maxie joked that the camp member who had given him the gun had gone over to Braddock's side. Baer missed a few days of training, but the real burn he suffered was from the stinging blows the 10–1 underdog Braddock administered while lifting his title at the Long Island City Bowl.[34]

Like *Taxi, Lucky Smith* was a promotional tie-in used to promote a Baer title fight. It is possible that the shooting incident was no more than a publicity ruse used to promote attendance at the Braddock fight. As claimed many years later by John V. Grombach, Baer's radio manager, Max was "accidently" shot, and "the burned clothes, the blood, ambulance, and nurses, were all part of the plan and resulted in first-page stories everywhere."[35]

While heavyweight champion, Baer was all over the airwaves including shortwave. When former President Herbert Hoover spoke to Rear Admiral Byrd and his men at "Little America" via W2XAF in Schenectady (carried by WEAF in New York), Baer was given equal time with the ex-president and also conversed with Byrd.[36]

Baer was an early triple threat in radio, film, and television. He parlayed his extraordinary good looks and competence in acting, singing, and dancing to make more money in the entertainment field outside of the sport of boxing than any other boxer, whether a contemporary or predecessor.[37]

Comparatively speaking, Baer's conqueror, James J. Braddock, like most of his ring contemporaries, lacked the gravitas of Baer. After lifting the title from Max, Braddock would have his own opportunities on the radio. In 1947, the retired ex-champion would appear on the radio program *Gangbusters* as the special narrator for the episode "The Inside Case of the Jersey Butcher Bandits." Although Braddock seemed an "everyman," his voice was monotone and a bit on the gruff side. Combined with his unpolished delivery, it is easy to understand how Braddock did not have an extensive radio career.[38]

The heavyweight champion most identifiable with radio is Braddock's successor, Joe Louis. By the time Louis was champion, radio's top shows were competing for his services as one of sport's most bankable stars. Just a week or so after Louis dismantled Buddy Baer in a single round, comedian Eddie Cantor featured Louis on his radio program. At the same time, Cantor's competitor Fred Allen secured an appearance by Baer. Fred Allen's sponsors were understandably chagrined, presumably having been scooped by Cantor. However, it was Buddy Baer who proved to be the more capable comedian before the microphone.

Frankly, Louis was not a master of enunciation. His voice was an unbreakable monotone complicated by a thick Alabamian accent. "Now that I have taken care of the Baers I am going after the Snakes," he told Cantor's audience in a stilted manner. "What did you do on December seventh?" the champ was asked. "Used nothing but Jap sparring partners," Louis said, regurgitating his memorized lines.[39]

While Louis may not have been articulate in the traditional sense, he was not unintelligent. When he wasn't hampered by a script, his postfight interviews, for instance, illustrated a certain country wisdom "in their brevity, modesty and simple eloquence."[40] He had a natural inclination toward avoiding verbal communication when he was in the presence of white men of the media. Early in his career, he suspected that they were looking to make sport of him. Trust of his own role in the world of media and entertainment and the ensuing development of his verbal skills would come in time.[41]

Louis's caution was warranted. The history of early radio was replete with racial prejudice as the norm, a standard that seemed to operate hand-in-hand with an equally unenlightened press. It had been less than ten years since Jack Sharkey had grabbed a radio microphone while standing next to Harry Wills, the last great black heavyweight before Louis, proclaiming before their fight, "I'm going to lick hell out of this nigger." What was equally telling about the incident was the manner in which the press reported it—even the *Baltimore Sun*, a newspaper with a large African American readership. Wary of printing the word *hell*, the *Sun* was compelled to substitute *H—1*. Yet, Sharkey's racial slur was spelled out in its entirety, affording it the status of an acceptable social norm.[42]

At the time, the notion of making sport of black men was completely mainstream. Louis arrived on the boxing scene during the twilight of the "Battle Royal," an arresting display of several blindfolded boxers flailing away inside the ring until only one remained standing. Typically, the fighters were black. At its core was a shameful spectacle perpetuated for the amusement of whites. Ironically, "civic-minded" groups such as the Maryland Council, Knights of Columbus, would promote these contests. They featured fighters such as "Black Kid" Williams and "Black" Stanley Ketchel.[43]

The mere notion of having a black man and white man in the same ring in the mid 1930s was still risky social experimentation, particularly in the South. Even when Louis became heavyweight champion in 1937, mixed-race matches in Washington, DC were still prohibited.[44]

Joe Louis was plucked from the pale of this giant social shadow and thrust into a white spotlight. It would take a man of his grace and character to navigate its ire. Fortunately, Louis was also affable, a growing sports idol, and a burgeoning marketable commodity. He would continue to appear on the radio during his days as champion, often winning over the audience with his performance, as he had done so many times in the ring.

If Louis had faltered on Eddie Cantor's program, Fred Allen was not dissuaded. A few weeks later, he had the champ appear on his show and explain the training routine for his upcoming fight with Arturo Godoy. Allen used Louis as a straight man with effect, leaving the nuisance of timing for himself and getting the laughs and applause from the studio audience:

> **Allen:** It's certainly a pleasure to welcome the heavyweight champion here on a social call.
> **Louis:** Thank you, Fred.
> **Allen:** You know if you were here on business, Joe, I would just about be passing New Rochelle now.
> **Allen:** How many pounds do you lose during a fight?
> **Louis:** I probably lose six or seven pounds.
> **Allen:** Your opponents probably gain a few pounds since they naturally would weigh more with lumps.

And then it was Louis's turn to deliver the punch line.

> **Allen:** Do you have any favorite programs?
> **Louis:** Oh, we listen to your show, Fred.
> **Allen:** Oh, that's fine.

Louis: And I also listen to Jack Benny.
Allen: Oh, that's not so good, Joe. Say, tell me how come you listen to Benny.
Louis: Well, Rochester's a friend of mine.[45]

While these exchanges may not seem as humorous on paper more than seventy-five years later, the audience experiencing the live performance was both engaged and delighted.

Fred Allen took a passing fancy to the fight game. For a while, he took weekly boxing lessons at a Manhattan gym.[46] In 1942, he visited with Fritzie Zivic, the former welterweight champion, while he was training for a fight with Beau Jack at Madison Square Garden. The star of stage, screen, and radio clowned and shared trade secrets with Zivic before the largest crowd at Stillman's Gym in five years.[47]

Boxing techniques gleaned from Zivic might have come in handy against Allen's fellow comedian Jack Benny. The pair maintained the longest feud in radio history. They maligned each other on their weekly programs, carrying each other on the wings of feigned animosity to radio stardom.

In one of Benny's episodes, Jack claims that Fred has breached their already lax rules of comedic engagement. Jack is determined to fight Fred. Benny goes into training at actor Andy Devine's barn with his faithful man-servant Rochester. He appears in his boxing gloves and red velvet trunks and makes the mistake of asking the others how he looks: "My my . . . when you get off your clothes there just ain't nothing left," Rochester observes. And Devine: "Say, Buck, Fred Allen was right. Your chest does cave in a little."

The pair begins to spar cautiously, and Devine comments laughingly, "With you and Rochester sparring, it looks like you are shadow boxing." At one point, Benny hits Rochester with a cheap shot and tells Rochester he gave him a black eye. "Black eye?" Rochester responds, "You'll have to peel me to prove it." Getting revenge, Rochester dupes Jack and knocks out his bridgework.[48]

In 1945, a bit more polished from his years of experience behind a microphone, Louis went on the air with Jack Benny. In one skit, Jack wants Louis to be his bodyguard and Joe wants to become a comedian:

Louis: I want to make people laugh. I've been wanting to do that for years.

Rochester: Well, Joe, if you want to make people laugh, you have been going about it the wrong way.

Louis: Who told you that?

Rochester: Max Schmeling, Tony Galento, Jim Braddock, and Buddy Baer—that's who.

Louis: Well, those fellows have no sense of humor.

Rochester: Well, you know, it's pretty hard to laugh with a referee countin' over you.

Louis: I wouldn't know, that never happened to me.

Rochester: Never?

Louis: Never.

Rochester: Joe, remember that first fight you had with Max Schmeling?

Louis: Ah hmm.

Rochester: What happened in the twelfth round, what happened?

Louis: That's the one page I tore out of my scrapbook.[49]

The heavyweight champions were boxing's standard-bearers both in the ring and on the radio from the 1920s to the 1940s. However, other boxers and ring personalities made their own unique contributions to American radio.

In the winter of 1930, long after his stellar twenty-year ring career ended, Barney Lebowitz, better known as "Battling Levinsky," took to the airwaves of WELK. The former light-heavyweight champion was dismayed with the present crop of heavyweight prospects who were the heirs apparent to Dempsey and Tunney. Levinsky believed that fighters were rushed along too quickly in order to satisfy the public's appetite to see the big men in action. "Big purses are ruining American heavyweight fighters," he lamented. "Tommy Loughran is "the only heavyweight in this country today that knows the real art of boxing," he opined. "It will be impossible to keep Tommy from the title, for when you can't hit a man you can't beat him."[50]

Former lightweight king Benny Leonard used radio to remain relevant after his failed comeback against Jimmy McLarnin. The following year, he teamed up with radio host Morton Downey on WABC. Leonard performed a reenactment of his 1918 match against Willie Ritchie in which he rose off the canvas after a nine count to win the contest via knockout.[51] Even after his fighting days, Leonard was still an idol to millions. At the Boys Clubs of America's 1937 annual meeting at the Hotel Commodore, Leonard was proudly introduced to a WEAF radio audience as a former club member.[52]

At the height of his boxing career, middleweight champion Ken Overlin was able to parlay his ring notoriety into a regular radio gig. Shortly after losing his laurels to Billy Soose in a disputed decision, Overlin was pegged as a radio commodity by a trio of local bistros when he "unconsciously" gave them a plug on the radio. The bistros decided to sponsor Overlin for a thirteen-week run on his own full-time program weekdays on WWDC in Washington, DC. Overlin, in training for a rematch with Soose, expressed an interest in becoming a radio reporter postboxing.[53]

While most boxing celebrities used their radio exposure as a springboard for television acting, Rocky Graziano reversed the process. He capitalized on his fame garnered on the Martha Raye television show to pursue a radio career. Rocky received a live tryout for the position of early-morning disc jockey on WABC. "I used to get up early all the time when I was fightin' but now that I'm an actor I'm outta shape. It'll be a little tough," he joked. Rocky was hardly intimidated by the gig. "I'll have a writer fellow sittin' next to me and if I run outta something to say, I'll say, 'Hey, gimme something.'"[54]

While most boxers dabbled in radio and the entertainment world, others became regulars. A few even developed postboxing careers. The most popular of these fighters was "Slapsie Maxie" Rosenbloom, who gained his moniker for his open-gloved fighting style. He had an amazing career featuring more than 300 fights and a brief stint as the light-heavyweight champion. With his cauliflower ears and "dese" and "dose" manner of speaking, Rosenbloom was quickly found on camera in small speaking parts as a hoodlum or lackey, often in a comical role for Warner Brothers pictures. He later opened his own nightclub, "Slapsie Maxie's."

Maxie also appeared on *Bill Stern's Sports Newsreel* program, performing material in standup fashion for a live radio audience: "Yes, this is "Slapsie Maxie" Rosenbloom . . . I wasn't always a great fighter, no, as a child I was so sickly I had to suck my thumb through a straw. . . . Why, every morning I used to stand under a cold shower and wonder what would happen if I turned the water on. . . . And then I became a fighter. At first they called me the wallpaper kid. I took quite a pasting. In fact I lost so many fights that my manager, instead of throwin' in towels threw in paper napkins. . . . Now I am living well in a New York Hotel. . . . So nice that they got a sign in the lobby that says you got to throw your own bed and no opium smoking in the elevator. And my room, huh, you should see my room. It's so small the mice are hunchbacks."[55]

Bill Stern was not only one of radio's most engaging in-between-round fight reporters, he was also the master of the short, dramatic sports story featuring a major coincidence or ironic twist. His style was perfectly suited to his fifteen-minute radio program. Some of his vignettes were undoubtedly apocryphal—so much so that Stern would introduce them with a disclaimer that they might be "hearsay." But they were packaged so neatly, Stern made listeners want to believe them.

His technique involved telling the entire story and not revealing who the story was about until the very end. This created a sense of anticipation that would build throughout the story no matter how brief.

As with many radio programs, background organ music was utilized to help create a heightened sense of drama. The music would bellow through its pipes with the melody shifting moment by moment to reset the ever-changing mood, rising and falling, sometimes working towards a crescendo, other times trailing off into a whisper:

Stern: "Jack Dempsey had to battle his way to the top and there were many times when he must have felt like quitting." Stern now speaks softly with the organ playing a low, sentimental tone in the background: "One time in particular, Jack Dempsey was in Wilkes-Barre, Pennsylvania. He was just an unknown prizefighter in those days. This night he was alone, broken and hungry. A traveling vaudeville player staked him to a meal, and it was this vaudeville player who gave Jack Dempsey hope."

Music and Stern's voice both rising: "It was the vaudeville player who said [then a cut to an actor's voice]: "Look kid, don't be discouraged, I saw you fight tonight and I know some day you'll hit the big time. Take my advice and don't quit."

And then Stern again: "The man who said that was [music now rising with Stern pausing for effect] . . . Jack Benny."

Stern would often string a series of stories together using the subject of one as the springboard for the next. The bits are still surprisingly entertaining, if you can tolerate a healthy dose of historical leniency.

Stern continuing: "But Jack Dempsey was destined to meet other men who were someday to be famous. For one day in Baltimore, he took on a kid in an exhibition boxing bout . . . and because of the beating that boy took he never became a prizefighter. But I don't think that boy was ever sorry that he never became a prizefighter, you see that boy that Jack Dempsey beat was . . . Babe Ruth." And then the next sketch concludes: "And that sparring partner took Jack Dempsey's advice and did become a dancer. Today he is the most famous dancing teacher in the world, his name . . . is . . . Arthur Murray."

To conclude the program, Stern circled back to Dempsey, who appeared live on the air to accept an award.[56]

Stern was not afraid to embrace the strange or offbeat story, and he carried his liberal approach to all aspects of his program. The day before Christmas Eve, 1949, the recently retired heavyweight champion Joe Louis went on the air with Stern. Louis appeared for the sole purpose of reciting a portion of "'Twas The Night Before Christmas" to the children of the listening audience. "The stockins were hangin' by the chimney with care, in hopes that St. Nick soon would be there," the "Brown Bomber" assured the youth of America.[57]

Chapter 8

DON'T TOUCH THAT DIAL: BOXING AND THE RADIO SERIAL

The boxer, through his nonring, public personality, carved a deep niche in radio through comedy and variety shows, as well as the occasional talk program or drama. However, fighter-turned-entertainer represented only one aspect of radio's interest in boxing. The fight game itself—its colorful characters, unique rituals, and tendency toward lawlessness—provided an even vaster landscape. Within this realm blossomed the seeds of many fictionalized stories starring nonboxers. The popularity of fictionalized boxing-oriented programs on the radio from the 1930s through the 1950s is evidenced by the gamut of its genres. Everything from drama, adventure, mystery, and suspense programs to theatrical, anthology, variety, and comedy shows had boxing themes.

Principal among these boxing-infused programs was the detective show. This category's core group featured private detectives: *The Falcon*, *Philip Marlowe*, *The New Adventures of Nero Wolf*, and *Rocky Fortune*. Variations on the detective theme included traditional law-enforcement shows, represented by *Gangbusters*; those rooted in the legal profession, such as *Roger Kilgore, Public Defender*, and *The*

Whisperer; and the world of freelance insurance investigation, presented in *Yours Truly, Johnny Dollar.*

A close cousin of the detective show was the adventure program. As Simon Templar in *The Saint,* Vincent Price battled both cops and crooks as "the Robin Hood of modern crime." Orson Welles contributed a touch of his genius in *The Lives of Harry Lime,* a program inspired by his film classic *The Third Man. Nightbeat* chronicled the efforts of a socially conscious news reporter portrayed by Frank Lovejoy. Mystery and suspense programs of the period such as *Mr. and Mrs. North* and *Suspense* also fell within the sphere of this detective subgenre.

All these programs share a close affinity to noir. The fight game and its raucous inhabitants were natural vehicles for stories of this genre, seamlessly blending with their noir-styled gangsters, femmes fatales, gamblers, grifters, and hard-boiled detectives. Risk-taking boxers, the machinations of the "fixed fight," and the fixers themselves also meshed easily with aspects of noir and other elements of the detective genre. Producers, recognizing the symbiotic relationship between noir-flavored drama and the boxing world, liberally produced programming that combined the two.

The first line of *The Thin Man*'s episode "The Passionate Palooka" typified the kind of atmosphere these boxing-oriented "radio noir" programs would establish: "It's one o'clock in the morning of one of those sizzling July nights that makes the average New Yorker feel like a hotdog on a griddle with mustard."[1] To further advance the desired ambience, dramatic organ music was used throughout each episode to set the changing moods and punctuate dialogue and action.

The opening narration of *Suspense* starring Dick Powell in the episode "Slow Burn" serves as a good example for these boxing-related dramas: "It all started the day I fought in Deville, Pennsylvania. My wife . . . didn't want me to fight, but to me it was the fastest way to make a buck. I was just beginning then, right after the war, and the coal town was the best I could do."[2]

The boxers and ex-boxers of these yarns were driven to acquire wealth and love but were frequently downtrodden or embittered.

Since they were facing dilemmas or in trouble with the law, their aspirations were often reduced to instinctive acts of survival. Their program titles reflected their themes: "The Bellicose Boxer," "The Passionate Palooka," and "The Ring of Death."

These fighters bore monikers as diverse as their stories—each colorful in its own way: "Punchy," "Kid Nebraska," the "Singing Slugger," and the "Atomic Bomber." The women of their world were consistently loose and self-interested, rarely trustworthy or genuine. They were typically characterized by their physical beauty and allure. They carried the scent of their seedy world.

In "The Gladiator," an episode of *Escape*, the fighter sees his fatal attraction for the first time: "And then I saw her, dark she was and pliantly slender . . . the most beautiful girl I had ever seen. She sat amongst the ringside bloodsuckers with the arch lights on her white face as calm and curious as a queen . . . and even a cold shower could not get her out of my mind."[3] In "Slow Burn," listeners are told of a woman who "had on a gown that had no straps and didn't need any. There was sweet rhythm in her walk and she wore a hands-off look that beat blood into a guy's head."[4] And in *Night Beat*, "Gunner's Last Fight": "She was in evening clothes, wearing a gown showing everything but good taste."[5]

On a subconscious level, many of these stories bore the stamp of "Beauty and the Beast." However, regardless of whether a woman had a role, there remained the tendency to cast the fighter as subhuman. In *The New Adventures of Nero Wolfe*'s, "The Case of the Deadly Sell-Out," starring Sydney Greenstreet, the boxer is referred to matter-of-factly as "a young savage animal."[6] In *Philip Marlowe*, "Angry Eagle," the physical characteristics of a fighter are described as "a nose spread over half his face" and a "hand that could pass for half a catcher's mitt."[7] Other fighters were depicted as less animalistic but were equally disparaged as punch-drunk or ignorant. At best, they were disembodied and amorphous entities such as the boxer who was "a lot of muscles in sweatpants."[8]

Portraying fighters as detached from their humanity was part and parcel of their regular treatment. In *Suspense!*, "Maestro and Man," a boxer, portrayed by radio "newcomer" Richard Conte, learns he has been sold by his manager. He expresses his anger at being treated as "so much beef on the hook, so much a pound." "Buy me and sell me until I can't take any more punishment," he rails in acknowledgment of his plight as perishable goods of the fight market.[9]

The notion of boxer as commodity was repeatedly reinforced in many programs with a storyline featuring a fixed fight. In these stories, boxers were reduced to indentured servants who had temporarily ceded their freedom and free will to another, typically a gangster, manager, or promoter who acted as his surrogate.

While these boxers struggled to achieve autonomy and choose between morality and materialism, writers entertained audiences with one-liners on the boxing "fix." In a 1948 episode of *Philo Vance*, a fighter asks, "Do you want me to lay down?" "That's right, on a golden pillow with an awful lot of cash as a blanket," the fixer replies.[10] In "The Case of The Deadly Sell-Out," listeners are told that a gambler "dropped a sizeable piece of change on last night's two-step," and that the boxer "laid down like a dog."[11] And in an episode of *The Adventures of Frank Race*, the tried-and-true fix analogy of the period was conjured up again: "He went into the tank like Esther Williams."[12]

Colorful and playful descriptions were utilized in boxing drama stories beyond that of the fixed fight. In *Rocky Fortune*, an NBC detective program starring Frank Sinatra, the typical colloquial dialogue of the period is utilized to embellish characterization in "Prizefight Set-Up." "The bell rings and I'm on my bicycle trying to keep away from 'Kid Cool,' who's after me like I was the mechanical rabbit at the racetrack," Sinatra says of his boxing match. After Sinatra's character scores a knockout, he further advises that "'Kid Cool' is still laid out like a dressed-suit when I stagger back to my corner."[13] Some of this language plays somewhat comically today, but it was apropos for the time and has acquired a certain historical linguistic charm.

The spoken word was indispensable in radio, and when radio dramas took to the ring, their visual activity would need translation into an audio experience. Writers cleverly utilized the character of a ringside announcer to call the action. This spared the audience the unwieldy and unrealistic recitation of the ring action by the story's characters. Those sitting ringside were used to provide complementary description. "To the labanza, Freddie" a male voice is heard in the audience from the distance, urging his charge in the earlier referenced episode of *The Adventures of Frank Race.*

References to the fight game in these programs were tossed about as liberally as Graziano's overhand right to assure the audience of the characters' authenticity. In *The Falcon,* "The Case of the Bellicose Boxer," the fighter is described as "the slickest thing to hit the ring since Benny Leonard."[14] In *Philip Marlowe,* there's a promise that *this time* the prospect is the real McCoy: "He's another Barney Ross, believe me."[15] Episodes of other programs evoked the signature signposts along the boxing trail such as Jacobs Beach, The Bronx Coliseum, and St. Nick's Arena.

An interesting and successful use of radio took the form of the audio dramatization of popular boxing films. During the late 1930s and 1940s, such radio programs as the *Lux Radio Theater, Theater of Romance, Screen Guild Theater,* and *Screen Directors Playhouse* aired thirty- or sixty-minute versions of famous boxing movies. These featured *The Champ, City for Conquest, Kid Galahad, Gentleman Jim, Champion,* and *Body and Soul.*[16]

Such programs attempted to remain true to the successful original movie versions by retaining specific dialogue whenever possible, and using the original lead actors to vocally reprise their screen performances.

Kirk Douglas and John Garfield would recreate their leading roles for *Screen Directors Playhouse*'s renditions of *Champion* and *Body and Soul,* respectively. Similarly, Wallace Beery appeared in two radio versions of *The Champ* for *Lux Radio Theater.* In these instances, the radio renditions maintained the clout of their film predecessors.[17]

Stars could not always be secured. Sometimes, as a result, program quality suffered. In *Lux Radio Theater*'s version of *City for Conquest,* James Cagney and all of his costars are sorely missed. Similarly, in a *Theater of Romance* performance of *Kid Galahad,* Edward G. Robinson, Humphrey Bogart, and Bette Davis are all conspicuously absent.[18] Still, a legitimate effort was usually made to replace original stars with worthy substitutes, such as Cary Grant for Robert Montgomery as the lead in *Lux*'s *Here Comes Mr. Jordan.*

In the main, these theatrical programs were neatly packaged radio entertainment. "Lady Esther presents the Screen Guild Players" was the introduction for one typical program. The announcer then cued in the stars of the evening's show, each of whom introduced themselves to the radio audience: "This is Errol Flynn," "This is Alexis Smith," "This is Ward Bond," and "This is Grant Withers." And so the broadcast of *Gentleman Jim* was officially underway.[19]

While scripts were truncated due to time limitations, they retained the key dialogue from the original screenplay: "Those fat bellies with the cigars ain't going to make a bum out of me," Kirk Douglas cries at the end of *Champion* before succumbing to a cerebral hemorrhage.[20]

At the end of *Screen Directors Playhouse* programs, the stars would come out of character and speak a bit to the audience. "Sure Peg, I'm alright, I never felt better in my life," John Garfield said triumphantly at the conclusion of *Body and Soul.* Moments later, he greeted his radio audience: "Thank you. Any realism you might have found in *Body and Soul* was partly because of a couple of ex-Eastside kids. A long time ago they made some admirable efforts at beating each other's brains out in the boxing ring. I was one of them and the other was the director of *Body and Soul,* Robert Rossen. Bob was a pretty lousy fighter, but he became one of Hollywood's most gifted writers and directors. Now ladies and gentleman, I would like you to meet Robert Rossen."[21]

Movie studios were able to compel many original stars and directors to perform in the radio versions. Their ability to use their film talent to exploit the medium for their marketing illustrated where the true power in the entertainment industry lay.

These radio programs were also important enough to draw the personal attention of such film greats as famed director-producer Cecil B. DeMille, who produced many of the radio versions of boxing films and served as the master of ceremonies for the *Lux Radio*

Theater broadcasts. He was committed to these broadcasts and pedaled Lux Toilet Soap with the same earnestness and gentlemanly demeanor he used when introducing Fred McMurray or Cary Grant to a program's audience.

It is fair to say that some radio versions of boxing films do not play today with the full impact and level of credulity as when originally broadcast. This is due to the dramatic writing style of the period that has since become inescapably clichéd. In the 1946 *Theater of Romance* broadcast of *Kid Galahad*, the kid levels the heavyweight champion, and we are told that he "knocked him colder than . . . ice cubes."[22] Lines from *Screen Directors Playhouse*'s 1950 version of *Champion*, such as "They brushed me off like dandruff," are now unintentionally funny.[23] However, much of the writing still holds up. We are told in another *Screen Directors Playhouse* performance of the effects of the punishment that protagonist Charlie Davis receives in *Body and Soul*: "his body reddening under the leather shock, the split lip with the crimson welt, the eyes tired . . . tired."[24]

Not all of these radio "theater" programs were based upon major motion pictures. Other programming, such as those presented by *Mystery Theater* and *Heartbeat Theater*, focused upon nonfilm, boxing-themed fictionalized stories. Although these programs were technically "theater" programs, in many ways they were indistinguishable from other boxing-related fictionalized dramatic stories. They were of an inferior quality to those written for the big screen, not unlike many other pedestrian detective stories of the period. *Mystery Theater*'s 1952 entry, "The Case of The Tell-Tale Tie," is illustrative. The story dredges up the well-worn theme of the down-and-out ex-fighter. In the episode, as the title suggests, the boxer's tie proves the definitive piece of evidence for the crime at hand—used in the strangulation of a woman by her boxer-husband.[25]

While theater and anthology programs provided some of the best boxing fiction on radio, nonfiction boxing stories were also successfully dramatized in a number of original scripted shows. One of the more interesting efforts notable for its progressive theme was a program called *Destination Freedom.* These educational programs broadcast over the NBC network were stylized with catchy titles such as "Shakespeare of Harlem" and "Negro Cinderella." Each program began: *Destination Freedom*: dramatizations of the great democratic traditions of the Negro people is brought to you by station WMAQ as part of the pageant of American history and America's own destination freedom."[26]

Three episodes of the series, each written by Richard Durham—"The Saga of Melody Jackson," "Premonition of the Panther," and "Little David"—focused on the three greatest African American fighters of the mid-twentieth century: Henry Armstrong, Sugar Ray Robinson, and Joe Louis. In each, both the life and ring career of the boxer is chronicled. What distinguished these episodes from most other programs of the time was black perspective with a frank social tone. In "The Saga of Melody Jackson," a young Henry Armstrong's dreams of higher education are dashed when he is told by a Washington University admissions official, "Of all the nerve, we don't take Jews, Negroes, or Mexicans."[27]

In "Little David," the title serves as an analogy between Joe Louis and David of the bible, both of whom we are told rise up and challenge the world. Louis is also an underdog, a member of a disadvantaged breed whose "genes have been juggled and blood mixed."[28] In "Premonition of the Panther," Robinson bristles at the notion of being "owned" by the white establishment, even if it is only his boxing contract that is at stake.[29]

Similarly, a moral drama, *Lest We Forget: The American Dream* (1943–48), a program created by the Institute for Democratic Education and Boston University Radio Institute, took a cutting-edge look at race in America. In a boxing-themed episode, "The Carolina Kid," Canada Lee portrays a black boxer who prefers to become a mathematician but is told, "It's not for Negroes, kid . . . why break your heart?" At the end of the episode, Lee steps out of character to address the audience: "And I wonder how many there are like the Carolina Kid, boys and girls of every faith, color, and national background who are being prevented by prejudice from making their maximum contribution to our community, our nation. As Americans isn't it about time we gave all of them a chance?"[30]

Whether fiction or nonfiction, most boxing dramas were single, episodic shows. However, *Joe Palooka* was one regular boxing feature that played for several years. From modest origins as Ham Fisher's comic-book character in 1930, Palooka would become an effective piece of American propaganda as the first comic strip character to join the US Army. His newspaper readership would eventually reach 40 million. After World War II, he would expand into radio, movie shorts, feature films, and, finally, television.

Ham Fisher and Philip Gelb scripted 260 fifteen-minute radio episodes that were broadcast on fifteen different radio stations. Norman Gottschalk played the boxer/American hero, and Hal Lansing spoke for the irrepressible sidekick, Knobby Walsh.

"The winner and still champion, Joe Palooka," the radio broadcast began. These words from a ring announcer were complemented by the clang of a ringside bell and the roar of the crowd. The narrator would continue: "In this corner in top fighting form, coming to you every Monday through Friday at this time in thrilling, action-packed stories, America's idol and number one hero, world's champion of boxing and fair play, Joe Palooka."[31]

Joe Palooka provided light entertainment, blending drama, action, and adventure with the sporadic use of comedic elements. Strict comedy programs on the radio featuring boxing material were almost exclusively "one-offs." They were highlighted in situation comedies such as *Easy Aces*, *My Friend Irma*, *Life of Riley*, and *The Adventures of Maisie*. They also showed up in variety programs with comedic skits including *The Red Skelton Show* and *The Jack Benny Program*.

During the '40s, *The Red Skelton Show* featured the actor as his signature, dim-witted fighter Cauliflower McPugg—a rare reoccurring boxing character on radio. Comedian Pete Hayes would exploit the same theme with "Punchy Callahan" as a guest on *The Ford Show*.[32]

With both genders equally represented in comedy program audiences, analogies between the universal topic of marriage and the ubiquitous sport of boxing were inevitable.[33] In an episode of the

Lou Holtz Laugh Club, Holtz tells his audience, "I've discovered marriage is often like boxing, the preliminaries are often better than the main event."[34] In a skit, after Red Skelton purchases a boxer named "Slugger Bozo," he is asked by a friend if he thinks he is a good fighter. "I think so," Skelton replies, "he's been married for ten years."[35]

As with his later TV show, the comedy of Skelton's radio program was often rooted in topical trends and events. During the early-1950s, televised boxing was at its height, with programs frequently sponsored by beer companies such as Pabst and Ballantine. Skelton spoofs this trend explaining in one radio skit, "I can't stand the fights myself, I can't stand the sight of beer."[36]

Topical themes and spoofing the sponsor were also part of the approach in a pair of boxing-themed episodes of *The Jack Benny Program.* In one episode, Benny lampoons the success of two recent boxing movies, *Champion* and *The Set-Up.* The sketch opens with a re-creation of the opening of *Champion*: "My name is Midge Benny. I'm the middleweight champion of the world. People say I'm a heel. They say I'd slug my own grandmother. But they are wrong. Grandmother is a heavyweight."[37]

As part of the skit, the Gillette Safety Razor Company, sponsor of the *Friday Night Fights,* is lampooned by Benny: "Look sharp, feel sharp. Use a wherever grindstone and sharpen your silly face off," the audience is told.[38]

A few months later, *Champion* was nominated for an Oscar for Best Picture, and Benny decided to take advantage of the film's increasing popularity by revisiting the skit. The now extraneous reference to *The Set-Up* was dropped.

Quite possibly, there was legal blowback from Gillette, because the second time around, Gillette's signature tagline, "Look sharp, feel sharp," was dropped entirely. The sponsor gag now focused on the fictitious Safe Rush Soap Company, urging listeners to "Look clean, feel clean, be clean." Benny's new version of *Champion* also added some new boxing one-liners. After "Midge Benny" kisses the femme fatale, she says in a husky voice, "Hmm, still a preliminary boy."[39]

Short sketches such as those in variety and anthology programs seemed best suited for boxing-based humor. Situation comedies of a longer format often stretched material noticeably. Writers could not be faulted. The popular topic of boxing was another angle from which writers could create possible scenarios, fortifying a star character that needed a weekly infusion of intrigue. For example, instead of the program's star purchasing a car or a washing machine as in previous episodes, a program could feature her buying a piece of a fighter. All the comedic results built into the script could be maintained with a slight twist of humor fashioned along the lines of the fight game.

Typically, these situation comedies were good for at least one boxing reference. The level of comedic appeal was debatable. In *My Friend Irma*, when Irma's boyfriend Al looks to bankroll a fighter, her friend berates him, informing him, "This is not an annex of Stillman's gym."[40] In an episode of *The Adventures of Maisie*, starring Ann Sothern, a fighter's lax training leads to his admonishment: "By the way you are training, by the second round you're gonna be hearing bells. And I don't mean from St. Mary's."[41]

Both boxing-themed programs highlighting the sport's personalities and other fiction and nonfiction programming with the fight game as its subject left an expansive imprint on radio during its golden age. Unfortunately, the pioneering efforts of the 1920s have been lost to the dustbin of history. Surviving programs from the '30s, and more abundantly those of the late- '40s and early- '50s, have left a rich legacy for the radio and boxing fan alike.

Chapter 9

TALES FROM RADIO LAND

An invisible veil separates the brightly lit ring and the darkened arena just beyond. On rare occasions, the activities outside the ring pierce this veil and become part of the fistic action. In these cases, the protocol calls for the fighter to dismiss such intrusions.

However, when Marty Servo challenged Freddie "Red" Cochrane for the welterweight championship in 1946, he took a markedly different approach. One would have expected Servo to ignore the prattle of the ringside announcer, letting it blend with the rising voices of the throng beyond. Instead, he was drawn to the announcer's voice like a fog-shrouded ship seeking a singular beacon of light. In one of the ring's more surreal moments, Servo would attempt to listen to the radio broadcast of his title match as he fought it.

After lifting the title from Cochrane, the twenty-six-year-old ex-guardsman from Schenectady, New York, explained the unusual phenomenon to a reporter: "I heard what they were broadcasting most of the time. About half a dozen times when we were on that side of the ring, I heard it real good. Once, when we were right over them, I heard the fellow say, 'Cochrane landed a solid left hook to

Servo's head.' I was so surprised I almost laughed. He didn't hit me with no left at all. He swung and missed by a mile."[1]

Servo had been cocking his head from time to time in an unusual manner. It appeared to ringsiders that he was trying to get a look at the clock, but he was actually trying to focus on the broadcast. "It was a lot of fun," the new champion stated, "Say, I wonder if that's the first time a fighter listened to himself fighting . . . at the same time, I mean."[2]

As part of its broadcast of Primo Carnera's 1934 title defense against Max Baer, the NBC Blue Network decided to expand its coverage. Not only would they broadcast Graham McNamee's blow-by-blow description of the fight, but for the first time they would provide live postfight coverage from the champion's dressing room immediately afterward. To accomplish this, NBC assigned broadcaster George Hicks and an equipment-touting engineer to the task.

Of course, Carnera's consent for the interview was required. Before the fight, Hicks attempted to secure the needed approval, but the champion's manager was noncommittal. Carnera took an unprecedented drubbing at the hands of Baer, and the possibility of a postfight interview grew dim. After the fight, Hicks watched as Carnera ducked and dodged a sportswriter's questions. Still, Hicks made another bid for the radio interview. This time he was admonished by Primo.

Clearly, Carnera was physically and psychologically battered. His pride was stung deeply. One might even say the ex-champion was suffering. However, he eventually gave Hicks his interview. Sitting on his dressing room table, his large head hung low, Carnera began to answer a number questions. Suddenly, the Italian behemoth began to cry. As Hicks would later explain, "No big tears came, but it was the simple, small crying of a boy who had never wished harm to anyone and who had just been terribly mistreated." "For Chrissake," McNamee was shouting. "Get this on the air! It's great! Primo Carnera is crying!"[3]

But McNamee's serendipitous scoop did not materialize. The on-air broadcast had moved away from ringside and was not switched back to the Garden City Bowl dressing room. They were not on the airwaves. A few who huddled around Carnera, McNamee, and perhaps some in the control room heard the historic moment. Unfortunately, millions of radio listeners had been denied a poignant moment and a rare occurrence in sports: the heavyweight champion weeping in public after a fight.[4,5]

With Jack Dempsey and Gene Tunney stepping off the stage, and Joe Louis still a twinkle in the eye of Mike Jacobs, boxing during the Depression entered an era in which its "little men" gained increased notoriety. Fans followed the talented featherweights, lightweights, and welterweights enthusiastically, with their rooting interests often tied to a fighter's ethnicity and place of origin.

One of these early post-Dempsey era matches featured local Chicagoan standout, the Jewish Jackie Fields, and West Coast African American clouter Jack Thompson. The fight was contested at the Chicago Coliseum over ten rounds for the world's welterweight championship. In a bout described as "one of the best welterweight ring struggles in fistic history," 10,000 attending fans and many more listening on the radio at home participated firsthand or vicariously in one of the most bizarre fight nights in ring history.[6]

During the eighth round of the fierce battle, a row of temporary bleachers in the rear of the arena collapsed. Almost simultaneously, the boom of a cameraman's flashbulb and shouts of "Fire!" were heard. Billows of smoke fueled the audience's fear and panic. Afterward, it was explained that some had feared that the animals from the nearby zoo outside of the Coliseum might have escaped.[7]

In what can easily be categorized as *not* one of Chicago's finest moments of chivalry, "in a panic, men rushed the ring, pushing aside women or bowling them over in a mad dash." As the crowd, unaware of what had started the riot, surged toward and then into the ring, the nearly oblivious Thompson and Fields continued to fight until the crowd was upon them.[8]

A later investigation revealed that the human stampede ensued when an individual engaged in a fight pulled a gun. The incident resulted in eighteen people being injured, including a man with life-threatening injuries who was pushed or fell from a balcony. Several others were hospitalized with broken bones.[9]

The Associated Press described radio's role in reporting the incident: "Press wires were interrupted and typewriters were trampled in the melee. For a time the only word of the panic and the interrupted fight was carried dramatically by microphones knocked to the floor and plucked up by radio announcers who leaped to the ring and kept up their story. Listeners heard the thunder of the stampede and the broken narrative of the broadcasters from the focal point of the frenzied crowd."[10]

In a fight that would otherwise have been remembered for its fistic prowess, Fields won the decision and the vacant N.B.A.

Jack Thompson, seen here with his parents, waged a memorable battle with Jackie Fields for the N.B.A. welterweight title at the Chicago Stadium, March 25, 1929. The bout, won by Fields, was overshadowed by a riot. Early radio captured the drama. *Photo courtesy of the Boston Public Library, Leslie Jones collection.*

welterweight championship in what was probably radio's first broadcast of a major boxing riot.

Perhaps there is no greater illustration of the public's changing tastes regarding boxing than its abandonment of the once-beloved amateur boxing program. Today, it is somewhat hard to comprehend that in their heyday in the 1930s and 1940s, lanky, pimple-faced teenage boys with little or no exposure could draw over 50,000 fans.

During this era, amateurs of all types boxing in myriad tournaments could be found in the ring. The iconic Golden Gloves bouts were featured annually, representing the pinnacle of the "simon-pure" ranks. Its fighters participated on a parochial level as well as in intercity and international competitions. There were also tournaments for the coveted Diamond Belt, an achievement on par with the Golden Gloves. Other youngsters aggressively competed in Catholic Youth Organization (CYO) and American Athletic Union (AAU) championships, significant honors in their time.

Collegiate fighters put down their books and traded hooks for NCAA honors in a league of their own. Faceless business and municipal employees formed teams and battled one another for bragging rights at the water cooler. Members of every branch of the Armed Forces competed amongst themselves and against each other for national honors.

The participant's lack of talent, or at least the lack of experience, did not dissuade the public interest in these contests. Sometimes the stakes in local, ethnic, or national pride was in itself enough to pique interest. On other occasions the sheer enthusiasm and grittiness of the bouts were more than sufficient to endear the participants to the fans.

With such a strong following, amateur boxing found a solid niche on the radio. Chicago became a national hub for the nonprofessional ranks, featuring many local, intercity, national, and international contests.

In the early '40s, WGN listeners in the Windy City area, and a broader audience over the Mutual Broadcasting system, could follow all of the action from the likes of radio reporters Dave Driscoll and Stan Lomax. The pair broadcast intercity bouts with the *New York Daily News* team.[11]

International Golden Gloves contests were also aired over the Mutual System and locally on WGN with stalwart Chicagoan boxing announcers Bob Elson and Quin Ryan giving the blow-by-blow and color analysis, respectively.[12]

International amateur contests had always been big news. In 1932, the German amateur boxing team arrived in Chicago for international Golden Gloves bouts. Its members were immediately whisked off to the radio studios of WGN. The boxers' limited English did not seem to hamper their popularity. Heavyweight Heinrich Kohlhas mustered a few words for the broadcast. "I am the baby of the team, heavy but good." It was reported that Kohlhas received more fan and love letters during his stay in Chicago than a popular screen star. When asked what he liked more than anything in the world, his teammate Joseph Schleinkofer responded, "Beer. I am from Munich." The public found these youngsters irresistible. Soldiers Field expected upward of 60,000 in attendance.[13]

The large crowds these amateurs drew for competition was noteworthy. However, the fanfare and enthusiasm displayed by the public when the fighters were not even in the ring was incredible. In 1940, the Hawaiian boxing team flew to Chicago to battle the Chicago Catholic Youth Organization at Soldiers Field. Several days before the bouts, the Hawaiian boxers were greeted by a crowd of 25,000 fans in the Westside of Chicago at Garfield Park. The Hawaiian squad received a rousing welcome as they marched onto the reception stand with the CYO's 100-piece band playing *Blue Hawaii.* As if this greeting weren't enough, another introduction, for the benefit of the Southside boxing fans, followed at Davis Square Park.

For those who could not attend in person, radio station WGN offered its own preliminaries with *Tribune* sports editor Arch Ward interviewing captains and coaches of the two teams. It was anticipated that when the fighters finally entered the ring at Soldiers Field, they would fight before an audience of 30,000.[14]

The enthusiasm for amateur boxing, particularly the Golden Gloves, would be reflected in its greatest audiences during the era of the combined radio and television coverage of the 1950s. The two mediums would bring the bouts "to millions of fight fans for the first time in the history of the event." [15]

In 1957, the New York City-Chicago Golden Gloves intercity tournament marked its thirtieth annual program. Alternating the location of the event annually, that year the Chicago Tribune Charities, Inc., hosted the event at Chicago Stadium. Three hundred radio stations participated in the program. The event was so significant that the International Boxing Club relinquished its television date to accommodate the event. Television stations in twenty-eight states and Alaska carried the bouts over the ABC Network.[16]

Several years later, the amateur game, like the general sport of boxing, would face the harsh consequences eroding support for both radio and TV broadcasting. Reduced media coverage contributed to a slow decline in the popularity of amateur boxing. While an interest in Olympic boxing would periodically forestall this trend, the ultimate decline in public interest was never reversed. Amateur boxing, like radio itself, continues to this day, but the fruitful marriage of the pair has long since passed into history.

Epilogue

RADIO RECORDINGS

There are no known statistics as to the percentage of boxing radio broadcasts that were made. Likewise, no hard information exists regarding the number that survived through recordings. Of the hundreds of thousands of radio programs broadcast on all subjects during the golden age of radio, the 1920s to the1950s, the majority have probably been lost. The Radio Yesteryear archive, for example, which holds the entire spectrum of radio programming, contains only 61,000 recorded broadcasts during this period.[1]

Other large historical holdings exist in the National Archives and the Library of Congress, but with an overlap of programming in the major archives and corporate collections such as Radio Yesteryear. The number of surviving boxing recordings is at best proportional to the overall industry survival rate, which is to say, only a minority remain.

It is clear that the technology to make radio recordings probably did not exist prior to 1923.[2] The first successful attempt to make a clear-sounding phonographic record by the transference of "radio sound vibration" to wax discs was made at the Democratic National Convention in Kansas City on June 26, 1924. At that time, Warner Recording Laboratories used "an amplification device constructed on the principal of a loud speaker and connected to the phonographic recording device."[3]

Therefore, it can be concluded that boxing history from ringside before the Dempsey-Firpo era simply does not exist in sound. The survival of radio recordings of any kind from the 1920s is also rare. Consequently, it is reasonable to assume that boxing is devoid of an audio history until the start of the Depression and the reign of Max Schmeling.

Recordings made during radio's Golden Age were captured by a number of methods under a variety of circumstances. Recordings were made by radio networks, their affiliated stations, or at a recording studio. Some industrious individuals even recorded from the radio in their homes. Methods used to make the recordings evolved along with technology and the industry.

From 1924 until approximately 1931, a recorded radio program was made on 78 rpm records, either ten or twelve inches in diameter. Two types of recordings could be produced. The first was called a "pressing." Pressings were mass-produced from master dies. They required a chemical and physical processing that needed more time to manufacture. As a result, there was a lag time between the actual broadcast, the production of the recording, and its ultimate availability.

The second type was called "cuttings." With a cutting, the grooves of the record were made as the program was heard. These were also referred to as "instantaneous" recordings because one could listen to the record immediately after it was produced. However, because only one cutting could be made at a time, the pressing or mass-produced version was much more commonplace in the industry.

In 1931, a new method called the "electrical transcription" (ET) became popular. It was produced on a record of sixteen inches in diameter. Like its predecessors, it could be either mass-produced through pressing or instantaneously "cut." The advantage of these records was their slower speed of 33 and 1/3 rpms, allowing a full thirty-minute radio program to be recorded on a single disc (fifteen minutes per side). Electric transcriptions remained popular until shortly after World War II with the introduction of magnetic tape recordings and persisted in use at a declining rate into the 1960s.[4]

PART II

TELEVISION

TELEVISION PROLOGUE

There is a tendency to distill one's memories of the Golden Age of televised boxing to a select handful of fighters who left an indelible mark. This cadre of boxers typically includes Chuck Davey, whose novelty as college graduate eclipsed his ring talent; "Kid" Gavilan with his famed "bolo" punch; and Art "Golden Boy" Aragon, the popular West Coast sensation. Others such as Ralph "Tiger" Jones, Joey Giardello, and Dick Tiger are equally memorable, if not for their skill and tenacity, then for their unmatched familiarity with the viewing audience.

However, early televised boxing also brought into the home the likes of Bob Satterfield, Coley Wallace, Charley Norkus, Danny Nardico, Jimmy Slade, Freddie Dawson, Bobby Dykes, Pierre Langlois, Al Andrews, Paddy DeMarco, Lauro Salas, and a host of others. Their ring exploits spanned almost an entire generation.

While the fighters were the stars, television itself, particularly in its early years, was the uncredited costar. Televised boxing during its Golden Age also brought to audiences what might be described as boxing's lost world—the fluttering white moths against the dark sky during the "outdoor" season; the referee's scorecard and pencil protruding from his back pocket, tools of his trade; the giant ring microphone magically appearing and then retracting into oblivion; a ring completely devoid of advertisement; boxers' trunks without embellishment; their gloves only dark brown or black; male "round card girls," whose singular purpose was to identify the upcoming stanza; newspapermen clanking away at their typewriters just beyond the ropes, frantically trying to make deadline; flashing blubs from the oversize cameras at ringside, creating bursts of brilliant, blinding white light; photographers scrambling to change their spent bulbs and used film so as not to miss the next dramatic moment; a single announcer who carried an entire broadcast without graphics, punch stats, or slow-motion replay; and the fighters themselves, who were referred to as "the boys," regardless of their age.

Indeed, vintage boxing television broadcasts were different from those of today in many respects. Limited production values were the standard. Primitive graphics started on cards that were moved by hand, for example. Grainy pictures were tolerated. Announcers went it alone; sometimes it appeared they were winging it.

Perhaps what was *not* part of the broadcast during the call of the fight is what contrasts so strikingly with the present telecasts—the incessant discussion of what the fight means to a fighter's career, the rampant speculation on what might happen after the fight is over, who might face who next, where the fight might rank in the history of the division or even in the sport itself.

Objectively speaking, today's broadcasts are eons ahead in their technological sophistication, in their coverage and content, in their elocution and delivery. In the early days of television, the announcer simply called the fight. Consider these broadcasts basic, even crude, if you like. But they represented a time before the pendulum of analysis had swung a bit too far in the opposite direction.

Most important, they are still ours. They represent our history and our culture. We can enjoy their ingenuity, salute their triumphs, and revel in traditions created and preserved.

Chapter 10

THE ERA OF EXPERIMENTAL AND AMATEUR TELEVISION: BOXING LEADS THE WAY

The invention of television—the electrical transmission and reception of transient images—was brought about by the collaboration of many who traveled a myriad of paths.[1] All of the elements of a practical transmission system for moving images over an electrical wire had been identified by 1880. However, it would take more than a half-century of hypothesis, experimentation, and discovery by a multitude of inventors on both sides of the Atlantic before operational, practical, and economically feasible systems for both transmission and reception were realized.[2]

Seminal names for early experimental devices included "telephoto" and "telectroscope." Such terminology became a footnote to history when Constantin Perskyl introduced his paper entitled "Television" on August 25, 1900.[3] By the mid-1920s, primitive but operational television systems, both mechanical and electronic, were being publically demonstrated.

A decade later, television moved beyond the experimental and amateur stages when public service television in England and Germany was offered.[4] Television in the United States reached a similar stage of development in 1941 with its first commercial telecasts.

As early as 1928, while television was still a child of the laboratory, the suitability of boxing with television was recognized. J. Andrew White, then-President of the Columbia Broadcasting System, was an early prognosticator: "The first and most logical application of television apparatus, I think, would be for events, such as championship boxing matches, or the picture story of the arrival of Lindbergh."[5]

Three years later, television was the fancy of the American amateur radio enthusiast, with an estimated 500 receivers in the New York area and 500 to 1,000 in the Chicago area. Signals broadcast by W9XAO AND W9XAB, two pioneering television stations in Chicago, were being plucked out of the airwaves by receivers tucked in between the wheat fields of Iowa and scattered amongst the cornfields of Kansas and Minnesota. Michigan, Ohio, and Missouri were also within the reach of the broadcasts, and some images were received as far west as Arizona. Early television viewers expressed a preference for "boxing matches and performances which feature plenty of action."[6]

Similarly, a New York station, W2XAB, was beaming its signal into the heartland of America, with one viewer from Manhattan, Kansas, reporting clear reception and the enjoyment of the Thursday night boxing matches.[7,8]

In 1932, station W2XAB began receiving fan mail regarding its television broadcasts. One viewer from Middlebury, Vermont, wrote, "Of the six television stations that I receive regularly, yours gives the greatest detail. I have especially enjoyed the dancer and the boxing bouts."[9] The following year, a Bristol, Tennessee, viewer of the same New York station commented that "I have noticed the boxing bouts, and have received quite a bit of entertainment."[10]

Boxing was not only one of television's earliest entertainment products, but also served as one of its earliest and most frequently used guinea pigs. In a 1928 Bell Telephone Laboratory experiment, images that previously captured only the heads and shoulders of the subjects now contained full figures on a screen of about two by three inches. "At today's demonstration a man served tennis balls, drove a golf ball, boxed a companion and went through other motions on a laboratory roof," it was triumphantly reported.[11] The following year, it was reported that "the demonstration of a thrilling boxing contest in silhouette form can be readily followed on the televisor screen."[12]

Several years later, William Schudt, who directed certain tests for W2XAB, noted that "When we projected the boxing match last week, it was discovered that greater clarity of images could be had when a heavy black curtain was spread across the entire rear of the ring. It was necessary to shake considerable white powder into the hair of the contestants, since it was too dark to make any showing at all in the television camera. The slight contrast that the addition of white powder made saved the night and made history of boxing by television."[13]

In August 1931, Benny Leonard became the first fighter of note to box before a television camera. The former lightweight king boxed an exhibition against Golden Gloves featherweight champion Jimmy Martin at the Columbia Television Studios on Madison Avenue in New York City. The quality of the transmission made by W2XAB varied. At its worst, it reproduced fighters who "seemed to be struggling through a severe blizzard."[14]

After Leonard knocked out his opponent in the third round, he proceeded to give the first postfight interview in boxing history. Justifying his comeback to the ring after a six-year hiatus, he noted that he had always "lived clean and fought clean." His trainer, Teddy Hayes, referee Jimmy De Forrest, and William C. "Wild Bill" Lyons also addressed the audience.[15]

The following year, another television experiment was performed at famed department store Gimbels, in New York City. Fifteen hundred curious onlookers observed an eclectic live program featuring fashion demonstrations as well as a three-round boxing match conducted in a miniature ring that was three feet square. The crowd that had assembled in an improvised television theater cheered the spectacle.[16]

In 1936, in a televised experiment conducted in Philadelphia by the engineers of the Philco Radio and Television Corporation, welterweights boxed on the roof of the company plant, entertainment bookended by musical solos and a musical quartet.[17] In England, boxing also served as fodder for an experiment called "slow-motion" television. A successful lesson of the art of self-defense was conducted by two boxers, "Dusty" Miller and Sergeant Wheeler, who dressed in black and white, respectively. They exchanged a series of blows and then repeated their punch sequences in slow motion, which were critiqued by former English amateur heavyweight champion, Captain D. S. Lister. The *London Observer* noted that boxing proved one of the best subjects yet chosen for the experiment."[18]

As visually compromised as the images of early boxing matches may have been, when compared to other sports, boxing was still an ideal subject. The stationary aspect of the ring, its small size (usually no more than twenty by twenty square feet), and the limited number of participants—two—made boxing something that television's early engineers could navigate. For example, in the Leonard-Martin exhibition, the television camera was mounted on a moving stand that allowed the engineers to easily traverse the perimeter of the small ring, mimicking the mobility of a motion-picture camera.[19] On the other hand, football was a perfect example of the difficulties that other sports presented and the dogged creativity of the broadcasters who tried to master these sports.

In 1931, it was readily conceded that television was "not eagle-eyed enough to follow a football game on the field." However, to deal with television's inability to reproduce the football itself, W2AXB, developed a miniature gridiron board to show every position of the ball: "A small football cut from sheet tin and painted white is moved by invisible wires and magnets to various positions on the field, always in synchronization with the voice of the announcer which comes from the scene of the contest."[20]

Despite the enthusiastic and hopeful start of television, it remained a scientific and amateur endeavor during the 1930s. Early television apparatuses were cumbersome, featuring mechanical parts not unlike those found in movie projectors. A major step was taken when General Electric began developing picture tubes. In the summer of 1934, the first public demonstration of an all-electric television was made by Philo Farnsworth at the Franklin Institute in Philadelphia.[21] Several years later, in 1938, the first relevant boxing matches were televised in the United States, originating from the Ridgewood Grove, Jamaica Arena, and The St. Nicholas Arena, all in New York. Radio announcer Sam Taub was behind the television microphone. Nevertheless, these were still local club fights, albeit of New York quality.[22, 23]

Finally, on June 1, 1939, a major step forward was taken for both television and boxing. Many of those seeking entertainment in New York that Thursday evening tuned their radios to WEAF to *The Good News of 1939*, featuring Frank Morgan, Fanny Brice, Meredith Wilson and His Orchestra, and Robert Young, followed by *The Bing Crosby Variety Hour* with Walter Huston. Others selected the popular *Major Bowe's Amateur Hour* on WABC. Sports fans undoubtedly opted for the 9:18 P.M. start of the Dodgers-Cubs baseball game on WOR. At 10 P.M., those fans preferring boxing switched over to WJZ for the bout between heavyweight contenders Lou Nova and Max Baer.

These listening choices were par for the course, except for a very select few. Those who owned a receiver with special capabilities could tune in at both 45.25 megacycles and 49.50 megacycles, respectively, for not only a "sound" broadcast of the fight, but a "picture" one, as well. This receiver-synchronized sound and video broadcast is generally recognized as the first major televised broadcast of boxing in America.[24]

As reported by the *New York Times*, boxing on television made a dramatic entrance. Observing from a darkened room in Great Neck, Long Island, Orrin E. Dunlap, Jr. explained that a radio audience that now has eyes looked on amazed and bewildered by the magic of it all. "To see a broadcast is ten thousand times more interesting than listening sightless to a broadcast announcer," he opined in his comparison to radio. Recognizing the suspense in viewing the action live,

On June 1, 1939, Max Baer and Lou Nova fought at Yankee Stadium in the first major televised American boxing match. The *New York Times* explained that "a radio audience that now has eyes looked on amazed and bewildered by the magic of it all." *From the author's collection.*

he said, "this seeing by radio is far more interesting than watching a belated and cut newsreel of such warfare."[25]

Despite the fact that Baer was seen climbing into the ring, and was easily distinguished from his opponent when the announcer identified him as "the giant with the towel wrapped around his head," the clarity of the broadcast left something to be desired. It was far from what a modern audience would probably consider viewable. "Television is not quite clear enough as of yet, to show swollen eyes and lacerations, but the different colored trunks are a great aid to the spectator," explained the *Times* observer. Despite these deficiencies, Dunlap concluded that "the first American bout by television was over, leaving evidence galore that boxing is a natural for television."[26]

With very few people owning their own television, curious onlookers jockeyed for position in public venues to catch a glimpse of the action. In the "smoking room" of the New Amsterdam Theater, 300 people crowded around a small set to watch the fight. One viewer noted: "fortunately the camera had been set up on the east side of the ring, near Baer's corner, so that the feverish activity of Baer's seconds at the end of the closing rounds was clearly caught."[27]

The first Baer-Nova affair, won by Nova via an eleventh-round knockout, is recognized as the first major American boxing match ever televised. However, it was not a commercial broadcast and was produced as a "courtesy arrangement." As an NBC representative at that time stated, no contract was signed, nor was any fee charged by the promoter for the rights of the telecast.[28] The Baer-Nova rematch two years later would earn credit for another milestone in television history—the first televised boxing match from Madison Square Garden.[29]

The televising of boxing at the time was a speculative affair at best. Some early bouts were listed for the public as "tentatively scheduled." With the technology unproven, the sponsorship concerns nonexistent, and the audience sparse at best, the telecast of fights was considered a serendipity.

In some respects, boxing on television in England actually predated that of the United States. In 1929, pioneer experiments were being conducted at the Baird Studio in London. Transmissions were made of enthusiastic employees who were willing to "take and receive black eyes"—subjects who were more cooperative than "a horse who was coaxed half-way up the stairs to be televised, but upon seeing the machinery . . . turned and fled."[30]

The following year, the first boxer of note to appear before a television camera lens in any capacity was "Bombardier" Billy Wells, former heavyweight champion of England. Viewers gathered at the London Coliseum and watched individuals "in a building some distance away." Wells was one of several speakers and discussed an upcoming sporting event.[31]

In October, 1931, the London television schedule for the *Daily Mail, Atlantic Edition,* listed the scheduled telecast of a four-round exhibition between Fred Dyer of London and Billy Overton of Wales. The signal for the television portion of the broadcast was to be made on the 261.3m wavelength. Strangely, this bout is not generally recognized as England's first televised bout. Perhaps it did not occur.[32]

The first confirmed televised bout of any description in England was an exhibition bout between Archie Sexton and Laurie Raiteri from the Broadcasting House in London on August 22, 1933.[33] In addition to the exhibition, another bout scheduled for four rounds, between flyweights Freddie Baxter and Teddy Lewis, both from Bethnal Green, England, was televised.[34] A twelve-foot ring was erected at the studio at the Broadcasting House. The boxers fought under dim lights to accommodate the television cameras. Viscount Scarsdale and Jim Mollison called the bout.[35, 36]

The British light-heavyweight championship between Jock McAvoy and Len Harvey staged at Harringay Arena in London on April 4, 1938, is considered to be the first televised, nonexhibition professional bout. This match was also the first BBC boxing telecast.[37] However, it was not a commercial broadcast for public television viewers.[38, 39, 40, 41]

The distinction of the world's first commercial television broadcast belongs to the telecast of the Eric Boon-Arthur Danahar fight in London four months prior to Baer-Nova. At that time, the London area boasted approximately 8,000 television receivers whose owners enjoyed the BBC's daily television service. Unfortunately the BBC, with its limited television budget, was unable to pay the 1,000 pound ($5,000) fee to promoter Sydney Hulls for the right to televise the broadcast. However, Gaumont-British, a newsreel company, which was also the firm behind the television system offered by Scottish engineer John Baird, purchased the rights.[42]

The fight, which was shown at two of Baird's theaters, the Tatler and the Marble Arch Pavilion, as well as at the theater of rival television company Scophony, was such a hit that "they had to call out the mounted police to control the crowds." Nonpaying fight fans entered the theaters, and although willing to pay for their seats, when none were available, they took seats anyway, showing little inclination to yield their spots to the rightful paying customers.

While confusion reigned amongst the overflowing television viewers, the 14,000 spectators at the fight itself were dealing with their own ramifications brought about by the telecast. Ringside officials announced that patrons should refrain from smoking in the interest of improving the picture, a request that was met with howling disapproval.[43]

The Boon-Danahar bout, won by Boon by a fourteenth-round technical knockout, would now be considered a closed-circuit TV broadcast and not television per se. Regardless, the Baer-Nova and Boon-Danahar efforts were watershed events in which the feasibility of both home and theatrical boxing were brought to the fore.

Just weeks before the Baer-Nova bout, RCA president David Sarnoff had appeared on television from the World's Fair in New York. At a dedication of the new RCA building, he heralded television as part of "The World of Tomorrow." Sarnoff could be seen, along with NBC president Lenox R. Lohr, on an eight-by-nine-inch screen in the New York studio. The transmitter on top of the Empire State Building would spread the signal for a radius of fifty miles.[44]

Sarnoff began the telecast with a simplicity that belied its profundity: "Now we add sight to sound," he explained. Then he went on to predict the far-reaching impact the industry would have: It is "a new art so important in its implications that is it bound to affect all of society."[45]

After a brief introduction at Radio City by famed boxing announcer Graham McNamee, the camera was switched to Flushing for a live view of George Hicks, another familiar boxing voice. The signal was eventually switched back to New York. There, an amateur bout between George Pemperton and Pat Dunne was televised from a ring at the studio, with Max Baer judging and Bill Stern at the microphone. The new era of television had been officially launched, with the sport of boxing at its forefront.[46, 47]

Sarnoff's new product was put on display on the sixty-first floor of the RCA building and made available to the public May 1, 1939. Consumers had a choice of a 5 x 7 television "tele-picture" (an attachment to radio receivers) at $199.50 or a 7 x 10 stand-alone model at $1,000. The economics of the industry were clearly not yet in sync with the desired commercial demand.[48]

Television in the late-'30s and early-'40s was still in its technological infancy, notwithstanding some of the clear studio transmissions at the World's Fair. This is evidenced by the fact that, in 1941, boxing ring canvases in New York were still painted brown to improve the visibility of the images to be telecast. However, the landscape was evolving rapidly. During the summer of 1941, when Joe Louis and Billy Conn waged their classic battle, another milestone was reached with the beginning of commercial television in New York.

An NBC study of the New York television audience at that time revealed that 4,500 home receivers and 600 public receivers were in use, servicing an audience of approximately 90,000 people. WNBT Channel 1 in New York boasted four paid sponsors during the first month of commercial television and anticipated more. Although television sponsors were few in number, they appeared to be highly pleased with the initial results. The broadcast networks were even more enthusiastic. "Our belief in the commercial advantages of television has been fully confirmed," said Alfred H. Morgan, NBC vice president in charge of television. Gilbert Seldes, director of television programming at CBS, noted that just thirty days ago, "we seemed to be producing for a non-existent audience . . . to our great pleasure we have found that our programs are being seen, and are being given satisfaction."[49] WCBW Channel 2, the CBS television station in New York, was quickly scheduled to go on the air as a commercial concern that September. The NBC-CBS competition had now spread from radio to television.

The commercial draw of boxing on television was also being confirmed—at least anecdotally. One report indicated that a New York suburban tavern owner drew 163 patrons to his bar for a boxing match, which increased his regular take at the register by 300 percent.[50]

Boxing insiders also seemed to grasp the financial potential of television. In April 1941, boxing's biggest promoter, Mike Jacobs, viewed a highly successful experimental broadcast of a boxing match on a giant sixteen-by-twenty-foot screen at the New Yorker Theater. This broadcast of the Billy Soose-Ken Overlin middleweight title bout was sent by wire from Madison Square Garden. Jacobs fully embraced the new medium, exclaiming, "it's worth a million." On the subject of commercial television, which was just weeks away from receiving the green light from the Federal Communications Commission (FCC), Jacobs said, "It will be a big thing, and I will be for it."[51]

Just two months later, another innovation for the medium was utilized in connection with the Melio Bettina-Red Burman bout from Ebbets Field in Brooklyn. Sitting in an office at Radio City, several miles from the ball park, Eli Canel, head of NBC's Spanish section, watched the bout on a television screen and then broadcast it by shortwave radio transmission to South America.[52]

The technological and financial potentialities of television had been revealed, and other locations were quickly brought into the fold. In late 1941, NBC and National Sports Enterprises, Inc., signed a one-year deal for the right to broadcast radio and television for fights in the Cleveland area, one of the more active boxing markets in the country. The first bout scheduled was the Abe Simon-Lem Franklin heavyweight contest.[53]

Commercial television, which debuted on July 1, 1941, broke out of the gate fast, but its vision was hampered by blinders in the form of Defense Department limitations on the industry. The availability of materials to produce transmitters and receivers was an issue even prior to December 7, 1941.[54] Like all aspects of American life, both the sport of boxing and the television industry would quickly reflect the effects of the United States' entry into World War II. The War Production Board, which was established on January 16, 1942, would halt all manufacturing of radio and television broadcast equipment for civilian use. The ban would be in effect from April 1942 until August 1945. The war, which brought broadcasting limitations to the civilian sector, would ironically spawn technological advances through military applications, which would boost television in the postwar period.[55]

Six stations remained on the air during the war, but most were broadcasting only a few hours a day and primarily for civil-defense purposes.[56] Just weeks after the Japanese attack at Pearl Harbor, the New York television listings for January 23 told the story: WCBW offered the *National Defense Program* at 8:15 P.M. Boxing from Ridgewood Grove could be viewed the following evening on rival station WNBT.[57] On Monday, February 9, 1942, WNBT aired only two programs: *Air Raid Instructions with Lieut. William F. Maley* at 8 P.M., followed by boxing bouts from Jamaica Arena at 9 o'clock.[58] On Friday, May 8, 1942, WNBT aired the interservice boxing tourney. That same day, WCBW showed an entire day of *Light Rescue Squads Training Courses.*[59]

At the time America entered the war, New York boasted two commercial television stations, WNBT Channel 1, formerly known as W2XBS, and WCBW Channel 2. Television would go into a state of stagnancy, and the station line-up would struggle to sustain itself during the war period.

During 1943, WCBW Channel 2 in New York was only airing on a limited basis on Thursday evenings. Continued broadcasts were planned, but, as a station representative explained, only "as long as the available materials and manpower hold out." As those trying to broadcast struggled with the process, the potential receiving audience was experiencing similar difficulties. For those with television sets in need of repair, the outlook was bleak, with manpower and materials unavailable to meet existing needs. It was estimated that between 1,000 and 2,000 receivers were inoperative in the New York area and might remain so indefinitely.[60]

The ability to transmit a television program required great resources, and the dual constraints of the war crippled the availability of both manpower and material.[61] Nevertheless, boxing continued to make its presence known on television. The *Cavalcade of Sports* radio program, expanded to television in 1943, broadcast boxing matches over WNBT New York. Their telecast of the George Kochan-Jake La Motta middleweight bout was a belated Christmas gift delivered on December 29, 1943.[62] Just two weeks later, WNBT was back at the Garden with its broadcast of the Bobby Ruffin-Tippy Larkin match. As with most major boxing bouts of the day, the fight was also broadcast on the radio, this time on WOR.[63]

WNBT continued to team up with Madison Square Garden, broadcasting the memorable match in which Willie Pep took the featherweight title from Chalky Wright on November 11, 1942.[64] WNBT and the Garden also offered the public amateur boxing, including the prestigious intercity Golden Gloves finals, which pitted New York and Chicago champions against each other.[65]

Despite television's limited amount of air time, boxing on television was also made part of the war effort. Beginning on October 25, 1943, NBC began televised programming from Madison Square Garden, which included boxing. The telecasts were noncommercial and were designed for the viewership of servicemen who were convalescing in local New York hospitals. NBC had the receivers hooked up at no charge to the government.[66]

The following year, NBC scheduled the broadcast of a series of fifty boxing matches from Madison Square Garden for the benefit of serviceman, which began with the aforementioned Pep-Wright battle for the featherweight championship.[67] That contest was the first time a television contract was signed for an American boxing bout.[68]

Commissioner John J. Phelan is flanked by challenger Willie Pep (left) and featherweight champion Chalky Wright (right), who sign to fight at Madison Square Garden, 1944. MSG matchmaker Nat Rogers looks on. It was the first time a TV contract was signed for an American boxing bout. *AP Photo/Tom Sande.*

These weekly contests, which began airing locally in New York in 1943 over WNBT, were eventually broadcast by the NBC network over many of their stations beginning with those located in Philadelphia and Schenectady. The Gillette Safety Razor Company continued on as the sponsor, and on November 8, 1946, the series was renamed *The Gillette Cavalcade of Sports.* The program became the longest-running series on any kind on television and did not sign off until June 24, 1960. The series began in 1946 with Bob Stanton at the microphone. He was joined by Ray Forrest in 1948, and Jimmy Powers took over the broadcasting duties in 1949.[69]

As the war began to wind down to its conclusion, speculation focused on what postwar television might look like. Noted inventor and engineer Alfred N. Goldsmith, speaking at a Television Press Club luncheon in March, 1944, explained the tremendous advances that lay in waiting. "We are on the verge of some remarkable new services in sight and sound," he explained. "Radio electronic facts for use, when the demands of war relax, are being accumulated at a staggering pace."[70]

The next month, James D. McLean, a commercial engineer for General Electric, informed an audience at the Waldorf-Astoria hotel that his company foresaw the manufacture of forty-five transmitters over the next eighteen months servicing upwards of 30 million viewers. He also predicted that as many as 100 transmitters would be made within five years, with an anticipated audience of 67 million.[71]

The willingness to invest so heavily in this infrastructure was based on a new confidence in the picture quality. Discoloration and lack of clarity had been improved over the past three years. Engineers indicated that "the pictures are now in black and white with good gradation between highlights and shadows."[72]

In anticipation of the brave new world of television, forward-thinking leaders of both radio and the fledging television industry began to ramp up. In 1944, radio station WGN in Chicago announced its intention to enter the field of "visual radio" by placing an order for a 40,000-watt transmitter and filing an application for a television wavelength and construction permit with the FCC. At that time, radio manufacturers were exclusively engaged in the mandatory production of war communications equipment. WGN's request would be the first filled when the requirement was lifted.[73]

While Chicago waited to be outfitted for television, New York City continued to carry the torch. In 1944, the Eastern Tournament of Champions was televised in its entirety with Bob Stanton at the microphone. The following week, through local station WNBT, NBC televised the intercity Golden Gloves matches between New York and Chicago, live from Madison Square Garden. "This was just a prelude to the telecasting of sports events after the war," the *New York Daily News* commented. "What only a few hundred pioneer television fans saw was a mere overture to what millions will see a few years from now."[74]

Chapter 11

BOXING AND TELEVISION FORGE A GOLDEN AGE

On June 19, 1946, less than one year after the bombing of Hiroshima and Nagasaki ended the war, the predicted technological advances were brought to television during the coverage of the Joe Louis-Billy Conn rematch. The fight marked the first time that a heavyweight championship boxing match was broadcast on television. NBC recognized the magnitude of the event from both the sporting and broadcasting perspectives. A staff of fifty special engineers and cameramen worked the telecast at Yankee Stadium that evening to bring the public this first mega postwar sporting event.

Materials previously reserved for the war effort were now available to RCA engineers. They exploited the new technology by building three "image orthicon" cameras with "turret" lens systems, offering the television audience varied shots of the action. New cameras with sensitivity 100 times greater than prewar cameras provided better ability for close-ups.

A camera booth was constructed in the stadium's upper right-field stands 145 feet from ringside, providing the television audience with a view equal to thirty feet from ringside. Another camera angle was made by a separate unit situated forty-five feet above the playing field level, directly behind home plate.[1] The telecast was of such importance that on the eve of a United Nations session, RCA removed ten television sets and one camera from the UN's conference rooms, so that the equipment could be utilized for the more valued engagement of Louis-Conn II.[2]

Depending upon where the telecast was received, viewers enjoyed the fight on either a traditional home television set (probably no larger than nine inches in diameter) or a large screen of a closed-circuit-style broadcast. Numerous "boxing by television" parties were staged in homes, clubs, hotels, and radio headquarters in New York, Schenectady, Philadelphia, and Washington, DC, cities serviced by NBC. One elated viewer observed: "It was as if you were sitting in an armchair at ring level and not even Mike Jacobs had a seat at ring level at Yankee Stadium. He had to crane his neck like everyone else."[3]

NBC staged a party for hundreds of invited guests, including newspapermen, who viewed the fight on a battery of eighteen prewar receivers. Sets were installed in the Hotel Statler, in Washington, DC, where hundreds of top officials watched the fight. "Remarkably clear" reception was reported from the nation's capital. At the RCA laboratory, an audience of over 3,000 people watched a "twice life-sized" image of Joe Louis dispatch an equally large Billy Conn, their likenesses projected on an exterior wall of the laboratory. A new projection tube helped deliver an "excellent" picture.[4] Despite the limited number of television receivers at the time, patrons packed their local bars. A broad estimate of between 100,000 and 300,000 viewers were believed to have watched the fight on commercial television. Bob Stanton made the call, and the preliminaries were also telecast.[5]

Despite its huge success, the broadcast still had several technological failures. There was a noticeable inconsistency in the images, with those produced by the prewar units still appearing fuzzy. Ringside microphones also failed; and the cheers, boos, and other atmospheric sounds so crucial to the ambiance of a prizefight were lost to the television audience.[6]

On the day of the fight, the *New York Times* reported that television had "undoubtedly . . . hurt the ticket sale," citing the fact that some fans were rebelling against Mike Jacobs and the Twentieth Century Sporting Club's unprecedented $100 ringside seats; they would stay home and enjoy the convenience and pricing of a seat on their couch. However, this opinion seems unsupported. The fight, which ultimately drew a large crowd of 42,266, set all-time high gate receipts of $1,925,564.[7] Even if some reduction in the gate existed, it would still be offset by the $125,000 that Mike Jacobs received for the sale of the telecast rights to NBC. He also received $100,000 for the sale of the radio rights. While it was reported that it was unknown whether Louis and Conn would share in the television money, such a concession by the promoter would soon become typical. Nevertheless, the fact that the television rights had exceeded the value of radio rights was a clear indicator of the immediate financial impact television was to have on the boxing world.[8]

The successful telecast of Louis-Conn II acted as a catalyst for the rapid technological refinement of televised boxing. Several weeks after the fight, a boxing broadcast carried by a local station from the Rainbow Arena in Chicago was temporarily suspended until an "image orthicon" camera, like the ones used for Louis-Conn II, could be obtained. Audiences in the arena had become annoyed by the glare created by the enormous amount of light necessary for prewar cameras to illuminate the ring. Such inconveniences would no longer be tolerated.[9]

The Louis-Conn event was also confirmation for business executives that televised sporting events were the wave of the future. The Gillette Safety Razor Company had already secured the sponsorship of Madison Square Garden boxing matches, broadcast in New York over WNBT, the local NBC station. This early television arrangement was proving prophetic for the razor company, whose substantial investment in the unproven medium had been a risk.

Not to be outdone by NBC and Gillette, just weeks after the Louis-Conn rematch, the Ford Motor Company and CBS entered into their own joint venture with Madison Square Garden. Ford would now sponsor all nonboxing sports television broadcasts for the Garden. The cornerstone of their programming would be basketball, hockey, and track events. The events would be broadcast in New York over WCBW, soon to become WCBS.[10]

The evolution of modern television was underway, and sports programming, spearheaded by boxing, was an early driving force. As 1946 drew to a close, the first televised basketball game in Chicago was telecast over WBKB. This was the first page written in local basketball history, which would culminate decades later with Michael Jordan becoming an institution, not only in that city, but the world over. The game followed programming that television's advertisers are glad to have left behind: the International Livestock Exposition, which featured "sheep skillfully herded by dogs."[11]

Even with technological advances such as the image orthicon camera, a glimpse into the future ten years forward was about to be revealed. In September, while Jacobs was still counting his receipts from Louis-Conn II, CBS engineers unveiled the next phenomenon: live color television. The technology was deemed commercially feasible, and a test transmission was made to a CBS studio with clarity that ranged from "excellent" to "remarkable." The studio audience thrilled to scenes featuring singers, models, Matisse and Van Gogh paintings, and "a brief but fast boxing match between two agile lightweights."[12]

Black-and-white television remained a staple for over a decade, and engineers and broadcasters continued to endeavor to increase the quality of the television audience's "colorless" viewing experience. In one bout, even the New York State Athletic Commission took action. In lieu of the use of the official black and purple trunks, commission chairman Eddie Eagan required Marcel Cerdan to wear black trunks with a white waistband and his opponent Harold "Red" Green to don white trunks with black trimmings. Eagan hoped that this change would provide a picture with better contrast. However, NBC, who had nothing to do with the effort, was dismissive of

Eagan's approach, explaining that off-white was the preferred lighter color.[13]

Predicted television growth had taken root in New York, and by autumn of 1947, the city boasted 51,500 television receivers in 40,100 homes and 4,000 taverns, with the remaining 7,400 with dealers. Most of the home receivers were owned by high-income individuals. However, the heavily attended bar crowd made the viewership in the taverns about equal to that at home. New York carried three commercial television stations, including two that featured regular boxing shows. WNBT Channel 4, the local affiliate of NBC, broadcast bouts from Madison Square Garden that eventually became the longest-running program on television. In 1946, NBC also became the first station to carry bouts from the St. Nicholas Arena, with their coverage lasting into 1948. Another New York station, WABD Channel 5, an affiliate of the DuMont Television Network, carried fights from Jamaica Arena and Park Arena.[14]

As the mecca of boxing, Madison Square Garden's telecasts featured championship and contender-level matches along with undercard bouts. Some of the bouts featured during 1947 from MSG included Gus Lesnevich's tenth-round knockout of Billy Fox in defense of his light-heavyweight laurels, and the controversial first Joe Louis-Jersey Joe Walcott contest for the heavyweight championship. The St. Nicholas Arena, Jamaica Arena, and Park Arena offered bouts of the "club fight" variety featuring up-and-coming prospects, and/or veteran trial horses, such as the Julio Jimenez-Eddie Giosa and Tommy Garland-Billy Grant matches, both of which were contested at St. Nick's.

Out in the Midwest, in Chicago, the second biggest market in the country showed a more modest concentration of television sets, with a total of 6,636 including 3,850 in homes and 1,790 in restaurants and taverns.[15] In 1947, Chicago still had only one commercial television station, WBKB, which broadcast boxing from venues such as the Rainbow Arena and the Madison Athletic Club.[16] Nevertheless, Chicago was on the verge of a major expansion. During 1947, it was announced that the Windy City planned to add four commercial stations within the next year, including local NBC and CBS stations.[17]

In 1947, "Video station" WBKB—as television stations were sometimes being called—telecast the Chicago Golden Gloves Tournament of Champions and its finals for the very first time. Local competitor WGN covered all of the Golden Gloves bouts on radio with Jack Brickhouse providing the blow-by-blow, Harry Creighton adding the color, and the station's sports editor, Frank Korch, interviewing the boxers.[18]

WBKB also broadcast professional fights on Tuesday nights from the unlikely location of Michigan City, Indiana. "Pictures were relayed from a mobile car parked outside the site of the fights to a tower in Michigan City, then across the lake to a relay point in Chicago's Lincoln Tower, and finally to WBKB's transmitter at 190 N. Lake Street." Newspapers referred to the process as "a boxing relay."[19]

Excitement regarding televised boxing ran high. Tony Zale made an appearance on the evening of the first telecast, and the hope was to broadcast a fight pitting the "Man of Steel" against Rocky Graziano in Michigan City. Apparently, the promoters, in their euphoria over the industry's possibilities, had lost sight of the fact that they were staging contests at the Isaac C. Elston High School Auditorium!

In those days, sponsors' commercials were presented live during the fight card. Away from the WBKB's studios in Chicago, where commercials were typically made for other programming, the stage of the high school auditorium would have to suffice. Veteran radio and "video star" Helen Malone admitted it was not easy for her to convincingly plug the sponsors' product just moments after watching a boxer being rendered unconscious in the flesh.[20]

Early television broadcasting was like the Wild West, with engineers playing sheriff to create order out of anarchy. But anyone with a solution could become the hero in the white hat. On one occasion, the Libertyville Boys Club requested that WBKB telecast their bouts against the Toronto YMCA. Because of the earth's curvature, engineers required an antenna with an elevation of about 100 feet so the video signal could transmit above the horizon. However, without a tall building in sight, engineers were left scratching their heads. Boxing coach Frank Gilmer came to the rescue by commandeering a friend's giant power crane. WBKB also had a backup plan: return to Chicago and televise the equally enthralling Central AAU amateur wrestling matches from the Rainbow Arena.[21]

Stations in mid-America had barely begun to erect their own transmitters and delight their respective communities with local fare when blueprints for network television had already moved from design to application. The zeal to establish a national network had already existed for a number of years. Attempts at defeating the transmission limitations created by the horizon had led to some extreme proposals. One enterprising group offered a system called Stratovision: a 300-mile-high transmitter to be located in Kansas boasting "a system of thirty-three airplanes flying in constant 20-mile circles 20,000–25,000 feet above the earth to cover the entire USA."[22]

Common sense would prevail. The first attempts at a network occurred in 1940, when NBC, located in New York City, began relaying some of its early programming to the General Electric station in upstate Schenectady. The following year, some telecasts were also sent to the Philco station in Philadelphia. However, these "networks" were merely one station retransmitting the signal it had picked up from the originating station. The quality of the rebroadcasts was lacking, with no potential to create an extensive network.[23]

The groundwork for a long-term solution occurred in 1944, when AT&T began laying coaxial cable to connect various cities on the Northeastern seaboard. In 1946, the New York-Philadelphia-Washington, DC, line was completed and in use for Louis-Conn II.[24] The following year, the Illinois Bell Telephone Company announced that coaxial cables linking the East Coast to Chicago would be laid that year, effectively bringing the core of the television industry and the epicenter of the boxing world from New York to the Midwest.[25,26] Simultaneous with the creation of the infrastructure for network television, various television stations across the country were obtaining commercial broadcast licenses and bringing local boxing to their communities.

The immense popularity that boxing on television enjoyed from the late-1940s through the mid-1950s is not easily attributable to any single factor. It was, more likely, a situation in which the whole was greater than the sum of its parts.

To start with, television executives favored boxing due to certain production advantages. From a technological standpoint, boxing's stationary ring avoided many problems presented by larger or more mobile subjects. Also, there were relatively low production costs associated with the telecasts. Perhaps, most significant, boxing already had an audience. With the exception of baseball, boxing had the best argument for being the country's favorite sport. And that audience could more easily follow the action of flying fists on a small screen than the rapid movement of a tiny ball on a field.

Some believe that certain social aspects of the period made the American male predisposed to an attraction to the sport. For example, it has been argued that boxing's inherent violence served as a natural draw for returning veterans of World War II and the Korean War. Author Troy Rondinone summarized that general proposition writing, "Cold War hypermasculinity combined with live war memories to provide a potent cultural milieu in which boxing found a comfortable place."[27]

Regardless of the impetus behind the burgeoning boxing television audience, television manufacturers were there to meet the demand. By 1948, the total number of televisions in the country would expand to accommodate the rapidly evolving industry, reaching approximately 1.75 million, with a projection of five million sets by year's end.[28] In April of that same year, WGN in Chicago began telecasting for the first time, helping to catapult Chicago into position as the number two boxing center in the world. "Tomorrow WGN-TV presents the miracle of postwar television to Chicago audiences," lauded the *Chicago Tribune* newspaper, owner of the station.[29]

In New York during the late 1940s, boxing permeated every corner of the television world with both local and national telecasts originating from multiple venues. With two of New York's three television stations broadcasting boxing in 1947, an early tone had been set for boxing to establish itself as an integral part of television's rapidly expanding landscape. In the summer of 1948, the city's third station, WCBS Channel 2, jumped on the bandwagon. With its partner, the Tournament of Champions, and its sponsor, Ballantine Beer, major bouts including Charles Fusari-Tippy Larkin II were featured.

In addition to broadcasting bouts from the Jamaica Arena and Park Arena, WABD, Channel 5, offered bouts from Ridgewood Grove. In February 1948, the station would telecast the semifinals of the New York Golden Gloves.[30] DuMont telecast regular boxing shows from the Jamaica Arena in 1948 and 1949. It also featured another boxing program, *Amateur Boxing Fight Club*, which aired on Friday evenings in direct competition with Gillette's "Friday Night Fights." And in 1949–50, DuMont set up their cameras on Thursday evenings in Sunnyside Gardens.[31] In 1950, DuMont televised bouts from Dexter Arena on Thursday evenings, as well.[32]

WPIX was the television station of the *New York Daily News*. Each year, the *News* sponsored the Golden Gloves Tournament. Unfortunately, WPIX was unable to televise its own fights, as the station was still several months from going on the air. WABD acted as surrogate telecaster of the matches.[33] Shortly after WPIX went on the air on Channel 11, the station broadcast boxing from Ridgewood Grove. The bouts were telecast on Saturday evenings during the 1948–49 indoor season, which ran from September to May.[34] WPIX immediately followed with Metropolitan Amateur Athletic Association boxing matches from the same location on sixteen consecutive Saturday evenings during the summer of 1949.[35]

In the fall of 1948, WCBS began televising bouts from the Westchester County Center, in White Plains, New York. The bouts aired on Wednesday evenings, directly competing with DuMont's matches from the Jamaica Arena.[36] The contract gave CBS the exclusive rights to broadcast matches for the 1948–49 indoor season. The White

Plains fights would feature Russ Hodges at the mike with televised dressing-room interviews.[37] Hodges would also serve as announcer for CBS's Wednesday night fights, which aired in the fall of '49 from St. Nicholas Arena. The heavyweight contest between Tami Mauriello and Cesar Brion kicked off the telecasts.[38]

In the spring of 1949, WPIX expanded their boxing broadcast coverage, telecasting the finals of the Continental Air Command boxing tournament from Mitchel Field, Long Island, and airing professional fights from the Coney Island Velodrome in Brooklyn.[39] WABD, the DuMont affiliate, began televising boxing bouts in the summer of 1949 from Jerome Stadium in the Bronx, with Dennis James handling the ringside descriptions.[40] A fifth New York station, WJZ, an ABC affiliate, under the sponsorship of Camel cigarettes, also telecast boxing during 1949. This featured coverage of the Golden Gloves from Chicago, an early benefit of the recently established coaxial cable connection between the East Coast and the Midwest.[41] *Tomorrow's Boxing Champions* aired each Tuesday night on the ABC Network.[42]

WOR, New York's seventh station, which hit the airwaves in 1949, also featured boxing. The following summer, it would establish telecasts during the outdoor season from the Fort Hamilton Arena in Brooklyn. Stan Lomax and Dick Nesbitt called the action for bouts from that venue during the early-1950s.[43] As the new decade approached, all seven of New York's stations were broadcasting boxing.[44]

New Yorkers enjoyed local boxing from 1947 to 1949, originating from as many as half-a-dozen localities. Manhattan, Queens, Brooklyn, the Bronx, White Plains, and Jersey City all provided a diverse geographic base for the local televised bouts. However, with the exception of the Chicago metro area, those outside the New York metropolitan area had fewer opportunities to view televised boxing.

Nevertheless, during 1948, through its television network, WNBC was regularly providing New York fights from Madison Square Garden and the St. Nicholas Arena to more remote viewers up and down the Northeast corridor. They reached them via their affiliate stations located in Richmond, Washington, DC, Baltimore, Philadelphia, Wilmington, Delaware, Schenectady, and Boston.[45] DuMont also provided their own bouts to viewers in its own network, which provided programming to Philadelphia and Washington, DC.

After the telecasts of the Friday night fights on NBC, the network often featured a fifteen-minute boxing show titled *Greatest Fights of the Century*. These filmed fights from years gone by were aired from 1950 to 1953 sponsored by the Chesebrough Manufacturing Company.[46]

In January, 1949, a coaxial cable link joining the eastern and midwestern television networks went operational. Twelve new programs quickly hit the New York airwaves, including Monday night bouts from Chicago over the ABC Network.[47] The next month, DuMont began televising regular Monday night matches from the Philadelphia Arena. The first card, which featured former lightweight champion Lew Jenkins versus Percy Bassett, was not only enjoyed by those in New York, Baltimore, and Washington, but also entertained new audiences in Chicago, Cleveland, Detroit, and Pittsburgh.[48] By June, 1949, the expanded NBC Network carried the Joe Walcott-Ezzard Charles contest for Louis's vacated title to sixteen eastern and midwestern cities. Chicago was the only city excluded due to the local television blackout, which was implemented to protect the live gate.[49]

Also that June, CBS sealed a deal with the Madison Square Garden Corporation for all radio and television rights for the weekly boxing bouts at St. Nick's Arena and for the Garden's promotion of fights in its outdoor arenas and bouts in venues in other cities.[50] The new decade was shaping up with CBS and NBC sharing the Garden's boxing programming. CBS would also pay $115,000 for the right to televise the Garden's Saturday evening bouts, with NBC continuing the Garden's Friday night telecasts.[51] When the International Boxing Club (IBC) announced its indoor season schedule for the 1950–51 season, more than half of the seventy scheduled shows would be from Garden arenas.

Twenty-four of these programs were scheduled for the Garden itself and eleven for St. Nicholas Arena, all on Friday evenings, with another ten for St. Nick's on Wednesdays. The remaining twenty-five shows were split between the IBC's various Midwest venues, also for Wednesday night broadcasts. Ten shows apiece went to the Chicago Stadium and the Olympia in Detroit, and the remaining five to the St. Louis Arena. The sale of television rights would bring the IBC $788,000. Of that sum, $288,000 would pay the fighters—part of their share of television money per the new contract between the IBC and The Boxing Managers' Guild.[52]

The new Wednesday lineup that began in 1950 would soon be commonly known as "The Wednesday Night Fights" or "The Pabst Blue Ribbon bouts." The series would continue, on ABC under other sponsorship, from the mid-'50s through 1959, making it second only to Gillette in its importance and duration.

Networks jockeying for opportune position to telecast boxing was merely a subplot to the main storyline. Beginning in 1949, the IBC had embarked on a crusade that would reach deep into the corporate structure of boxing arenas and the management of fighters. It would culminate in its monopoly of the promotion and telecast of the sport. The IBC would prove to be both the Alpha and Omega of boxing during television's Golden Age (see Chapter 14).

Contemporaneous with their receipt of boxing matches from New York and Chicago, the cities of Baltimore, Philadelphia, Washington, and Boston began their own television broadcasting that featured local boxing. In Baltimore, station WMAR TV was integrating boxing into its telecasts featuring newsreels as early as 1947. By the early-'50s local bouts were being broadcast live from the Baltimore Coliseum and The Squires Club.[53]

In Philadelphia, local fare included the 1951 "Kid Gloves" program in which the son of future heavyweight champion Jersey Joe Walcott was a participant. The bouts were recorded on kinescope and aired at a later time so that the pint-sized fighters could watch themselves on television.[54] Several years later, Philadelphia Enterprises telecast local bouts on Channel 12 from the Cambria A.C. that specialized in "negro fighters who never got a break on television and their negro managers, who never shared in any of the money or glory of TV boxing."[55]

The nation's capital was also an early entrant into the televised boxing phenomenon. Station WNBW received its official launch in June 1947 as an affiliate of the NBC Network and featured weekly bouts from Madison Square Garden in New York.[56] WTTG Channel 5 telecast fights over the DuMont Network from the Eastern Parkway Arena in Brooklyn.[57]

During the late-'40s and early-'50s WMAL TV Channel 7 offered both local boxing from the Turner Arena and amateur and professional boxing matches piped in from Chicago. When nonboxing events were scheduled at Madison Square Garden and the St. Nick's Arena, CBS and NBC would utilize Washington locales as substitute venues.[58]

Fight fans in Boston warmed up to televised boxing before it went commercial by eavesdropping on bouts telecast from New York. In January, 1948, 400 public officials and representatives of the business community gathered at the Hotel Bradford to view bouts telecast from St. Nick's Arena.[59] The following month, WBZ's Studio A picked up the telecast of the Beau Jack-Terry Young bout from Madison Square Garden.[60] Later that year, WBZ would obtain its commercial license and become an NBC affiliate, carrying weekly bouts from Madison Square Garden.[61] Another early commercial station, WNAC-TV, picked up bouts from the Rainbow Arena in Chicago and broadcast local bouts from the Boston Arena and the Callahan A.C.[62]

Out in the Midwest, in Cincinnati, station W8XCT, owned by Crosley Broadcasting, signed on the air as a commercial station in February 1948. The Golden Gloves bouts—which the experimental station had periodically televised in the past—were so popular that the station took to the airwaves a week earlier than originally scheduled so that they could telecast the opening round of the 1948 tournament. In effect, boxing ushered commercial television into Cincinnati.[63]

Amateur boxing was extremely popular with the public at the time and in favor with broadcasters and sponsors, who did not have to bear the expense of paying the participants. Like Cincinnati, other midwestern cities featured local boxing as part of their early telecasts. In Pittsburgh, the Booker T. Washington Center boxing team was given its moment in the sun when six of its members were featured in an amateur show.[64]

In the early-'50s, television was hurting attendance at matches staged at the Olympia Stadium in Detroit. However, local televised boxing thrived with the weekly cards promoted by Julius Piazza in the tiny venue of the Motor City Gym. Despite the steady television viewership, attendance increased, and the bouts were moved to service a larger live audience. For over two years, local Detroit boxers entertained television audiences until the bouts where discontinued when Pfeiffer Beer withdrew its sponsorship.[65]

Out on the West Coast, Los Angeles spearheaded television broadcasting. Boxing in that city also predated commercial television and was featured on Don Lee's station W6XAO.[66] The first telecast of a boxing match in Los Angeles was on May 10, 1940, as Jimmy Garrison squared off against George Latka.[67] It was the beginning of a rich local television history during the era that featured bouts from the Hollywood Legion Stadium, the Olympic Auditorium, and the Southgate Arena.

Down South, viewing opportunities of local matches were not always readily available, but boxing fans with a keen interest could still find them. In the small community of Marathon located in the Florida Keys, fans pointed their antennas in the direction of Havana, Cuba, 140 miles away in an attempt to pick up the Wednesday and Saturday night fights. Word quickly spread that at the local tavern, free beers were waiting for the viewer who could translate the bouts, which were broadcast in Spanish.[68]

By the early-1950s, boxing had established itself as a premier form of television entertainment on both a local and regional level. As CBS's 1949 foray into boxing on Saturday evenings had proven, the Garden's regular Friday night programming on NBC, sponsored by Gillette, could not cover all of the action from the world's most famous arena. While the CBS Saturday series was short-lived, during the winter of 1950–51, boxing was also featured on the multisubject *Saturday Night at the Garden* series aired on DuMont with Dennis James at the microphone.[69]

Although boxing was enjoying a meteoric rise to television prominence, like all early television programming, its telecasts were not without their share of engineering and production setbacks. For example, in a heavyweight encounter at the venerable Laurel Gardens, WATV, an independent station in Newark, New Jersey, delivered its television audience a pair of Willie Huff's knockdowns of Ben Miller but cheated their viewers of the climatic knockout due to a transmission failure.[70] However, these and other sporadic miscues did little to hinder boxing's seemingly preordained appointment with the nationwide spotlight.[71]

On October 3, 1951, the first coast-to-coast home broadcast was achieved with the telecast of the Dave Sands-Carl "Bobo" Olson bout aired from Chicago Stadium. The television signal stretched eastward to New York and westward to California.[72] The following month, the second Jimmy Carter-Art Aragon bout, an IBC promotion for the lightweight championship of the world, became the first West Coast-to-East Coast home television broadcast. The fight, promoted by Cal Eaton and held at the Olympic Auditorium, was blacked out for a 150-mile radius of Los Angeles but viewed by the rest of the nation courtesy of CBS Television. To accommodate the New York television audience, which was accustomed to a 10 P.M. viewing time, the bout began at 7 P.M. Los Angeles time. From this point forward, boxing was primarily a nationally televised sport.[73]

NBC and its sponsor, the Gillette Safety Razor Company, would remain a staple of the Friday night fights, religiously renewing their relationship with the Garden. In June of 1952, NBC and Gillette teamed up with the IBC and local Philadelphia promoter Herman Taylor to televise the fourth and final Walcott-Charles match.[74] The 1952–53 indoor season opened with Jimmy Powers calling the Bobby Dykes-Gil Turner welterweight contest.[75] In the summer of 1952, CBS, with Pabst Blue Ribbon Beer and the IBC, televised sixteen major fights over the course of the summer on Wednesday nights, with fourteen of the sixteen bouts originating from Chicago Stadium.[76] ABC, a later entrant to network boxing telecasts, began telecasting fights nationally on January 24, 1953, promoted by Famous Sports Enterprises, Inc., a group headed by trainer Ray Arcel and sponsored by Bayuk Cigars.[77]

By the early-1950s, public appetite for the sport had grown so powerful that television stations expanded their boxing content beyond live coverage. CBS, under the sponsorship of Pabst, began presenting kinescope film recordings of bouts that had been telecast

Early commercial television, with its ubiquitous boxing broadcasts, captured the imagination of the American public. The author's great-grandparents, Francesco and Anna Romano, proudly pose with the family's first television (1950). *From the author's collection.*

live the prior season. The replays would air on Wednesday evenings, when no live bout was being presented. The CBS/Pabst catalog was only a year old, and they had already found the economic justification for the making of the kinescope recordings.[78] For a brief period in the fall of 1951, Madison Square Garden also capitalized on its portfolio by airing a fifteen-minute program on the DuMont Network titled *Famous Fights from Madison Square Garden.*[79]

In May 1952, promoter Emil Lence brought televised boxing to the 6,000-seat Parkway Sporting Club in the Brownsville section of Brooklyn. The building, better known as the Eastern Parkway Arena, had been formerly used as an indoor skating rink. The Monday night fights, which would be televised by DuMont for a two-year run, featured Ted Husing as the original announcer.[80] In 1954, the Eastern Parkway matches moved to ABC, and DuMont returned to St. Nick's, going head-to-head with bouts from its former venue.[81] A few years earlier, boxing had achieved the distinction of reaching the airwaves of every television station in New York. With these broadcasts, television was now in every major fight arena in New York City.[82]

In Chicago, boxing remained eminently popular. Even the Windy City's number one television comedian David Garroway was forced off the air, as both the local and national NBC stations opted to pick up boxing broadcasts rather than his program.[83]

In 1952, ABC and the IBC hooked up to televise local boxing every Monday night from the Rainbow Arena, over WBKB Channel 7 in Chicago, with Jack Drees providing the commentary. ABC affiliates also carried the bouts to other cities via coaxial cable. A bout between Chicago's South Side welterweight Freddy Dawson and Norman Webb of Detroit opened the series. Each received the additional sum of $150 for going before the television lens.[84]

The following year, Rainbow Arena promoter Irving Schoenwald struck a deal with Ray Arcel and Dewey Fragetta. The pair owned the exclusive rights to air the Saturday night fights over the ABC Network. The new contract was in addition to the existing promotion by Schoenwald of the Monday night fights from the Rainbow Arena.[85]

In 1954, Schoenwald, still partnering with the IBC, switched networks, completing a deal for a series of televised bouts with CBS. The promoters not only pegged the oft-used Rainbow Arena as a site for their matches, but they also utilized the Garrick Theater in Chicago's Loop, a CBS television studio. It was ironic that a television studio was used to buttress the local fight club arenas; in the near future, televised bouts emanating from near-empty arenas would disparagingly be called "studio fights."[86]

At the time, it appeared as if the importance of the arena and live audiences in the sport of boxing were diminishing with each passing moment. Another important innovation of commercial television that could only serve to further this trend was the debut of color television.

In 1954, two middleweights, Gustav "Bubi" Scholz of Germany and Al Andrews of Superior, Wisconsin, faced off on a *Cavalcade of Sports* broadcast carried on WNBQ in Chicago, and other stations, in boxing's first "colorcast." In order to enhance the viewers' experience, the corner stools were covered in orange material for the occasion, and Sholz wore blue trunks with gold trimming while Andrews wore gold trunks with blue trimming.

One critic dubbed the telecast "less than sensational." He noted that while "a ringside doll" wore "a crimson camellia against her white stole," there wasn't enough color in or around the ring to justify "color cameras." He also lamented that an opportunity to view red blood was not taken advantage of by cameras, which failed to provide close-ups of Bubi's cut under his left eye. Further, the ring lighting at Madison Square Garden appeared to be inadequate for color TV, with a haze of tobacco smoke further obscuring the color.[87,88] Apparently, arena promoters would receive a temporary reprieve. It would be another decade before color TV would become a staple of commercial broadcasting, and a regular part of boxing telecasts.

Such advances in television such as the "colorcast" proved to be secondary to the fortunes of the boxing world. Unfortunately, the television industry at large had already predetermined the sport's future. The rapid growth of the medium of television in its early years was so profound that in the autumn of 1948, the FCC implemented a freeze on the issuance of further licenses to operate individual stations. Time was needed to figure out the most equitable way to issue the licenses, as well as how to avoid problems with transmission interference between existing stations. The freeze lasted for four years. During that time, national network television arrived.

In 1952, when the freeze was lifted, the FCC assigned each metropolitan area a maximum of three VHF stations. NBC, CBS, and, to a lesser degree, ABC quickly secured the available spots on that band for the large metro areas. By lining up affiliates for their networks in these lucrative population centers, the networks squeezed out many small independent stations and the smaller DuMont Network, all of whom could not compete economically. UHF stations were an option for local broadcasters, but not feasible due to its inferior reception.[89] Unwittingly, the FCC had made boxing primarily a nationally televised sport.

By the mid-1950s, boxing was experiencing unparalleled popularity on television. However, television provided a free and convenient viewing option that was rapidly eroding boxing's live audiences. Consequently, local fight venues, the lifeblood of the sport, were being put out of business.

Simultaneous with this phenomenon, the FCC's method of station assignments, which led to network domination, further fueled the decline of local boxing. The national character of the sport proved significant when the networks began pulling out in the late-'50s and early-'60s. With financially self-sufficient live audiences already a thing of the past, the exit of television and its sponsors from the national scene would leave boxing homeless.

Chapter 12

A SECOND FRONTIER: THEATER AND CLOSED-CIRCUIT TELEVISION

Theater television, a.k.a. closed-circuit television, had been technologically feasible for almost as long as traditional broadcast television itself. As early as 1939, Gaumont-British, a newsreel company, had enticed a wildly enthusiastic audience to the Eric Boon-Arthur Danahar fight in London theaters. No home television was available. This scenario—which offered theater television in lieu of home television rather than as a competing option—would become the basis upon which theater television would be successfully established.

In England, the strict governmental regulations limited the BBC, the country's regular television broadcaster, to a maximum budget of 200 pounds to purchase television rights. The rights to a big fight at Wembley Stadium, for example, broadcast on television, could cost as much as 25,000 pounds ($100,000 US). Therefore, motion picture theater broadcasting in England, at least initially, was not born of competition, but of necessity, and a means of circumventing the limitations of commercial television.[1]

However, in the United States, the use of theater television operated under laissez-faire conditions. If a promoter felt that the net take of a boxing promotion would be greater with a theatrical broadcast than with commercial TV, then the fight would be shown in the theater accompanied with advertising clearly indicating that no home television or home radio (in some instances) would be available.

Closed-circuit television was not be used exclusively for boxing matches. As the technology developed, businesses discovered that it provided a financially beneficial way to reach large business audiences. Among the companies who utilized such telecasts were General Motors, Chrysler, Upjohn, and IBM.[2]

The first theater television broadcasts in the United States were conducted in 1939 as demonstrations by RCA to the Society of Motion Picture Engineers on a screen of approximately three by four feet. In December 1940, a system was installed by RCA in the New York Theater in Times Square that featured a nine-by-twelve-foot screen. During the next year, private screenings were conducted for governmental officials, leaders of the motion picture industry, and press representatives.[3,4]

On May 9, 1941, an attempt at a comprehensive theatrical broadcast was undertaken when a full evening of programming was presented. Significantly, its audience would also include some members of the general public. The first half of the evening featured programming originating from the NBC Television Studios in Radio City. Ray Forrest served as the television announcer. After the intermission, the Billy Soose-Ken Overlin middleweight championship fight from Madison Square Garden was presented. Jack Fraser handled the blow-by-blow description with William Spargrove providing the between-rounds commentary. The evening program noted that the bout was being shown through the cooperation of Colonel John Kilpatrick, president of Madison Square Garden, and Mike Jacobs, president of the Twentieth Century Sporting Club.[5] Depending on the source, the attendance that evening was between 1,000 and 1,600 people.

As reported by one science magazine of the day, "close-ups of the fight action projected on a 15 by 20 foot screen afforded an audience a better-than-ringside view of the action."[6] Another magazine noted that "three-dimensional" sound equipment, through a special installation, "brought . . . all of the crowd noises of the fight so as to create an almost perfect illusion of being at ringside."[7] Engineers also utilized a chocolate-covered canvas to enhance the picture quality by creating the proper contrast.[8]

One report found the pulse of the future in theatrical television: "The telephone wire from the Garden to Radio City and the telephone wire from there to the theater is a miniature of the television networks, which RCA engineers predict will someday make theater television available all over the United States."[9] Yet another magazine article erroneously touted the broadcast as "a foretaste of the day when television would bring to neighborhood movie houses football and baseball games."[10]

Although John Kilpatrick widely missed the mark in his assessment that Garden events such as dog shows and horse shows were fodder for theatrical television, he clearly understood the power of the medium with respect to boxing. It could increase the Garden's seating capacity "from 25,000 to a million or more," he assessed. While an RCA representative noted that a television cable had already been installed between New York and Philadelphia, the intercession of World War II would make theatrical television, like commercial broadcast television, a postwar phenomenon.[11]

In the US, theater television, utilizing a full motion picture screen, would have its first official public showing in April 1948 at the Paramount Theater at Broadway and Forty-Third Street in New York City. The audience that day only expected to see a feature film and a stage show. But much to their surprise and delight, fifteen minutes of live boxing were broadcast on the theater's eighteen-by-twenty-foot screen. Paramount utilized a special film recorder that allowed television images received from the live event to be transposed onto standard 35mm film. The film was then incorporated into the Paramount newsreel that was being featured at the theater and shown to the live audience on a sixty-six-second delay.

The audience witnessed three rounds of boxing from the Navy YMCA in Brooklyn. The telecast, which concluded with a boatswain mate scoring a technical knockout over a ship fitter, was greeted with spontaneous applause from the Manhattan audience. Although the movie audience was not predisposed to viewing a boxing match, it still held the broadcaster, the legendary Don Dunphy, to a standard equal to that of an experienced fight fan at the Ridgewood Grove Arena. When one of the fighters was knocked down for a count of seven, and Dunphy remarked that the fighter was not hurt, his call evoked "titters" from the crowd.[12,13]

This blend of a prerecorded newsreel and a live broadcast was merely a dress rehearsal for a similar broadcast two months later. On June 25, 1948, Joe Louis faced Jersey Joe Walcott at Yankee Stadium in a rematch of their bout that had yielded a controversial decision in Louis's favor the previous December. Paramount used its Theater Television System to capture "a live television signal by recording it on motion picture film. The film was fed through a developer and then into a projector allowing spectators to see a 35mm kinescope some sixty-six seconds later" on a twenty-four-foot movie screen.[14] This presentation was also held at the Paramount Theater in Times Square. What distinguishes Louis-Walcott II and its predecessor test from subsequent theater television is that at the time they had no means by which to project a live video signal onto a large screen. Their imperfect solution was the film method with the brief time delay. These limitations would soon be remedied to produce live projected telecasts.[15]

Once theater television began, it had an immediate and profound impact upon the sport of boxing. Paul Raibourn, head of Paramount's television activities, indicated that regular television stations, not surprisingly, had been reluctant to cooperate with theater telecasting and echoed a growing concern of the two factions' competing interests.[16] Within less than three years, it would progress from Paramount's experimental single theater showings to the very top of the sport. The die had been cast—pitting commercial television concerns against those with theater interests: "The first significant economic challenge to television in the home came yesterday with the announcement that a group of motion picture theaters had bought exclusive rights to cover next Wednesday's heavyweight fight between Joe Louis and Lee Savold at the Polo Grounds," boxing fans were informed.[17]

Not only would Paramount theaters participate in the telecast, but the Loew's, RKO, and Fabian circuits would also be included. While not every theater that was equipped with the technology was participating in the broadcast, there would be fight coverage in theaters in Albany, Washington, Baltimore, Cleveland, and Chicago. New York City and its surrounding vicinity would be blacked out. "This will mark the historical first network of theater television," declared Nathan L. Halpern, who represented the theater companies.[18]

The architect of boxing's latest revolution was its new power broker, James D. Norris, president of the IBC. Norris explained that the alternative medium was the key to solving the television-sports dilemma of how to gain additional television revenue without adversely affecting the live gate.

It was anticipated that by the early part of the following year, 100 theaters with a capacity of 200,000 seats would be available for use. Future availability was exponential, with the nation's 18,000 theaters with a seating capacity of 13 million waiting to be exploited. The new medium offered potential gates that Jacobs and Rickard could only have dreamed of.

The groundwork for the future of theater television had already been laid, with the Louis-Savold contract covering additional outdoor fights to occur that summer. However, those with interests in home television were not ready to cede their lifeblood to their competitors. In fact, they had already been preparing for such an eventuality by working on their own systems—the precursors to today's pay-per-view television.

Simultaneous with the breaking news of the Louis-Savold theater coverage, The Radio Corporation of America, parent of the National Broadcasting Company, formally confirmed for the first time that it was working on its own system of "subscription television." The

Zenith Radio Corporation had already been testing "Phonevision," another subscription system, for some time. Paramount Pictures Corporation, which had a substantial investment in the DuMont Television Network, had already purchased an interest in "Telemeter," a coin-operated device attachable to a home television receiver. The Columbia Broadcasting System was also known to be watching developments in the industry closely.[19]

The Louis-Savold theatrical gambit proved a huge success for Norris and the IBC. The first goal of protecting the live gate was not only met, but exceeded all expectations. The bout, which was switched from the Polo Grounds to Madison Square Garden due to rain, had a record one-day indoor ticket sale of $43,000. A standing-room-only crowd of 18,179 fans watched an aged but still capable Joe Louis advance on his comeback trail, producing a live gate of $93,918.[20]

As part of the contract for this experimental broadcast, the IBC was guaranteed a minimum of $10,000 for the additional take from the theaters. This was just the tip of the iceberg. The fight was only broadcast in limited locations, and future bouts would service a much larger audience, providing more weighty financial returns.[21] This point was not lost on Wall Street. Stock for the Madison Square Garden Corporation rose $1.87.5 to $8.87.5 based upon the Street's acknowledgment of the experiment's success and its future potential.[22]

The salve on the wound of the home television audience deprived of a live showing of Louis-Savold was the later telecast of a nonkinescope film version of the fight announced by Dennis James. However, the salt in the wounds of both The Pabst Sales Company, sponsor of the film presentation, and commercial television interests at large was that Pabst reportedly paid $20,000 for the rights to the delayed telecast. This amount was double what the theatrical interests paid to show the fight live.[23]

Norris was salivating over the IBC's prospects. The promotional concern had just closed a contractual arrangement to broadcast 102 fights for the coming year. Exercising control over arenas in Chicago, St. Louis, Detroit, Indianapolis, and Omaha, as well as Madison

Square Garden, Norris dreamed of a future in which he would be puppet master of both live television and theatrical broadcasts. Norris described the industry's potential as "fantastic." Despite the fact that the upcoming Jake La Motta-Bob Murphy light-heavyweight match was only ten days away, Norris was already scurrying about to bring the IBC's next big match to the theater.[24]

During June 1951, the same month in which Louis-Savold was contested, the talk of the boxing world was Randy Turpin's stunning victory over Sugar Ray Robinson at Earl Court in London. The highly anticipated rematch was quickly scheduled in September at the Polo Grounds. This would be the first megafight in which Norris could test the financial mettle of the theater television industry.

The bout would be the fourth match in which the IBC would be offering theater television to the exclusion of home TV that summer. Regular television interests were still in competition for bouts but were being outbid. Pabst negotiated with the IBC but was unable to consummate a deal. NBC, taking the creative approach by trying to interest television set manufacturers in acting as a collective sponsor, was (at least for the time being) also unsuccessful.

In the early years of theater television, the rivalry for elite matches was akin to trench warfare. Commercial television would advance a few precious steps forward with its latest broadcast of a Louis bout, only to be pushed back an equal distance by theater TV, which scooped them for the rights of the next big fight featuring Willie Pep.

Motion picture distribution rights were often a decisive factor in the television bidding wars. Those rights offered the IBC a two-for-one bargain: show the fight live in theaters and then rebroadcast it at a later date as a filmed telecast through the same medium. The supposition was that if a fight was kept off free television and it proved to be a good one, there would be plenty of paying customers willing to buy a ticket for a second theatrical showing. The rebroadcast option for the first Robinson-Turpin fight had been successfully exploited through the distribution of a film of the fight by Republic Pictures in 400 theaters throughout the US. Norris would do the same with the motion picture distribution rights from the rematch.[25]

Excluding motion picture rights, home television actually had the better offer for the Robinson-Turpin bout. While theater television was willing to pay $25,000 for the rights based upon the capacity of its "wired" theaters, one home television sponsor was willing to pay more than $300,000 for television and radio rights. But the theater television package, once the motion picture distribution rights were included, appeared to be more lucrative. RKO agreed to provide a guarantee of $200,000, plus a percentage of profits from the movie film's rentals worldwide. Additionally, the IBC would also retain ownership of the film negatives. Finally, by keeping the bout off home television, it was estimated that a loss of $150,000 in live gate receipts could be avoided.[26]

Robinson-Turpin II brought on a firestorm by "free television" proponents who collectively railed in objection. One member of Congress found the issue worthy of the House of Representatives, launching an investigation into sports. Another asked the same body to determine if the depravation of home television constituted "unreasonable restraint." Another called for a determination of whether the radio and television blackout violated "a right that should not be denied the tax-paying public of America." One state senator, no doubt a boxing fan, suggested to the FCC that "an event of this importance might well fall within the public domain." Watchdog groups such as the Fair Television Practice Committee in New York received many calls protesting the blackout. In Cleveland, a group called the TV Owners and Viewers League indicated that its 300 members would boycott a local theater that had shown the fight.[27]

Norris and his partners were unperturbed. The match, which was carried by closed circuit at thirteen theaters in eleven cities, had fetched up to $2.60 a seat, with 35,000 paying customers.[28] Protests over the home television blackout notwithstanding, crowds in Chicago were so anxious to see the match that they smashed through the theater doors of one sold-out screening. Some New Yorkers, rejecting bleacher seats at the Polo Grounds, headed to the nearest closed-circuit theaters in Philadelphia to watch the bout. Upon their arrival, many who had not secured a reserved seat in advance were stunned to learn that both the Stanley and Royal theaters had been sold out ten days before the fight. The weary travelers might have consoled themselves with a famous Philly cheesesteak, because they definitely missed the fight.[29]

Those who abandoned the Polo Grounds were comparatively few. The live gate was so well protected that 61,000 fans attended the match, to the tune of $768,000. Factoring in the $200,000 movie rights and $50,000 from TV, the fight created the first million-dollar gate for nonheavyweights in the history of the sport.[30]

Basking in the glory of its recent financial triumphs, Madison Square Garden's public posture that television was more of a savior than an assassin was gaining credibility. "They have been educated by video," said Garden vice president Ned Irish commenting on the contemporary boxing fan. "They learned about boxing at home and this proves that, given a good attraction, they will leave the home and go to the arena." Harry Markson, IBC director, recognized that the quality of the fight influenced its popularity just as much as the general exposure provided by television, finding proof in what he had been repeating ad nauseam: "Boxing is not dead."[31]

The IBC quickly followed up on the Robinson-Turpin affair by expanding its closed-circuit coverage for the third Pep-Sandy Saddler match at Yankee Stadium. The contest was brought to twenty theaters including smaller population centers such as Minneapolis and Binghamton. Consistent with the developing pattern, there was no home radio and television, and a closed-circuit blackout for the New York City area applied. The combined theater television and motion-picture rights fee from RKO brought in a total of $110,000.[32]

With the outdoor season of 1951 concluding, the 1951–52 indoor season would see the temporary return of major fights to home television. The most important of these bouts was the clash between two legends: the comebacking Joe Louis and the rising contender Rocky Marciano. This swing of the broadcasting pendulum back toward commercial interests was not due to the hue and cry of the free television rights contingency. It was a somber reaction of television set manufacturers responding to a legitimate fear of stark financial consequences presented by theater TV's encroachment.

When the threat arose, the Radio-Television Manufacturers' Association moved quickly to organize a special committee to strategically keep sporting events within their sphere. A possible long-term strategy included the formation of a multimillion-dollar pool to be established through either a voluntary or contributory tax on the television manufacturers.[33] Several months earlier, eight television set manufacturers had formed an alliance raising sufficient funds to purchase the television rights to the third Jersey Joe Walcott-Ezzard Charles match, to the exclusion of the theater television interests. To the boxing fans' delight, the upset of champion Charles, which made Jersey Joe the oldest heavyweight champion of all time, was carried to a national television audience of 60 million by DuMont at no charge.[34] It was estimated that a staggering 85 percent of the nation's 13 million sets were tuned into the fight.[35] The all-time record television audience enjoyed the prefight rant of Ez's manager Jake Mintz objecting to a Philadelphia official, as well as the sizzling left hook of Jersey Joe that rendered Charles unconscious.[36]

A group of eighteen TV-equipped theaters had previously won the exclusive rights to the Louis-Savold and Bob Murphy-Jake La Motta bouts for $10,000 each, but their bid of $65,000 for Charles-Walcott was topped by the TV manufacturer consortium that ponied up $100,000. A representative of one of the set manufacturer theorized that it had an obligation to the purchasers of their product but also admitted that the broadcast of these major fights stimulated further sales of their sets.[37] What was most unusual in this promotion was that the money was not provided by typical advertising sponsors such as a Gillette or Pabst, but by outside parties who had a greater monetary stake.

For the highly anticipated Rocky Marciano-Joe Louis contest, a similar joint venture was established. Seven major television manufacturers—Admiral, Philco, RCA, Sylvania, Motorola, Crosley, and General Electric—joined with Gillette to pay a substantial fee in excess of $100,000 for the television rights. The bout would be televised by NBC during Gillette's Friday night *Cavalcade of Sports* program, with its regular partner, the IBC, as promoter.[38] Norris had crunched the numbers. With the combined television and radio fee in the $150,000-to-$225,000 range, and with an expected live gate of $150,000, home television was the more profitable move.[39]

In the spring of 1952, the Ray Robinson-Rocky Graziano middleweight title tiff found its way to broadcast television, save the local Chicago blackout, which applied to television, but not radio. Television and radio rights were sold for $80,000, with Robinson and Graziano to receive 30 and 25 percent, respectively, of both gate receipts and TV-radio receipts.[40]

Jim Norris's careful eye on the turnstiles meant that the live gate vs. "free" television issue would be analyzed and configured on a fight-by-fight basis. After Charles-Walcott III had somewhat surprisingly taken the free television route, Norris warned, "This does not set a pattern for future fights."[41] Not only would theater television continue as the new alternative, but the option of a complete blackout of both home and theater television was still very much alive. A complete blackout was utilized for the third Pep-Saddler fight, contested on September 8, 1950. That match, however, was held prior to the existence of theater television. Future bouts would have to weigh the new option of theater TV in the equation.

In the summer of 1952, the IBC returned to this formula for the Rocky Marciano-Harry Matthews heavyweight match, providing a complete blackout for radio and both home and theater television. IBC director Harry Markson predicted that the bout would even surpass the live receipts of $421,000 recently made by the Sugar Ray Robinson-Joey Maxim light-heavyweight contest. The predicted healthy live gate intimated the financial analysis behind the strategy of a complete blackout. Norris had placed the boxing audience under his thumb. "The only way fans can see the fight will be to come to the Stadium," he declared.[42] That summer, Norris would utilize this very same approach for Kid Gavilan's third title defense against Billy Graham. A fan either purchased a ticket to the fight or read about it in the newspapers the following morning.

One of the summer's other hot tickets, the Robinson-Maxim over-the-weight battle, was carried by Theater Television Network, Inc. (TNT) in thirty-nine theaters in twenty-five cities, with a local New York blackout.[43] The now-fabled Robinson-Maxim affair illustrates how the finances of a theater broadcast of a major fight worked on a local level. With no home television or radio available, the bout played in four movie houses in Chicago. Balaban and Katz operated three: The Tivoli with a capacity of 3,600, and The Uptown and Marbro with 4,000 seats each. The Paramount Theater in nearby Hammond, Indiana, also carried the fight. Each ticket cost $2.40.

The Essaness Theater Corp. presented the bout at the 1,600-seat Crown Theater on the near North Side of Chicago for a pricey $3.60 per ducat. From each ticket, the IBC would collect $1.05. American Telephone and Telegraph would receive thirty-five cents per seat for providing the coaxial hookup, with the remainder going toward other expenses.[44] Considering the number of limited theatrical seats compared to the potential audience in Chicago for commercial television at that time, it is obvious why theater television was assailed as undemocratic.

The summer's other top headliner, Rocky Marciano's challenge of Jersey Joe Walcott for the heavyweight championship, was also put on the theater track.[45] The rapid expansion of the theater network would extend to a record forty-nine theaters in thirty cities for this bout. Not only was the network reaching into the innards of the country to places like Hammond, Indiana, and Omaha, Nebraska, but the first coast-to-coast theater hookup was realized. Marciano's famous "Suzie Q" would distort Walcott's features on giant screens as far west as Seattle, Sacramento, and Los Angeles.[46]

The first theater showing of a world heavyweight championship in Los Angeles took place at the Orpheum Theater in front of 2,200 fans. Despite the fantastic achievement of a coast-to-coast hookup, all theaters west of Kansas City, including the Orpheum, received the broadcast on a forty-five-minute delay, as a "real-time" broadcast was still not feasible. Remaining in sync with the Orpheum, radio station KMPC in Los Angeles provided a re-creation radio broadcast of the bout.[47]

An interesting variation on theater television was the big-screen outdoor broadcasts. For the Marciano-Roland La Starza heavyweight championship match in September 1953, a drive-in movie theater in Commack, New York, served as one of the forty-five national closed-circuit locations. Located fifty miles from the Polo Grounds, it was the closest venue in the country from which anyone could see a contemporaneous view of the fight without being there in person.[48] A similar telecast was held the following year at a drive-in theater in Hillside, Maryland, when Marciano met Charles for the first time.[49]

In general, those who did not purchase a theater ticket, but who demanded immediate fight results, were accommodated by alternative sources. It soon became commonplace for the switchboard of the *New York Times* to be bombarded by hundreds of calls for the result of a major "theater only" fight. So many people had made inquiries for the Robinson-Maxim bout that the *Times* was prompted to assign three telephone operators and seven other employees to handle the calls for Marciano-Walcott.[50]

While the IBC dictated which alternative would be fostered upon the boxing fan, on occasion the fan was able to beat the system. For the Robinson-Maxim row at Yankee Stadium, shown only in theaters, the IBC decided to pick up some additional money by selling radio rights to the Dominion Network of the Canadian Broadcasting Corporation. Gillette served as the sponsor. Since radio waves know no borders, listeners across that country, as well as some in New York, were able to catch Don Dunphy's radio blow-by-blow account of the historic fight on CJBC, Toronto; CHML, Hamilton, Ontario; and a Canadian station operating on the six-megacycle band. Joe Hassell urged Canadians "to look sharp," as Dunphy reported the dramatic collapse of Robinson. Eavesdroppers only needed to filter out some rhumba music from Cuban stations that occasionally interfered with the broadcast.[51]

For the most part, the IBC attempted to maintain strict control of the radio and home television blackouts of their theater television broadcasts. During "theater television only" telecasts, radio stations were restricted to providing a summary at the end of each round, or every three rounds. Running radio commentary was banned. Nevertheless, for the Marciano-La Starza championship match, a number of radio stations defied the restriction.

One station, WOV, planned to foil the IBC by arming their personnel with binoculars and sending them out onto the rooftops of buildings near the Polo Grounds. Their observations could then be transmitted on their radio broadcast. In the end, several stations did provide "blow-by-blow" reports of the match taken from wire service reports in contravention of the IBC's wishes. Those more ambitious stations even provided "canned" crowd noises to enhance the running commentary.[52]

The minor machinations of radio interests were no match for closed-circuit television, which operated on the cutting edge of technology and sport throughout the 1950s. For the price of a seat ranging from three to six dollars, Godzilla-sized Marcianos and Moores, and Rodin-proportioned Robinsons and Fullmers, could be experienced on screens as large as fifty by sixty-five feet. As an added free attraction, a feature film was sometimes shown before or after the fight. Like their contemporary monster screen stars, boxers were even featured in 3-D. Such was the case of Marciano-Walcott II—a fight that many critics have claimed as boxing's own version of a horror show![53,54]

For a typical telecast by TNT, one of the premier theater television networks of the era, three conventional cameras were situated over the ring to feed a black-and-white picture into a control room at 32 Avenue of the Americas, New York City. The picture was then sent out by AT&T's "long-line division." TNT utilized their own private channel consisting of long-line telephone equipment and 25,000 miles of phone wire. These phone lines along with coaxial cable carried the fight to each theater in the network. Atop the roof of each theater, a round metal disc set to the specified channel would pick up the signal and beam it inside the theater.[55]

Two days before a fight, all lines received a final check, and five hours before the fight, a test pattern was sent from the fight location to all of the theaters to confirm reception. Fifteen hundred engineers

Closed-circuit/theater television existed on a dual track with its competitor, free television. The former exclusively broadcast most of the megafights of the 1950s and early-1960s. Here, a closed-circuit camera is trained on the ring for Ali-Liston I. *AP Photo.*

and technicians worked the telecast with 100 mobile projectors waiting on standby as emergency equipment.[56] These precautionary measures were not unfounded. The picture quality at theatrical presentation of the Floyd Patterson-Sonny Liston rematch at the Stanley Warner Theater in San Pedro, California, was so poor that the police were called in to quiet down the customers who were promised a refund.[57, 58]

Promoters of the day went to great lengths in an attempt to recreate the atmosphere of a genuine boxing match. In addition to movie theaters and drive-in theaters, large screens were also set up in civic auditoriums, armories, and gymnasiums. Configured in a square made by four screens at the center of the venue, they provided any seat in the house with a head-on view of the action. Perhaps taking the illusion a bit too far, the screens were sometimes arranged around a boxing ring for effect.[59]

In the few short years prior to Rocky Marciano's ascension to the heavyweight throne, James D. Norris and the IBC, through their contracts for radio, television, theatrical television, and movie distribution, had fashioned a new media configuration from which the sport of boxing would be carried to the public. Part and parcel of this new order was the manipulation and strategic elimination of commercial television broadcasts in favor of theatrical television.

The intrusion, however, was acutely selective. Amateur boxing, club fights, virtually all matches between contenders, and the majority of championship contests would remain within the realm of free television. Only a very small percentage of bouts made their way to the big screen. They were almost exclusively the cream-of-the-crop championship bouts. For these matches, the appeal factor was potent enough to lure the average boxing fan out of their easy chair and into the theater.

Most times, bouts simply did not have the economic drawing power to warrant theater television. In 1954, the first Marciano-Charles match was put on the big screen for obvious reasons. The other top matches of that summer were low-hanging fruit passed upon by the high-soaring theatrical concerns and left for commercial television to harvest. Therefore, the July 14 match between Archie Moore and Harold Johnson, as well as the Paddy DeMarco-James Carter and Kid Gavilan-Johnny Saxton bouts, were all aired by CBS, with NBC kicking in with Bobo Olson-Rocky Castellani.[60]

When theater TV did trump commercial television, the IBC would often grant a minor dispensation to the home audience who did not get to the theater by providing them a radio broadcast. This approach was used for Marciano's swan song versus Archie Moore, both Sugar Ray Robinson-Carmen Basilio matches, and the first Patterson-Liston encounter, as well as other matches.[61]

Whereas free television was a direct competitor of radio in that both offered the consumer the product gratis, theater television actually benefited radio. By freezing out free commercial television, it allowed radio to capture an audience it had lost to free television. By the early-'60s, theater television featuring boxing's best was drawing upwards of a million viewers, but those numbers paled in comparison to the audiences lost by radio to commercial television, which sometimes counted in the tens of millions.

Radio might have lost all its relevance to television by the mid-1950s, but theater television breathed new life into the medium, keeping radio an important part of the sport for an additional decade, albeit only for a few megafights a year. In 1955, for example, the Marciano-Moore bout reached a staggering radio audience of one-quarter of a billion people in five continents.[62]

The expansion of closed-circuit hookups reached a new plateau with the utilization of coast-to-coast theatrical venues, as seen in such bouts as Marciano's title-winning effort against Walcott and his defense against La Starza. The almost exponential increase in additional seating offered an increase of potential revenue for theatrical promotions in like proportion. The economic balance of power for boxing's biggest attractions would irrevocably tip in favor of the big-screen telecasts.[63]

Each big-screen telecasting package was specifically crafted around the geographical circumstances surrounding the bout and its featured personalities to guarantee the maximum financial return. Marciano's second bout against La Starza and his first encounter with Charles, both contested in New York, were "theater only" affairs. In both instances, a maximum return was guaranteed through the use of the local blackout. Not only was it utilized in the New York City area where the matches were contested, but selected areas of New England that were staunch Marciano territory. The strategy would prompt the Brockton Blockbuster's large parochial following to make the road trip to the Polo Grounds or Yankee Stadium to purchase the more expensive stadium tickets.

Marciano would become an economic property exclusively in the pocket of theater television. All of his title defenses, with the exception of his first defense against Walcott, were staged without coverage by free commercial television.

Norris was not alone in his recognition of the linear incline in the financial returns that theatrical broadcasts were producing from major boxing events. Chief amongst these other observers were the boxers themselves, who sought to grab a larger piece of the financial pie. At the forefront of these boxers was middleweight champion Sugar Ray Robinson, who reemerged as boxing's greatest attraction after the retirement of Rocky Marciano in April 1956. Robinson's innate sense of how to make a buck was no less acute than his natural ability to maneuver around the ring. He knew how to leverage his importance as a commodity and was not afraid to exercise that advantage. One might even say he was an opportunist.

A month prior to his September 1957 title defense against Carmen Basilio at Yankee Stadium, Robinson put his business savvy on display. It all happened quite unexpectedly—so the champ claims. Robinson was approached by Teleprompter Corporation, Inc., a closed-circuit broadcaster, who offered him a sizable return for the bout's closed-circuit rights. Although Robinson was under contract with his promoter, the IBC, who in turn was in contract with TNT, the dominant closed-circuit provider of the day, he balked at the TNT deal. "Robbie" claimed the IBC had no authority to bind him. Further, he threatened that if the bout did not proceed with the Teleprompter group, which had made the more financially lucrative offer, he simply would not go through with the fight.[64]

Robinson had executed two contracts with the IBC, and he needed to find a loophole. He put his attorneys to work perusing the agreements until they found one: the scope of the term *ancillary rights* was not clear. The term *ancillary* was therefore deemed by Robinson's legal brain trust to include closed-circuit rights, which could only be exercised by the promoter with Sugar Ray's approval.[65]

The facts now fit squarely into Robinson's narrative. Exploiting his own celebrity, he made a plea to New York Governor Averill

Harriman to prevent the IBC and the NYSAC Commission from depriving him of his "rights as a citizen."[66] Taking his grandstanding to the next level, Robinson went public, feigning the belief that no theater television coverage of the bout at all would be a reasonable solution to the conflict.[67] It all played out over an exhausting nine-day battle during which the champ claimed he needed to take medication to cope with the ordeal. A compromise was ultimately reached. Robinson would receive a guarantee of $255,000, a sweeter deal than originally planned, and Teleprompter would join TNT as a junior partner in the telecast.[68]

During the period of contractual strife, Robinson claimed that he had read and become well versed with McKinney's Digest, a legal volume comprised of New York statutes. With the acumen of a member of the New York bar, he would return to training. Basilio remained silent throughout the entire affair. He would receive $110,000 for his portion of the theater rights, but the payday was always secondary to him. Basilio's talent was strictly as a prizefighter. It may have been a singular ability, but it was stellar. He would lift the middleweight title from the great Robinson in an all-time classic.[69]

For the Robinson-Basilio encounter, 173 theaters across the US and in Canada comprised the closed-circuit network, surpassing the 133 sites in ninety-three cities utilized for Marciano-Moore. The combined seating capacity of 500,000 would have made even the late Rickard and Jacobs, both masters at packing a site with patrons, green with envy.[70,71]

When the rematch between Robinson and Basilio was scheduled for the following March, another twist to closed-circuit television was unveiled. Promoter Norman Rothschild successfully petitioned the New York State Athletic Commission to allow his closed-circuit telecast of the bout from Chicago Stadium to be combined with live fights from the War Memorial Auditorium in Syracuse, New York. The plan called for twenty-eight rounds of preliminary boxing to be followed by Basilio and Robinson on the screen.[72] San Francisco's Cow Palace jumped on the bandwagon and also showed a live card with their closed-circuit telecast.[73,74]

Sugar Ray Robinson was a man who knew what he wanted. He campaigned for and succeeded in getting the Teleprompter Corporation a piece of the closed-circuit pie in the first Basilio rumble. For the rematch in which Robinson regained the title, Teleprompter promoted the event exclusively. There were 173 locations in 140 cities, including four Canadian provences, with a seating capacity of 514,000, with tickets scaled at $3.00 to $7.15. The closed-circuit return was a staggering gross gate of two million dollars, larger than any live gate in the history of the sport up to that time, with the exception of Dempsey-Tunney II.[75]

Whereas commercial television receipts represented earnings that were merely supplemental to a bout's live gate, the closed-circuit take had become the primary source of a fight's revenue. Closed-circuit television was also increasing the gross revenue for prizefights in general. High-profile bouts of the period such as Marciano-Moore and the two Robinson-Basilio affairs offered no regular television and could only be watched on closed-circuit television, which capitalized on these increased revenues.[76]

When the US Supreme Court affirmed its decision adjudging the IBC as a monopoly in early 1959, the organization was dissolved. A crop of newly formed promoters rushed in to fill the vacuum and partner with the handful of closed-circuit operators who dominated the industry.

Practically overnight, the closed-circuit operators became the lions and the fledgling promoters the fleeing gazelles. "What happened," explained Olympic Auditorium copromoter George Parnassus, "is that some eggheads with money got into the promotional business. They put on two of Patterson's fights but now they're just window dressing. Teleprompter has taken over. . . . Even Patterson can't say who he will fight. It all up to the new 'octopus,'" he lamented.[77] National Boxing Association president Abe Greene feared that the new threat would reduce boxing commissions to "underling vassals of money-minded theater-TV potentates."[78]

Fresh off the protracted legal battle with the IBC monopoly, courts were wary of a repeat scenario in the boxing industry. In 1960, the New York Supreme Court enjoined Teleprompter Corporation and its president, Irving B. Kahn, from engaging in monopolistic practices, canceling all existing contracts and requiring an open-bid process on all future bouts, including Ingemar Johansson's first defense of his heavyweight championship.[79]

Indeed, the stakes were rising. With the closed-circuit gross increasing with each additional seat added to the theater network, the combined revenue of the live gate, closed-circuit TV, and other ancillary rights also seemed to increase for each major bout. By the time Patterson stepped into the ring against Liston for the second time in 1963, the combined receipts reached a sum in the range of 3.8 to 5 million dollars.

In their first fight, Liston was the challenger and a heavy favorite. Because the promoter of the contest, Championship Sports, Inc., had failed to file a tax return for the previous year, IRS agents were dispatched to the 260 theaters showing the contest. Anyone could foresee that an early ending to the match was a distinct possibility. Well, almost anyone. Notices of Lien were to be served by the agents on theater owners during the bout, but some were slow in fulfilling their duties. Surely there was time for a hot dog and coffee first, they must have reasoned. To the shock of no one, except some of the agents, Patterson was knocked out in a single canto, concluding the match before many of the notices were served. As the agents scrambled to effectuate service, Patterson, in even greater dismay, left the arena in a disguise. To add to the vanquished champion's woes, his purse was frozen as part of the assets seized by the government.[80]

The rematch the following year was held in Las Vegas, Nevada. It was a sign of the times. Boxing was going west. It was also the beginning of a new era in which Las Vegas would begin to vie with New York as the fight capital of the world. It was a competition that Vegas would win in the ensuing decade. In the early-1960s, the population in Las Vegas was insufficient to consistently fill a large stadium for boxing matches. However, such demographic limitations were becoming moot. The anticipated 8,000 attendees at the second Liston-Patterson match would generate a live gate of $200,000. This sum was a mere one-fifth of the anticipated closed-circuit revenue that would be derived from attendees from 109 cities in thirty-five states in 143 theaters.[81] In the first Patterson-Liston bout staged the previous year, the closed-circuit receipts from theaters in Los Angeles alone doubled the live gate receipts produced at Chicago's Comiskey Park. Closed-circuit television had become the great equalizer in the promotion of the sport.[82]

Of course, the receipts from the closed-circuit broadcasts would be divided amongst the theatrical concern, the promoter of the fight, and the fighters themselves. Typically, the closed-circuit operator would receive less than 25 percent. Teleprompter received 22 percent of the receipts from the first Patterson-Liston bout. For the return bout, GRS Enterprises agreed to take 15 percent.[83]

Even with a lesser-grade event, a closed-circuit broadcast could do fair business. A few years earlier, when Floyd Patterson put the heavyweight championship on the line against unheralded Roy Harris, the promotion still drew 196,762 viewers with a gross closed-circuit take of $763,437. Harris hailed from arguably the most memorably named city in the history of boxing lore—Cut and Shoot, Texas. A prohibitive underdog, Harris was given little or no chance to beat Patterson, except perhaps by a few partisans from his uniquely named hometown.

Irving B. Kahn, who handled the closed-circuit promotion of the bout, surmised that the loyalty and enthusiasm of Harris's contingent would create a keen local interest in the bout. Kahn set ticket prices in the large drive-in movie theater in Conroe County, the county seat in which Cut and Shoot was located, at a pricey ten dollars per seat for the best tickets. That price was almost triple the $3.88 average ticket price in the country. A sellout of the 10,000-seat drive-in theater was predicted by Kahn. However, when the dust cleared from the streets of Conroe, all that was left was a bloodied Harris on the giant screen and a paltry 1,800 tickets sold at the box office. Cut and Shoot might not have produced great fighters, but apparently it knew its boxing.[84]

The disappointing local theater gate notwithstanding, the fact that the closed-circuit network could reach innumerable paying audiences in such remote places as Conroe County reaffirmed that the site of a match itself was no longer the dispositive factor in determining where a prizefight could be successfully staged.

From its most recent incarnation at Eighth Avenue between 49th and 50th Streets, Madison Square Garden had been operating as the centerpiece of the sport for two generations. It reached its peak in attendance just prior to World War II, when well over 20 million fans were shoehorned into the arena for an Armstrong-Zivic bout. Those days were long gone. By the early-1960s, typical professional shows were drawing a scant 2,000 per event. There was the attendance of 8,000-plus fans for the Carmen Basilio-Gaspar Ortega match, but such welcome anomalies were infrequent.

Additionally, the Garden was no longer a cinch to stage the big fights. It failed to secure the site rights for the finale of the Patterson-Johansson trilogy, which landed in the new Convention Center in Miami Beach. It was probably a bittersweet moment for the Garden when it announced that for the very first time it would be joining the closed-circuit ranks. Floyd Patterson, a native New Yorker, would defend his title 1,000 miles away and appear on a television screen in their arena, purportedly still the world's most famous.[85,86]

This change was another step in the Garden losing its financial hold on the sport. Years ago, Jacobs had seized the promotional reins from the Garden, leaving it to play landlord; now the Garden would be playing second fiddle to the landlord.[87]

As commercial broadcast television, closed-circuit TV, and radio diminished the importance of the once-mighty arenas, promoters sought to further exploit the financial power of these vehicles through cross-pollination. For example, Irving Kahn and his Teleprompter group promoted their closed-circuit TV-only broadcast of the second Patterson-Johansson fight by airing a one-half-hour program featuring highlights of the exciting first bout in which Ingo annexed the title on free ABC television the night before the match. ABC also had skin in the game, as they held the radio broadcast rights to the fight.[88] The anticipated combined take from the live gate, closed-circuit TV, and other ancillary rights was two to three million dollars.[89]

At least initially, introducing a little of commercial television's DNA into the closed-circuit gene pool seemed to yield a palpable mutation. When television was a fledgling industry, WNAC-TV in Washington teamed up with the Pilgrim Theater to show the intercity finals of the National Golden Gloves on their screen, along with a regular two-feature screen bill, Humphrey Bogart in *Chain Lightning* and *Dakota Lil.*[90]

However, by the early 1960's, when promoters attempted to crossbreed the two media, audiences bristled at such miscegenation. In yet another technological experiment, General Electric created a system that would reproduce television programs on the closed-circuit theater screen. The process was called Talaria, and it was a dud. As usual, boxing was used in one of the product's demonstrations.[91]

Agreeing to combine television and theater may have been a bad idea, but at least in this instance, no rights seemed to have been violated. Fifteen years earlier, RKO theaters, without any permission, planned to present the telecast of part of a professional boxing match by projecting it onto a large screen as part of a double feature with a regular theater screen show. NBC, the commercial broadcaster, was forced to intercede.[92]

It is no wonder that closed-circuit promoters such as Teleprompter zealously protected their rights, just as Rickard and Jacobs had before them. In one such instance, Teleprompter held the exclusive rights for the Patterson-Harris bout and planned to present it as a "closed-circuit only" affair. With no radio broadcasts, radio stations in New York seized the opportunity to fill the vacuum. Similar to the situation with Marciano-La Starza II five years prior, WINS, WOR, and WOV planned to give "accounts" of the fight. Ostensibly, they would be just reporting the fight, but their true objective was to create the illusion that they were broadcasting the fight live so that they would capture and maintain a larger listening audience. Teleprompter was successful in having the State Supreme Court block the radio stations' use of any presentation resembling "live" broadcasts or "blow-by-blow accounts in the present tense." Radio stations were held to have the same rights as newspapers. They could carry the fight as news only. However, undaunted by the limitations imposed, three to five minutes after the start of the fight, WINS and WOR respectively were on the air using information received from the United Press International service, giving a blow-by-blow description of the fight—in the past tense![93]

Radio may have taken a subordinate role to commercial and theatrical television in the broadcast of boxing during the era, but its continued presence outpaced the efforts of the fledgling pay-TV industry. In fact, pay-TV would never take root during boxing's Golden Age of television. However, the story of its failed struggle against commercial television is a fascinating part of television history, made even more noteworthy by its wildly successful reemergence in the boxing world a generation or two later. It would be accurate to say that if closed-circuit television was the flamboyant cousin of broadcast television, known for its occasional but dramatic appearances, then pay-TV was its shy sibling who turned into a very late bloomer.

The notion of being paid for a television program, which competed with free television in the same home, quickly moved from a financial whimsy to the testing stage at the same time commercial television began to become popular. Zenith began conducting public tests of its Phonevision system as early as 1946. At the time, the economic viability of nationwide advertisement-supported network television was in doubt, and the notion of pay-TV was seen not as a threat, but as a potential economic solution.[94]

The basic concept was elemental. The provider of "Pay-as-you-see TV," which the service was sometimes called, would send out a scrambled signal. If the television owner was a subscriber to the service, a decoding device would allow them to descramble the signal and view it. A bill would be generated after the fact. Strangely, this was a concern at the time, apparently because a "box-office" fee was always paid prior to the event.[95]

Early resistance to the concept came from outside the entertainment industry. Practically from its inception, proponents of free television marshaled their forces to squash any type of pay television or television that alienated the purported rights of free television viewers. When Phonevision charged viewers one dollar per movie presentation in a pay-TV test in Chicago, businessmen responded by creating the Fair Television Practices Committee. The committee sought to petition the FCC to suspend the license of any commercial broadcaster who participated in box-office television by challenging the legality of the premise. They cited the theater presentation of the Joe Louis-Lee Savold bout as a form of discrimination against TV-set owners in its deliberate channeling of broadcasting away from designated areas into restricted areas.[96] However, the argument against theater television as an infringement on viewers' rights did not persist, leaving the dispute exclusively in the realm of the small screen for commercial and pay-TV interests to contest. This gave boxing, for better or worse, an opportunity to become a multimillion-dollar theatrical business bifurcated from commercial television, which could advance alongside it on a dual track.

By the mid-1950s, commercial television broadcasters were able to support a national sponsorship model, and the pay-TV concept morphed from a beneficial piece of the financial puzzle into a major economic threat. Just when pay television was ready to roll out, commercial broadcasting interests successfully launched a vigorous public relations and political campaign against its implementation. In a 1955 CBS pamphlet, typical of commercial broadcasters' rhetoric, network president Frank Stanton bemoaned that pay-TV "would highjack the American public into paying for the privilege of looking at its own television sets."[97]

Pay-TV interests were also losing the battle over critical source material. The broadcast of old Hollywood films was pegged to be a bountiful and steady largesse for exploitation. However, when commercial television began snatching up the movie studios' portfolios in 1955, showing them for free, a core product for pay-TV interests vanished. By the turn of the decade, much of the attractive product for pay-TV had been diverted into the hands of commercial television interests.[98]

The pay-television industry was stuck in a perpetual dress rehearsal as the understudy of commercial television. It developed new affectations, none of which seemed to garner favor with the FCC, a casting director who had already turned a blind eye to their performances. Telemeter, a subsidiary of Paramount Pictures, for example, offered a system that contained a coin box. The viewer was required to deposit the coins before the program could be viewed. Still, another

Pay TV, sometimes outfitted with coin-operated receivers, remained a novelty during the Golden Age of boxing on television. It resurfaced decades later to become a financial juggernaut in the sport. A woman is shown dropping a coin into the control box of a Telmeter Pay-TV in 1957. *AP Photo/Dan Grossi.*

system, Teleglobe, would offer a nonscrambled video signal, which would add sound to those who subscribed—a fatally flawed system for boxing that could still be enjoyed to a great degree for free without the sound. Notwithstanding the new and sometimes unwieldy methods of payment, the technology was more than sufficient. However, a strong lobby of commercial broadcasters and theater owners kept the FCC in their court and kept Congress legislatively impotent. This resulted in the successful restraint of the application of pay-TV during television's Golden Age.[99]

In reality, the birth of pay-television in the 1950s was stillborn. The concept would have its day, albeit a generation or so later. Once again, it was boxing that would drive the success of a major communication medium. The quaint "coin box," now an anachronism, was discarded. The fuzzy pictures of closed-circuit TV and the travel time to and from the theater would be vetoed by a public that had become indoctrinated by cable television to pay for programming. Audiences preferred to stay in the comfort of their family rooms, and later on their media rooms and man caves, to indulge in "pay-per-view."

The 1990s and the new millennium would see staggering viewership and receipts from pay-TV broadcasts such as Mike Tyson's return against Peter McNeeley in 1995 and Oscar De La Hoya vs. Floyd Mayweather Jr. in 2007, which set all-time records with gross revenues of $96 and $136 million, respectively.[100] In 2015, the concept would reach its apex with the Floyd Mayweather-Manny Pacquiao bout. An estimated 4.4 million "buys" in the U.S. alone helped yield gross worldwide receipts in excess of $500 million.[101] Boxing and "pay-as-you-see TV" proved to be a dream deferred and not a lucrative dream denied.

Chapter 13

SHOW ME THE MONEY: THE LIVE GATE VS. TELEVISION MONEY CONUNDRUM

As early as 1946 and the Louis- Conn rematch—the start of the modern era of boxing and commercial TV—the debate raged over whether television reduced attendance and gate receipts to the extent that it is financially counterproductive. It was the old Tex Rickard radio conundrum recast in a new medium.

The end of the war had taken all the shackles off promoters. Their talent returned from the service. The champions' titles were unfrozen, and lucrative championship bouts such as the Tony Zale-Rocky Graziano matchup were staged. In 1946, in the state of New York, a staggering 599 boxing and wrestling shows were held. The state's net receipts doubled from the previous year.[1]

While the partnership between commercial television and boxing showed steady growth, its ripple effect began to make unwelcome waves in the boxing community. The live gate for those matches televised by Madison Square Garden during the summer of 1947 was down, and the grumbling from the fighters, managers, and trainers who claimed to be financially damaged became more vocal and more organized. At this juncture, the live gate was still overwhelmingly the most important source of revenue. The live gate at the Garden for 1947 was close to 2.2 million dollars as compared to radio and television revenues, which were $220,000 and $100,000, respectively.[2]

Opponents of televised boxing matches contended that the drop in the live gate was directly related to television. However, there were other potential contributory factors. The quality of the bouts, competition from other forms of entertainment, the weather, even a wife's refusal to let her husband go out on a particular evening, might have an effect. Therefore, it was difficult to prove a direct correlation between television and declining gate receipts.

The Twentieth Century Sporting Club, Inc., promoter at Madison Square Garden and other important locales in New York, skirted the issue altogether, citing existing television contractual obligations. The Garden's contract with WNBT, New York's NBC affiliate, was in effect until May of the following year. From the promoters' perspective, the contract was to be honored and bouts broadcast regardless of any perceived or real financial effects.[3]

The following month, welterweights Tony Janiro and Tony Pellone fought in a televised match from the Garden that drew a solid showing of 15,000 fans with a healthy gate of $55,000, rainy evening and all.[4] Some of those concerned gave a temporary sigh of relief. While the managers, trainers, and fighters in New York hunkered down for the winter and waited for their next opportunity to state their case, the television issue was brought front and center on the West Coast.

The popularity of the fight game in Los Angeles never approached that of New York, but similar to Chicago, St. Louis, Detroit, Cleveland, and several other cities around the country, a thriving postwar boxing community existed. In the Los Angeles area, the Olympic Auditorium, Hollywood Legion Stadium, and Ocean Park regularly hosted matches featuring such standouts as Enrique Bolanos, Jackie Wilson, and a young Lauro Salas.[5]

Like the televised bouts at the Garden in New York, those from Hollywood Legion Stadium, although on the air for just six months, were quickly criticized by boxing managers as the cause for the reduction in live gate receipts. Reduced receipts were a concern because the stadium compensated main event fighters based on a percentage of the gate receipts. More proactive then their New York counterparts, the Los Angeles managers threatened to pull their fighters from further action unless the television broadcasts ceased.[6]

The television contract between the Don Lee Television Company and the Hollywood Legion Stadium still had two and a half years remaining. A meeting was held between representatives of these concerns as well as a committee representing the managers headed by George Parnassus, who would later become a famed Los Angeles promoter.[7] When Legion representatives were unable to break their contract with the television company, the boxing managers held steadfast. They wouldn't sign any more fighters to appear there after the upcoming Friday night card unless the contracts contained antitelevision clauses.

In the face of the managers' continued threats, a spokesman for the Legion board claimed they would continue to hold regular bouts. Where the fighters would come from was not disclosed.[8] In one recruiting effort, Hollywood Legion matchmaker Bobby Jackson journeyed to San Francisco. Managers in that city uniformly rebuked Jackson, joining their Southern California brethren and refusing to allow their fighters to participate in televised matches.[9]

Vowing that the show would go on, Jackson recruited talent from as far east as Washington, DC, Baltimore, and Brooklyn.[10] A meeting of Los Angeles managers was held at the famed Main Street Gym and included former middleweight champion Gorilla Jones. Former heavyweight champion Jack Dempsey addressed the group, encouraging managers to keep the fighters working at Legion Stadium while they pursued a settlement.[11] The Dempsey charisma did not fail. Soon after, it was announced that a temporary agreement had been hammered out for the duration of the next eight shows. Television revenues would be split evenly between the stadium and the boxers, provided sponsors for the shows were secured. A new and more lucrative purse schedule was also established.[12]

Back in New York, the Boxing Managers' Guild, 122 strong, perhaps emboldened by the success of their West Coast counterparts, did not wait until the expiration of NBC's television contract to take action. They staged their own strike in the spring of 1948. The target of their walkout was Mike Jacobs's Twentieth Century, the promoter of fights at Madison Square Garden and St. Nicholas Arena. Twentieth Century's financial partner, Madison Square Garden, also controlled St. Nick's Arena and by virtue of their association with Twentieth Century became an adversary of the managers, as well.[13] New York managers began holding back their fighters from the regular weekly cards at the St. Nicholas arena. To counter the boycott, which successfully caused the cancellation of several shows, Twentieth Century began to import fighters from out of town. None of the fighters on the card for St. Nick's' strikebreaking show were handled by the managers of the New York guild including the headliner heavyweights, Bill Smith of Oakland, California, and Colin Chaney of Indianapolis, Indiana.[14]

Neither faction could deny that out-of-town fighters paled in comparison to the local hero at the box office, and this continued practice would benefit neither party. Less than a week later, representatives of the Boxing Managers' Guild and Twentieth Century agreed to negotiate. When the discourse broke down, Garden Vice President Ned Irish threatened to pull the plug permanently. "We can do without boxing in the Garden, if the managers continue their unreasonable demands," proclaimed Irish in response to the guild's demand of 50 percent of the television receipts.[15]

In support of his position, Irish cited the 1.25 million dollar take of boxers and managers at the Garden during the previous year, which had accounted for two-thirds of the live gate receipts. Further, Irish claimed that main event fighters were already getting additional compensation related to television, as their percentage of the live gate had increased during the last few years, and higher percentages were being facilitated by the television money.[16]

The biggest stumbling block during negotiations was not the Twentieth Century Sporting Club. Acting President Sol Strauss, while initially adamant about not giving away money directly tied to television revenue, would eventually indicate that the promotional company was amenable to a 50–50 split.[17] However, Irish appeared resolute in his position that the Garden would not yield a penny. "We'll put professional basketball in on Friday nights, formerly allotted to boxing, and we'll televise it, and we'll make more money," Irish said.[18]

Irish may have been cavalier in public, but the circus was going to finish its run at the Garden the next week, and several lucrative upcoming dates were now in jeopardy. Missing the gate at a few small shows at St. Nick's was one thing; losing the gate at the Garden was something else entirely.[19]

Negotiations quickly resumed without success. Not having boxing at the Garden would be sacrilegious in New York. So a week later, Eddie Eagan, the state athletic commissioner, opened his doors for an informal session with the principals. The guild came en masse: President Charley Johnston and their Vice Presidents Frankie Jacobs, Irving Cohen, Bill Daly, Tex Sullivan, and Lew Burston. Sol Strauss led the Twentieth Century contingent. Testimony to the fact that the commission wielded great power in New York, the ailing Mike Jacobs briefly appeared, as well.

As the commission had no legal power to negotiate with the guild, it informally brokered a deal. The strike was not officially settled, but immediately the word was out that managers would take a 25 percent cut of television revenues.[20] The full membership of the Boxing Managers' Guild of New York quickly accepted a 50 percent take of the Twentieth Century Sporting Club's income from television, which, after the Garden split, amounted to 25 percent of the total revenue. It was estimated that the next year would bring the managers an additional $25,000 in revenues.

The guild's motivation for the strike was not one based on principle. Nor was obtaining the agreed-upon settlement its primary goal. The strike was a maneuver to position themselves for potentially lucrative television money down the line. For Twentieth Century, the settlement served to remove an immediate ancillary problem: its inability to fulfill its radio contract and deliver boxing matches for a national radio hookup every Friday evening.[21]

The increase in live gate receipts experienced at the end of the war was short-lived, and the television issue was again front and center at the annual dinner of the Boxing Writers Association at Toots Shor's in January, 1949. The New York State Athletic Commission's perspective was provided by Commissioner Eddie P. Eagan, who offered the financial stats for 1948. The State coffers, filled through the collection of tax money, showed a decrease in the sum of over $23,000 for boxing matches, presumably from a decline in gate receipts. However, for the same period, there was an increase in gains from motion pictures, television, and radio of over $61,000, showing that the gains offset the decreases.

Keynote speaker Harry Markson, acting promoter of the Twentieth Century Sporting Club, hypothesized that television was only one cause for the decline in boxing attendance, citing a shortage of talent, business decline, and adverse publicity. Markson did not subscribe to the belief that television was killing boxing. "There will always be people who want the personal touch and who will want to be present at a good boxing attraction," he reasoned.[22]

That summer, the issue of television revenues resurfaced with a second lockout. Markson, who was then in the position of managing director of boxing at the Garden, announced the cancellation of all boxing promotions at the Garden, St. Nick's, and outdoor venues for the summer of 1949.[23]

The dispute had already prevented the signing of the Ray Robinson-Kid Gavilan welterweight title fight scheduled for June 17 and led to the cancellation of the June 3 bout between welterweight Billy Graham and lightweight Enrique Bolanos.[24] In an effort to save the remaining two-thirds of the summer season, the Boxing Managers' Guild of New York and the Madison Square Garden Corporation reached an agreement in which the main event fighters of televised Garden programs would receive $1,000 each above their regular purse as their share of television and radio income. The same agreement was made for the Friday night St. Nicholas Arena shows, with a lesser sum of $350 for the main event fighters on Tuesday's St. Nick cards.[25, 26]

In Los Angeles, a series of strikes would continue to plague the fight game during 1948 and 1949. One of the strikes would drag on for a full five months. By this time, Hollywood Legion Stadium matchmaker Bobby Jackson had been replaced by Baron von Stumme. The lengthy walkout was resolved with a uniquely Southern California flavor, with the wax-mustachioed von Stumme and members of the Southern California Boxing Managers' Association gathering under a group of pepper trees in front of the stadium in a self-congratulatory session. However, their celebration was premature.[27] By January of 1949, the managers were boycotting Hollywood Legion Stadium for the fourth time over the issue of fighters' TV compensation.[28]

Meanwhile, in New York, the latest television fee contract had another year to run and would expire May 31, 1950. During that period, the television money grew into an even larger pie. Shortly before the expiration of the agreement, the membership of the New York Boxing Managers' Guild voted unanimously that they wanted a bigger piece. The fixed rates established in 1949 would no longer suffice, and the guild's demand reverted to the 50–50 split that they had originally sought. The manager committee that was formed to carry on negotiations with Twentieth's Century's successor, the IBC "big-money boys," as guild president Charlie Johnston called them, included Johnston, Tony Lento, George Gainesford, Eddie Walker, Irving Cohen, Hyman Wallman, and Jackie Levine.[29]

Cooperation in the boycott was pledged from the heads of similar manager groups in Chicago, Pennsylvania, and Connecticut.[30] The first and perhaps most enduring result of the threatened boycott was the failure to consummate a deal that would have placed Jake La Motta and Rocky Graziano in the same boxing ring. At the time, La Motta had already been signed by the IBC to defend his title at Yankee Stadium on June 14. Graziano's camp appeared to be agreeable with the terms offered to fight Jake. However, with the match only several weeks from the first bell, Graziano's advisers refused to let their charge sign a contract until the IBC and the Managers' Guild reached a new agreement on television revenues.[31]

The La Motta-Graziano match, a wildly popular pairing, particularly for New York fight fans, could have been a classic. Instead, it became a pawn in the guild's crusade for control of television money. Without regard to complete accuracy, Johnston, as the guild president, represented that the managers and trainers had taken a collective stand that sparring partners would not be made available for Graziano and La Motta.[32] As if the posturing of Johnston were not enough to discourage the bout, Graziano was under increasing pressure from National Boxing Association (NBA) President Abe Greene to name an opponent for the June 14 date. Greene sent his demand in writing via telegram, which Rocky failed to answer promptly.[33]

The IBC, which had replaced the Twentieth Century Sporting Club as the promotional counterpart of the Managers' Guild, had planned to run thirty-five consecutive Friday night cards from the Garden and St. Nicholas arena. With no new contract during June, and with the scheduling of the 1950–51 indoor boxing season imminent, the IBC had offered the guild 25 percent of the TV receipts with a guaranteed minimum of $4,000 to be split between the two main event fighters. In the St. Nick's arena, the same 25 percent would apply with a no-guarantee clause. The managers rejected the offer.[34] The strike was settled a couple of weeks later, ending the forty-four-day walkout under the same terms as the prior offer, but the minimum figure for Garden bouts was raised to $4,500.[35]

Another important feature of the settlement was the handling of "delayed" television, or the telecast of a filmed version of the fight. In an effort to avoid guild fighters financially competing against each other, it was agreed that no film recording of a fight would be shown on the same evening in which live bouts were taking place in that city. Additionally, the earliest a filmed fight could be shown was seventy-two hours after the match. A filmed fight could only be shown once in a city, unless consent was given by the Managers' Guild for subsequent showings.[36]

The television dispute was not settled until July, and the whole sordid affair had Frankie Carbo's fingerprints all over it (see Chapter 15). The fight fans' dream of seeing irresistible force Graziano take on immovable object La Motta had passed into the realm of boxing's great "what ifs."

Like the potential heirs of a stock portfolio of fast-rising issues, it was to be expected that boxing's promoters, managers, and fighters would each stake their right to the anticipated fortune left to them by television. What was at stake was obvious. In fact, before managers in New York and Los Angeles sought to protect their interests, even the smaller boxing fraternity of Cincinnati had grasped the issue. Representatives of the city's fight venues sought to protect their own financial hides by informing W8XCT, the Crosley Broadcasting Corporation's television station, that its cameras would be banned from all contests in which the television broadcaster did not guarantee the payment of all unsold tickets.[37] Whether it reared its head in New York, the fight capital of the world, or Cincinnati, one of the sport's satellite outposts, television revenues became the first issue for boxing during the television era and only one of several major hurdles that the union of television and boxing would have to overcome.

The cycle of boycotts, negotiations, and settlements resurfaced periodically during the late-'40s and early-'50s to realign the distribution of the increasing pot of money. The International Boxing Guild, through its various local chapters in New York, Chicago, and other cities, was the only real counterweight in the fighter's corner in its ongoing battle with promoters for a share of television money. Unfortunately, the guild's loyalties were suspect. Its managers were under the influence of crime figure Frankie Carbo, and the IBC's and the guilds' actions were often driven by conflicting motives.

Beginning in the late-1940s, the International Boxing Guild's predecessor, the Boxing Managers' Guild of New York, had effectively raised the television/radio fee for each main event fighter at the Garden from $186.60 to $212.05 as of June 4, 1948, to the $1,000 in effect until July 12, 1950. The Guild strike of 1950 resulted in a television fee increase to $2,250. The following year, the figure hit

$3,000, with the main event fighters for the IBC of Illinois Wednesday night Pabst fights on CBS receiving $1,500. Television revenue of $570 went to the headliners on their less lucrative Monday night fights from the St. Nicholas Arena. After the IBG came into the picture in 1952, the Garden fee would be raised twice more to $3,600 on September 1, 1952, and then $4,000 exactly one year later. Club fight television fees around that time increased as well, with the television fee for main-eventers set at the Eastern Parkway Arena at $2,900.[38]

The influence that Carbo and Norris exerted on the New York Boxing Managers' Guild and later, to an even a great extent, upon the IBG was strongly self-motivated. Nevertheless, it can be argued that the managers' guilds in their various incarnations successfully advocated for their fighters during the seminal years of television. A telling statistic supporting this idea is the proportion of the television fee paid to the fighter in relation to the television sponsorship money paid to the promoter. When Norris and the IBC arrived on the scene in 1949, main event fighters were paid $1,000 each out of the $18,500 rights fee paid by Gillette. In 1953, the television fee was only slightly higher, at about $22,500 per week, yet the fighters' share had increased to $4,000. However, if you examine the fighters' take as a percent-basis of the gross television fee received from the sponsors, you could make a strong argument that the fighters were still underpaid for their services.

Lack of financial transparency favored the promoters. The IBC's Truman Gibson was a master at the use of multiple corporations to control and obfuscate the flow of television money. However, the artistry he so deftly displayed within the Chicago-IBC could not be applied at the Garden. At the time, the Norris-Wirtz combination was not yet a majority stockholder, and they had to answer to the board of directors of that publically held corporation. Thusly, sponsorship fees paid by Gillette went directly to the IBC of New York, who in turn paid Madison Square Garden. At least in New York, fighters and their managers had a reasonable idea of the total amount of television money available for distribution.[39]

Significantly, the fixed television fees for boxers applied only to nonchampionship fights, and a free market still existed for championship contests. Television money was funneled into a multifaceted matrix. The fighters' cut that emerged was dependent on a number of potential factors created by the various parties associated with the bout—the promoter(s), venue, television broadcaster, and sponsor were each a contributory factor. On occasion, this dynamic would lead to forum shopping.

When Lauro Salas sought to defend his lightweight title against James Carter, Gillette, the sponsor of the Friday night fights telecast from Madison Square Garden on NBC, offered the fighters a maximum of $3,600 each for the television/radio portion of the proceeds. The Pabst Brewing Company, sponsor of Wednesday night fights from Chicago Stadium on CBS, offered each fighter 30 percent ($9,000) of the $30,000 they were putting up for the telecast and radio broadcast. The sponsor with the higher offer determined which network would telecast the fight. The bout's financial dynamics served as yet another illustration of how much power TV exerted on the sport.[40]

While various boxing manager strikes of the late-'40s and early-'50s would address how telecasters, promoters, and fighters should share television profits, the larger litmus question of whether or not to televise a match in the first place would remain an open issue for many years.

Regardless of which side one supported in the argument of profit sharing, the financial indicators of the sport were changing. During the late-1940s, Promoters decided whether or not to televise bouts on a case-by-case basis whenever possible. The financial variables of television promotion were still uncertain. One significant variable was the wide range of fees the promoter might receive for television rights. While the Jimmy Bivins-Ezzard Charles match had a price tag of $3,500 and the Beau Jack-Ike Williams $6,000, the Louis-Walcott rematch, which was also televised, carried a whopping $100,000 return.[41]

In an effort to hedge their bets, one of the promotional strategies promoters implemented was waiting until the last moment to decide whether or not to televise a match. It was a gambit utilized for years in regard to radio broadcasts. Sadly, the rubber match of the Zale-Graziano trilogy, one of the greatest in boxing history, fell victim to this approach. While the promoter, the Tournament of Champions, Inc., did have Ruppert Stadium in Newark, New Jersey, wired for a television broadcast, it decided to forego a $30,000 television fee and bank on the gate receipts instead. The potential television audience was cheated of a ring classic.[42]

The public was dissatisfied when the promoter would forgo television, and conversely, promoters balked when the gate suffered due to a telecast. The echo of Herman Taylor can still be heard in Philadelphia railing against the evils of television, which put his

The Tournament of Champions, Inc. (T of C), had the third Graziano-Zale fight (1948) wired for television but made a financial decision not to proceed with the broadcast. Shortly afterward, the International Boxing Club outdueled T of C for control of boxing promotion and its television empire. *AP Photo.*

promotion of the Ike Williams-Beau Jack lightweight championship fight in the red to the tune of $10,000. Taylor was justifiably distraught that the match produced only about half the gate that Williams drew with Bolanos in a nontelevised match the previous year in Los Angeles. He vowed never to allow television on one of his promotions unless the television sponsors provided a guarantee against financial loss.[43]

Fear of financial reductions or losses often led to the draconian approach of banning television. Some high-profile fights of the era were sorely missed by the new television audience. In addition to Zale-Graziano III, some of the major matches that were not seen on television during the close of the decade were Ray Robinson against Steve Belloise, which finally occurred in August of 1949; La Motta's memorable victory over Cerdan for the middleweight title; Robinson outdueling Gavilan in defense of his welterweight crown; and Ezzard Charles defending his newly won NBA heavyweight laurels against former light-heavyweight champion Gus Lesnevich.[44]

An equitable promotional approach to the problem, which would endure for many years in boxing and other sports, was the "local blackout," which permitted the telecast of the bout in all locations but the city of the telecast's origin. The local blackout, a logical middle approach for providing television while potentially protecting the gate, was implemented by the IBC for the Walcott-Charles battle for Louis's vacant heavyweight title. Unfortunately, in that instance, the dull affair was displeasing to the live audience and television viewers alike.[45]

Boxing on television was like free Halloween candy, and those who were imposed with the blackout were the unfortunate souls given a rotten apple. Some fans, however, were unwilling to accept the "trick" and demanded the "treat."

Because of a local blackout when Joe Louis fought Ezzard Charles in Chicago for his newly earned laurels, the nearest locations that offered television were Milwaukee, Kenosha, Racine, Waukegan, Kalamazoo, and Indianapolis. The closest city telecasting the fight was Milwaukee, ninety miles from Chicago. Many set owners in the

Utilization of the "local blackout" often provided promoters and venue owners the best opportunity to maximize revenues from both television and the "live gate." This approach was used when Bobo Olson defeated Randy Turpin for the vacant middleweight title at MSG, October 21, 1953. *AP Photo/Marty Lederhandler.*

Windy City purchased boosters and could be found climbing onto their roofs and turning their aerials toward Milwaukee in an attempt to receive Channel 2 and the fight. It wasn't a particularly convenient or safe way to tune in, but televisions that typically had a range of fifty miles were known to receive signals from twice the distance. It was worth a shot to avoid a three-hour round-trip drive for a seat in a strange bar.[46]

The local blackout was televised boxing's great compromise. It would be strategically used in the years to follow. In 1953, Bobo Olson banged out a unanimous fifteen-round decision over Randy Turpin on a nationally televised match. The bout, which drew a capacity crowd of 18,869 with a live gate of $167,651 and TV-radio rights of $60,000, met promotional expectations. It also kept the vast majority of the viewing audience happy except the New Yorkers who were blacked out. Similar results were garnered when Kid Gavilan trounced Johnny Bratton over fifteen rounds before a live crowd of 19,260 at Chicago Stadium, drawing $176,390 and $40,000 from Gillette for the national telecast. This time, the odd man out was the Chicagoan who stayed at home.[47] The use of the local blackout typically pitted the local promoter, who favored a broader blackout because it protected their live gate, against competing television interests, most notably the sponsors, who desired the broadest television audience possible.

With the local blackout, often the devil was in the details. In 1956, when lightweight champion Wallace "Bud" Smith met local hero Tony DeMarco in a nontitle bout at the Boston Garden, the bout was telecast nationally. The IBC insisted on a local blackout of Boston stations only. Channel 9 in Manchester, New Hampshire, was only about fifty miles away. Promoter Sam Silverman had a good track record with the IBC, having promoted three title fights with them the previous year. He argued that the station was powerful enough to be received on most Boston television sets and therefore should not air the bout.

The IBC refused to yield to Silverman's logic. "Get yourself another fight for that date," Silverman countered. Casting the television issue in light of the sport's most recent developments, he attempted to rally his constituency: "It's about time boxing promoters in this country got wise to themselves. Why should buildings like Madison Square Garden [New York], Cleveland Arena, Chicago Stadium—all with vast seating capacities—be used as studios? If they televise locally, I can't make any money, the fighters can't make any money, and these huge buildings end up empty."[48] Under such conditions, it was the local promoters, who were forced to copromote with the IBC for televised matches, who suffered the most financially from the loss of the live gate.

Silverman was not overstating his point. That same summer, eight televised boxing shows at Chicago Stadium featured such talent as Johnny Saxton, Gil Turner, Holly Mims, and Bob Satterfield. They drew a total of only 14,521 patrons—less than 2,000 attendees per card. Even Frank Gilmer, chairman of the Illinois Athletic Commission, had to publicly concede that "This isn't the best encouragement."[49]

On other occasions, television interests did capitulate to the local promoter in realization that if they backed their counterpart too close to the edge, they might go over the financial cliff together. In 1955, ABC announced that there would be a New York–area television blackout of future Monday night boxing matches originating from the Eastern Parkway Arena in Brooklyn, while the arena's promoter attempted to increase its live attendance. In lieu of the lost on-site television revenues, the network looked to raise its income by expanding its national television network.[50]

As early as 1953, when the boxing-television combine was still at the height of its powers, the International Boxing Club realized the danger of the depletion of talented fighters for television consumption. In order to build new prospects, on one card from the Rainbow Arena in Chicago, the IBC televised four six-rounders, one including newcomer Floyd Patterson, but did not televise the main event.[51] However, even with such legitimate talent as Patterson, the overall supply of worthy boxers could not keep up with the demands of boxing's television schedule.

Additionally, there was the related problem of the erosion of boxing's "farm system." By the mid-1950s the fallout of television's effect on the sport at the grassroots level was substantial. During the pre-television era, New York City had been bursting with small clubs: the Broadway Arena, Ridgewood Grove, Dexter Park, Fort Hamilton, Pioneer, Coney Island Stadium, Henderson Bowl, the New York Coliseum, Rockland Palace, Manhattan Casino, Lenox, Sunnyside Gardens, Queensboro Arena, Eastern Parkway Arena, and St. Nick's Arena. By the end of 1953, only the Eastern Parkway Arena and St. Nick's remained as active fight clubs.[52]

With the live gate increasingly diminished as a financial component of boxing productions, alternative models were explored. In

1953, a Chicago firm rolled out a plan to move boxing from the arena to television studios. "Boxing is now a segment of the television industry," it was explained by one of its proponents. "Is there any good reason why major prize-fights shouldn't be held in television studios?"[53] Three years earlier, the concept had already been tried in Baltimore on a small scale, in a program sponsored by a Baltimore brewery, where the only live viewers of an eight-bout card on WAAM were studio technicians and nonpaying guests.[54] However, studio bouts in Chicago were short-lived, and the concept never gained significant traction nationally, seeing only sporadic use. For example, in a variation of the concept, a small fight club in Philadelphia, "The Met," held a nationally televised card on September 1, 1954. Two thousand patrons were admitted for free.[55] However, the fundamental idea that the promoter and the arena owner could be circumvented by a system in which the television broadcaster and its sponsor dealt directly with the fighter would not be permitted by the International Boxing Club, the many arenas it controlled, and the managers beholden to them.

The persisting television problem could be stated easily, but the solution was vexing: How could a TV audience be satisfied while still drawing patrons to the arena? In early 1954, St. Nick's took the major step of banning television and radio coverage from its bouts in an attempt to draw fans out of their living rooms and back to the arena.[56] This measure was short-lived, with DuMont providing regular telecasts from the arena from 1954 through 1956. The network signed off the air on the evening of August 6, 1956; their final broadcast was a fight card from St. Nick's. The seemingly impenetrable fortress built by boxing and network television had been breached.[57]

At that time, the Eastern Parkway Arena in Brooklyn was the only other remaining active fight club in New York telecasting bouts. The Eastern Parkway fights were also carried by DuMont. When promoter Emile Lence's contract with the network expired in May of 1956, Joe Arata took over the promotional reins and struck a new deal with ABC to telecast their bouts.[58,59]

In 1956, with the supporting timbers of America's few remaining small fight clubs already rotting from within, Teddy Brenner took over matchmaking duties of St. Nick's Arena from the deposed Tex Sullivan, who had received a lifetime suspension from the NYSAC for violation of its rules. "It's a paradox," Brenner posited. "Boxing has more fans today than ever before. But they won't pay to see a bout. Local arenas, where fighters used to learn their trade, have been choked out like weeds."[60]

Brenner explained the quandary that television had created. Whereas a fighter in the old days was brought up slowly, the present crop was rushed along with unrealistic expectations. "A few knockouts in prelims and they push him on TV. One lousy showing before twenty million people and he is done for."[61]

TV's financial aspects also directly affected the style of boxer chosen for a particular bout. Brenner noted that people loved to see a first- or second-round knockout but admitted "the sponsors hate it." "They feel they haven't received their money's worth." Brenner candidly explained that matchmakers were now avoiding matching two sluggers. "A lot of good punchers have been finished in boxing when they should have been in their prime," he complained.[62]

While television's implications continued to reshape the sport during the mid-1950s, the role of the International Boxing Guild and the New York Boxing Guild was called under scrutiny. By 1954, the IBC was two years deep into a Federal lawsuit alleging that it ran an illegal monopoly of professional boxing. In an effort to control the sport, it had forged an unholy alliance with middleman and underworld figure Frankie Carbo. The sway that Carbo held over the International Boxing Guild and its New York chapter would lead to severe consequences for the sport's rank and file, as well.

The spoils of television were at the heart of the problem. In November of 1954, the New York State Athletic Commission opened an inquiry into charges of monopoly and discrimination levied against the International Boxing Guild and its New York guild. Accusations were brought by the Metropolitan Boxing Alliance, a new managers' group, as well as others. Specifically, the New York guild was charged with blackmailing main event television fighters to pay a kickback fee of $100 to participate in television fights. Additionally, they were accused of blacklisting managers who were not members of the guild.

The International Boxing Guild had been formed in 1952. At least ostensibly, one of the IBG's primary goals was the same as that of all labor unions: obtain the best possible financial arrangements for its members, in this case, managers and their fighters. The Guild had sixteen chapter members in the US, and by the mid-1950s virtually all of the important managers in the country were members, particularly those located in New York. Two of the more notable members of the New York chapter of the guild were Al Weill, pilot of heavyweight champion Rocky Marciano, and Charley Johnston, manager of both featherweight kingpin Sandy Saddler and light-heavyweight ruler Archie Moore.

Television generated the money to pay the fighters, and James D. Norris controlled the TV contracts. Guild members would periodically deal with the IBC in negotiating these contracts. They would also have to interact with them anytime a fight was promoted by Norris at the Garden or in one of his other arenas located in Chicago, Detroit, or St. Louis. If you wanted your fighter in an important fight, Norris was your partner. As the IBC lined its pockets with television money, influential managers in the guild looked on with a jealous eye. Self-interest would get the best of some of them.

In an effort to buttress the charges put forth by the commission, attorneys for the guild argued that the $100 "kickback" fees were actually voluntary. Further, they produced records to prove that many nonguild managers had actively participated in televised bouts during the past year.

Some of boxing's most legendary figures were involved in the scandal. Cus D'Amato, manager of Floyd Patterson, a contending light-heavyweight at the time, admitted to being " a solicitor of television donations." On behalf of the guild, he collected from both guild and nonguild members, explaining that the money was used to

James D. Norris, president of the International Boxing Club, created a boxing empire during the 1950s that controlled boxing on television. It was eventually adjudicated a monopoly and dismantled. *Photo courtesy of the Library of Congress.*

defer the organization's expenses. And in what was clearly an "end justifies the means" rationale, fellow manager Ray Arcel explained the $100 "donations": "If it wasn't for the Guild our fighters would still be getting about $250 for TV fights in Madison Square Garden, instead of the $4,000 that they are paid now."[63] Arcel was the trainer of countless champions including Ezzard Charles, and at the time he was the promoter of the *Saturday Night Fights.* He had paid the guild $13,000 to advertise in its publication before it was discontinued. Arcel's position was that "it was not tribute." However, the true purpose of that large sum was also under investigation.[64]

Other influential individuals caught in the scandal included Tex Sullivan, matchmaker of the London Sporting Club, which promoted at the St. Nicholas arena. Whereas D'Amato acted as the "bag man," Sullivan was taking money off the top, deducting fighters' purses to the tune of $100. He justified his actions by claiming that they were at the request of the managers and fighters involved.

With the charges of blacklisting and monopoly still pending, the New York State Athletic Commission began issuing suspensions. In addition to D'Amato and Sullivan, this included Sullivan's assistant matchmaker Angelo Pucci and managers Lippy Briedbart and Bill Daily. Daily was the treasurer of the guild and pilot of welterweight contender Vince Martinez.

In a bizarre twist to the investigation, Al Braverman, president of the Metropolitan Boxing Alliance and the principal complainant against the two guilds, was also suspended. The suspension of Braverman, who had admitted that he had twice been convicted on bookmaking, was a slap on the wrist. Through the commission's discretionary power, he avoided a lifetime suspension.

Along with the suspensions came a warning from commissioner Robert K. Christenberry: "The commission will not tolerate any blacklisting or boycotting. The Commission, and not any [other] group, has the authority to regulate boxing in New York."[65] The commission followed the suspensions with a $1,000 fine of promoter London Sporting Club, and a refund of $100 each to nineteen boxers was ordered. Sullivan's suspension was then lifted. Pucci was not as fortunate. His suspension led to a revocation of his license for blacklisting and dealing with unlicensed managers to book preliminary bouts at St. Nick's.[66]

The New York State Athletic Commission's investigation lasted for seven months. During that period, the United States Supreme Court found that the profession of boxing was a business within the meaning of the Sherman Anti-Trust Act, and the government proceeded with its prosecution of a case claiming that the International Boxing Club was running a monopoly. The New York State Athletic Commission's lengthy investigation concluded with a declaration by its new commissioner, Julius Helfand, that "the Boxing Guild of New York, affiliated with the International Boxing Guild, is a continuing menace to the integrity of boxing in this state."[67]

Included in the commission's findings was 1) a conspiracy to boycott certain noncooperative fighters, specifically a boycott of welterweight Vince Martinez, who could not get bouts in New York when he refused to renew his contract with manager "Honest" Billy Daily and attempted to guide his own career; 2) the requirement of payment by out-of-state managers before their fighter could obtain a fight in New York; 3) the guild's absolute control of television contracts to the exclusion of fighter and promoter;[68] 4) memberships admitted association with underworld figure Frankie Carbo; 5) Ray Arcel's $17,000 payment to conduct business as a promoter, disguised as publication costs at $1,500 a page for a nonsubscription magazine; 6) the continued collection of $100 fees in circumvention of a prior commission order.[69]

Running parallel to the misdeeds occurring in New York were the transgressions of the IBG's Ohio chapter, which was guilty of barring its managers from matching their fighters with any boxer who was handled by a non-IBG member. The Ohio Guild also boycotted studio fights from television station WEWS in Cleveland. Based upon these facts, and on the coattails of its favorable court decision that found the International Boxing Club was illegally monopolizing boxing, the Federal government brought similar antitrust charges against the IBG.[70]

The New York State Athletic Commission, the most powerful boxing body in the world, wanted to distance itself from the stain on the sport that these disputes had created. The existing debacle in New York and the Cleveland incident were illustrative of the woes the guilds could cause. Clearly, the New York guild was far from considered sacrosanct. The tentacles of the federal government could reach New York next, and the commission did not intend to be within its reach. Outwardly, the commission recognized none of this and took the position that its actions regarding the guild were based upon their attempt to usurp the commission's power.

On December 14, 1955, commission chairman Julius Helfand declared that no boxing manager licensed in New York would be permitted to operate in the state if they remained a member of the New York guild or the International Boxing Guild after January 15, 1956. Doing so would be considered "an act and conduct detrimental to the interests of boxing."[71]

The implications of the commission's actions on the sport and televised boxing in New York were potentially far-reaching. While the NYSAC's move only applied in New York, the National Boxing Association, whose rules were followed by most other state commissions, had a frosty relationship with New York. It was quite possible that New York managers would take their business out of state without consequence of reciprocity. Along with that business, the television contracts would disappear. This would please no one, except perhaps the television industry. TV did not necessarily favor New York as a live venue to start because the oft-utilized blackout of home television resulted in the loss of its largest market.[72]

Guild managers felt that they had the better hand to play. They controlled the New York fighters. They reasoned that, if necessary, their fighters could box on televised shows for Jim Norris at his non-New York venues, effectively freezing out New York State. Since its inception in 1952, the IBG had been negotiating its television contracts through the IBC to establish standard television fees for fighters. The guild perceived Norris as sympathetic. After all, he had gone on record stating, "I've always dealt with the Guild as if it was a union.

I've always found its members fair and cooperative."[73] He had also made statements that suggested that he was perturbed with the commission's recent ruling, lamenting that "We don't know what fight managers to deal with now, and we have fights to get up for next month."[74]

The guild called the commission's bluff. Acting president Cus D'Amato announced the vote—66–0 in favor of ignoring the commission edict of dissolution. A formal guild statement explained its position: "No manager or promoter wants to shut out boxing from New York. Most of them are native New Yorkers and do not wish to leave their hometown, but Helfand's boycott order against the guilds in this state leaves them without a choice."[75]

Jimmy Johnston, a New York chapter member who was also president of the entire IBG, assailed Helfand for his "blanket indictment of the honesty of the guild members."[76] As part of the New York contingency's willingness to eschew New York State, two guild members, Tex Sullivan and Willie Gilzenberg, attempted to move their boxing promotion out of New York's St. Nick's Arena and present five shows at the Baltimore Coliseum starting January 23.[77] Whatever feelings of self-assurance the guild and its members may have held, they would soon evaporate. Just two days later, Norris went public with his position on the commission's edict. He was a man in a protracted legal struggle with the US government with his entire boxing empire at stake. His business was alleged to be an illegal monopoly. Locking horns with the State of New York at this time would not be a prudent move.

Norris met at length with Commissioner Helfand and offered the IBC's full and continued cooperation with the NYSAC and its laws. He assured that the IBC would continue to promote in New York. Two cards, one at the Garden and the other in Syracuse, were already being touted.

Adding to the wound inflicted by New York State was Governor Theodore McKendlin of Maryland. He persuaded the boxing commission of that state to deny boxing promotional licenses to Sullivan and Gilzenberg.[78] The commission had already approved the

Baltimore promotions. However, through his relationship with the Baltimore Chief of Police, Helfand was able to uncover a connection between Frankie Carbo and Sullivan and Gilzenberg's new Baltimore promotional partners, Benny Trotta and Angelo Munafo. When the name of the notorious Carbo reached the ears of the governor, he intervened with the commission.[79,80] Acknowledging potential retribution from local managers, Norris indicated that he had already informed his sponsors to be ready to broadcast substitute programming in the event of a last-minute "illness" on the part of one of the scheduled boxers.[81]

Almost immediately, Al Weill, manager of the most important fighter in the world, Rocky Marciano, whisked a telegram from Los Angeles to the guild advising of his resignation. Cagey as always, Weill was vague regarding motive: "I wanted to do it. I have no other comment." None was needed. It was simple. No Norris, no television contracts. No television contracts, less money.

If Norris was the financial steel that had given the guild its inner strength, then Weill was the cement that symbolically held together its façade. Without either, it would collapse. When Weill exited, managers Chick Wergeles, Bobby Gleason, Hymie Wallman, and Eddie Walker were right behind him. Others followed. Soon, there was nothing left for the sport to do but bulldoze the remnants of the guild.[82]

The demise of the guild, and that of the International Boxing Club a few years later, were each, in part, byproducts of the greed to control television money. The issues of whether to televise a bout or not based upon TV's effect on the live gate, and the distribution of television money, would be placed on hold as boxing ebbed from the national television scene in the early-1960s. During the 1950s, it was established that the additional revenue obtained by a closed-circuit telecast of a major fight could carry the financial aspects of a promotion, making theatrical television the preferred option in those instances. The size of the live gate became a secondary matter (see Chapter 12).

When television reemerged during the Muhammad Ali era, the economics of boxing on commercial television had changed. Because of the continued growth of the potential television audience and a greater abundance of sponsorship money, commercial television would also become a more viable option. As with closed-circuit broadcasts, the money generated from the live gate became a less significant factor in determining whether a bout should be telecast on commercial television.

This is not to say that in all instances the television model was preferred, only that television was more frequently a favored choice due to the size of the related money. Additionally, transactions were packaged to better insulate the boxer against anomalous financial results. This alleviated the prior problem of a smaller live gate or token television fee that adversely affected the boxers' overall compensation. And whether a fight was broadcast on commercial television, via closed-circuit or not at all, the common refrain of "Show Me the Money" would continue.

Chapter 14

THE RISE AND FALL OF A BOXING MONOPOLY

In June 1937, Joe Louis knocked out a game but outclassed Jimmy Braddock to win the heavyweight championship of the World. Eleven years later, Louis made his twenty-fifth consecutive title defense by knocking out Jersey Joe Walcott in their rematch. During all that time, Mike Jacobs, through his Twentieth Century Sporting Club, was the foremost boxing promoter in the world. With the promotion of the Louis-Conn rematch in June, 1946, a financial juggernaut, it appeared that "Uncle Mike"'s grasp on the boxing world was firm, and his longevity as top promoter certain.

This dominance would change in December, 1946, when Jacobs suffered a stroke. During 1947 and 1948, Jacobs was forced to take a more behind-the-scenes role in the company's operation, and Twentieth Century pushed forward with Jacobs's cousin, Sol Strauss, as acting president.

With Jacobs ailing and the retirement of Louis imminent, a power vacuum was forming. Simultaneously, the new medium of television was changing the promotion of boxing. Not only did TV have far-reaching financial ramifications, but it was poised to revolutionize the very depiction of the sport.

Jacobs, through his relationship with Madison Square Garden, and its contracts with NBC and DuMont, was in control of the majority of televised boxing. Other players such as CBS, a national network, were waiting in the wings. Local stations sprinkled along the Eastern seaboard and throughout the Midwest were arriving on the scene. With Jacobs's power waning, it was all ripe for the taking.

The first group to attempt supplanting Jacobs as boxing's latest power broker to capitalize on television's financial promise was the Tournament of Champions, Inc. (T of C). The Tournament of Champions, organized in 1947, was led by seven wealthy individuals including Lawrence Lowman of the Columbia Broadcasting System. While none of the members had a boxing background, the entrepreneurial group realized the sport presented an excellent opportunity to exploit the television industry. To advance their cause, they secured Andy Niederreiter as the matchmaker.[1]

This new promotional group quickly drew attention when it outbid the Garden and staged three bouts in the Garden's backyard across the river in New Jersey. Its biggest show was the promotion of the memorable third Graziano-Zale fight in Jersey City. However, the fight was a nontelevised affair.[2]

The outfit offered its first indoor show on October 21, 1948, in a welterweight match that pitted the "blonde and lanky" Charlie Fusari of Irvington, New Jersey, against another local hero, Tippy Larkin of Garfield. Referee Paul Cavalier stopped the televised match in the sixth round, with a battered and reeling Larkin still on his feet. It was the second trouncing that the veteran of over 130 fights had taken from his younger opponent in as many years.

The first Larkin-Fusari bout was held at Madison Square Garden, and the use of these two particular fighters by T of C in the rematch signaled to Jacobs and the Garden that they had direct promotional competition. By selling the television rights of the event for $7,500, it was clear that T of C could compete for the promotion of televised contests, as well.[3] T of C furthered its promotional position by televising other bouts in a deal with CBS, airing its contests in direction competition with the Garden's Friday night Gillette fights.[4]

Fusari, young and a hot prospect, was a sound future investment for T of C. Still, in order to rapidly breach the upper echelon of talent for its televised bouts, they needed an established star attraction. The solution was their promotion of a bout between Sugar Ray Robinson, the biggest draw of the new post-Louis era, and Bronxite Steve Belloise. The match would be televised by CBS, who already owned an interest in the Garden. Playing both ends against the middle, and believing that T of C was on the verge of supplanting Twentieth Century as the Garden's partner, CBS now acquired partial ownership of T of C.[5]

At the time of CBS's acquisition, the fate of T of C was in the balance. George Kletz was the only surviving investor of the original seven millionaires. However, CBS and Kletz, along with two other new partners, Music Corporation of America and Allied Syndicates, Inc., were anticipating their financial exploitation of the new television network, which would be extending from New York to St. Louis the following month.[6]

While the Robinson-Belloise match was to take place in New Jersey, T of C had no intention of remaining on the other side of the Hudson River. They announced their plan to apply for a license from the New York State Athletic Commission with their sights set on promoting top boxing matches in New York, including heavyweight championship bouts.[7]

The assault on Twentieth Century by T of C had been revitalized, but when Andy Niederreiter quit as matchmaker, T of C suspended its operations through the end of 1948. T of C maintained a skeleton staff of three. Somewhat embarrassingly, one was a ticket seller charged with refunding tickets for the company's stellar attraction, Robinson-Belloise, which had been cancelled.[8]

A month later, Twentieth Century countered its reconstituted rival by showcasing Belloise in a Garden main event against Frenchman Robert Villemain in his American debut. Maintaining its course, T of C forged ahead, making inroads into New York with the completion of plans to lease the Manhattan Center with its seating capacity of 5,000.[9]

In January of 1949, T of C made its New York debut by televising the heavyweight rematch between Curtis "The Hatchetman" Sheppard and Rusty Payne. The first fight was a Pittsburgh brawl in which The Hatchetman, living up to his name, floored Payne with his famous right, requiring the limp body to be dragged back to his corner.[10]

The boxing vultures had arrived at Jacobs's doorstep, waiting with eager anticipation for his fistic demise. However, while Jacobs was being scrutinized by T of C to see just how much life was left in him, a more potent adversary emerged from the wilds of the boxing world: the International Boxing Club.

As mentioned earlier, the IBC was a triumvirate of business and sporting personalities including James D. Norris, Arthur M. Wirtz, and Joe Louis. Norris and Wirtz were well situated to commandeer boxing's promotional reins due to their extensive control over major American fight arenas. The pair owned, or had a controlling interest in, the Chicago Stadium, the Detroit Olympia, and the St. Louis Arena. They had made a substantial investment in the Cincinnati Gardens and held leases to promote in the Omaha Coliseum and the Indianapolis Arena. The duo also owned a sizable amount of stock in the Madison Square Garden Corporation. Through the IBC, Norris and Wirtz paid Louis a six-figure sum to retire and become a director of the IBC. The recently retired heavyweight champion "personally hand-picked" Jersey Joe Walcott and Ezzard Charles to fight for his vacated title in June, 1949, at an IBC promotion in its stronghold of Chicago.

Irving Schoenwald and Jack Begun had previously held exclusive rights to promote professional boxing shows in Chicago Stadium since November 1942. When the IBC promoted the Walcott-Charles fight at Comiskey Park, the two important Chicago promoters were dealt out by Norris and Wirtz. Not only did they run the IBC, they also held high-ranking positions with Chicago Stadium. The result was the termination of the contract with Schoenwald and Begun and Chicago Stadium's new agreement with the IBC to promote ten dates in the 1949–50 indoor season. Beginning in September, all of the bouts would be broadcast on radio and televised pursuant to contracts that the IBC held with NBC and CBS.[11] The IBC's ability to use its multiple positions of power in concert with one another, as they did with the forcing out of Schoenwald and Begun, would become its modus operandi.

Just a month prior to the IBC's promotion of the Charles-Walcott contest, an era in boxing ended. An already physically spent Jacobs, abandoned by his meal ticket Louis, who had retired and aligned with Norris, had neither the strength nor the emotional will to continue in the fight game. For $100,000 he capitulated to the Garden and agreed to the cancellation of the Twenty Century's exclusive lease to promote boxing at the arena.

After twelve years, Madison Square Garden needed a new dance partner. The IBC was waiting. As it already possessed expansive promotional ties to other arenas throughout the country, New York was the only jewel missing from the boxing crown it desired.[12] Although the T of C was still an obstacle for the IBC, its meteoric rise was fading over the horizon. After only promoting two championship bouts for its investors in two years—Zale-Graziano III and Zale-Cerdan—its financial backers, CBS amongst them, had become disenchanted and unsupportive.

As the decade of the 1940s was drawing to a close, the state of promotional affairs was formalized. An announcement by MSG president John Reed Kilpatrick that Twentieth Century was "voluntarily" relinquishing its rights to promote at the Garden to the Madison Square Garden Corporation itself was coupled with the news that the Tournament of Champions, Inc., was up for sale and might be absorbed by a newly formed Garden-IBC promotional combine. The timing of these developments could not have been better for the International Boxing Club. The next month would bring about the expiration of the existing NBC television contract, allowing for a fresh deal with the new promotional lineup. With the soon-to-be absorbed T of C being partially owned by CBS, it was anticipated that both NBC and CBS would figure in the new television arrangement.[13]

When the details were finally ironed out, NBC would continue to televise all Friday night Garden bouts, including those from St. Nicholas Arena, with the Gillette Safety Razor Company as its sponsor. (ABC would carry those same fights on the radio, also partnering with Gillette.) CBS was given both television and radio rights for the Monday night fights from St. Nick's. Tentatively, the two networks were to share the television rights for "outdoor championship bouts."[14] The IBC would be the new television lineup's promoter.

T of C still held lease rights to the Polo Grounds and was planning to stage the La Motta-Cerdan middleweight clash there. As part of the realignment, the Garden secured the leases to both the Polo Grounds and Yankee Stadium through 1952.[15] In a most prophetic statement regarding the purchase, one journalist wrote, "The greatest monopoly in the history of boxing will be created with the purchase of the Tournament of Champions by the new Madison Square Garden-IBC combine."[16]

When T of C was moved aside, the La Motta-Cerdan fight was switched from New York to Briggs Stadium in Detroit. Significantly, the IBC. did not promote the bout. Instead, the match was staged by The Olympia Stadium Corp. of which James D. Norris was vice president.[17] The choice of venue appeared to be a mere technicality, the significance of which was undoubtedly lost upon the pedestrian boxing fan. However, it underscored an important fact: the real individual power in the new order lay with Norris, who would do business with the Garden's Kilpatrick but was unquestionably the more dominant of the two. Similarly, Norris was equal partners with Wirtz in name only. It was Norris who pulled the strings. James D. Norris *was* the IBC and had become boxing's biggest power broker.

In the beginning of its promotional reign, before it was disparagingly called "Octopus, Inc.," the International Boxing Club enjoyed a honeymoon period with the press. This enabled them to maintain a positive public image for a couple of years. Norris was viewed by many as a multimillionaire sportsman who wasn't in the game to exploit the sport for money. He was educated, polite, and could be charming when desired. His criminal associations within the sport of boxing were not yet front and center. The bottom line was that the IBC had successfully courted the public's favor by providing an unprecedented amount of boxing through the new medium of television. By 1951, its promotions could be found on all three major television networks: NBC, CBS, and DuMont.

Ironically, as television brought boxing to new heights through its cameras in the ring, its lenses were simultaneously tearing down the sport through its scrutiny on the outside.

On a televised debate carried over NBC in September of 1951, Truman Gibson, the attorney and secretary of the IBC went head-to-head with US Senator Harry P. Cain, a Republican from Washington, in a program titled *Should Professional Boxing Be Investigated?*[18] Negative depictions of boxing on television would continue throughout the decade, reaching their zenith in 1959 with a Congressional investigation commonly known as the "Kefauver Crime Hearings."

In the early-1950s, boxing wasn't the only big game the government hunted. Similar to boxing, the National Football League (NFL) and other sports leagues used television restrictions as part of their business models. The Justice Department developed a keen interest in their affairs, as well. In October 1951, Assistant Attorney General H. Graham Morison, in charge of the Antitrust Division of the Department of Justice, filed a lawsuit against the NFL. Morison alleged that its twelve teams violated the Sherman Antitrust Act by boycotting select stations and "blacking out" telecasts and broadcasts of their games in certain areas. Morison noted that the suit was brought against the NFL because it presented its best legal case.

It was revealed that success in this action would lead to suits in other sports' telecasts and broadcasts that were restricted, including college football, professional baseball, and boxing. Further, Morison explained that legal action was prompted by complaints from the public to the antitrust division.[19]

In fact, the Justice Department had already launched its official attack on boxing. A day before the suit against the NFL was filed, a grand jury had been convened to hear evidence regarding whether a monopoly existed in the sport of boxing. During the inquiry, which lasted five months, officers of the IBC appeared before the grand jury. While other promoters also appeared, they were not the actual target of the investigation. However, they served to provide crucial evidence regarding practices in the sport. This evidence advanced the grand jury's actual focus, which was squarely on the IBC. However, at no time was the IBC actually named as the government's target.[20] Some of the notable members of the fistic fraternity to give testimony during the inquiry were Sugar Ray Robinson; his manager, George Gainsford; Nat Fleischer, the editor of *The Ring Magazine*; and Dan Dowd, Executive Secretary of the New York State Athletic Commission.[21]

At the time, boxing was a multimillion-dollar business. The IBC was the recipient of a substantial portion of the industry's revenues. Its contracts for the broadcast of Wednesday and Friday night fights alone totaled more than an estimated million dollars.[22] In the face of a potential lawsuit, the IBC maintained a sunny facade with front man Norris, who stated, "We're in the clear and welcome the investigation. My door is open all the time and we're prepared to give wholehearted cooperation."[23] Behind the scenes, the IBC was bracing itself for what would prove to be a seven-year siege by the Justice Department.

In March of 1952, a civil suit was filed in Federal Court charging the IBC of Illinois and New York, two of its directors, Norris and Wirtz, and the Madison Square Garden Corporation with conspiring to restrain professional championship boxing matches in the United States. At the time, Norris and Wirtz controlled 20 percent Class A common stock and the Garden owned 40 percent, giving those defendants a majority of stock in the IBC. Joe Louis owned 20 percent of the Class A stock; he was not named as a defendant, as he was expected to be called as a witness.[24]

The government contended that the conspiracy was advanced through the promotion of twenty-one major professional championship bouts beginning in June of 1949. These matches produced a gross income of 4.5 million dollars from radio, television, and motion-picture fees as well as live gate receipts. This figure was substantial considering that the entire sport generated revenues of 15 million dollars for that same period, much from nontitle bouts that were not the subject of the suit.

The government alleged that the conspiracy was furthered by a number of actions. Cited were some of the preliminary moves made by the IBC: the elimination of its major competitor for the promotion of championship matches, the Tournament of Champions, Inc.; and the acquisition of its exclusive lease to promote matches at the Polo Grounds and promotional rights to middleweight champion Marcel Cerdan.

It was also alleged that the conspiracy was furthered through the IBC's numerous exclusive contracts. Principal among these was its exclusive promotional rights. These were held on most, if not all, of the major arenas where successful promotion of championship matches could be staged. Equally instrumental were the exclusive contractual agreements maintained with six of the eight champions and many of the contenders for each weight class in the sport.

The suit claimed that the conspiracy almost entirely excluded other promoters from promoting championship bouts. Additionally, it was maintained that fighters were excluded from competing for championship bouts unless they agreed to a three-year exclusive contract. The contracts, it was argued, had the effect of preventing the fighters from using other promoters should they win the title. It was also claimed that the benefits of competition had been denied to radio broadcasters, television stations, motion-picture manufacturers and distributors, other arena owners, and the public at large.[25] The New York State Athletic Commission piggybacked on the government's suit, scheduling a hearing to determine whether the IBC's license should be revoked or suspended on the grounds that its acts were detrimental to the sport of boxing.[26]

For once, boxing was in prestigious company, albeit under dubious circumstances. Other commercial industries sued for violation of antitrust laws in 1952 included major manufacturers and motion-picture companies. It was alleged that well-known soap makers Proctor & Gamble, Colgate-Palmolive-Peet, and Lever Brothers had successfully conspired for a quarter of a century, reducing their competition's share of the market to less than 1 percent. Columbia Pictures Corporation, Twentieth Century Fox Film Corporation, and Warner Brothers Pictures Inc., along with nine other major motion-picture studios and distributors, were also sued by the government for an alleged conspiracy to prevent the use of 16-millimeter feature films on television programs.[27]

While claims that professional boxing constituted a monopoly arose contemporaneously with antitrust claims levied against pro football, boxing's fate was integrally bound with legal precedents involving the sport of baseball.

In 1922, Supreme Court Justice Oliver Wendell Holmes, a fan of the national pastime, took the position on behalf of the court that baseball was not "trade or commerce among the states" within the meaning of the antitrust laws. The travel of the players between states was found to be "incidents" of otherwise local exhibitions. In subsequent years, other sports were not brought squarely within this ruling. This created an open issue as to whether or not their professional businesses might constitute a business that could be in violation of the Sherman Act and deemed an illegal monopoly.[28]

In February of 1954, James D. Norris and the other boxing defendants won a major victory when the US District Court, following Holmes's precedent and its recent confirmation, ruled in their favor. Professional boxing, like professional baseball, was adjudged not to be a business within the meaning of the antitrust laws and thus exempt from those laws. While the government had argued that the new issues of broadcasting and television had distinguished their case from the court's 1922 decision, this court was not willing to make such a distinction. The Justice Department promptly appealed the court's decision to the United States Supreme Court.[29] Attorneys for the boxing defendants claimed that the federal government was using its case against boxing to get at baseball through the back door. It was argued that if boxing was found to be a business under the purview of antitrust laws, it could serve as a basis to mount an offensive to reverse the existing baseball ruling.[30]

The district court's ruling would be the last major decision in favor of the defendants. Less than a year later, in January of 1955, The United States Supreme Court reversed the district court's decision, ruling that boxing was a business under the Sherman Act. Therefore, boxing concerns could now be sued for violation of those laws. In support of the court's 6–2 decision, Chief Justice Earl Warren found that the 1922 baseball decision did not exempt all businesses "that involve exhibitions of an athletic nature" from the Sherman Act. In sum, boxing was found never to have been exempt from those laws. Whether an exemption should be granted presently was a separate issue entirely that only Congress—and not the court—could decide.[31] This court, unlike the lower court, believed that television broadcasting was a factor. They acknowledged the government's contention that 25 percent of revenue for championship fights made from radio and television in and of itself constituted interstate commerce.

The decision was a pivotal blow to the boxing defendants. Now that boxing was categorized within the scope of antitrust laws, the government could proceed with its suit in the Federal District Court. They would be given the opportunity to prove its claim that the defendants were violating those laws by operating a monopoly. In response to the decision, the IBC's Chicago office issued the following statement: "We are confident that the court will vindicate our position that, in presenting seven or eight championship fights a year, we do not operate an illegal monopoly within the meaning of the Sherman Act."[32]

Reactions to the court's decision depended on the source's perspective. George Barton, former president of the National Boxing Association and boxing commissioner in Minnesota, felt the ruling would bring about the eventual determination that a monopoly existed and that it was "the first step in the rebirth of the small fight promoter." This notion echoed the sentiments of many boxing industry members and dyed-in-the-wool fans who felt that the

IBC-television era had suffocated the fight club circuit, casting aside promoters and practically eliminating the life blood of the sport—the fighters themselves.[33]

However, others did not subscribe to the notion that the IBC was at the root of all of boxing's ills. To the contrary, one astute scribe, Arch Ward of the *Chicago Tribune*, believed that the promotional group had served the interests of the national boxing community by breaking the long-time stranglehold that New York had on the sport. He noted that the IBC had brought ten championship fights to Chicago, while in a similar time span, its predecessor, Mike Jacobs and the Twentieth Century Sporting Club, had only promoted two in the Windy City. The argument that cities like Philadelphia, Detroit, and San Francisco had similarly benefited through the diffusion of boxing to their local venues was also offered. "If current operation is a restraint of trade, let's have more of it," the sardonic Ward offered.[34]

"So the court voted six to two. Well, at least it was a split decision," Norris had quipped in private after the court had ruled against the IBC[35] Outwardly, Norris may have been glib, but serious times were ahead. Fifteen months later, on April 25, 1956, Norris and Wirtz sat in Judge Sylvester J. Ryan's courtroom in New York's Foley Square, to face the government's contentions: "This case presents classic instances of violations of antitrust laws. A group of men have banded together to seek domination of a field. In this, they have succeeded. It is submitted that the equity powers of this Court should be invoked to dissolve that amalgamation of powers and to enjoin the illegal practices through which it was achieved."[36]

On March 8, 1957, the court found that the defendants had acted in concert to conspire to monopolize the sport of boxing. This was achieved through stock ownership and voting power that the defendants used to dictate not only the elections of directors, officers, and management of various corporations under their control, but the functioning of these corporations that were specifically interrelated for the purpose of establishing and maintaining a monopoly. In other words, Norris and Wirtz controlled boxing in Chicago and the Midwest, as the Madison Square Garden Boxing Corporation did in

New York, and purposefully worked together to the illegal exclusion of their competition.[37]

Central to the monopolistic claim against the IBC was their control of television and radio rights. In an effort to create the illusion of separation of control, they had set up a corporation called Telradio Promotions, Inc. The court saw through the ruse. In an outline of his decree, Judge Ryan detailed how the complex matrix of corporations, principals, and stockholders acted in concert to control boxing on television: "With respect to the control of television and radio rights, a mere corporate structure change has taken place. A new corporation has been formed, Telradio Promotions, Inc., and its entire issued capital stock is owned by Chicago Stadium Corporation. To Telradio has been given the right to sell television and radio rights in connection with the Wednesday night television series. Thus Wirtz and Norris (the sole shareholders of the Chicago Stadium Corporation) control Telradio and IBC-Illinois through Chicago Stadium Corporation, and with it the Wednesday night television series, and through IBC-New York and Madison Square Garden (where Norris, Wirtz, and their allied interests still hold a controlling interest), these same combinations control the Friday night series. Truman Gibson is still found as one of the liaison between New York and Chicago. He is still an employee and Secretary of IBC-NY and IBC-Illinois, and is now, in addition, an employee and secretary of Telradio Promotions, Inc."[38]

The court determined that these interlocking individuals and corporations acted in concert to monopolize the promotion of championship boxing contests. Since May 15, 1953, the date of the Marciano-Walcott rematch, there had been thirty-seven championship bouts contested in the United States. The defendants had exercised promotional control over twenty-four, or about two-thirds of these contests.

The promotional monopoly was significant, but the monopoly of television broadcasts was even greater. Thirty-two of the thirty-seven championship bouts during that period—all but the five that were outdoor contests—were telecast by the defendants on their Wednesday or Friday night shows.[39]

In December of 1957, the IBC announced a two-year extension to the Friday night fights series with Gillette. The contract appeared encouraging; it was the first time in the history of televised boxing that a contract was made on more than a year-to-year basis. The new deal would bring the sponsors $10.4 million, and the IBC $24,500 weekly.[40] The Wednesday night fights were no longer associated with the Pabst Blue Ribbon Brewing Company. Under the sponsorship of Mennen Co. and Miles Laboratories. the telecasts were also recently extended through May 1959, with an option through September of that year.[41]

Another TV milestone occurred in September 1958 when Mickey Crawford met Ralph "Tiger" Jones in a ten-round contest at the Chicago Stadium, marking the 400th bout telecast in the weekly series that began on CBS in May1950 and moved to ABC in June of 1955. The contest also marked Jones's forty-sixth nationally televised fight.[42]

Such obvious signs of a healthy relationship between boxing and television were nothing more than a cheap veneer. Judge Ryan's decision against the IBC and its affiliated interests had both immediate and practical implications. The decree had enjoined the Garden from promoting more than two championship fights a year for the next five years. Wirtz and Norris were placed under the same promotional restraints.[43,44] The IBC was no longer in control of the promotional end of the sport; it had been reduced to a mere player.

Apparently emboldened by the success of the federal suit, the Callahan Athletic Club of Boston and its matchmaker, Sam Silverman, sued the IBC, Norris, Madison Square Garden, and others for nine million dollars for attempting to keep the Callahan from promoting title fights and selling related radio, television, and movie rights.[45] Later that year, the National Hockey League Players' Association filed a $3 million antitrust suit in federal court against the NHL, Madison Square Garden, and Norris, who held interests in professional hockey concerns. Norris was under siege from all quarters.[46]

The diminished role of the IBC was on display in October 1958, when Virgil Atkins signed to fight Don Jordan in a welterweight match in Los Angeles that would have undoubtedly been promoted or copromoted by the IBC. Instead, the event was promoted solely by the Olympic Auditorium. The IBC, however, remained in the media realm and obtained the television and radio broadcasting rights to the fight.[47] It merely played the last good card it held in what was, ultimately, a losing hand.

The death knell for the various corporations of the International Boxing Club, James D. Norris, and Arthur M. Wirtz came on January 12, 1959, when they lost their appeal to the US Supreme Court. In accordance with the final judgment issued in the antitrust case, the IBC began the process of dissolution. At the end of January, Wirtz, president of the Chicago Stadium Corporation, which owned the IBC stock of the Illinois faction, announced the dissolution of one of the pillars of the IBC empire, the IBC of Illinois. The IBC of New York was also required to dissolve immediately. Additionally, Norris and Wirtz were ordered to sell all of their stock in the Madison Square Garden Corporation. A new era of independent boxing promotion had officially launched.[48,49]

Cus D'Amato, long-time opponent of the IBC and manager of heavyweight champion Floyd Patterson, found the court decision to be "the first good break I've gotten. . . . It may force one of the weekly television shows into the hands of an independent promoter to whom I will make available the heavyweight champion, providing I can trust the promoter," he explained.[50]

The democratization of boxing promotion was fraught with the same political pitfalls as the democratization of nations. Stability, security, and the delivery of services inherent under the dictatorship of Norris now became glaring concerns. True, independent promoters would have their opportunity. Nevertheless, Norris left an enormous vacuum to fill. Without a large central power such as the IBC, it was unclear who would provide the programming which the networks and sponsors required. A voluminous product would be needed. It would have to be delivered consistently and made available prepackaged well in advance of the programming season so as to provide the financial security that television sponsors demanded. An additional pitfall of the new competition was that it would undoubtedly spawn self-interest. As promoters each vied to develop their own provincial empires, interests of the sport as a whole might be compromised or forgotten completely.

Norris declared that the Supreme Court ruling would prevent a promotional organization from growing large enough to guarantee regular fights, thus leaving sponsors scrambling to deal with a different promoter week to week. "I don't see how any promoter can guarantee continuity. That's what we sought—continuity. We had two weekly TV fight programs for nine years. That's 104 fights a year. In nine years, we never missed a fight. We had substitution on top of substitution, but we never missed a fight."[51]

With the demise of the IBC, the Garden reconstituted itself, stylized as Madison Square Boxing, Inc., with Harry Markson as general manager of boxing. Friday night fights from the Garden televised by NBC continued. However, the demise of the IBC had been a continuing factor in the precipitous decline of televised boxing, which began to unravel that same year—1959—with CBS dropping its national TV coverage of the sport.

Gillette had sponsored fights regularly on NBC television since 1944 with the telecast of the Pep-Wright contest. In the beginning of 1960, NBC informally advised Gillette that it no longer was interested in televising the bouts from Madison Square Garden. NBC gave no reason for their decision, but it was reported that they were dissatisfied with both the quality of fights and the ratings. Gillette had a separate contract with Madison Square Garden, and Markson reported that they had received no word from the sponsor, but, television or not, bouts at the Garden would continue.[52]

Gillette eventually struck a new one-year deal, with an option to renew, with ABC to keep their boxing series alive. ABC would telecast the bouts and move the fights to Saturday evenings. The last Friday NBC television and radio broadcasts would be held June 24 with the ABC bouts commencing in September. ABC would not be carrying the fights on radio. The bouts would continue to originate from the Garden. Yet another reason for NBC's departure was reported: corruption and the involvement of organized crime in the sport.[53,54]

On October 8, 1960, Saturday fights were launched with Kenny Lane squaring off against Len Matthews in Los Angeles. ABC reverted the series back to Friday nights with the Willie Pastrano-Gregory Peralta fight at Miami Beach on September 14, 1963.[55] Shortly afterward, it was announced that the following fall, ABC would terminate its boxing coverage. A number of familiar woes was cited as the reason: waning interest in boxing, the lack of quality fighters to sustain championship and other high-level matches, the existence of an unsavory element in the sport, and the economics of television.[56]

The historic Gillette Safety Razor Company-Madison Square Garden run bowed out on August 21, 1964, with the Johnny Persol-Henry Hank bout. Gillette's last fight under the Garden contract, featuring Wayne Thornton vs. Bobo Olson, was not staged at the Garden, but in San Francisco. ABC finished the series two weeks later, without the Garden or Gillette, by telecasting the Jose Torres-Gomeo Brennan bout from Miami Beach. Gillette's former cosponsor, the General Cigar Company, acted as the lone sponsor.[57]

A multitude of factors brought about the end of national televised boxing. The removal of the International Boxing Club from the scene undoubtedly made it more challenging to consistently fill fight dates each week on one or more programs. Also, the death of the small fight clubs, once the breeding ground for new talent, made it increasingly difficult to consistently provide a product for television regardless of the promoter. Concomitant with this was the reduced pool of quality fighters, another harsh effect of the reduced number of fight clubs.

These problems on the supply side were balanced by an equal number of issues regarding demand. Quite simply, the public had reached a juncture at which they were losing interest in televised boxing. Whereas the Friday night fights' share of the television audience was 31 percent in 1952, a decade later it had dropped to 11.2 percent.[58] Here, too, there were many contributing factors. Naturally, the quality of matches was also an issue for the viewers. Other influences were more tangential but no less significant. Concern over criminal involvement in the sport had increased throughout the 1950s and was only punctuated to millions by Senator Estes Kefauver's probe on live television.

Parallel to the violent overtones outside of the ring was that which occurred on its inside. The ring death of Benny "Kid" Paret at the hands of Emile Griffith a few years after the Kefauver hearings was one of the most graphic to date. Improved camera work featuring close-ups were repeatedly pounded into the consciousness of the television audience through the use of videotape replay.

Interests and tastes were also changing. The 1958 NFL championship game between the Baltimore Colts and the New York Giants elevated professional football to new heights, contributing to a reshaping of viewer sports preferences. The debut of *ABC's Wide World of Sports* in 1961, with its diverse sports programming, would have a similar effect.

Changes in viewing habits were partially a function of changing demographics. At the end of boxing's Golden Age on television, over 40 percent of the US population was nineteen years old or younger, and advertisers were taking note.[59] For all of these reasons, sponsors found that associating their products with the sport of boxing was no longer a profitable approach to doing business.

The end of network television coverage saw a sharp divide in opinion in regard to its effect on the sport. One faction was comprised of reactionaries who believed the end of television as a force in boxing would create a revival of grassroots talent, live audiences, and improve the general health of the game. Joey Giardello was of this mind. "At first a lot of guys are going to starve," the middleweight champion at the time admitted in 1963, "but then the little clubs will spring up again, boxing will get to be a neighborhood thing again, and promoters will have to come up with good fights to pack a house."[60]

Independent promoter Murray Goodman predicted that the long-term effect would result in the renaissance of boxing. He believed in the promotional competition the new open market would provide and that closed-circuit bouts would continue to support the upper echelon of the sport.

Others believed that television had become an indispensable part of the sport. It was true that Madison Square Garden had exerted a disproportionate influence through its television ties extending beyond New York, often to the chagrin of fighters, managers, and promoters. But without them in place, benefits would have been lost.

The Garden had been spending $100,000 annually to subsidize more than a dozen small boxing clubs throughout the country. They were amongst the few that the sport had not cannibalized. Locally, they had subsidized St. Nick's Arena until a few years earlier, and they were still providing aid to Sunnyside Gardens in Queens and the Union City State Garden in Union City, New Jersey. "Without television revenue," John F. X. Condon of the Garden explained, "it wouldn't seem feasible to support those clubs or even continue our own regular weekly boxing shows."[61]

The demise of televised boxing would prove to be short-lived. Despite all of boxing's self-inflicted wounds, the incessant adverse publicity, a seemingly indifferent public, and the abandonment of the sport by networks and sponsors, this Rasputin of sports would soon rise again to exert its influence on the televised sporting scene.

Chapter 15

THE INFLUENCE OF ORGANIZED CRIME ON TELEVISED BOXING

The criminal element and organized crime have always been a part of boxing. Highly unregulated, particularly in its early years, the sport was the perfect landscape for criminals to operate from within yet still remain under the radar of law enforcement. Fixed matches were not uncommon during the early days of gloved fighting. Several major scandals led to legislation that prohibited or proscribed boxing in the United States for the first quarter of the century.

In New York, corruption contributed to the repeal of the Horton Boxing Law in September 1900. This ushered in an eleven-year lull of fighting under the Lewis Law, which only permitted boxing on a club membership basis.[1]

In Chicago that same year, the Joe Gans-Terry McGovern fiasco saw the "Old Master" Gans "knocked out" in two rounds. Immediately after the fight, the city council banned all boxing in Chicago except for club membership bouts. This scandal put big-time boxing out of business in the Windy City until it made its dramatic return with the "Battle of the Long Count" a quarter-century later.[2]

Even as late as the early-1930s, the fixed fight was selectively utilized at the highest level of the sport. Corruption would play an instrumental role in positioning Primo Carnera to become the heavyweight champion of the world. Televised boxing merely inherited this legacy. When the television industry became commercially relevant at the end of World War II, boxing became an early, but dubious, business partner.

Legitimate and criminal members of the boxing community were transposed upon one another in such a way that, in many instances, they became indistinguishable. In this sense, boxing's field of play was resolutely fixed. In order to build his boxing television empire during the 1950s, James D. Norris, who exploded onto the boxing scene at the very moment that television arrived in earnest, had no choice but to navigate this reality. Years later, Norris would sum up the gravity of the challenge that he undertook: "Even if Cardinal Spellman got into boxing, in two weeks he would be a discredited man."[3]

Long before Norris became a major player in boxing and television, the seeds had been sown for Norris's contact with the fight game and ultimately its underworld. In 1935, his father purchased Chicago Stadium, a major fight venue. Sitting at ringside, Norris came into contact which many fight managers. He would soon open his large wallet to Nate Lewis and Jack Hurley in their steering of their heavyweights, Harry Thomas and Lem Franklin.[4]

Norris was a legitimate businessman, and his eventual involvement with those in organized crime, while not unforeseeable, can be viewed as somewhat of a seduction. Truman Gibson, Norris's right-hand man at the International Boxing Club, served as his prime liaison with the unsavory side. He would bring Norris shoulder-to-shoulder with the notorious yet intriguing Frankie Carbo.

Carbo had both the connections and the credentials of an underworld heavyweight. He was a soldier in the Lucchese crime family and, in his darkest moments, a cold-blooded killer. He was also as elusive as Willie Pep. He was indicted several times for murder including the killing of Murder Incorporated's Harry Greenberg a.k.a. "Big Greeney."

Fellow gangster Al "Tic Toc" Tannenbaum testified that Carbo had put five bullets in "Big Greeney," but the verdict was a hung jury. Another underling of Murder, Inc., Abe "Kid Twist" Reles, was to testify against Frankie in a second trial but ended up splattered on a Coney Island street. The most convincing evidence suggests he was tossed from a window of the Half Moon Hotel. Carbo was never retried.[5]

Carbo, who was known as "Mr. Gray" for his mane of steel-gray hair, was a holdover from the pretelevision era of Mike Jacobs. He began his twenty-year boxing odyssey alongside other mob-connected manager-types such as Ettore "Eddie" Coco, the manager of Rocky Graziano; James "Jimmy Doyle" Plumeri; Frankie Palermo; Harry "Champ" Segal; and Felix Bocchicchio, the manager of Jersey Joe Walcott. Collectively, they were known as "The Combination."[6]

During his run as the czar of the boxing underworld, Carbo was said to have some measure of control over Joey Giardello, Harold Gomes, Joe Brown, Davey Moore, Jimmy Carter, Virgil Akins, and Sonny Liston, or their managers.[7] New York detective Frank Marrone went so far as to say that "there was not any prominent fighter . . . he did not control or have a piece of."[8]

From the dining room of the Forrest Hotel down the street from Madison Square Garden, Carbo operated openly as the emperor of boxing's underworld, directly and indirectly controlling many of the top-level fighters in the sport. Paradoxically, he was both at once under the regular scrutiny of boxing journalists, assailed as a criminal bane, and yet seemingly immune from the power of boxing commissions and law enforcement.

During the early days of his influence, when the New York District Attorney or the New York State Athletic Commission did act, Carbo went into his "Will-o'-the-Wisp" act. The two august bodies were unable to connect the hoodlum to a bribe offered Rocky Graziano in his bout with Reuben Shank. Graziano was banned in New York, but when he defeated Zale at Chicago Stadium, Carbo could be found celebrating in Graziano's hotel suite.[9]

Around the same time, the New York District Attorney launched a massive investigation of boxing corruption in the state. Carbo was called to testify, as was one of his fighters, Johnny Greco, a Canadian welterweight. They appeared without consequence.

Carbo often seemed to be one step removed from the questionable activities of boxing. Lurking in the shadows of the sport, he was just deep enough in their murky cloak not to be identified as its assailant. This particular probe burrowed no deeper than Nat Rogers, the matchmaker of the Twentieth Century Sporting Club.

Rogers was forced out of boxing when the New York State Athletic Commission refused to renew his license for acts detrimental to the sport. He was found guilty of doing business with hoodlums who controlled prizefighters.[10] On the one end, he was the front man for Twentieth Century's promoter Mike Jacobs. On the other, he was the go-between for men like Frankie Carbo. His deliberate removal was a classic example of "killing the messenger." It highlighted the unwillingness, or at the very least the difficulty, authorities had reaching the criminal element lying beneath the surface of the sport.

The streetwise Carbo was a deft operator. He seemed to instinctively know when to press his advantage and when to assume a low profile. However, even when his judgment failed him, boxing's *omertà* seemed to provide the needed insulation. A case in point was an evening in 1947 when Carbo and underworld partner "Blinky" Palermo met with Jake La Motta in the basement of the Park Arena. It was just a week prior to La Motta's scheduled meeting with "Black Jack" Billy Fox. Fox was the gangsters' fighter, and the fix was in. In a lax moment, Carbo held the meeting in a public place, and at a fight area no less.[11]

The stink of the fight was palpable long before it was contested. The bout bore out all of the prefight suspicions, with La Motta going limp in the fourth round in a painfully obvious fraud. La Motta, Carbo, and Palermo were all called on the carpet. Carbo is said to have sauntered into the New York District Attorney's Office to give testimony. The trio gave the investigators nothing. Many others were called to testify. Little of value was given in return. La Motta received a small fine for failing to disclose a supposed spleen injury. Carbo, arrogant as ever, skated once again.[12]

James D. Norris inherited a multimillion-dollar sports empire from his father, but he was also bequeathed Frankie Carbo by the boxing world. Consequently, the IBC's recent business triumphs created only a façade of complete control of the sport. True, they had successfully toppled the Twentieth Century Sporting Club, and outmaneuvered the upstart Tournament of Champions to become the sport's premier promoter. They had also hijacked the porthole to Madison Square Garden and the opportunity to exploit the new medium of television. However, boxing's complex hierarchy was laced with interdependency. The IBC had merely inserted itself as its top rung.

Boxing during this era was as much about the acutely personal and codependent relationships of the fighters, their managers, and the de facto managers who were connected to organized crime as it was about the promoters, their licensed matchmakers, and the new medium of television and its sponsors.

So the die was cast for the television era with James D. Norris and the burgeoning IBC balancing precariously atop a deceitful foundation laid long ago by Frankie Carbo and his underworld cohorts.

The clear practical need for this construct was enough to justify its continuance. Norris and his IBC were new to the sport of boxing. Having squeezed Jacobs out of the Garden, only the talented Harry Markson remained for guidance. The IBC could tinker with—or even replace—parts of boxing's infrastructure, but operations at the ground level proved to be amorphous.

In and around the gyms, small fight clubs, and bars where fighters, managers, hoodlums, and hangers-on congregated, the sport of boxing was pollinated. This process was not only beyond the long reach of Norris, but perhaps best left untampered with.

Norris would yield to the practicalities of deferring certain responsibilities to Carbo and his kind, albeit unofficially. It was they who could maintain the sport's underpinnings—it was they who would, at least temporarily, ensure his own personal success. In testimony given to a Senate subcommittee years later, manager Herman Wallman would sum up the balance of power in boxing's new dual monarchy: Norris was the "big boss," and Carbo the "small boss."[13]

Organized crime influenced the telecast of boxing through several different means, and Carbo was the mob's chief manipulator of the new medium. At the end of Carbo's run as the "underworld czar of boxing," Senate subcommittee hearings would publicly confirm what every boxing insider already knew: Carbo had exerted a "wide influence . . . on the scheduling of televised bouts."[14]

While Carbo influenced what boxing was aired on NBC's Gillette-sponsored bouts, amongst other telecasts, the idea of complicity of the broadcasters and sponsors with Carbo would be specious. However, there was speculation. A typical joke of the time was that TV sponsors would suggest that "a bout last five commercials . . . I mean, at least five rounds." After the promotion of the Floyd Patterson-Pete Rademacher bust in Seattle in 1957, Jack Hurley was to have hinted that he could have received $200,000 from the television interests if he had guaranteed the fight would last six rounds. Patterson, in fact, retained his heavyweight title with a sixth-round knockout against Rademacher, who was making his professional debut. When a writer asked Hurley point-blank: "Did the television people suggest that the fight be fixed to last six rounds?" the wily old-timer backtracked, stating, "Well no, but they didn't unsuggest it, either."[15]

Notwithstanding Carbo's sway in bout selection for telecasts, the critical matchmaking function itself was never directly ceded to organized crime. Even the hoodlums realized that a certain expertise was required to keep the public interested in the steady diet of fighters for the television audience to feed on.

One of Harry Markson's early moves in his alliance with the IBC was to have Al Weill inserted as the Garden matchmaker. Not only did "The Vest" have a keen eye regarding fighters and their styles, but he had held the very same position several years prior. Carbo was friendly with Weill, so the decision would guarantee that Carbo's fighters would receive regular work on Garden cards.

In this manner, Carbo would gain influence over boxing's most important television program, the Garden's weekly Friday night fights, which were aired on NBC. The same preferential treatment could be relied on at the Garden's lesser television plants such as the St. Nicholas Arena.

Carbo would generally leave Weill to his own devices, but special circumstances would require Norris to call upon Carbo from time to time to exert his influence over Weill. On one such occasion Carbo facilitated a solution that helped the IBC repel congressional pressure and secure its relationship with its television sponsors.

Jack Hurley had instigated the crisis. The cantankerous manager was on a rant because his fighter, Harry Matthews, could not secure a title shot against light-heavyweight champion Joey Maxim. "We will never get the chance," Hurley told the press, "because Jim Norris and those people run a nice little store and monopolize everything." Hurley's seething resulted in a Senate probe followed by a federal grand jury investigation of the IBC. It also spawned a harsh reaction by the IBC's television sponsors.[16]

The sponsorship of their weekly televised bouts was now in jeopardy, so the IBC promptly offered Matthews a match against Maxim, but Hurley rejected its terms. With the federal investigation looming large, Norris concocted a Marciano-Matthews fight as a panacea. Now it was Weill's turn to pass. Norris had had enough. Carbo had a talk with Weill. A few days later, Weill came into Norris's office and said, "I'll take the match. If I hadn't talked to certain people, I would never have taken that match for you."[17]

Carbo was notorious for shifting alliances to satisfy self-interest. He would broker a deal in favor of his close associate, Walcott's manager Felix Bocchicchio, which would provide Walcott with a whopping $250,000 guarantee for the Marciano rematch. Weill's fighter, Marciano, despite being the champion, was given the short end of the stick, receiving his fee on a percentage basis of radio and television that amounted to only $166,060.30. "Norris did that to me," Weill bemoaned. Norris would later describe it as "a very foolish deal." Carbo had duped Weill and, as a consequence, Marciano.[18]

Al Weill served only a few years as the IBC matchmaker. He was a seasoned boxing expert and bended to the will of the IBC when it counted, but he was operating under a grave conflict as both Rocky

Marciano's manager and the matchmaker at Madison Square Garden. Weill hid behind his son, Marty, the manager of record for Marciano. He was eventually given an ultimatum by Robert K. Christenberry, the New York State Athletic Commissioner, who grew weary of the charade.

To replace Weill, who exited in 1952, the IBC pegged assistant matchmaker Billy Brown. Brown, whose real name was Dominick Mordini, also had experience as a manager and a promoter. He was previously involved in the management of heavyweight contender Nathan Mann, who was under the thumb of the powerful Dutch Schultz gang. Brown did not have the gravitas of a Weill in the boxing world. Carbo would exploit Brown's weaker status.

Norris described Brown as a man over whom Carbo had "considerable influence." In this respect, the IBC matchmaking change was a windfall for Carbo. It would help lead to a six-year run in which "Mr. Gray" would cut an even greater swath through the sport, before finally being brought to justice.[19]

Carbo always seemed to be bubbling just beneath the surface of an IBC promotion or the handling of one of their fighters. Frequently, he acted as a go-between for boxing's rank and file and Norris. Herman "Hymie the Mink" Wallman, a successful furrier who made a stab at the fight game, wanted Johnny Bratton as his fighter. The IBC delivered strictly on Carbo's say-so, and fronted the $12,500 purchase price for Wallman. In effect, Carbo was providing personal guarantees on IBC investments. Of course, a favor from Carbo meant you were beholden to him—or else. As Wallman later explained, if Carbo chose to oppose him, the chances of his fighter participating in bouts at Madison Square Garden would have been "zero."[20, 21]

Norris and Carbo were inextricably bound, and the pair took on the daunting task of attempting to keep their relationship clandestine, particularly from boxing and law enforcement officials. At the Louis-Bivins match, Norris was careful to meet with Carbo at the Lord Baltimore Hotel, and not at the fight. And when Carbo plunked himself down in a first-row seat at the match, IBC staff diplomatically relocated him out of view of the camera to avoid the possibility that the IBC's theater television lens might unwittingly feature him on their telecast.[22]

Another means by which Carbo exerted his influence on boxing, which affected the telecasting of the sport, was his manipulation of the various boxing guilds comprised of the sport's managers. New York was home to the Boxing Managers' Guild, which had butted heads with the IBC over television revenues. It became an IBC target. In April 1952, it was succeeded by the more IBC-friendly International Boxing Guild, with a local chapter named the New York Boxing Guild. Many of the new members were aligned with Carbo and would readily do his bidding. Carbo was able to use the guild to advance the interests of fighters in whom he had a stake, securing television dates and title opportunities.

Exercising his duplicitous nature, Carbo would play the guild and the IBC against each other. One scenario occurred at the end of the IBC's first year of operation, when Carbo spearheaded a strike against them over the split of television revenues. In one stroke, he caused the strike, and in another he resolved it. The maneuver was an example of his ability to influence aspects regarding both television fees and the decisions regarding the telecasts themselves.

The scenario concerned an upcoming title defense for Rocky Graziano. Graziano had pulled out of a match with Jake La Motta. Ostensibly, his withdrawal was due to an injury. In reality, it was a maneuver orchestrated by Carbo and backed by the guild to pressure the IBC with regard to television fees.

Carbo then turned around and used his relationship with La Motta to have the champ proceed with a nontelevised IBC promotion against a Graziano substitute, Tiberio Mitri of Italy. Keeping the bout off television proved financially successful for the IBC and was also a snub to the managers regarding the issue of television fees. A week later the two parties, each of whom believed that Carbo had gone to bat for them, struck a new agreement regarding fighters' compensation for televised bouts. Carbo's duplicity brought him favor on both ends of the boxing fulcrum.[23]

Underworld figure Frankie Carbo was instrumental in creating the machinations leading to the cancellation of the intriguing Rocky Graziano-Jake La Motta bout. He spearheaded organized crime's influence on televised boxing during the 1950s. Pictured is a "phantom" ticket from the unrealized fight. *From the author's collection.*

Just as Norris had Truman Gibson as his right-hand man on the corporate rung of the boxing ladder, Frankie Carbo had a criminal partner in his manipulation of the sport, the aforementioned Frankie "Blinky" Palermo. Sporting a prominent nose, raspy voice, and signature peering eyes, the diminutive Palermo had a criminal dossier including assault and larceny and was widely known in Philadelphia as its "numbers king."[24] In fact, Palermo had larceny in his heart. Even as a middle-aged man, he could not resist boosting a newspaper and a package of gum, a flight of fancy resulting in Palermo being picked up by law enforcement at the Los Angeles International Airport.[25]

Despite his physical and social shortcomings, he could exude considerable charm. He used it with great effect on the Pennsylvania Athletic Commission, cajoling them into issuing his manager's license to represent Ike Williams, who became lightweight champion of the world.[26]

In addition to Billy Fox and Williams, other prominent fighters under Palermo's control included Johnny Saxton and Virgil Akins—each of whom held the welterweight title under Carbo's watchful eye—heavyweight contenders Coley Wallace and Clarence Henry, and future heavyweight champion Charles "Sonny" Liston.[27]

To complement his role as manager and de facto manager, Palermo attempted to exert his influence through his relationships with promoters. From his home base in Philadelphia, he sought control over local Philly fight promotions through his relationship with Allentown promoter Pep Barone. At the time, Barone, along with Jimmy Toppi, was close to sealing a TV deal with Bayuk Cigars. However, the venture was squashed by John "Ox" DaGrosa, the Pennsylvania commissioner who was aware of the Palermo-Barone affiliation. Undaunted by this setback, Palermo would pressure other promoters—an approach that would eventually lead to his boxing demise.[28]

During this period, the most notorious incident involving the mob and a promoter was the brutal attack on Ray Arcel, brashly perpetrated in midafternoon on a busy Boston street. Arcel, promoter of the Saturday night fights, had had the audacity to challenge the

IBC monopoly, although he posed only a minor financial threat. Ironically, the act occurred just hours before Arcel was to appear at Boston Garden for a TV fight show.

While the attack was never directly connected to Carbo, Palermo, or their cohorts, it was widely accepted by the public that they were behind the act. A *Look* magazine article, "The Slugging of Ray Arcel," explained how "the New York fight Mob includes a ready supply of behind-the-scenes managers capable of ordering or executing a murder." No one was ever held responsible for the crime.[29, 30]

Nevertheless, acts of extreme physical violence in the boxing community were an anomaly. For Palermo, the fixed fight was more to his suiting, and he was one of its more unabashed purveyors. Shamelessly, he had no reservations in fixing his own charge. On several occasions, he delivered Ike Williams offers to throw major matches. Williams was offered $100,000 for the "Kid" Gavilan fight at the Garden in 1949 and $50,000 against Jimmy Carter two years later. Each time Williams demurred. In both instances Williams lost anyway, and he regretted not having taken the money.[31]

In 1954, several years after Williams's bouts, a series of notorious matches occurred involving Palermo's charge Johnny Saxton. In the first, Saxton was pitted against Johnny Bratton. After the listless bout, won by underdog Saxton by decision, Bratton sat in his dressing room and offered the anticipated alibi: "I hurt my hands, both of them." However, an examination by commission doctor James J. Simkin proved otherwise. After the dressing room emptied, Palermo appeared with Norris to collect their charge Saxton. As one reporter covering the fight noted, "Wherever Blinky puts in an appearance, there's justification for rare surprises."[32]

The Bratton bout did little to enhance the reputation of Philadelphia boxing, and it served as the ignoble debut for the city's first major televised bout.[33] Pennsylvania State Boxing Commissioner Frank Wiener was not at the fight but watched it on television 1,500 miles away in Hot Springs, Arkansas. After the bout, he immediately contacted his colleagues by public pay phone and ordered them to suspend Bratton and fine him $3,000 for his "poor showing."[34]

The opening position adopted by Norris and supported by the Pennsylvania commission was that "Johnny (Bratton) was still suffering from the effects of the beating he took from Gavilan," in a prior championship bout. Although the commission upheld Bratton's purse of $4,900 from the gate and $4,000 from the television sponsors pending a commission hearing, the powers that be were already foreshadowing a predisposition toward leniency.[35]

Later that year, Palermo, Carbo, and the IBC matched Saxton with Gavilan. Prior to the fight, New York bookies were only taking action on Gavilan. The decision in favor of Saxton was received by a shocked American television audience.[36]

A few days after the fight, both Gavilan and Carbo were at a party at the St. Moritz Hotel in New York City. Gavilan sought out Carbo and told him in broken English, "For what they do to me (meaning if the first bout was fixed) I want a return match. Mr. Blinky Palermo told me they do whatever you want." "Right," Carbo answered. But Gavilan was never given his rematch.[37]

The manipulation of Saxton's bouts continued. His fight the following year, in which he regained the middleweight title against Carmen Basilio, was also widely recognized as suspect.[38] New York State Athletic Commissioner Julius Helfand would bar Saxton from fighting in New York until he separated from Carbo.[39]

That same year, as part of a broader investigation on boxing, the New York State Athletic Commission questioned James Norris regarding the Gavilan bout and his connection with Carbo. He was asked, "Have you ever discussed with Mr. Carbo, fights or fighters?" "No," Norris responded, issuing a patent denial of their business relationship.[40]

In the pretelevision era, many "tank jobs" could be contained within the confines of the arena. But the proliferation of televised bouts had made it virtually impossible to fix a major fight without that bout finding its way before the television camera lens and millions of critical viewers.

Bouts such as Saxton's trio with Bratton, Gavilan, and Basilio created the perception that the fixed fight was regularly in play.

But contrary to the popular public perception of the mid-1950s, perpetuated by such Hollywood films as *The Harder They Fall* and a steady diet of weekly radio and television dramas, fixed fights at the top echelon of the sport were actually a rarity. Considering that thousands of fights were telecast during boxing's Golden Age without the slightest indication of tampering, it is clear that the fix was not prevalent.

IBC Vice President Truman Gibson explained the ramifications of the fixed fight when he testified before Congress: "If there were fixed fights we would be out of business, so we try to protect ourselves in every way against the possibility of a fixed fight . . . you only need one or two and you have no more boxing." In his autobiography some years later, he offered that fixed fights "would have been death to TV ratings."[41]

While the specter of physical intimidation remained, the fix had been replaced by a more subtle and insidious manipulation. Carbo and Palermo held a stranglehold over the lightweight and welterweight divisions, ensuring that the titles would remain under their control. They often secured a piece of a challenger before he was even permitted to fight for the title. This was frequently accomplished by making side deals with the fighters' managers, some of whom were intimidated into the conspiracy.

Such arrangements might occur without knowledge of the fighters themselves. At the very least, they were far removed from the specifics of the deal. Because Carbo and the interests that he represented were often guaranteed a part of the championship before the bout was even held, by the time the "friendly" matchmaker at the IBC, Weill or Brown, would officially make a match, the corruption had already taken place.

While the nexus between the fight game and organized crime during the 1950s is quite clear, the economic motivations and implications are frequently misunderstood. Films and television programs created the image that the top "Dons" were puppeteers of the boxing world. Additionally, publishers who loved to sell newspapers would link a Mafia kingpin to a boxing scandal, regardless of how tenuous the connection might be. While it is true that Carbo had associations with such criminal heavyweights as Albert Anastasia and Vito Genovese, the involvement of such high-ranking members of organized crime in the sport has never been proven to be more than peripheral.[42]

The reason for the mob's outlying involvement with boxing was purely economical. Boxing was not a top moneymaker. Loansharking, gambling, prostitution, labor racketeering, and the control of construction, garment, and waste industries were all infinitely more lucrative than the take from the occasional fixed fight.

Organized crime, however, would never pass on a money-making opportunity. It seemed to have an unshakable ability to weather changes in times or circumstance in order to maintain its position. In 1957, when the Justice Department began to dismantle the IBC for operating as a monopoly, boxing's criminal element seamlessly attached itself to the new promoters who attempted to fill the vacuum.

In 1959, following the recent Supreme Court affirmation of the decree that limited the IBC to the promotion of two championships contest per year, Bill Rosensohn entered the boxing game at its top tier by independently promoting the first Patterson-Johansson heavyweight title encounter under the banner of Rosensohn Enterprises, Inc.

Cus D'Amato, Patterson's manager, was close to two New York gangsters, Anthony "Fat Tony" Salerno and Charlie Black. It was not long before the pair had muscled their way into Rosensohn Enterprises and were holding two-thirds of its stock. As Rosensohn described it, the two gangsters, in association with attorney Vincent Velella and Irving Kahn, the head of closed-circuit outfit Teleprompter, Inc., had tried to push him out of his own company before the second Patterson-Johansson fight.[43]

Throughout the early television era, Carbo had threatened, duped, bribed, and cajoled his way through the boxing world, but behind-the-scenes law enforcement was building its case against him and his cronies. In mid-1958, Carbo was indicted and charged with ten criminal counts including conspiracy, undercover management of fighters, and acting as an unlicensed matchmaker for IBC contests.[44] The bout that ultimately sealed Carbo's fate was a televised match between Virgil Akins and Issac Logart at Madison Square Garden. The match was an elimination contest to determine the successor to Carmen Basilio's welterweight championship. Logart was the favorite, but in the lobby of the Garden before the bout, the "smart money" was on Akins, who scored the upset knockout. The spector of the fix had appeared again.[45]

Frankie Carbo, "on the lam" for over a year to avoid prosecution for conspiracy, undercover management, and unlicensed matchmaking, is finally captured by law enforcement. Here, Carbo is booked at New York's Beach Street police station, August 7, 1959. His $100,000 bail request was denied. *AP Photo/John Lindsay.*

Carbo went on the lam, and New York County District Attorney Frank Hogan tried to corner his opponent by issuing a national bulletin for his arrest. The ducking and dodging finally ended on May 29, 1959, when Carbo was surrounded in a New Jersey home by detectives from Hogan's office. Carbo tried to slip out of a rear window but ran headlong into two detectives waiting for him with sidearms drawn.[46] "I didn't know you were cops," Carbo would later explain to law-enforcement officials, "I thought it was a rubout."[47,48]

The Carbo swagger was now gone. He uncharacteristically pleaded guilty to the extortion and illegal matchmaking and management charges, each of which carried a one-year jail sentence. Specifically, Carbo admitted to acting as a manager for fighters under the wing of Herman Wallman, acting as a manager without a license for the match between Jimmy Peters and George Chimenti on February 21, 1958, and acting as a matchmaker without a license for the Akins-Logart bout on March 21, 1958.[49] New York would be first to officially dole out justice to Carbo. On November 30, 1959, Carbo, now a white-haired diabetic with failing kidneys, was compassionately given two years at Rikers Island by Judge John Mullen. "You had a terrific, improper, and illegal influence in the fight game. You enriched yourself to a degree I can't contemplate," he noted.[50]

While under indictment in New York, Carbo, along with Palermo, Truman Gibson, and two others, was named in a ten-count indictment in Los Angeles. The charges involved conspiracy to violate the federal antiracketeering act, extortion, and conspiracy. One of the government's allegations was that "Carbo and Palermo used Gibson and the IBC in their extortive activity."[51] The situation had become so dire that Gibson later admitted that at one point he was compelled to tell Palermo to get out of California "for the good of boxing."[52]

At trial, Jackie Leonard, a former Hollywood boxing promoter, testified about how Carbo exerted pressure to dictate which fighters were used on Hollywood Legion Stadium programs. Specifically, he pushed fighters managed by Al Weill, and those under the wing of Chicago promoter Ralph Gambina. The most damaging facts that came to light at the trial indicated that Carbo had attempted to extort the earnings of former welterweight champion Don Jordan, and that he had threatened the life of Hollywood Legion Stadium promoter Jackie Leonard.[53] Leonard had previously gone into hiding after a mysterious fire erupted at his home. He fled "to protect his family from the vengeance by underworld mobsters."[54]

While Carbo was still incarcerated at Rikers Island, a Senate subcommittee lead by its chairman, Tennessee Democrat Estes Kefauver, began its investigation into the sport of boxing. A parade of boxing notables was called to testify including Jack Dempsey, Jack "Doc" Kearns, Carmen Basilio, Sonny Liston, and Jake La Motta. Carbo's witness testimony was saved for the final day of the eight-day hearings conducted by the Senate's Anti-Trust and Monopoly Subcommittee.

Carbo, with his Los Angeles extortion case still pending, invoked the Fifth Amendment throughout his thirty-five minute appearance. He offered not a solitary word on his boxing associations or activities. "I cannot be compelled to be a witness against myself," he repeated over and over in a gravelly voice as he read from a piece of paper. Carbo did go through the pleasantry of congratulating Kefauver on his recent reelection, to the delight of the press.[55]

Frankie Palermo was also called as a witness at the hearings, and he too sought protection under the Constitution. Testimony was given by Truman Gibson, once Secretary of the since-dissolved IBC. Gibson explained how the IBC advanced as much as $350,000 to various fighters, including a one-time payment of $90,000 to Sugar Ray Robinson for the purpose of keeping the boxers "married" to the IBC and their promotions. The information, while enlightening, was passé from the standpoint that the IBC had already been dissolved.[56]

Kefauver noted that Carbo's "influence with promoters, managers, and match makers continues to this day," even while incarcerated. His involvement with the control of heavyweight contender Sonny Liston was cited. Blinky Palermo and John Vitale, also exploiting Liston at the time, were characterized by the senator as "as vicious a group of racketeers as ever appeared on the boxing scene."[57]

The senate hearings would prompt the first of many proposals for a federal boxing commission. The proposal brought with it implications for the telecast of boxing. Since all but the most local of televised boxing would constitute interstate commerce, under Kefauver's proposal all televised officials, "particularly [those] in closed-circuit TV," would now need to be licensed.[58] Despite invocations of its need, which persist to this day, a federal commission was never implemented. The Kefauver hearings, which were televised nationally to an audience of millions, became one of the most significant factors in damaging the sport's public image and bringing its national television coverage to an end.

Carbo would return to his cell at Rikers Island. On December 2, 1961, after a three-month trial in the conspiracy extortion case prosecuted by US Attorney General Robert Kennedy, the Los Angeles judge sentenced Carbo to twenty-five years in prison. Palermo was given a fifteen-year term. Carbo was sent directly to Alcatraz prison on San Francisco Bay. Truman Gibson of the IBC received only a five-year suspended sentence. The authorities had finally pulled Carbo and Palermo out from the dark shadows.[59, 60] At the time of the sentencing of the trio, the IBC had already been dissolved for its monopolistic practices for almost three years. Three years hence, in 1964, boxing would no longer be aired nationally, marking the official end to boxing's Golden Age of television.

Chapter 16

THE ORWELLIAN REALITY

A. Keep It Clean . . . Big Brother Is Watching

By 1948, just two years into the commercial broadcasting boom, a consensus developed that television would change the social fabric of the nation. However, the opinions regarding the effect of television ran the gamut from positive to negative. Some of the more fundamental social questions raised were whether or not television would strengthen or weaken the family unit and marriage, and whether it would lessen juvenile delinquency or, alternatively, distract youngsters from their studies. Other pundits asked whether television would create a better-informed and educated public or stunt social growth through the reduction of human interaction and reading.

One critic, in a chauvinistic tone not uncommon for the times, queried: "By distracting women from household duties during the day, [will television] promote domestic rifts?"[1] Another "expert" offered, in resignation, "The housewife who is accustomed to listen to soap operas while she washes, irons, and does the house work, cannot watch a visual program while she does the chores."

The impact of television could not be ignored. In London, the wife of an engineer threatened to put an axe through her husband and the television set one night while he was watching a boxing match. While she never carried out her threats, a subsequent evening of television led to an exchange of blows. A judge issued the couple a divorce, citing television as a contributing factor.[2]

The new art and science of television also proved a learned activity. Boxing fan Leo McCarey, the movie director of *Going My Way* and *The Bells of St. Mary's,* had difficulties mastering the new technology. After inviting friends over to watch the second Walcott-Charles fight, McCarey struggled to tune in "Jersey Joe" and Ezzard. McCarey's wife, actress Helen Hayes, admitted that her spouse regularly called in their thirteen-year-old son to get the set working.[3] Advice on how to operate and interact with television was doled out liberally. A writer for *Parents* magazine even counseled her readers that "it is not advisable to wear sunglasses while watching television."[4]

While time would ease television audiences into conventional viewing habits and provide the answer to the broader social questions raised, the new commercial industry was having an immediate and demonstrable effect on popular entertainment. In Chicago, a survey was done of homes new to television under the sponsorship of *Television Forecast* magazine in 1949, the start of that city's television boom. The study found that radio listening after 4 P.M. had declined by 62.2 percent, movie-going was down 58.3 percent, magazine reading 32.7 percent, newspaper reading 22 percent, and sports attendance 7.8 percent.[5]

As a new epicenter of entertainment, the TV set soon spawned a virtual cottage industry of complementary items including trays, coasters, and drink holders. "Many of the new gadgets are made of nonbreakable plastics, on the ground perhaps that someone in the crowd is apt to follow the motions of a prizefight too intently," one observer quipped. Something called the Serv-All Tray was representative of the new television viewing conveniences. "The Serv-All Tray is one of the latest accessories which should prove handy for the housewife who does not want to skip a television program for lunch in the dinette or for the men who do not want to miss the knockout blow of a boxing match," one sales pitch explained. The trays, which fetched approximately two dollars each, clamped onto the arm of an upholstered chair and were available in red, yellow, and green.[6]

As the armchair viewer with a Pabst Blue Ribbon beer or Ballantine ale in hand was being whisked via television into arenas such as Ridgewood Grove, the Baltimore Coliseum, and Chicago Stadium, the often crude atmosphere of these boxing venues was brought into the very living rooms of these viewers. Sometimes their entire family was among those subjected to the less-than-savory content.

Televised boxing and its viewers formed a relationship with characteristics not unlike the call and response dynamic found in an African American church. Uncompromised truths were being laid right before the audience's eyes, and emotional reactions and pointed perspectives were bellowed in refrain.

During a 1950 boxing telecast by WEWS, viewer Howard L. Smith from Cleveland Heights, Ohio, became incensed. During the playing of the national anthem, just prior to the main event, the television camera picked up shots of a seemingly uninterested audience. "If the lazy indifference, disrespect and evident boredom displayed by this crowd during the playing of the anthem is a sample of our national spirit it is no wonder that subversive agents can bore into our national 'innards,' railed Mr. Smith in a letter to the *New York Times* that flouted boxing fans and Communists alike.[7]

Other early observers riled by fight telecasts were the members of the Women's Christian Temperance Union. Its president, Mrs. D. Leigh Colvin, accused boxing telecasters of "glorifying bloodshed" to sell their beer. Regarding one telecast, she complained that "the announcers themselves took a drink of beer and yelled praise for it each time. Naturally there was a different announcer every two or three rounds to preclude one from burping or staggering before the camera," she surmised.[8]

As viewers grappled with the emotions evoked by boxing telecasts, boxers were attempting to navigate the medium's newfound consequences and opportunities. Fabela Chavez attempted to bar television from his featherweight bout against Buddy Jacklich at Hollywood Legion Stadium, claiming a right of privacy. However, a judge found that an individual's right of privacy is waived the moment he enters the ring unless that right is specifically reserved by contract.[9]

As resolute as Chavez was in not wanting to be seen on television, another contender, Gil Turner, was adamant about getting on the air. In 1951, Turner took a fight with Vic Cardell in Madison Square Garden during the week between Christmas and New Year, a date guaranteed to be financially weak, to experience a televised match.[10] Turner was not unaware of the power of the camera, commenting after the fight that he was "real nervous . . . with that television and all that."[11]

Savvy fighters realized that television was ripe for exploitation, although their efforts were sometimes half-baked. When Rocky Graziano was banned from fighting in New York because of the suspicious nature of his match with Reuben Shank, the boisterous middleweight pursued a creative idea that interested hopeful sponsors. He aspired to fight a series of "studio bouts" within New York State that would be televised. It was naively hypothesized that they would be allowed by the New York State Athletic Commission, his suspension notwithstanding, because the public would not be admitted and no admission would be charged.[12]

Boxers also learned that television created unintended consequences—both good and bad. In a serendipitous moment, twenty-six-year-old welterweight Danny Taylor was making his debut in a televised match from Madison Square Garden when his mother spotted him from her living room in San Pablo, California. They had not seen each other in five years. "I thought I'd jump out of my skin. I knew it was you the minute I saw you on television, she would later tell him."[13]

While middleweight Holly Mims was fighting an eight-rounder at Turner Arena in Washington, DC, the television camera delivered a close-up of him in his corner. An ex-army "buddy" from Fort Devens recognized Mims and immediately called the office of the Provost Marshall General. Mims was wanted as a deserter, and he was promptly picked up by agents of the Criminal Investigation Division and placed in the stockade at Fort Belvoir.[14]

The boxing fraternity at large was also taking notice of television's transparency. "Television may revolutionize the entire concept of boxing," noted Abe J. Greene, who served as president of the National Boxing Association and later as the state boxing commissioner in New Jersey.[15] According to Greene, "Boxing no longer is confined to the arena in which it takes place. . . . Television is taking the sport into homes, and boxing must make its participants and their assistants presentable to persons in all walks of life."[16]

Greene advocated the neat attire of boxers, seconds, referees, and announcers and the correct usage of grammar and "proper" language. In an effort to cleanse the sport of boxing, one of Greene's edicts required New Jersey seconds to "wear gray, button-front sweaters and carry white towels into the ring for all bouts."[17]

Even before Greene's proclamations, cornermen had been known to enter the ring with spotless white towels, only to leave with them grotesquely bloodied. The nature of early live television was not dissimilar, in that planning for a sanitized broadcast never guaranteed its delivery. This point was most dramatically illustrated when the death of a fighter occurred during a televised bout.

The fact was that Greene was poking around the base of a volcano that had already begun to erupt. In the summer of 1947, a national radio audience listened in as Cleveland challenger Jimmy Doyle was taken from the ring unconscious after a battering from welterweight champion Sugar Ray Robinson. The boxer was given his last rites in the hospital and died.[18] Future carnage of this type would be delivered much more graphically through the lens of the television camera.

A few years after Robinson-Doyle, in a televised contest from St. Nicholas Arena witnessed by millions, Percy Bassett of Philadelphia met Alfred "Sonny Boy" West from Washington, DC. West rose to prominence through his frequent appearances on local television.

He achieved the rank of sixth in the world in the lightweight division, but his climb was derailed by Bassett, a future world champion.

After suffering a knockout at the hands of Bassett, West was carried from the ring unconscious and rushed to St. Clare's Hospital.[19] The incident was so disturbing that announcer Ted Husing was momentarily shaken from his professional persona, confiding in his audience: "It's the last time I'll ever let my kid sit up to watch a fight on TV."[20]

West's parents, who had witnessed the fight on television, flew to New York unaware of the critical nature of their son's condition. Two unsuccessful operations failed to save West's life. Dr. Vincent Nardiello of the NYSAC was one of the doctors at his bedside when he died.[21]

Sympathetic television viewers raised $11,000 for a fund for the West family, and Pabst Blue Ribbon beer, the fight's sponsor, made an additional $1,000 donation. The IBC also sent a high-ranking official to attend the funeral.[22] In a display of good taste, CBS television, which normally rebroadcast kinescope versions of its Wednesday night fights anywhere from a day to a week after its original telecast, cancelled all subsequent telecasts of the fight.[23]

The bout was the second tragedy televised from St. Nick's that year. In February, Texas lightweight Laverne Roach died of injuries suffered at the hands of Georgie Small.[24] The ex-Marine had been ahead in the bout. He was bloodied in the eight round and downed twice in the tenth, pitching face-forward on his second trip to the canvas before the referee finally halted the bout amid cries to stop the contest. Roach arose and was helped to his stool. "Damn it, my luck is running out," he mumbled. He then slumped over and lapsed into unconsciousness. The next day, he died.[25] As with the West bout, Pabst cancelled the rerun of the match.[26]

Like the West tragedy, Roach's death shocked the boxing world and the television audience at large. Perfunctory investigations were launched by both the New York State Athletic Commission and the New York District Attorney's office.[27] However, the two deaths would quickly be forgotten. They also did little to quell the appetite for televised boxing and seemed to have no effect on the censorship of future live broadcasts.[28]

Some of the violence during boxing telecasts was less tragic, but still disturbing.

Lightweight champion James Carter squared off against local hero Tommy Collins at the Boston Garden. Collins would hit the canvas several times before the bout was finally stopped in the fourth round. The public outrage was as voracious as any that had been seen to date. Joseph C. Nichols of the *New York Times* called the bout "one of the most reprehensible mismatches in modern ring history." Dick Friendlich of the *San Francisco Chronicle* characterized the spectacle as "an incredible display of callousness and stupidity on the part of both referee Tommy Rawson and the seconds of battered Tommy Collins." "The worst black eye on boxing ever delivered over the national television network," decried Lewis Burton of the *New York Journal-American*.[29] Fans calling the *Boston Globe* from far-off locations in Virginia and North Carolina described the bout as "murder" and "the most sickening, disgusting thing I have ever seen."[30, 31]

For once, a calamitous bout did have a silver lining. Collins-Carter became the impetus for the establishment of the three-knockdown rule requiring a bout to be stopped when there are three knockdowns of a fighter in a single round.[32]

Even when the boxers were not involved in generating violence, the sport's other participants found a way to contribute to its brutality. In a televised middleweight scuffle between the hard-punching Ernie "The Rock" Durando and Rocky Castellani, a near riot and assault and battery were beamed into living rooms and parlors across the nation.

The violence erupted unexpectedly. Castellani was ahead in the bout but suddenly encountered disaster. He went down from a right hand in the sixth round and was again dropped to the canvas in the seventh by a right uppercut. Castellani appeared groggy and unable to defend himself, and referee Ray Miller prudently halted the contest and awarded Durando a TKO victory. Tommy Ryan, Castellani's manager, immediately attacked the referee, raining punches down upon him. Bedlam broke out at the Garden with both men and women climbing onto their seats and shouting protests, mixed with applause for Durando's victory. Special police, commission deputies, and referee Al Berle all entered the ring intent on subduing Ryan and any other upstarts. New York boxing commissioner Robert K. Christenberry immediately suspended Ryan and held up Castellani's purse pending an investigation. In a statement mimicking many a Garden fighter who had just taken a whipping, referee Miller, who did not throw a return blow, was pleased to report that none of the punches landed by "his opponent" had hurt him.[33]

One reporter described the incident "as one of the most disorderly scenes ever beheld in a New York ring." Concerned with the effect that the melee may have had on the home audience, Christenberry stated that "Such an incident like this is bad not only for the people watching it about ringside, but from the standpoint of those who were viewing the bout on television and listening to the broadcast of events. . . . I shall exert all my power to see that the incident is not repeated."[34] Apparently, the violence in the Garden that night was infectious and beyond the declarations of the commissioner. At the conclusion of the evening, Garden matchmaker Al Weill was beaten up in the dressing room by unknown assailants.[35]

Ray Miller, like an earlier day Richard Steele, seemed to be a lightning rod for controversy. In a match held at the Garden in December of 1952, welterweight Joey Giardello was awarded a split decision over Billy Graham. Judge Joe Agnello, along with Miller, scored the fight for Giardello, while judge Charley Shortell gave the nod to Graham.

The decision was announced to a disapproving crowd of 3,228. Some of them greeted the decision by hurling beer, popcorn, and whatever else they could get their hands on. In boxing's version of "Dewey defeats Truman," the TV audience went to sleep that evening believing Giardello was the victor.

The saga at ringside continued. In an unprecedented move to undo a perceived wrong, as well as to quell the rowdy audience, commissioner Christenberry authorized the announcement that the first decision was "unofficial pending revision by the commission." One half-hour later, Agnello's scorecard was revised, changing his 6–4 vote for Giardello to five rounds apiece by flipping the tenth round to Graham's favor. A second adjustment was made on Agnello's card for the fourth round by giving Graham two additional points on New York's supplementary point system. Agnello's card now showed an even score in rounds but a tiebreaking vote of 7–6 for Graham on the supplemental system. It was now Graham who was the split-decision victor.[36]

The next day, unaware of the reversal of the decision, irate members of the television audience sent telegrams to the New York State Athletic Commission, calling the decision a farce. However, once the word of the reversal spread, the commission was flooded with telegrams from television viewers from all over the nation in support of its reversal.[37]

Fans may have liked Christenberry's bold actions, but many of those affected found the reversal to be fascist in nature. Judge Agnello, who had his card reversed, explained that he was not even consulted regarding his scoring before the commission made its change. He expressed interest in retiring. "If I can't call them as I see them, what's the use of it," wondered the twenty-five-year veteran. Giardello's manager, Tony Ferrante, instituted legal proceedings against Christenberry and the NYSAC to have Giardello reinstated as the winner.[38] Three months later, far away from the television lens and irate Graham fans, the Supreme Court of New York reversed the actions that gave the bout to Graham and reinstated Giardello as the winner.[39] The bout may have been poorly judged, but there was no corruption involved.[40]

The boxing fraternity was learning that at one moment television could instantly popularize its most noble characteristics, and in another lay bare its most corrosive elements. Indeed, boxing on television would periodically generate negative exposure throughout the medium's Golden Age. Even the sport of amateur boxing, which has always stood for clean sportsmanship and providing positive direction to America's youth, was not beyond this taint.

Unlike today, amateur boxing was once an extremely popular televised sport, with thriving broadcasts at both the local and national levels. For several years, WFMB-TV in Indianapolis regularly televised local teenage amateur boxing matches. But all was not right in Boys Town. After a lengthy investigation, police arrested the two promoters of the television bouts. A police raid had discovered eleven boys playing poker at Bland's gymnasium. The youths also informed the police that they had been turning over to the promoters, five to fifteen dollars a fight, money tossed into the ring by appreciative fans for the fighters. The promoters were charged with child abuse. In something out of a Bowery Boys movie, Eugene "Tiny" Bland, one of the promoters, attempted to square things with the coppers: "I don't smoke and I don't drink and every kid I got is straight."[41]

Television not only placed a spotlight on small-time corruption in the amateur ranks, but on the darker misdeeds in the professional ranks, as well. In a 1955 bout, twenty-two-year-old Cuban heavyweight Julio Mederos scored a surprising second-round knockout over future light-heavyweight champion Harold Johnson in Philadelphia. He had lost to Johnson just six months earlier. Johnson was carried from the ring on a stretcher and taken to the hospital from ill effects that did not appear to be caused by Mederos.

The fight's large national television audience was soon following their newspapers and the actions of the Pennsylvania State Athletic Commission. The fight was investigated on the grounds that Johnson had been drugged prior to the bout. Potential evidence included an orange that Johnson ate about an hour before the fight, which made him feel ill. The fruit's remnants were retrieved and tested.[42]

Johnson testified that he had seen Louis Black, Mederos's former manager, in Johnson's dressing room just before the fight. Black vehemently denied this, claiming he was nowhere near the arena. His alibi was that he had watched the fight on television in Miami with friends. Black's veracity was suspect; he had been convicted ten times for narcotics trafficking, hardly the type of reputation one wants when you are suspected of "doping." The incident proved to be part of another televised match that cast aspersions on the sport.[43]

One might argue that boxing on television was a victim of bad public relations. Even when a boxing telecast was completely incidental to a negative news item, it seemed to become an integral part of its pall.

In one ghoulish news story that cropped up with televised boxing as a backdrop, a former "peeping Tom" and convicted arsonist was confined to a Philadelphia sanatorium. After watching boxing matches on television one evening, the man proceeded to take a pack of matches and set fire to a pile of clothes. Nine people perished in the fire, and sixty more were injured.[44] In another incident in Jersey City, New Jersey, the site of the Dempsey-Carpentier affair, an ex-Marine angered by his ejection from a tavern shot a fusillade of rounds from his Springfield rifle into the bar full of customers watching a boxing match on television. A fatal wound to the chest of one of the men viewing the bout resulted.[45]

One of the most gut-wrenching stories featuring a televised prizefight involved a distraught twenty-two-year-old man. One evening, he arrived at his brother's home with a horrific tale. The man, however, was unable to get the attention of his brother or his wife, who were absorbed by a fight they were watching on television. "Watch the television," and "look at that left," the brother exhorted. Finally, at the end of the bout, the frightful news was revealed: the man had just taken his own baby daughter's life.[46]

Another tragedy involved Benjamin "Chippy" Weiner, whose moniker belied the fact that he was a one-time associate of Louis Lepke, the notorious gangland figure. One evening, Weiner was enjoying some televised bouts in his living room on First Street in Manhattan. Two visitors dropped by to catch a few rounds. Their names were Eddie Rosenberg and Santo Bretagna, two gentlemen Weiner had met in Sing Sing prison.

As Weiner headed to the kitchen via his bedroom to prepare Rosenberg a drink, Rosenberg turned up the volume of the boxing broadcast full blast. While the announcer, perhaps Bob Stanton, belted out his ringside call, Bretagna unloaded five shots on Weiner from his .38-caliber gun. Three struck Weiner, killing him.[47] Even years later, it is hard to ignore these tragic incidents or separate them from their boxing-related settings.

Television's exposure of the darker side of the sweet science reached its apex with its coverage of the Kefauver hearings in 1960. As a parade of boxers and organized crime members came before the senate subcommittee to give testimony in the government's investigation of the sport, boxing fans and the general public alike were crestfallen to hear firsthand the great familiarity members of the two seemingly disparate groups had with each other. The manipulation, undue influence, and criminality in the sport could no longer be denied.

Already reeling from the taint of the Kefauver hearings, a death blow to the public image of boxing was dealt both literally and metaphorically, on March 24, 1962. Periodically, ring deaths had been aired on television throughout the 1950s. While these incidences evoked concern and even elicited adverse reactions, they did little to affect change. The third fight between Emile Griffith and Benny "Kid" Paret would be different.

Not only was Paret's welterweight title at stake in this fight, but an ugly dimension appeared when Paret attacked Griffith's sexuality. The bout reached its climactic finish in the twelfth round, when Griffith pinned the champion in a corner and pummeled him into unconsciousness. While it was, unquestionably, brutality at the highest level, it was not dissimilar to other ring deaths previously broadcast on television. However, as a nationally televised fight contested for a world's championship, the bout carried a greater significance, featured a higher profile, and reached a larger audience.

Television's ever-improving technology would compound the tragedy through the use of the slow-motion replay. After the knockout, ring announcer Don Dunphy joined Emile Griffith in watching a slow-motion replay of the carnage with the pair providing commentary to a shocked national audience.[48] As ABC continued to replay the massacre, word spread from viewers to their friends, who joined in to watch the postfight telecast and its slow-motion replays.

The postfight ratings would exceed that of the bout itself. Boxing's reputation had been irreparably harmed.[49]

After the bout, Paret was carried unconscious from the ring to his dressing room on a stretcher. Later, he was taken to Roosevelt Hospital where he underwent three hours of brain surgery.[50] While Paret lay in a coma the public assault on boxing began. On March 30, four days before his death, the New York Senate and Assembly adopted a resolution creating a special joint legislative committee to investigate prizefighting. The committee would be empowered to delve into all aspects of boxing including "ascertaining the degree of danger which fighters are exposed and the effect of professional matches on radio and television," and whether or not "boxing as a licensed public attraction" should continue.[51]

Paret passed away on April 3, 1962. The *New York Times* coverage of the funeral included an article with the headline "Clamor Grows Here and Abroad For End to Professional Boxing; As Thousands File Past Paret's Bier . . ." In addition to the state legislative investigation, legislation was introduced at the federal level to ban radio and television of boxing matches. The ripple effect of the bout even reached the Vatican. Its weekly publication *L'Osservatore della Domenica* declared that fight promoters and boxers must remember the Fifth Commandment, "Thou Shall Not Kill."[52]

The media would perpetuate the political persecution of boxing with television coverage such as David Brinkley's television documentary *The Last Round.* The piece was a scathing indictment of the sport, pandering to the emotions of his audience complete with an interview of Paret's widow. It also went for the visceral jugular, with images of gangsters and downtrodden ex-fighters such as "King" Levinsky selling neckties to swimmers sitting poolside in Miami.[53]

As with so many political actions regarding the regulation of boxing, the latest effort to ban boxing was never taken to fruition. However, boxing at the time was already a stuck bull pierced time and again over the years by other televised deaths, the recent ring death of Davey Moore, and the incessant taint of organized crime. The Paret tragedy was the final banderilla plunged into a dying animal. All that remained was the slow bleed. Boxing's metaphorical death would come by the end of the next year when ABC dropped its national television coverage.

B. The Lighter Side of Televised Boxing

In spite of, and perhaps partially due to, its inherent high drama, frequent tragedies, and a flavor of unsavoriness and criminality, televised boxing was a multifaceted phenomenon ripe for lampooning. Comedy television programs, topical comedians, and social pundits brought both lighthearted and caustic approaches to boxing satire during the Golden Age of television.

A number of contemporary comedic stars of the period, including the duo of Bob Elliott and Ray Goulding, took their turn poking fun at the sweet science. In one WNBQ episode reminiscent of passé vaudevillian or radio-boxing shticks, Bob and Ray spoofed the stereotypical TV pug: Announcer: How did you get into the boxing game, anyway? Boxer: My goil gave me a robe wid my name printed on the back. Announcer: What's your most important punch? Boxer: The one I hit'em wid.[54]

Frequently, however, the comedy focused upon the social effect televised boxing was having on its audience. For example, the *Saturday Evening Post* weighed in on the subject by fashioning a set of rules to follow. One rule that commented on televised boxing's effect on family life required that "in one of the later rounds, both fighters should retreat warily from each other, striking no blows, and permitting television watchers to say good-night to their kiddies or let out the cat."[55]

Undoubtedly, boxing was having a mesmerizing grip on television audiences. This fact did not escape the writers of *I Love Lucy*, the premier television comedy of the 1950s. In one episode, the program spoofed the hypnotic effect that televised boxing was having on its audiences. In between rounds, Ricky and Fred are able to conduct ordinary conversation with their wives, but once the bell sounds for the start of a round, their laser-like focus on the fight on the television set makes them oblivious to the rest of their surroundings. The only recourse available to Lucy and Ethel to snap their husbands back to reality is to cut the building's electrical power.[56]

If boxing was turning viewers into its own army of "Stepford Wives," one could easily cite its almost daily presence in the American home as the reason. This fact, in and of itself, was fodder for comedic exploitation. Commenting on the omnipresent nature of televised boxing, Red Skelton wittily offered that "The Monday night fight, scheduled for a Tuesday this Wednesday, has been postponed till Thursday and rescheduled for Friday this Saturday because Sunday is a holiday."[57]

While parodies peppered the boxing world, further humor in the form of whimsical curiosities was organically created by the marriage of boxing and television. Boxing's ubiquity, for example, would create television scheduling conflicts, placing the fight game at odds with political heavyweights in an unusual number of incidents.

The December, 1950, featherweight ten-rounder featuring European champion Ray Famechon against Del Flanagan headlined the card at Madison Square Garden's twenty-fifth anniversary celebration. In an effort to conclude the show as quickly as possible so the audience could return home for President Truman's televised national address, the Garden effectively sabotaged its own party.

Introductions were abandoned, and the traditional singing of the National Anthem was also eliminated. Paul Berlenbach, who fought Jack Delaney in the Garden opener twenty-five years earlier, was at the event as a special guest but was not even afforded the normal "in the ring introduction" to the crowd. The bout proved as dull as the planning of the event was poor. Many of the crowd of 4,742 seemed to take advantage of the Garden's deferential treatment, bolting early in an effort to make Truman's speech.[58] Less than three months later, the broadcaster of the Fritzie Pruden-Tony Janiro bout abruptly ended the telecast, depriving the audience of the last three rounds in favor of a televised speech given by a government official.[59]

Turnabout is fair play, and a little over a year later, a political telecast was compromised by a boxing match. On an early February evening in 1952, 15,000 supporters of presidential candidate Dwight D. Eisenhower assembled at the Garden to attend a "Serenade Ike Rally." Many more gathered around their sets at home to join in on the festivities. However, the opening program of the rally and the frequent "I like Ike" shouts were delayed. The Eisenhower supporters could not get into the Garden on time, courtesy of the Chico Vejar-Johnny DeFazio crowd still filing out of the same arena. Apparently, the bout, which was won by Vejar by ninth-round TKO, did not fully satiate five hundred of the fans who saw it, because they remained in the Garden to join Ike's supporters for a few more hours of shouting.[60]

A few years later, politics would score a pair of knockouts over boxing. The Ridgewood Grove in Brooklyn cancelled its televised Tuesday night fight because of the extensive television coverage of the coronation of the Queen of England,[61] and President Eisenhower's announcement that he was running for a second term delayed CBS's broadcast of the Johnny Holman-Joey Rowan heavyweight clash.[62] Royal and presidential diversions aside, boxing on television was building a large and inordinately diverse viewership. Octogenarians Arturo Toscanini, the world-renowned conductor, and legendary baseball manager Connie Mack were counted among the ardent fans of boxing "video." Other viewers were less famous but more curious.

Frisky, a five-year-old terrier and roommate of Mr. and Mrs. Frank Trubl of Chicago, knew a good show when she saw one. Frisky, so it was claimed, showed a preference for boxing on television. A student of the squared-circle, she liked boxing but drew the line at wrestling. By wagging her tail and making shimmies, shivers, and noises this television enthusiast had the ability to distinguish a good row from a stinker. It is a shame that Frisky was only a puppy at the time of Louis-Walcott I, for her obvious skills might have brought Walcott the heavyweight championship four years earlier.[63]

Apparently, Frisky was not the only terrier to poke its nose into the sweet science. According to Daisy Evans, an owner of a fox terrier from Davenport, Iowa, her dog Midgie was not only "the smartest pooch in these United States," but had a great disdain for boxing. Midgie was known to "stalk away in disgust" when it came on the television. Her favorite TV shows, well—those featuring dogs.[64]

While this pair of terriers might have been the most vocal animals ever to offer an opinion on televised boxing, the title of most articulate and compassionate box judge of the animal kingdom undoubtedly goes to Tippie, an eighteen-month-old self-educated parrot who watched a match with the educated eye of ringside physician Dr. Vincent Nardiello. "His nose is bleeding!" Tippie was known to screech upon sighting the flow of blood.[65]

Other less learned animals eschewed a passive role and took to the television screen to display their own boxing skills. On CBS-TV's *Big Top*, the weekly television circus that aired from the Camden, New Jersey, Armory, Dellan's Boxing Cats exhibited the feline version of the manly art of self-defense.[66]

While the antics of the cats and dogs of the boxing world never quite brought them celebrity status, television did have the power to manufacture boxing celebrities, albeit sometimes in an exploitive fashion. In the late-1950s, when boxing in France was on a respirator, manager Phillippe Filippi needed a savior. If he could not find a fighter, he would create a story. Seducing the great French champion Marcel Cerdan's son, Marcel Jr., with a chance at earning money and glory, Filippi drew the young man away from his home in Casablanca to Paris to embark on a boxing career of his own.

As the tenth anniversary of Cerdan Sr.'s tragic death neared, Filippi arranged a television broadcast of the son in training for his first fight. A single camera focused on the back of the fighter punching the heavy bag. Suddenly, he spun around to face the camera, which drew in for a close-up of his face. "This man is . . . Marcel Cerdan!" the announcer dramatically revealed. A second camera was also situated in Casablanca trained on the boy's mother. "I never wanted him to box. Boxing took my husband. I will know the same suffering with my son," she told an audience of millions in an anguished voice.[67]

Milking the drama for everything it was worth, the announcer coaxed Mrs. Cerdan: "On what you say to him now could depend his entire career. Speak to him now." And so, as millions of Frenchmen sat riveted to what was unfolding on their television screens, Mrs. Cerdan responded softly, as only a mother could, delivering the emotional coup de grâce: "It is cold in Paris, my little one. Be careful. Dress warmly." If there was a dry eye left in France, it probably did not survive the closing salvo delivered by Filippi himself: "I am a religious man and I know that Marcel up there is watching me and that he is happy about what I am doing for his boy."[68]

Another boxing personality who would reach pseudocelebrity status was organist and singer Gladys Goodding. Ironically, she was "created" by television, but she was never seen on it. Goodding was the organist not only at Madison Square Garden, but at Brooklyn's Ebbets Field, as well. It was promoter Mike Jacobs who green-lit her singing of the "Star-Spangled Banner" at Garden boxing shows. However, due to the ban on live music on television by the American Federation of Musicians, NBC's televised fights of the 1940s did not include her musical accompaniment of the anthem over the air. A studio recording was substituted.[69]

In the fall of 1951, the live music ban was lifted, and engineers began cueing Goodding for sound tests. With the national television hookup occurring at about the same time as the use of live music, Goodding's organ performances, which had previously entertained several thousand in the arena, now reached several million. Ironically, just two years prior, the IBC took over the promotional reins from Mike Jacobs, and Goodding's vocals were discontinued for boxing matches at the Garden. While boxing fans of the Golden Age of television may never have seen her face, they experienced some version of her performances prior to each night's main event.[70]

Goodding was not the only musical act in the Garden's repertoire. William J. Ferrall was an assistant corporation counsel of the City of New York. He was also at one time a member of the Coast Guard, along with Marty Servo. When Servo was matched to defend his title against Rocky Graziano in 1946, the Guardsmen's publicity director convinced Harry Markson to allow Ferrall to sing the national anthem at the bout. Servo was knocked out in the second round, but his fellow serviceman was so good, he became a regular. Like Goodding, Ferrall also became familiar to millions of television fans of the NBC/Gillette Friday night fights for his rendition of the national anthem.[71]

These behind-the-scene contributors to televised boxing may have been tangential, but they added to an allure that was all too real—sometimes so much so that the attraction of watching boxing on television could become a compulsion. Such was the case with Betty Upton.

Any good detective knows that a criminal can be had, if you just learn his propensities. The downfall of Upton, a check thief, was her unbreakable habit of watching boxing on television at her local taverns. A tip regarding Upton's viewing addiction led police to one such tavern. They walked into the bar during the Kid Gavilan-Chuck Davey fight, and, sure enough, there was Upton. Engrossed in the fight, she was exhorting Davey. "Come on Chuck," she pleaded as her opportunity for escape slipped away. Later, while under arrest, Upton learned the real bad news: she had also lost her bet on her blond hero.[72]

One of the most memorable and enduring celebrities associated with boxing and television was neither a boxer nor a man, but a twenty-eight-year-old female psychologist. In 1955, contestant Dr. Joyce Brothers chose the unlikely topic of boxing on the popular television game show *The $64,000 Question* and went on to shock and amaze the nation on her climb to the final question.

On the evening of her final show, many American homes tuned in to see if the pretty young contestant would go for the $64,000 question. One of the American families to catch the telecast was the Robinson family of Chicago. Actually, the man of the house, Sugar Ray, was busy with his training for his upcoming middleweight title fight with Carl "Bobo" Olson.

At home that evening was Mrs. Robinson and her six-year-old son, Ray Robinson Jr. A small party soon joined them. Publicist Harry Mendel, IBC secretary and attorney Truman Gibson, Ted Becker, and a few others from the Chicago fight crowd dropped by the Robinson's hotel room to watch Dr. Brothers display her curious talent. After a one-dollar payoff to little Ray, and the assurance that the Mickey Mouse show was not on, the gang tuned into the quiz show. Flopping on the beds, teetering on suitcases and occupying stray chairs in the room, they surrounded the television set and began to make bets as to whether or not she would go for the ultimate prize.

Dr. Brothers explained to the audience that last week she and her husband had been taken to Boston as guests of the IBC to see the middleweight bout between Tony DeMarco and Carmen Basilio. "Why doesn't she tell them where she is going next week?" Gibson decried, "It's this Ray Robinson-Bobo Olson fight we are selling tickets for."[73]

The program permitted the assistance of an expert consultant, and Dr. Brothers chose Eddie Eagan, former commissioner of the New York State Athletic Commission. In order to win the top prize, which had only been done once before, Dr. Brothers was required to answer a series of diverse questions that spanned the gamut of boxing history. Not a problem. Dr. Brothers knew the exact duration of the Dempsey-Firpo clash (3 minutes 57 seconds), the site of the Carnera-Uzcudun heavyweight bout (Rome), the full name of the Marquis of Queensberry (John Sholto Douglas), and she also identified the cestus as the type of glove used in ancient Rome.[74, 75]

Other questions were even more difficult—but not for Brothers. The first scientific boxer to win the championship in England? Daniel Mendoza, she replied. The English champion who taught boxing to Lord Byron? "Gentleman" John Jackson, she answered correctly. She then turned to Eagan, who was in the soundproof booth with her, and smiled.

Dr. Brothers was racing against the clock. In a real stumper, she named the essayist who wrote "The Fight," after having seen Bill Neat defeat Thomas Hickman in 1821—John Hazlitt. She also knew Hickman's nickname, "Hickman the Gasman."[76]

Having answered the final question correctly, those in Robinson's hotel room, little Ray included, exploded in applause, mimicking the national salute that the doctor received. The television broadcast had been purposely extended to include the program's finale, but apparently without an extra second to spare. Just as the master of ceremonies Hal March bellowed, "You are correct for $64,000," the telecast was promptly cut off, depriving the audience of Brothers's "postfight" interview.[77]

Dr. Brothers became a local celebrity in New York. She signed autographs for fans at Madison Square Garden fights, which she regularly attended, and received their hardy cheers when she was spotted in the crowd.[78] Capitalizing on her status as the only woman to win the $64,000 question, in a predominantly male-oriented category no less, the doctor landed a position as a commentator on a sports-talk television show. The program, *Sports Showcase*, was aired

By winning the grand prize on *The $64,000 Question* in the category of boxing, TV game show contestant Dr. Joyce Brothers became a national celebrity. The twenty-eight-year-old psychologist is shown reveling in her victory with her "staff" of boxers. L to R: Marty Sommers, Tony Canzoneri, Gus Lesnevich, Dr. Brothers, Bob Olin, Mickey Walker, and Eddie Eagan. *AP Photo.*

by WATV and originated from Al Schacht's restaurant on East 52nd Street near Park Avenue in New York. The one-hour show was hosted by Max Kase, the sports editor of the *New York Journal-American*. Dr. Joyce Brothers's role was to discuss and report on sports events and interview sports celebrities and personalities, with her boxing expertise at the forefront of her contributions.[79]

Television quiz shows were all the rage during the 1950s before the famed scandal in 1959 ended their brief but wildly popular run.[80] A year after Dr. Brothers's triumph, two New Yorkers, Harold Craig, a twenty-six-year-old farmer, and Hank Bloomgarden, a public-relations consultant, locked horns on NBC's television quiz show *Twenty-One*. Bloomgarden had racked up $119,000 in earnings and looked unstoppable as he vied to top the show's record winnings of $129,000. The question that toppled him concerned the June 21, 1932, heavyweight championship in which the loser's manager cried "We wuz robbed." While Bloomgarden named the manager who uttered the famous phrase, Joe Jacobs, and the winner of the bout, Jack Sharkey, he incorrectly pegged Primo Carnera as the loser instead of Max Schmeling. Craig answered the entire question correctly, eliminating Bloomgarden and picking up $17,500 for his efforts.[81]

Chapter 17

WHAT'LL YA HAVE?: THE ANNOUNCERS AND THEIR BROADCASTS

Not surprisingly, boxing's radio announcers served as the initial pool of broadcasters when television began its coverage of the sport. However, similar to actors transitioning from silent to sound films, these announcers were challenged by inherent differences between the two media. While the voice is the central tool for announcing on both radio and television, the process in determining *what* to talk about and *when* to speak is vastly different.

Announcing on radio and television were almost diametrically opposed in both pace and content. Radio required a certain rapidity and focused upon the description of specific punches, while television could be more deliberate and lent itself to the summary of the action.

During the television broadcast of the Louis-Charles match, the rapid and unbroken radio call of Don Dunphy can be faintly heard in the background during the periods of television silence. This anomaly provides a perfectly synchronized overlay of two simultaneous broadcasts. It also serves as empirical evidence of how the approach by both media to the same content differed so strikingly.

Just as Lionel Barrymore successfully moved from silent to sound films, boxing announcers such as Ted Husing and Don Dunphy effectively made the transition from radio to television. But many did not—the "John Gilberts" of their medium, temporarily relevant and then suddenly forgotten. However, it would be misleading to say that failure to adapt to the new media caused prevalent change in the roster of boxing announcers.

Significantly, a full generation had passed since the advent of commercial radio at the end of World War I to the proliferation of commercial television by the end of World War II. Consequently, there was a great deal of natural attrition. Ground-breaking radio broadcasters such as Major White, Graham McNamee, Phillips Carlin, and Clem McCarthy would be replaced as part of the natural cycle by such television boxing pioneers as Jack Drees, Russ Hodges, Chris Schenkel, and Jimmy Powers. In this manner, television brought a host of fresh faces to the boxing microphone.

Sam Taub was the first boxing radio announcer to be used in a meaningful way on television. While he was still one of the most recognizable radio blow-by-blow broadcasters, he handled some of television's very first boxing telecasts aired from the Ridgewood Grove, St. Nicholas Arena, and Jamaica Arena in 1938. Taub, however, did not endure as part of the postwar television boom.[1]

Bob Stanton was also a pioneering boxing television announcer. He participated in some of the seminal boxing broadcasts including those on NBC sponsored by Gillette. He was behind the microphone for the call of the 1946 Louis-Conn rematch, the first heavyweight championship bout to be televised. Later that year, the Gillette fights on NBC would become known as the *Gillette Cavalcade of Sports*, and the series would run until 1960. Stanton would remain behind the microphone for NBC through 1949, the year in which Jimmy Powers made his debut.[2,3] Taub and Stanton helped usher in televised boxing during a period of experimentation when there were relatively few television receivers. Others made their contributions to early televised boxing during the 1940s for noncommercial, commercial, and theatrical television broadcasts. This group included George

Hicks, who partook in the 1939 World's Fair experimental boxing broadcast;[4] Jack Fraser and William Spargrove, who covered the telecast of the first public theatrical television presentation featuring the 1941 Billy Soose-Ken Overlin middleweight championship fight;[5] and Ray Forrest, who partnered with Stanton on the Friday night fights in 1948.[6] A host of long-forgotten local television announcers of the period also enjoyed a fleeting moment in front of the television camera lens.

When the television boom arrived in the second half of the 1940s, one of the first faces to regularly appear on boxing telecasts was Dennis James. James was an early force in television—the first person to host a network game show, telethon, and variety show, and the first to appear in a television commercial and on videotape.[7]

James made the catchphrase "Okay, mother" common television parlance. He first used it during his wrestling broadcasts. "Okay, mother," James would begin, to preface his explanation of events happening within the roped square. He used the saying exclusively when he spoke to the female segment of his audience. The phrase became so popular, and so identifiable with James, it led to his own variety show.[8]

James, who was a middleweight boxing champion at St. Peter's College, was also closely associated with televised boxing broadcasts of the late 1940s on the DuMont Network.[9] His televised boxing contributions included *Boxing from Jamaica Arena, Amateur Boxing Fight Club,* and *Boxing From Sunnyside Gardens.*

James was succeeded on DuMont by Chris Schenkel, a unique broadcaster from the heartland. With a background in radio, young Schenkel started on the ground floor of network boxing on television. He announced fights over the DuMont Television Network on Monday evenings at 10 P.M. Eastern time from the Eastern Parkway Arena in Brooklyn beginning in 1952. By his third year with DuMont, Schenkel was announcing on its all-locally-sponsored coast-to-coast network. He remained behind the microphone at the arena, often called the "house of upsets," into 1954.[10]

Schenkel maintained a relationship with DuMont after it moved on from Eastern Parkway. From 1954 until the network went off the air in 1956, he provided the blow-by-blow for its bouts from the St. Nicholas Arena in Manhattan.[11]

Even as a young man, Schenkel's voice had a grandfatherly quality that provided a comforting calm. He only departed from this tone when a sudden rise in the action occurred. On those occasions, his voice would take on a more animated and steely quality. Although he never used phrases such as "Golly gee whiz," or "Aw shucks," he had viewers thoroughly convinced that he did. He offered that type of sensibility and also created a personal bond. "Let's watch round four," his whispering voice would invite his audience at the start of a round. He created the feeling that just the two of you were secretly peering into a silent movie set. "Ow, that right was a whisker taker," he would say on occasion. You could almost feel him jab his elbow into your side when he did.

Despite this certain type of informality, Schenkel was something of a stickler in the call of a bout. He was like the reliable bus driver, courteous, but more importantly always on schedule. At the beginning of each round, he would provide the fighters' names, their corresponding trunk colors, and their weights. The time remaining in the round was regularly provided. It did not matter when you stepped aboard the Schenkel express, you always knew where it was going.

Schenkel would go on to rival Don Dunphy as the most enduring boxing broadcaster in history, certainly for television. Finishing his career on ABC calling bouts on the *Schlitz Malt Liquor Professional Boxing* series, his career endured for almost a half century. He was also the last of the boxing announcers to call bouts solo. Befittingly, he concluded his career as he had started it.

While DuMont had its niche in early televised boxing, NBC was the standard-bearer for boxing broadcasts. NBC conducted experimental boxing transmissions even before World War II. By 1944, the network was telecasting bouts commercially sponsored by Gillette. They would bow out in 1960 with the longest-running boxing program in the history of the sport.

The simplistic beauty of the musical jingle for the *Gillette Cavalcade of Sports* program became one of the most memorable in sports history. "*The Gillette Cavalcade of Sports* is on the air !" the announcer would begin. Then the wordless beat would begin: Da-dat–da . . . da-da-da-da-da . . . da-dat-da . . . da-da-da-da-da . . . The jingle continued with its now iconic phrase: "You look sharp . . . and feel sharp too, choose the razor . . . that is built for you. Light . . . and regular . . . and heavy . . . hey . . . slick shaves for any beard." In conclusion, the wordless beat would return, while simultaneously a graphic appeared on screen: "From Madison Square Garden . . . Gillette Presents . . . This Week's Headline Boxing Event . . . Promoted by the International Boxing Club." The perfect segue into the introduction by Jimmy Powers.[12]

In 1949, at the same time that interregional network television came to the fore, Powers would take over the NBC/Gillette microphone from Bob Stanton. Powers, like many on the radio and television broadcasting tree, could trace his roots back to his days as a sportswriter. After thirteen years behind the typewriter, he began his boxing broadcasting career. Powers was friendly with James D. Norris of the IBC, and when Norris became the top man at Madison Square Garden, Powers found himself announcing for NBC/Gillette.[13]

Throughout the 1950s, he continued in the position as blow-by-blow announcer for the *Gillette Cavalcade of Sports.* These boxing telecasts on NBC on Friday evenings included bouts from both Madison Square Garden and St. Nick's Arena. Even while broadcasting, he maintained an important role in newspapers as sports editor of the widely circulated *New York Daily News.* As a dual force with NBC and the *News,* he became one of boxing's most influential reporters.

Powers's voice featured a nasal twang. When he became excited, it would take on something of a high-pitched, screeching quality. Today, it probably wouldn't survive a marketing director's vetting process. However, it not only endured for an entire decade, but it became synonymous with the Friday night fights.

One of Powers's best attributes as a boxing announcer, plainly put by one of his contemporaries, was his "realization that the fans don't want to listen to chatter about things that they can see on their screens." Powers valued an announcer's "restrained showmanship," which he considered even more important than his breadth of knowledge. Understanding the inherent duality of the television audience's rooting interests, he held objectivity to be paramount.[14]

He also knew how to protect the sponsors who signed his check: "No matter how dull the fight is, you just can't come out and say it's dull. If you do it's the same thing as saying, 'Listen folks, both of these guys are a couple of bums, why don't you tune into a better program?'" If a bout didn't provide visceral satisfaction, Powers looked beyond the surface to interest his audience by educating them. In a bout with a lot of clinching but little action, Powers explained he might say something like, "You know folks, the reason there is so much clinching going on here is because these two fighters have the same style. Boxing styles are like, gears on an automobile. If the two boxers have the same style, they mess and fall into a clinch. If they have contrasting styles they wouldn't clinch so much."[15]

Powers subscribed to an announcing etiquette when dealing with a losing fighter that he called a "hearts and flowers routine." "You try to give the loser a boost without being outlandish about it," he explained. He also recognized the powerful emotions at play in boxing, and the necessity for caution: "Boxing is an atavistic thing that churns people up inside. You can get in trouble so easily in this business by saying the wrong thing."[16]

During his run as the anchor of the Friday night fights, Powers called hundreds of bouts. He embraced the prevailing view that television both hurt the small fight clubs and "made stars out of average fighters." He also credited television with having "changed boxing completely."[17] Powers pegged the Basilio-Gavilan fight in 1953 as the most exciting he ever called. He had respect for Basilio, who he felt was "ugly" and "courageous," and ideal for the average fight fan. He also favored Art Aragon, who he found to be "magnetic, one of the few in sports who gives off sparks."[18]

Powers's nationally televised boxing broadcasts came to an end in 1959 when the NBC/Gillette fights from the Garden were dropped. When they reemerged in 1960 on ABC, Don Dunphy was at the mike. Boxing's premier radio announcer for the past two decades, Dunphy would finish out Gillette's run and the Golden Age of boxing on television calling bouts solo for the next five years.[19]

Dunphy was already a familiar face to television audiences. As early as the late 1940s, he was conducting postfight interviews in the ring that were carried simultaneously to the NBC audiences of both radio and television broadcasts.

During his tenure as TV's face of boxing in the early-1960s, he would provide blow-by-blow for all the era's greats, including Muhammad Ali fighting as Cassius Clay, Ray Robinson, Gene Fullmer, Carmen Basilio, Emile Griffith, Luis Rodriguez, Harold Johnson, Willie Pastrano, Carlos Ortiz, and Joe Brown.

On radio, Dunphy used detail to convey drama. On television, he dialed back his blow-by-blow description significantly, using words as signposts and letting the pictures write the script. Whereas factual information such as fight statistics and personal anecdotes were used in the prefight portion of a radio broadcasts, that information now peppered the telecast of the fight itself. Dunphy believed that radio broadcasts with their rapid-fire reporting were more physically demanding, but television—which required the continuous assessment of whether or not to speak—was more mentally taxing.

He also understood the fight game at a personal level. During the typical postfight interview, a well-spoken man in a suit and tie who is predisposed to inquiry and judgment enters the ring. There he encounters two men dripping with sweat, perhaps bloodied and still panting after an hour of fierce fighting. There is always a risk that this meeting will resemble the first confrontation of Eliza Doolittle and Professor Henry Higgins in *My Fair Lady*. But that was never the case with Dunphy. Don had a genuine respect for boxers and was never patronizing during his interviews. "You know, fighters in the main are good people," he said. "They're also gentle—and the guys named Rocky I've noticed are usually the gentlest of all away from the ring." Dunphy also valued the accessibility and generosity of boxers, comparing them favorably to the professional athletes in baseball, football, and tennis. "A fighter loses a bout, he wipes off his face, and he's ready to be interviewed," he pointed out.[20]

The secret to Dunphy's success, which spanned half a century, can be attributed to a palpable genuineness about him. He capitalized on this quality and his relaxed affability to create an earnest approach. It yielded the right balance of simplicity and sensationalism. In his later years, he developed a "Cronkite-esque" paternalism, soothing in both its integrity and trustworthiness. With Dunphy at the microphone, ABC was boxing's final television outpost. It was the last network to terminate boxing programming during televised boxing's Golden Age with their Saturday/Friday Night *Fight of the Week* programs going off the air in 1964.

Long before Dunphy became a familiar face to ABC viewers, Jack Gregson made his mark as the color commentator on ABC-TV's *Saturday Night Fights,* commonly called "the Philly Fights." The program aired from 1953 to 1954, making ABC the last network to begin telecasting boxing nationally during boxing's Golden Age.

Gregson, like other successful TV boxing announcers, respected the fact that what the home viewer saw on his TV screen was not necessarily what someone was seeing from a ringside seat. A former boxer, he would watch both the ring and the monitor so that he could adjust his commentary accordingly. "The home viewer is seeing the fight from a different angle than the ringsider, and frankly he's missing many small but important details. . . . The greatest camera coverage in the world . . . can't catch those quick, telling blows in the in-fighting, and no TV camera can register the glazed expression in a boxer's eyes which is a sure sign he is hurt."[21]

To Gregson's point, the savvy TV announcer would fill in details not always visible to the viewer. Likewise, he would bring attention or clarification to moments viewers could not experience on their own. The closed-circuit television call of Marciano-Walcott I, provided by veteran boxing radio announcer Bill Corum, finely illustrates this point:

Round 1 (after Marciano was downed by Walcott): "Rocky is bleeding inside his mouth, not outside it."

Round 2: "That was a good body punch by Marciano, I hope you saw it clearly."
Round 3: "In Marciano's corner they are yelling keep them up, but there is no low punch I assure you."
Round 6: "Walcott—his back to you—and you're probably not seeing these punches—they're hard by both fighters. Marciano is now cut on the forehead, Walcott is cut around the eye . . . that may be his blood on Marciano's forehead."
Between Rounds 6 and 7 (the TV camera trained on Walcott's corner): "I don't think that is a deep cut from what I can see."[22, 23]

The Marciano-Walcott match was sponsored by the Pabst Brewing Company, the host of the Wednesday Night Fights series that began in 1950. Like the Gillette theme song, the memorable Pabst jingles have become iconic.

In a typical ad, as the Pabst logo appeared on the screen, alternating with the words, "What'll You Have?" the catchy jingle would begin:

What'll You Have? Pabst Blue Ribbon
What'll You Have? Pabst Blue Ribbon
What'll You Have? Pabst Blue Ribbon
Pabst Blue Ribbon Beer
Smoother, smoother, smoother flavor
Zest and sparkle millions favor
Taste that smoother, smoother flavor
Pabst Blue Ribbon Beer.

"Finest beer served anywhere, Pabst Blue Ribbon" the announcer would conclude.[24]

Part of the reason why these ads are so indelible were the frequent "spot" mentions of the sponsor's product laced throughout the match: "One minute to go of the sixth round of this heavyweight championship bout here at Yankee Stadium in New York City, brought to you with the good wishes of Pabst Blue Ribbon Beer—

Yowsa, Yowsa!" and "Well, you can put your seal of approval on this bout just like you like to put that Pabst Blue Ribbon seal right in front of you on the table—yes, sir!"[25]

Ted Husing was one of the CBS Pabst Blue Ribbon TV announcers who began calling their bouts in 1950. One of the few top boxing radio announcers who successfully made the transition to television, in addition to his run at CBS, Husing covered boxing for DuMont on its *Boxing from Eastern Parkway* series from May 1952 to March 1953. His pedigree can be traced back to his mentoring by the father of boxing announcers, Major J. Andrew White, although White schooled him on announcing other sports.[26]

Authoritative and informative, Husing was the most articulate of his contemporaries. He displayed a facility and ease with language. He also held a greater understanding of pace and structure. Like

Opinionated and controversial, Ted Husing was also a multitalented broadcaster. He was a key figure for boxing broadcasts on both radio and television. *By Harris Ewing Collection via Wikimedia Commons.*

most of his television brethren, he avoided calling blows per se, but he was superior to them in his ability to avoid unnecessary or glaring dead time on the air. He achieved this mostly by providing a greater depth and breadth of information and insightful commentary while executing its delivery with proper placement.

Husing was something of a wordsmith, and he could provide a unique description and call the action all in one breath: "So, we always have the spectacle of the Louis milieu with that tremendous right—there he just threw it—and the constant application of the good blows with craftiness, agility, and fluidity by Ezzard Charles." He also never passed on an opportunity to turn a phrase: "Two minutes to go in the eleventh round in what has been a good fight, and that's not giving expletives away either," he would tell his Louis-Charles audience.[27] Husing would refer to the television camera as "our mirror." On one occasion, when a fighter gave his opponent a sound beating, he described it as "a great lathering." He once referred to the contending Argentine heavyweight as "the tiring yet tireless, if I can use the antitheism verb, Cesar Brion."[28]

Unexpected occurrences were of no problem to him, and he seamlessly worked them into his presentation as if they were scripted: "By the way, the action in the ring right now, as you see, is the midget who has come into the ring. And as he is in there wandering across, the boys are saying, 'Throw him out, throw him out.' The excitement, of course, is always attenuated upon one of these little pieces of side play."[29]

Husing could be "arrogant, coarse, and opinionated." He developed a fierce rivalry with NBC's Bill Stern, which started during their reporting days and carried over into later years when they both became their networks' sporting directors.[30] He suddenly left the telecast of Pabst's Wednesday night fights in 1951. The official explanation was that he resigned because the traveling requirements kept him from his commitments in New York. But insiders claimed that both Pabst and the television viewers were disenchanted by some of his actions, which included an altercation with a television technician and the on-air disparagement of an individual whom he called an "idiot."[31] He would return to announce fights from the Eastern Parkway Arena on DuMont before illness ended his career. Despite his relatively short run before the camera, he is a candidate for the best of the early TV announcers.

Husing was one of the four principal announcers used during the Pabst Blue Ribbon TV fight series. The others were Steve Ellis, Jack Drees, and Russ Hodges. This trio of colleagues also served double duty for Pabst, often announcing their radio broadcasts.

Ellis, who had a brief stint as an announcer for Gillette's Friday night fights, handled the blow-by-blow announcing for Pabst's Wednesday night fights during the early/mid-1950s.[32] He was affable, offered a friendly disposition, and immediately made the viewer feel comfortable. "Hello, there everybody," he would greet his audiences at the beginning of a Pabst broadcast.[33] Ellis seemed to have boundless energy. His gregarious nature gave the impression that he wanted to step right through the television screen and offer you a hearty handshake or give you a slap on the back. This characteristic distinguished him from his Pabst broadcasting colleagues, Husing, Hodges, and Drees, who were less personal in their approaches.

His economic descriptions of the action provided very little in the way of a blow-by-blow account. However, this was typical of the early TV announcers, who made a conscious effort to avoid describing the obvious. In this manner, his style was strikingly similar to that of Hodges and Drees. To Ellis, commentary was reserved for what the viewer could not see, as well as for clarification, general assessment, and the occasional factoid about the boxers.

During his tenure, boxing broadcasts were developing their prefight introductions as well as their in-between round segments. In those early days, the camera would somewhat awkwardly, almost intrusively, be thrust upon the announcer at ringside to provide the audience with a quick, in-between round interview. Ellis, unaffected by inferior production values, would handle these segments with a natural ease.[34]

Ellis was involved in one of the more bizarre telecasts of the era. Despite the fact that he was Chico Vejar's manager of record, CBS and Pabst put him before the microphone as the announcer for his fight against Chuck Davey. More incredibly, he would call the bout alone. After disclosing his dual role to the audience, Ellis told them, "May the better guy win."[35]

We will never know what Ellis's initial approach was to the call of the bout. The bell for the first round sounded, and Davey rushed in and began pummeling Vejar, quickly dropping him to the canvas. Ellis sat in virtual silence, managing to only offer: "We have two minutes to go in round one." Then Ellis's charge was deposited on the seat of his pants for the second time. "One minute to go in the round," Ellis explained matter-of-factly, giving only his second and final comment of the round. It is unclear whether Ellis had planned to strictly avoid commentary due to his flagrant conflict of interest or whether he simply was in a state of shock.[36]

Ellis was clearly on the spot. So as Chuck continued to rout Chico, the commentary remained sparse. "Davey is an exceptionally fast puncher," Ellis noted, providing only the subtext to the real story, and "Vejar is an NYU freshman," he inserted randomly. Ultimately, Davey received the ten-round decision, and an argument could be made that Ellis had a rougher time of it than his fighter.[37]

Ellis's colleague, Jack Drees, a lanky Chicagoan and former star center of the State University of Iowa basketball team, was another announcer of the Pabst Blue Ribbon fights during the mid-1950s. During the period in which he announced the fights on television, he also had the unique opportunity to speak about them as the daily host of his own sports show on WBKB in Chicago. In an unusual but successful scheduling maneuver, Drees would take over the Pabst microphone for Russ Hodges while Hodges was announcing for baseball's New York Giants.[38] In a rare treat, the pair could be found working together, as they did on the Ray Robinson-Ralph "Tiger" Jones telecast.

Drees had a knack for the use of the modifying adjective that allowed him to paint simple, yet effective pictures. Carmen Basilio was "gifted with an astounding toughness," or "He really took a slashing left hook," he explained. And similarly: "Carmen Basilio smashes

Tony DeMarco into a helpless condition." But these descriptions were used economically, and he was neither verbose nor intrusive during his telecasts.[39]

Because bouts of the time were often called by only one announcer, the in-between round commentary was also provided by the blow-by-blow commentator. On such occasions, as the camera trained upon the fighters' corners, Drees would describe the cornermen's actions with zeal and an attention to detail. Amongst the more notable bouts broadcast by Drees was the Basilio-DeMarco rematch, *The Ring* magazine's 1955 fight of the year.

Drees was conscious of how a television broadcast could influence the perception of its viewing audience, He even counseled the television boxing fan in a newspaper article, "How To Score A Fight On TV." Drees was concerned about the TV viewer's ability to determine the effect of a blow, which he explained was more difficult to assess than watching it from ringside. He emphasized how in certain instances during his broadcasts it was necessary for him to point out the relative power of a blow or that a punch did not actually hit the mark. "Because television is not three-dimensional, a near-miss can sometimes look like a hit to the viewer," he cautioned. Drees also explained how he made sure his call of the fight reported situations where he believed the camera angle might be misleading to his audience.[40]

Russ Hodges rounded out the Pabst foursome. Best known for his call of Bobby Thomson's pennant-winning blast for the Giants in 1951, Hodges was the blow-by-blow man for CBS's Pabst Blue Ribbon shows during the fall and winter. He alternated behind the microphone with Drees, who covered the other seasons.[41] Hodges could lay claim to a legitimate foothold in both the baseball and boxing worlds. He called the final game of the 1951 World Series and later that evening provided the blow-by-blow for the heavyweight match in which Ezzard Charles scored an eleventh-round TKO of Rex Layne in Pittsburgh.

Hodges offered a cool, steady delivery belying his frantic call of Thomson's "Shot Heard 'Round the World." His voice would deepen in moments of intensity, but he was not prone to hyperbolic descriptions and avoided feigned drama. On some occasions, he would call a bout on his own. On others, he had a partner, typically Steve Ellis.

More so than most of his colleagues, he unabashedly let the action on the screen speak for itself. He rarely called out combinations or even single blows as they were thrown, but intermittently he would provide a summarized assessment: "Robinson does not have too much of a defense against the left hand of Tiger Jones tonight, particularly against the hook." And "Over the first six rounds Robinson has certainly run into much more rugged opposition than he expected as Jones, in splendid condition, has been forcing the fighting." And "Right above our Pabst Blue Ribbon microphone is Robinson calling on all of his ring generalship . . . it's strange to see Robinson take two to land one, we have never seen him do that."[42, 43]

Whether it was the steady and stolid style of Hodges and Husing or the personal touch of Dunphy and Schenkel, the boxing fan usually identified a particular boxing series with a particular announcer. Of course, out of the camera's view was a multitude of engineers, technicians, producers, and other behind-the-scenes professionals responsible for delivering the telecast of a boxing match. These individuals were not only indispensable to the facilitation of the presentation itself, but they helped shape the very role of the boxing television announcer.

Hugh Beach produced ABC-TV's Fight of the Week program in the early-'60s. He was one of the many behind-the-scenes television participants who contributed to the success of televised boxing during its Golden Age. Beach fully understood the pitfalls of the telecast of boxing, a sometimes unique and complicated affair. He took a scientific approach to ensure that a telecast went smoothly and that the presentation of the ringside announcers would not be compromised. At ABC, he implemented a sixteen-page manual of commercial and camera instructions that contained all the basic information for the telecast except the names of the bout's winner. Supplementing these "house rules" were special instructions for several common permutations that needed their own approach.[44]

For example, if a fighter got tagged in the last ten seconds of a round, the cue for the commercial would need to be cut so the camera could stay with the corner. Once that commercial was cut, it would then need to be reinserted elsewhere in the telecast. If a fight ended early via a knockout, an entirely new procedure for the showing of the next televised bout, commonly referred to as "the emergency bout," was put into action. The emergency bout would require the reallocation of the original schedule of commercials. An early knockout in the emergency bout would trigger yet another variation of the broadcaster's approach.[45]

These strategies were helpful but could only provide structure, or perhaps a false sense of security, amid the wild unpredictability of a live boxing broadcast. Everything from benign gaffes such as camera miscues, to intermediate surprises such as profanity that went out on the air, to major calamities such as a riot or ring death could be only a round away. Producers were required to deal with such unpleasant occurrences. Perhaps the more difficult chore fell to announcers, responsible for simultaneously comforting and entertaining their large television audiences when such incidents happened.

Fights outdoors, for example, presented their own unique set of challenges, principally caused by the weather. In rare instances, the announcer was on his own. In a telecast of the welterweight championship match between Emile Griffith and Luis Rodriguez, a monsoon-like storm drenched Dodger Stadium in Los Angeles, leaving half a foot of water in the ballpark's dugouts. Instead of watching Luis and Emile swap blows for the championship, "viewers were treated to the sight of a soaking Don Dunphy commenting between rounds from a rain-swept perch in the center of the ring in an empty ballpark, not dryly, on a videotape account of Cassius Clay's encounter with Doug Jones." To avoid electrocution, Dunphy held the microphone in a slippery rubber glove.[46, 47]

The men behind the camera deserve their just due. However, the romanticism for the fan will always lie with the announcer. Ellis's enthusiasm, Husing's command, Dunphy's purposefulness, and

Schenkel's endearment resonated with fans on a visceral level and had a lasting effect on those who experienced them over half a century ago.

And just as the McNamees and Taubs and radio itself was revolutionized by the Dunphys and Powerses and the new medium of television, the post–Golden Age brought the further metamorphosis of the boxing television announcer. The rise of the color commentator, the elevated standards for preparation and presentation, and the unique "mirrors" of men like Howard Cosell, Marv Albert, and Larry Merchant would recall a proud legacy.

Chapter 18

OUT OF THE RING AND ONTO THE SMALL SCREEN

The exploitation of boxers in the entertainment world, whether on the stage, in films, or in front of the radio microphone, had already established an important axiom: most fighters can't act, but the popular ones can still make you money trying.

From the very beginning, promoters intuitively understood this. Men such as John L. Sullivan and James J. Corbett were quickly pressed onto the stage. Fighters could tour the country and make more money selling their persona than they did in the ring. During the next generation, it was the likes of Jack Dempsey and Gene Tunney in silent-movie serials, followed in the pantheon by Max Baer and Joe Louis in sound pictures and on the radio.

In the latest medium spotlighting boxers, fledgling television producers needed only to look backward for a blueprint for success. Perhaps more so than any previous media, early television was most like the stage. Unlike movies, they both demanded a "live" performance. Additionally, the stage and television each required a physical presentation beyond that demanded by radio. It was for this reason that many of the television appearances of boxers, not unlike many TV subjects of the day, were fashioned around vehicles reminiscent of vaudeville: interesting banter and a few jokes, a little singing and dancing, and perhaps a comical skit.

Boxing during its Golden Age on television from the late 1940s through the early-1960s facilitated these vehicles through several popular programming formats. Principal among these were the interview program, the game show, the variety show, and the situation comedy.

The interview program was the least risky in that it did not require a performance in the traditional sense—although cataclysmically dangerous in that it could expose a boxing hero to be devoid of personality. The game shows were essentially interviews in a more relaxed and entertaining atmosphere. The fighter needed only to defend against the prescripted questions or soft inquiries of the host or panel, easily navigated around like a pecking jab or a telegraphed overhand right.

The variety program was a grab bag of opportunities. If you were strong in elocution, naturally funny, or could sing and dance, you had a chance to shine. If you had none of these talents, it was time to cross your fingers and pray that the audience was blinded by your celebrity status and/or at least forgiving in their assessment of you.

The television situation comedy required some real acting. Comedy is often the most difficult form of acting to execute. Results were predictable. Performances were stilted, timing was sometimes painfully off, but hey, it was all in fun, audiences reasoned, so why not enjoy it? One can still imagine the typical scenario: *Hey, honey, put those dishes down and come in here, it's Maxie Baer with Abbott and Costello.*

Fighters were even passable when cast in television dramas, provided they were relegated to a cameo, or a small role in which their character closely mirrored their own persona. Serious drama was another matter. It was avoided with few exceptions. That was for . . . well . . . professional actors.

Television of the late-1940s quickly pulled boxing legends and recent champions into its orbit. Jack Dempsey was a logical early entry. One of his first appearances was in 1949 on KTTV, the

Heavyweight champions led the way for ex-fighters in their foray into both radio and television. Pictured is Jack Dempsey rehearsing with Bob Hope for Hope's television debut, October 14, 1951. *AP Photo.*

Times-CBS station in Los Angeles, on a show hosted by Braven Dyer. During the telecast, Dempsey regaled the audience with tales of his fights against Jess Willard, Georges Carpentier, and Gene Tunney.[1]

From time to time television, during its golden age, would call on Dempsey. And like a retired consigliere of the Mafia, he would return to counsel on present-day issues, and to remind the audience of the glories of the past. Jack Dempsey always appeared as Jack Dempsey. He eschewed assuming character roles. They could never do justice to his legend.

He worked the television circuit, appearing on mostly variety programs from *Texaco Star Theater* and *Toast of the Town* with Bob Hope and Ed Sullivan, to later appearances on their own programs, to *The Ken Murray Show*, *Art Linkletter's House Party*, and *The Jack Paar Show.*

Other former boxing champions appeared on early television in a variety of programming. In 1949, Jake La Motta provided a unique contribution to early boxing television history. He appeared with radio and television personality Tex McCrary on WNAC TV, Washington, DC, in a ring at the Brooklyn's Broadway Arena.[2] There they staged a four-round demonstration for early television viewers on "How to Watch a Prize Fight."[3]

That same year, former middleweight champion Tony Zale, whose career had ended only recently at the hands of Marcel Cerdan, was interviewed by Jack Brickhouse on a WGN-TV telecast from Chicago. Zale's new gig at that time was boxing director of the local CYO.[4] Former heavyweight champion Primo Carnera was recycled on television as a wrestler, appearing in matches from Madison Square Garden during 1949, when wrestling returned to the arena after a twelve-year hiatus.[5] Later, Carnera would secure some dramatic roles, such as his occasional appearances with John Bromfield in *The Sheriff of Cochise.*[6] In 1950, Gus Lesnevich, former world light-heavyweight champion, appeared as a boxer in the CBS television drama adapted from Paul Gallico's *The Winner and the Champion.* Joining Lesnevich was Johnnie Addie, the Garden's ring announcer.[7]

Joe Louis was the most prolific champion to make appearances on radio, and he carried the weight of his celebrity as an ex-champion into the realm of television. As a budding celebrity in the mid-1930s, his Alabama drawl, clipped speech, and lack of timing all presented challenges for him as a speaker on the radio. But after many years of experience in front of the microphone, his diction had grown a bit clearer, and his ear for the pace of scripted banter had somewhat improved. Objectively speaking, Louis was still quite limited, but his legend made that problem a mere technicality.

Louis parceled together a diverse minicareer on television as a professional wrestler, comedy and quiz-show guest, and dramatic performer, as well as behind-the-camera boxing consultant. His debt to the US government for back taxes had forced Joe into a wrestling ring. Even today, it is painful for some to watch the great Brown Bomber punching out his leotard-wearing opponents in the circled-square. Louis even appeared on a television quiz show that offered a $75,000 jackpot in a gambit to ameliorate his tax problem. One news article reporting the game show appearance featured a picture of the champ captioned, "Woe is me." The story explained that Louis was attempting to pay off his $1.3 million debt to Uncle Sam and that Rocky Marciano and Jimmy Braddock were providing moral support.[8] It was more fitting to find the champ acting as a boxing consultant on one of the fight-oriented episodes of the *Studio One* program.[9]

Money would remain a prime motivator for the Brown Bomber to continue his relationship with the television industry. In the early-1960s, he turned to boxing promotion to pay the bills. Louis promoted televised boxing matches from a Los Angeles night club, Moulin Rouge. The first televised main event featured future welterweight champion Curtis Cokes and Johnny Newman. Tom Malone provided the blow-by-blow, and Louis added the in-between round analysis. The series lasted a mere sixteen weeks. Like so many of Louis's other business ventures, his foray into the promotional world proved unsuccessful.[10]

As an adult, the champ had always been obsessed with golf, and he developed into quite a proficient scratch golfer. It was with great pride that during the 1940s, Louis began sponsoring the Joe Louis

Open, a golf tournament for African American golfers. Eventually, the event would make its way to television. In 1949, the tournament was televised from the Rackham, one of Detroit's municipal golf courses. Joining premier African American champions of the day were then-current boxing champions Sugar Ray Robinson, Ike Williams, and Ezzard Charles. Louis entered the open as the defending champion of its amateur division.[11]

Louis's notoriety made him a sought-after commodity. A couple of years later, the Dean Martin and Jerry Lewis show on the *Colgate Comedy Hour* was making a splash. Louis, then on the comeback trail, appeared on an episode with crooner Tony Martin. The pair was introduced as Martin and Lewis, with the audience expecting the appearance of the comic duo, only to be surprised with the boxer and the singer. The comedians soon appeared, and the script had the foursome in "debated" ownership of their hyphenated surnames.

As the taciturn Louis stands with his coat folded in his arms, Jerry Lewis attempts to remove him from the stage. "Get off the stage, get off the stage Joey," a hysterical Lewis shrieks at the Brown Bomber. The comedian then assumes his boxing stance, displays some fancy footwork, and launches a few hooks to Louis's body. "I keep hittin' him, I keep hittin' him, it don't bother him," Jerry cries, appealing to Dean Martin. "I like it, I like it," Joe responds, bringing raucous laughter from both the crowd and his fellow performers.[12]

In 1955, Louis appeared in a dramatic role on *General Electric Theater*. In the CBS presentation entitled "Gentleman Jim," the former heavyweight king James J. Corbett comes down from heaven to prove that he is a better boxer than the Brown Bomber. It may not have been Louis's finest moment on television, but it certainly was more dignified than being bounced about a wrestling ring.[13]

Long after his retirement, Louis, now truly comfortable before the camera, appeared on the game show *I've Got A Secret* with Ben Gazzara and New York Yankees pitching ace Whitey Ford. Gazzara in suit and tie sans jacket, and Whitey in a sweat suit and sneakers, showed some legitimate boxing acumen as they sparred a bit for host John Daly.

Of course, a sparring partner was needed for Daly. The host, fitted with boxing gloves but still wearing his inimitable bowtie, turns his face into the fist of Louis. Daly, Louis, and Gazzara retreat to a bench to discuss boxing of the day. Gazzara queries Joe about the rumor of a Marciano comeback. "Well, all I can say is that I made a comeback once and it wasn't so good," the champ responds. The trio fall into laughter as the actor embraces the boxer. Louis opines on the upcoming Patterson-Johansson rematch at the Polo Grounds. "They always tell me to bet on the champ because he can only lose once," Louis jokes, offering up the old boxing insider one-liner.[14]

The following year, Louis was made the subject of the biographical program *This is Your Life.* The program begins at the People to People sports banquet at the Hotel Astor in Time Square, where cameras lie in wait for the unsuspecting champion. The show opens for the television audience with suspense. Any of the famous celebrities at the event might be the show's focus. "Could it be Jack Dempsey or Don Budge or Althea Gibson or Kyle Rote or Robert Moses?" host Ralph Edwards asks, teasing television viewers as the camera focuses upon each celebrity. Edwards then bursts into the hotel and clearly surprises Louis. Dempsey, a subject of the program in 1957, is the first to congratulate Joe.

Louis is then whisked to a mobile studio backstage. He sits in his tuxedo on a tiny boxing stool in the middle of a makeshift ring, sagging ropes and all, creating a visual effect that is as amusing as it suggests. With sentimental music playing, six of Louis's living brothers and sisters join a beaming Brown Bomber in the ring. Next to appear is the grown-up version of the ten-year-old neighbor who carried his gym bag for him—none other than the irrepressible Ray Robinson. Sugar meets Louis center ring in a huge embrace. The Louis pantheon continues, all to the genuine delight of Joe: Ring pilot John Roxborough, comanager Julian Black, Max Schmeling, James J. Braddock, Ezzard Charles, and Louis's wife, Martha, with children and foster children in tow for the coup de grâce.[15]

As a radio celebrity, the only fighter who rivaled Louis in both popularity and ubiquity was Max Baer. Baer's fame had peaked before the television era moved into high gear, but he was still a familiar personality to American television audiences of the 1950s. After his bout with Tony Galento in 1940, Maxie had been interviewed along with Joe Louis by comedian Lou Costello before the newsreel cameras. Costello had always had an interest in the fight game, boxing briefly under the alias of Lou King.[16] Years later, as the star of his own television comedy, *The Abbott and Costello Show,* a more portly Lou would engage Max to appear in one of his programs.

In the appearance, an older but still-robust Baer portrays prizefighter Killer King, who is also the jealous husband of a blonde named Dixie. The pair rent an apartment in the boys' building, and Costello immediately bumbles his way into suspicion of amorous intents. "They're the scum of the earth," Maxie rails at his competition, "Next time I find a guy fooling around with my Dixie I am going to ram his head right down into his shoes."[17] Hjinks ensue, as unbeknownst to Max, Lou hides under a couch, which Baer alternately sits and stands on. Costello and Baer ultimately end up in a free-for-all at the gym in which Lou takes out Max with a flying kick only to be downed himself by Killer's wife.[18]

Baer's services were also called upon by producers in dramatic roles, and he was cast in several episodes of *Sheena, Queen of the Jungle* to portray a white hunter.[19] Baer's personality was also a natural for a variety show, and he starred in his own program out of Los Angeles, which aired locally on Channel 9. It was an opportunity for Baer to bring his larger-than-life persona to a new generation and share the spotlight with an array of guests including Jack Dempsey, Joe Louis, Jimmy Durante, and Jack Lemmon.[20]

Up until the week that Baer died from a heart attack at the age of fifty, he could be found in front of the television camera. He had recently arrived in Hollywood to film some television commercials, and just a week prior, he appeared as the referee of a televised ten-round bout between Zora Folley and Alonzo Johnson.[21]

Television cameras attracted many top middleweights of the era. In addition to numerous appearances by Ray Robinson, former middleweight contender Walter Cartier made his acting debut on *The*

Phil Silvers Show on CBS in a 1954 episode. Jack Healy, one-time manager of Rocky Graziano, also appeared.[22] Robinson opponent Joey Archer was featured on an episode of *Route 66.*

Perhaps the most celebrated ex-fighter to appear on television was former middleweight champion Rocky Graziano, who fell into acting to help a friend and did his first gigs for no money. Writer Nat Hiken liked what he saw, and when he needed a boyfriend for Martha Raye on her show, he pegged Graziano. "People saw me on *The Martha Raye Show* and said, 'Gee, you done great,' so I left fighting." "Television was the last thing on my mind, who thought I could do comedy?" Graziano quickly warmed to the etiquette of his new profession. "In Stillman's gym the guys yell, 'Hey, you bum!' In show business they say, 'Good morning, Mr. Graziano.'"[23]

Rocky, who had been trounced in front of the cameras in a boxing ring by Chuck Davey and Sugar Ray Robinson, found acting to be a cinch by comparison. Before going on the air, Martha Raye and Rocky's other new colleagues would rush over to him with words of encouragement. Graziano was perplexed. "I think to myself: whatta they mean? Nothing's gonna happen. Nobody's gonna get killed tonight." After his first show, Rocky watched a film copy at home and noted: "It's a wonderful experience. I'm glad my father took the boat. This is a hell of a country."[24] In 1961, several years after *The Martha Raye Show,* Graziano would reach the apex of his television run, appearing in thirty-eight episodes of the private investigative drama *Miami Undercover.*[25]

One of Graziano's more memorable appearances on television was when he was matched with former ring rival Sugar Ray Robinson on an episode of *Car 54, Where Are You?* starring Joe E. Ross and Fred Gwynne. Graziano plays Antoine, a hairdresser who paints, knits, bakes, and bird-watches. He is also one hell of a fighter. "Just a few more minutes," he tells one of his clients crowned by a hairdryer, "Oh, it's going to look ravishing."[26]

His girlfriend, with the assistance of Ross and Gwynne, tries to derail his Golden Gloves career by overmatching him. The foil is Sugar Ray Robinson disguised as an old man. At first, Robinson declines to help. "Why don't you get Archie Moore, he won't need a wig or makeup," Robbie quips. Robinson also hits the speed bag while being fitted for a new suit. "Leave a little room for me to do the 'lambo,'" he tells the tailor, as he breaks out into a little dance. Later, Robinson, in a bald wig and white mustache, thrashes the Rock. Graziano's character retires from boxing and is without an outlet for his frustrations, which he now takes out on his mortified customers.[27]

As was the case with every prominent boxer who crossed over into television during the era, Graziano was given his opportunity on a game show. Appearing on *I've Got a Secret,* the Rock enters the studio stage in full regalia of the Boy Scouts of America, including knee-socks and handkerchief with tie clasp, to salute National Boy Scout Week. Next, Graziano and host Daly, both in uniform, attempt to qualify for their badges as a troop of Boy Scouts stand behind them and assay their activities.[28]

Daly and Graziano make a fire from kindling, thrust axes into tree stumps, and flip flapjacks as the blindfolded panel tries to guess the activity. Johnny Carson is then guided off the panel to serve as a guinea pig for their first aid activity. The panelists could not guess Rocky's secret, but Graziano did earn his merit badge.[29]

The other Rock of the day, Rocky Marciano, was more polished and articulate than his *paesan* and certainly more phlegmatic. He also pursued an acting career shortly after retiring. "Fighting has given me all the confidence I need . . . I have the confidence to go before a camera as well as under the ring lights," the former champ explained after appearing on a TV show.[30]

Unlike Carnera and Louis before him, Marciano avoided the "grunt and groan" circuit, but on one occasion he did find himself on British television as the referee of a wrestling match between Fritz Von Erich and "Whipper" Billy Watson. After Marciano disqualified Erich, the wrestler closed in on the Rock, who then raised both fists, assuming his boxing stance. Erich wisely retreated.[31]

Marciano tasted the flavor of television outside the ring during his tenure as heavyweight champion. Shortly after winning the title, he made an appearance on *Four Star Review.* He was a guest on *Toast of the Town* three times, and twice on *The Colgate Comedy Hour*, including an appearance right after his second victory over Ezzard Charles. In that program he was joined by his manager, Al Weill, and singer Eddie Fisher, whom the champ knew from Grossinger's Resort Hotel in the Catskills, where Rocky trained and Eddie performed.[32] During that period, he also made his way onto *The Bob Hope Show, The Red Skelton Show,* and *Person to Person.* In each instance, Marciano appeared as himself.[33]

While considering a serious acting career, Marciano consulted such ex-fighters-turned-thespians as Victor McLaglen and Maxie Rosenbloom. He also spoke to television producers. One producer who seemed to have a good understanding of Rocky's out-of-the-ring demeanor believed he might excel in the role of a small-town policeman who helped friends and children with their problems.[34] While affable, Marciano never landed a starring role or even a steady part on a dramatic or comedic television program. He did make an uncredited appearance in an episode of *Combat!* titled "Masquerade." During the episode, in which Lee Marvin makes a guest appearance, Marciano has a few fleeting moments on screen as an ambulance driver.[35]

Marciano's likability was of value, and he displayed his appeal on Groucho Marx's *You Bet Your Life.*[36] As a preliminary to Marciano's appearance on the program, a young intern provides a bit of unintended humor by bungling two boxing questions. First, he mistakes Primo Carnera, whom he simply called "Prima," for the man who knocked Dempsey out of the ring, and then he misidentifies the boxer known as "Gentleman Jim" as the fictitious hybrid, "Jim Fitzsimmons."

Marciano then warms up with Groucho before his turn to tackle some questions. The Rock had an endearing, little-boy quality about him. He was sheepishly proud of his accomplishments. Groucho: "In your opinion, who was the greatest fighter of all time?" Marciano: "I think Joe Louis." Groucho: "How about Dempsey and Jim Jeffries, why do you say Louis is the best?" "Well, I like to say Louis was the greatest because I was lucky enough to beat Louis, so that makes me pretty good," Marciano explained, breaking into a little grin.[37]

It was this natural quality that helped Marciano find a niche on television as host of the boxing series *Main Event.* During the program, the champion watched films of great fights of the past with a guest star from the entertainment or sporting world. During the opening segment, and in between highlights of the week's featured fight, the Rock and his guest would pal around. On a couch flanked by a pair of lamps, in front of a wall-paneled backdrop, the likes of George Raft, Zsa Zsa Gabor, Tony Martin, and Jersey Joe Walcott would join him.

One week, Marciano and Walcott kibitzed about their first title bout. At one point during Walcott's appearance, Marciano points to a picture on the wall. It is the iconic shot of the thirteenth-round knockout blow of Jersey Joe, in which Walcott's features are greatly distorted. "Remember this picture here, it won the sports picture of the year." "Yeah, Rock," a reflective Jersey Joe responds, "We were no matinee idols that night."[38]

Main Event was written by a young Pete Hamill, a great author and lifelong patron of the sport. His professionalism provided a solid base for the show, and for the most part, Marciano was in his element. In one episode featuring Nat King Cole, Cole makes note of a picture of the Rock with Joe DiMaggio and President Dwight Eisenhower. Marciano explained to Nat how a number of awestruck sport figures met the president at the White House. Then Marciano related a short story. After meeting the president and returning to his Italian neighborhood, Rocky entered a local club ready to receive his props. There he overheard an old mustachioed man exclaim, "Hmmm, Marciano thinks he's a big shot now, just had his picture taken with DiMaggio."[39]

While *Main Event* mined the vast anecdotal experiences of Marciano and his guests with success, the program did have its maladies. The segments, which were undoubtedly produced on a slim budget, are extremely formulaic. It is also readily apparent that Marciano, on occasion, is reading from the teleprompter. However, years later, these curiosities only add to the program's charm. The show now serves as a veritable time capsule for America's entertainment world in the early-1960s.

One of Marciano's opponents, Roland La Starza, parlayed his disputed 1950 loss and spirited heavyweight championship challenge against Rocky into his own dalliance with the television camera. La Starza appeared in off-Broadway plays and in the movie *Reprieve,* as well as episodes of the television series *The Untouchables* and *Hennessey.* In 1962, this son of a Bronx butcher was cast in a new Warner Brothers TV show about World War II titled *The Gallant Men.*[40]

The show emphasized the personal stories of individual soldiers of the American 36th Division, from their landing at Salerno to their entry into Rome. La Starza was schooled in army firearms and combat maneuvers for the role, and endured twelve-hour filming days but was undaunted by the regiment. "I am having a great time in television. The way I feel now, I'd like to keep acting forever," the ex-contender explained. Apparently, his biggest difficulty was suppressing his natural fighting instincts. "The stunt men had to show me how to pull punches in fights. I was coming too close at first," La Starza admitted.[41]

Unlike La Starza, Ingemar Johansson did not wait for retirement to launch his television career. Clearly, his good looks gave him a distinct advantage over some in his profession, and he quickly signed with the William Morris Agency. In a surprising display of musical talent, the champ appeared on the *Dinah Shore Chevy Show* in 1959. Standing near a heavy bag, the champ and Shore exchange some awkwardly sweet banter. Johansson then takes to singing, and after he finished an unexpectedly moving solo in Swedish, Shore exclaims, "Perry Como look out!" She then asks Ingo to sing a duet, to which Ingemar responds, "Good, your singing always knock me down." The pair then belt out a Swedish toe-tapper.[42]

One television reviewer pegged Johansson as "an engaging stage personality with an attractively shy and diffident manner" and noted that "thanks to the sincerity and simplicity of his approach he projected a high degree of boyish charm" in his singing efforts.[43]

A handsome singing boxer from Sweden, however, did not an actor make. An appropriate vehicle would need to be found for American television. Years before, Ernest Hemingway had penned the story *The Killers*, the tale of an ex-boxer called the Big Swede. It was almost as if Hemingway had prognosticated Johansson's future need for a story. Ingemar played Ole Anderson, an ex-fighter pursued by gangsters. The drama marked the premiere of *Buick-Electra Playhouse*, aired on CBS.[44]

After receiving a positive response to his song-and-dance routines on television and his work in a motion picture, Johansson returned to New York to appear in *The Killers*. The boxing portions of the program were taped at the Eighth Avenue Gym in midtown Manhattan. Johansson was assuming Max Baer's old role as boxing's media playboy. He relaxed between takes, clowning with fellow actor Dean Stockwell, and, was playful with visitors, trying on their undersize hats. He even entertained the set by singing a Swedish version of "I Hear Music," and, of course, he took the phone number of an attractive female "in a feather-cut hairdo."[45]

The script called for Johansson to be floored by his opponent, played by another fighter-turned-actor, Henry Wallitsch, who ended up with a professional record of 14–13. Some of the fledgling pro's friends suggested that he hit the champion with a "cheap shot" and knock him out for real, a gambit that would bring him instant fame. "I couldn't do that," Wallitsch said, "In the few weeks we've been rehearsing, I got to like him too much."[46]

The Killers was the first of four Hemingway short stories adapted for television by A. E. Hotchner for *Buick-Electra Playhouse*. John P. Shanley of the *New York Times* found Johansson's portrayal as "natural and believable" but found that the adaptation was unsuccessful at capturing the distinctive quality of Hemingway's original.[47]

During the peak of his fame, Johansson was the most ubiquitous boxing television face to date. The champ appeared twice on the panel show *What's My Line?* In his first appearance, as a mystery guest, Johansson was not yet a world champion, but the heavyweight boxing champion of Europe. The clue given was that the subject was self-employed. The first panelist, Martin Gable, scored early with his questioning and had Johansson on the ropes when he asked, "Did you knock out an American boxer in one round not so long ago?

Was his name Eddie Machen?" Then, the knockout blow: "Are you about to fight Floyd Patterson next June for the heavyweight championship of the world?" After Johansson was exposed, host John Daly explained, "Floyd Patterson is an American. Of course we would like to see the crown stay here, but if it has to go I can't think of a better man for it to go to."[48]

Johansson sought a rematch with the panelists the following year as a mystery challenger. One of the blindfolded panelists, Amon Andrews, was introduced at the beginning of the show as the man who would announce the Patterson rematch from New York for the BBC the next day. Shockingly, Johansson was appearing on a TV game show the evening before defending his title! "Why aren't you home in bed?" panelist Arlene Francis asked incredulously, after Johansson was easily identified. Patterson would put him to sleep the next evening.[49]

In Sweden, Johansson appeared in numerous Volvo ads and was featured on a panel game show in Canada. In the United States, he made an encore appearance on *The Dinah Shore Show,* played on *The Steve Allen Show,* and was a "mystery guest" on *Masquerade Party.* The champ also had a brief stint in films, appearing in a Korean War film, *All the Young Men.*[50]

Johansson's ring rival Floyd Patterson was the complete opposite of Ingo, shunning any type of attention, no less that of the television audience. Patterson, however, did predate Ingo as a panelist on *What's My Line?* when he was the heavyweight champ. The program's format only requiring a simple "yes" or "no" response from the guest suited the painfully shy boxer fine.

In retrospect, the irony is apparent. Just as the panelists would don their masks, on occasion, Floyd would resort to the use of disguises to mask his identity following the loss of a bout. Patterson had recently won the vacant title against Archie Moore. "You did fight marvelously," Arlene Francis told the new champion after he was identified. "I bet on the other fellow, but you were just great."[51]

Perhaps fittingly, Patterson made his biggest splash on television by proxy. During the 1960 Emmy Awards telecast, Fred Astaire interrupted the proceedings to announce that Floyd had knocked out Ingemar Johansson at the Polo Grounds to regain the heavyweight championship.[52]

Whereas Patterson wanted nothing of television beyond its already intrusive lens, Sugar Ray Robinson was compelled to "act" before the audience. Performing was always in Robbie's blood. As a child, he danced at the Alvin Theater for two dollars a night. He even put his historic ring career on hold for a couple of years to pursue a full-time entertainment career. He debuted at a French casino with Joe Louis, Jersey Joe Walcott, Jackie Robinson, and Milton Berle to cheer him on. Sporting an eye-catching yellow-and-black tuxedo jacket, he danced, joked, and turned on his natural charm. He spent two years touring Europe and the United States. Dance practice was long hours, bus rides even longer. His urge to box and a cable received that said, "Hurry home. Business going to the dogs," sent him back into the ring.[53]

However, the ring's bright lights alone were never enough for Robinson, and from time to time he would seek out television. In 1957, Robinson appeared on *Person to Person* with Edward R. Murrow. Sitting cross-legged in a studio chair with cigarette in hand, the famed correspondent asked Robbie: "You give me the impression that you rather enjoy your work, is that right?" Robinson, appearing remotely from his home in accordance with the show's format, looked resplendent in his suede smoking jacket. "No, just the opposite, Ed," Sugar Ray replied, "I've never enjoyed boxing; it's just a business with me."[54]

In 1962, Robinson was to box former middleweight champion Terry Downes in England. Ten days before the bout, Ray could be found at the London Palladium singing before a television audience.[55]

Unlike the vast majority of athletes who ventured into the entertainment world, Robinson had some legitimate talent. What boxer would have the chops to go line-for-line with Laurence Olivier or sing with Frank Sinatra? Yet, Robinson danced with confidence beside the great Gene Kelly on *Omnibus*, the longest-running cultural series in the history on network television. "Now listen, Sugar, what's the most important thing a boxer's got to have?," Kelly asks

Robinson as they began their segment. "Rhythm, man, rhythm," a grinning Ray replied as the pair broke into a tap routine.[56]

Robinson was offered other opportunities to dance on television. Shortly after losing his middleweight laurels to Carmen Basilio, he was scheduled to replace Cab Calloway in the CBS drama *Green Pastures.* He would portray the King of Babylon in a role that included dancing. Like Calloway, Robinson abdicated his fictitious throne before it ever reached the small screen.[57] Several years earlier, Robinson, while on hiatus from the ring, also appeared in the drama *The Adventures of Huckleberry Finn* in the role of Jim. Interestingly, Archie Moore reprised the role in a major motion picture a decade later.[58]

Just like Patterson, Johansson, Walcott, Dempsey, and Tiger, Robinson, then middleweight kingpin, would have his turn as the mystery challenger on *What's My Line?* Sugar, capitalizing on his Parisian travels, adopted a French accent to throw off the blindfolded panel. "Have you ever been a champion?" asked Arlene Francis. "*Oui, oui, oui*" Ray responded.[59]

Not all boxers to appear on television had the pedigree of Robinson, Louis, or even Graziano. Early television was sprinkled with ex-boxers of minor fame who either found their true calling before the cameras or was afforded a second professional career. Hugh O'Brian was an amateur boxer in the Marine Corps. He amassed a record of 35–1 with 18 KOs before transforming into Marshal Wyatt Earp. Even to this day, he is probably remembered by those who wore Daniel Boone-like coonskin caps as kids, watching him cross-legged in front of their DuMont or Admiral set.[60]

Remembering a television star is one thing; recalling his boxing résumé is another. Only the true boxing aficionado will recall that Johnny Bromfield, who was seen on television as the leading man in the outdoor TV epic *Sheriff of Cochise,* was Golden Gloves champion his senior year at St. Mary's in Oakland, California, and an intercollegiate champion. Or likewise, that Dane Clark turned down a professional boxing career to eventually become the star of *Wire Service.* And only those with quiz show–level knowledge would be intimate with the television dossier of long forgotten amateur fighters such as University of Miami collegiate boxer Joe Cranston. Cranston appeared in numerous top television shows such as *Wyatt Earp*, *Climax!*, *Playhouse 90*, and *Ford Theater*.[61]

While Cranston may have worked the television circuit with effect, he was a mere novice in comparison to Vincent Barbi, early television's "face without a name." An ex-boxer who fought as a teenager for Italy in the 1932 Olympics, he later became a New York Golden Gloves champion under several ring aliases. In a three-year span, Barbi made an amazing 400 television appearances.

Barbi was compelled to act on television. He was disgusted with what he found to be the unrealistic portrayal of prizefighters. In addition to acting, Barbi also served as a technical boxing advisor for television programs and coached actors such as Gig Young, in an episode of *Robert Montgomery Presents*, and Tod Andrews on *Armstrong Circle Theater*.[62]

While in front of the camera, Barbi was often cast as a criminal. Barbi had the face for it. "I owe a lot to boxing," he explained, "but my nose owes it even more. I wanted a boxer's nose when I was fighting. I wanted it to get flattened. I accomplished that all right."[63]

Barbi performed his 100th television homicide on the popular television series *Martin Kane*. The actor's criminal actions on television were so ubiquitous that he was once picked up by two policemen in New York who mistakenly believed that they had seen his face on wanted posters. Barbi can be seen in the motion picture *On the Waterfront*. However, with all those pugs in the film, it still may be a challenge to identify him.[64]

Chapter 19

STAY TUNED: BOXING AND THE TELEVISION SERIES

The sport of boxing served the medium of television on two levels. In addition to lending its ring talent to the small screen, the fight game itself, with its seedy backdrop and edgy characters, was a natural for the dramatic exploitation of fictionalized stories. With its cozy relationship with the television industry and its larger-than-life characters, it was also fodder for comedic exploitation. In fact, no genre could resist the "boxing story." Dramas, particularly crime dramas and detective stories, theater anthology programs, comedy and variety shows, even adventure and science fiction stories all embraced the boxing world on television. From the late-1940s through the early-1960s, boxing-themed programs counted into the hundreds.

The amount of boxing content in these programs varied considerably. Some shows were completely tangential and raise the unanswerable question as to what constitutes a "boxing program." In an episode of *The Beverly Hillbillies,* we find Granny sparring for a few moments with a kangaroo.[1] On *The Jack Benny Program,* Jack attends a concert with a date who listens briefly to a fight broadcast on a transistor radio, driving the well-dressed audience out of the concert hall.[2]

Others shows used boxing to provide a deep background for a program that otherwise lacked boxing content. In the premiere episode of *The George Burns and Gracie Allen Show,* the comedy focuses on George's efforts to get out of the house so that he can go to the fights.[3] In an episode of *My Three Sons,* Bub is faced with giving up his fight tickets in order to help Robbie pursue a romantic interest.[4] And in an entry of the *The Untouchables,* the subject of the criminal activity is the theft of the gate receipts from the Baer-Schmeling bout.[5]

On other occasions, boxing was not the program's focus but was used to help advance a story or further develop a character's persona. When Ozzie Nelson decides to pursue new leisure interests, he finds himself woefully out of place at a boxing match caught between two patrons fistfighting in the stands. He returns to his routine of card playing and golf.[6] In *The Untouchables,* Frank Nitti is found at ringside firmly in charge of his underworld domain.[7]

Generally speaking, when dramatic programs delved into fight themes, they would make boxing central to the story. Additionally, it was almost guaranteed that a drama or crime drama series that had any longevity on television would eventually get around to airing at least one episode with a boxing backdrop. Dramatic programs such as *Racket Squad, The Untouchables, The Fugitive, The Public Defender, Peter Gunn, Tightrope,* and *Man Against Crime* were all amongst those shows contributing to the boxing subgenre.

Frequently, a "fixed fight," with a "dive," orchestrated by gangsters, with a possible "double-cross" was central to the plot. The 1961 episode of *The Untouchables,* "Ring of Terror," featured an introductory description by Walter Winchell that encapsulates the boxing crime drama and the world of corruption that it portrayed: the ring is "a place where tough young animals from reform schools and rotting tenements were willing to sacrifice their blood for a chance to lick the two phantoms of poverty and obscurity. It hardly mattered that in the process the Marquis of Queensberry got only lip service and that the men who got the big payoffs fought with machine guns instead of gloves."[8]

In 1959, Mike Connors starred in an episode of *Tightrope!*, "The Money Fight," which typified the standard "fixed fight" story. In the program, a fix is orchestrated by gangsters. However, the fighter refuses to go through with the fix and knocks out his opponent, completing the "double cross." Later, the fighter is strangled in the dressing room and then hung to make the murder look like suicide.[9]

The "fixed" fight also had a number of variations. In a 1954 episode of *The Public Defender*, "The Prizefighter Story," one can find a youthful Richard Jaeckel portraying an honest boxer who won't play ball with the syndicate. When he refuses to fix a fight, he is framed with a narcotics charge.[10] In a 1951 episode of *Racket Squad*, "The Knockout," the audience is taken into the world of confidence men, who bilk the mark of his money, through a staged fixed fight complete with a phony audience complicit to the con.[11] In *The Untouchables*' 1960 entry, "Head of Fire, Feat of Clay," a childhood friend of Elliot Ness uses the weight of their relationship for personal gain by blackmailing a Chicago gangster who regularly fixes fights.[12]

These crime dramas typically portrayed the gangsters' grip on the fight game as a stranglehold, telling us that "once those vultures get their dirty claws into one of your fighters they don't quit until they get them all" and that gangsters are "protected by a wall of silence, created by fear." The sport of boxing was also depicted as saddled with a certain degree of fatalism: "The fight game is like the weather, everybody talks about it, but nobody ever does anything."[13]

Paradoxically, while the overriding message was that the war on boxing corruption could not be won, these programs regularly portrayed law enforcement as victors in their individual turf battles against it. At the conclusion of "Head of Fire, Feet of Clay," we find the perpetrators of the boxing corruption to be punished by being beaten and bloodied. In *Tightrope!* we see police apprehending the criminals, and in *Racket Squad* we are told at the end that "the whole mob" was sent to jail. Similarly, in *The Public Defender*, prison sentences for criminal conspiracy and perjury are doled out as part of justice served.

The gangster, the fixed fight, and other stereotypical portrayals of the boxing world were themes to which television audiences had grown accustomed. An audience complicit with the storytellers on both radio and television had permitted these themes to persist for more than a generation. However, a shift in both the depiction of boxing and general social tastes was on the horizon. This new model was foreshadowed in the atypical boxing drama "Decision in the Ring," a 1963 episode of *The Fugitive.* While in pursuit of the one-armed man, Richard Kimble, played by David Janssen, takes a detour to serve as cutman for a black boxer, Joe Smith, portrayed by James Edwards. Smith contends with the specter of prejudice that has curtailed his willingness to pursue a career as a doctor, with the fugitive providing needed encouragement.[14]

However, throughout the 1950s, the utilization of common or topical boxing themes remained prevalent. Several programs of the adventure genre, a subgenre of television dramas, capitalized on their familiarity with audiences. In *Route 66*, the old standby, "the fighter on the comeback trail," is visited, with middleweight contender Joey Archer featured.[15] The ubiquitous self-serving promoter is found in a 1955 episode of *Sheena, Queen of the Jungle*, "The Ganyika Kid." In the story, which can fairly be categorized as the disgruntled boxer's ultimate fantasy, an African fighter who is also the head of his tribe literally hunts his ex-promoter, who is led through the jungle by a scantily clad Sheena.[16]

The always-topical ring death is featured, replete with the telling newspaper headline to memorialize the occasion in *Lassie*'s "The Fighter" in 1954. "I was a pretty good fighter, so good I killed a man with my fists," a boxer dramatically confides to Ellen of the "Lassie family."[17] In a 1962 episode of *Everglades*, "Young Osceola," the hot topic of boxing corruption and its related governmental hearings is utilized. "I'm not going to testify in front of that committee," a frightened boxer explains, before developing his courage with the help of the series star, Ron Haye.[18] In an episode of *Adventures in Paradise*,

"Once Around the Circuit," boxing's safety rules and regulations are touched upon in a story concerning a fighter who is banned in the US for health considerations and seeks ring action in the South Seas.[19]

These and other television dramas presented a wide variety of perspectives from which to glimpse the fight game. However, while they were numerous, they were not always qualitative. Without question, the boxing-themed programs of superior quality were most commonly featured on the "theater programs." During the 1950s, *General Electric Theater, Ford Theater, Four Star Theater,* and NBC's *Kraft Television Theater* offered programs with diverse subject matter that occasionally embraced a boxing-themed story. These and other dramatic anthology programs featured both well-known and more obscure boxing-oriented stories.

While not illustrative of their best efforts, like other dramatic television programming involving boxing, the portrayal of the fixed fight was well represented in "theatrical series." The theme of "the fix" was fertile material for laying the foundation for stories with tough characters, and writers had a penchant for endowing them with an uncanny knack for colorful expression. In *Stage 7*'s 1955 episode, "The Long Count," star Frank Lovejoy exposes the murder of a boxer for insurance money. Regarding a fixed fight, the boxer is warned, "You louse up this bout and I'll have a couple of my boys catch you in the alley and break both your arms."[20] In *Four Star Playhouse*'s "Knockout," starring Broderick Crawford, as an "arranged" bout is exposed, we are told "the whole thing started to smell rotten."[21] And in *General Electric Theater*'s "No Skin Off Me," a trainer portrayed by Ronald Reagan spots an obvious fix: "I saw our boy flick Grasso's whiskers with a right that was about as tough as a barber's brush."[22]

These theatrical programs stood at the edge of a slippery slope subject to the very same pitfalls of any other dramatic programs. At their worst, they could be stereotypical, with predictable plots laced with clichés. However, at their best, they featured writers and actors of considerable talent who represented the best of television of the era—much of which was still being performed live.

In 1955, the substantial writing talents of Budd Schulberg were capitalized upon in "Winner by Decision," presented by *General Electric Theater.* The program, hosted by Ronald Reagan, featured fine performances by Harry Belafonte and Ethel Waters. Here, the audience is offered a superior character study of a boxer of considerable natural ability who is thrust into the fight game by the other men of his family. "There's a boy fighting at St. Nicks, my boy," his father pronounces with a sense of lineal pride.[23]

Struggling with his desire to pursue an education, Belafonte's character is coaxed into the ring: "What about Vejar?" "He was at NYU and made big dough boxing all at the same time," he is told. Ethel Waters portrays the fighter's mother, who is disturbed by her son's lack of independence. Yet, she vigilantly protects him and even chastises his prospective manager: "You're talking about my boy, not a hungry animal. A person, not a pie to be cut into pieces." Ultimately, the fighter exerts his independence and eschews the ring.[24]

It was the straightforward dramatic theatrical programming such as "Winner By Decision" that produced the era's most compelling boxing stories. Other anthology series such as *Playwrights '56, The Buick-Electra Playhouse,* and *Robert Montgomery Presents* all made contributions to serious television drama related to the sport. One effort in particular has endured and stands amongst the best television would offer, not only as a boxing piece, but as an example of exemplary programming during television's Golden Age.

In 1956, when CBS launched their ninety-minute live drama program *Playhouse 90,* Rod Serling's boxing saga *Requiem For A Heavyweight* was pegged for the second episode. The program would star ex-boxer Jack Palance in the role of Mountain McClintock, a veteran heavyweight fighter coming to terms with the end of his career.[25, 26]

Palance, a son of Ukrainian immigrants, was a 6-foot-4-inch former football player, prizefighter, and bomber pilot. He fought as an intercollegiate boxer at the University of North Carolina. The press at the time stated that he boxed professionally for two years, working the fight club circuit from Louisville to the Broadway Arena in Brooklyn, compiling a mark of 18 wins in 21 outings including a draw with Joe Baski. Present record books show a limited pro career. Regardless, Palance admitted he "didn't have a real fighter's heart." He took the broken nose he earned in the ring to Stanford University, where he studied acting under the GI Bill.[27]

Palance had once described his acting philosophy as a belief that "anything that is really good must in some way be universal, however subtly or blandly."[28] It was the exact quality of universality that made *Requiem* resonate with both viewing audiences and those of the boxing community. The production worked expertly on two levels. It would lay bare the realities of the human condition with all of its frailty and fear, its desperation and yearning; and it would also vividly convey the heightened state in which these conditions existed in the sport of boxing.

Key to the program's success was Rod Serling's stark and pungent dialogue that was able to capture the essence of the fight game where so many others had failed. In one of the opening scenes, a spent Mountain McClintock is being stitched up by a veteran doctor. As the physician goes about his gruesome task, the Mountain's self-absorbed manager, Maish, and his concerned trainer, Army, look on. "When I first came in they laid them out in front of me," the doctor explains to his companions. "They were human beings then. Young men. You know what it's like now Maish? Its like a guy grating meat in a packing plant. They roll the carcasses down the line in front of them . . . and stamp them . . . beef."[29]

In *Requiem*, Palance gives a nuanced performance as a man who enters the ring as the one-time contender for the heavyweight championship and exits a human being without an identity. Palance endows Mountain with both a childlike need to understand and an adult's need to be understood. He strikes just the right balance of crudeness and warmth, of maturity and naïveté.

Comedian Ed Wynn also shined in a surprisingly multifaceted dramatic role as the sensitive and insightful trainer who loves Mountain more than himself. His real-life son, Keenan Wynn, also delivers as the conflicted manager whose self-interest outpaces his feelings of loyalty and sense of guilt. The fine cast was rounded out by Kim

Hunter, who warmly portrays a social worker who restores Mountain's faith as well as our own belief in the perseverance of human empathy. It was one of the last great live dramatic television programs. It was also boxing's finest contribution to the Golden Age of television.[30]

On occasion, an anthology series would serve up a boxing story that was pure fun. In *General Electric Theater*'s "The Return of Gentleman Jim," fans are treated to a boxing fantasy. The deceased heavyweight champion, "Gentleman" Jim Corbett, portrayed by George Montgomery in his television debut, returns from the great beyond to settle the age-old argument: Are fighters of the past better than their contemporaries? To answer this question, a match is arranged with Joe Louis, who portrays himself in the program. However, Corbett's return to earth brings two personal restrictions: no money and no women. As Louis waits for Corbett in the ring, sitting on a stool, Corbett kisses his new love. The crackle of thunder whisks Corbett away and along with it, the chance to see whether Louis or Corbett is the better man. While waiting for Corbett, Louis, who was privy to the otherworld dynamics of the situation, had a moment to reflect. He told the promoter he desired to meet Corbett's foe, the deceased John L. Sullivan. "I'd like to talk to John someday. Of course, I'm not in a hurry."[31]

Other lesser known works of the theater variety fashioned for the small screen included *Kraft*'s playfully named "In the La Banza," in which a boxer is overmatched by his brother and incurs severe injuries, which ends his career; and *Silver Theater*'s "Never Hit a Pigeon," a Runyonesque tale involving a pigeon-breeding boxer from New York who loves a girl who loathes the prize ring.[32]

A serendipitous benefit of boxing-themed programming was its development of future television stars. In the 1957 episode of *Telephone Time*, "Fight for a Title," lightweight champion Benny Leonard is portrayed in a tragic tale. A youthful Michael Landon appears as his opponent, "Kid Lombard." An overmatched Lombard is seriously hurt in the ring by the champion. To make amends, Leonard fights

Lombard in a mock fight held at the gym. Leonard "loses" his title to his mentally diminished opponent, who revels in his victory. A skinny and big-eared Landon looks a bit mechanical in the ring during an earlier bout in the program in which he fights earnestly.[33]

Interestingly, boxing-themed programming served as an even more fertile breeding ground for future movie stars than television stars. Not surprisingly, it was serious actors who performed in dramatic roles who rose to screen stardom, not their ex-fighter counterparts.

The legendary Charlton Heston made an early television appearance as the protagonist in George Bernard Shaw's *Cashel Byron's Profession,* which was adapted for television in a *Robert Montgomery Presents* episode in the early-1950s. A prefilm Paul Newman appeared in the second episode of *Playwrights '56* a.k.a. *The Playwright Hour,* in Sidney Carroll's adaptation of Ernest Hemingway's story *The Battler.* The 1955 episode, which was directed by Arthur Penn, was a remake of a 1953 episode of *Omnibus* with the same name in which Chester Morris played the Hemingway subject.

The most ubiquitous movie star to box on television early in his career was Charles Bronson. Bronson appeared in no less than eight televised episodes of an eclectic group of boxing-related programs from the early-1950s through the early-1960s.

Bronson the boxer was introduced to television audiences in January 1952 on *The Red Skelton Hour.* His magnificently honed physique, muscular yet lean, was perfect for the portrayal of a fighter. Skelton utilized Bronson in a boxing skit with his reoccurring character Cauliflower McPugg. Bare-chested, dressed in his boxing trunks and shoes, and wearing a pair of boxing gloves, Charles faces off against the fully dressed and laconic McPugg in a sparring match held in a locker room. The encounter ends with a knockout scored by Bronson. Bronson's comedic skills never were his forte. Nevertheless, he was able to break Skelton out of character and draw a laugh from him earlier in their scene when he hits Skelton over the head with a newspaper.[34]

In December of that same year, *The Roy Rogers Show* presented the episode "Knockout," which not only featured Trigger, but the recently discovered Bronson, who was billed at the time as Charles Bucinski. In the episode, Bronson is part of a group who sets up a boxing training camp on Rogers's property to facilitate the retrieval of buried loot stolen from a bank. It is both a curiosity and a hoot to watch Rogers knock out Bronson, even if it was staged. Of course, every story has a moral, some more corny than others: "You know we can all be champions at something," Rogers explains, "if we just keep at it and don't throw in the sponge."[35]

In 1954, Bronson appeared on *The Joe Palooka Story*. In the episode, "Two Rings for Eddie," which also features "Slapsie" Maxie Rosenbloom, Bronson's character is a welterweight who seeks to preserve his honor in a grudge sparring session with a heavyweight. Predictably, Bronson gets trounced and Palooka ultimately settles the score. Rosenbloom sets the testosterone-driven fight fan at ease early in the episode by claiming that golf "is a sissy game for my dough."[36] The following year, in an episode of *Public Defender*, "Cornered," starring Bart Matthews, Bronson is a boxer who breaks probation. Despite his efforts to turn over a new leaf, he must resort to attempted armed robbery and kidnapping. In a rare directorial decision, the chiseled Bronson is asked to keep his shirt on for the entire episode.[37]

A few years later, in 1958, Bronson was called upon to portray a boxer in the *Playhouse 90* episode "No Time At All." In the story, Bronson is a boxing champion who is sympathetic to the plight of an opponent who faces the unexpected crisis of having a wife and child on an airliner in peril.[38]

Due to these and other television roles, that same year Bronson was given his own television series, *Man with a Camera*. In the premiere episode, Bronson, who portrays cameraman Mike Kovac, takes his superbly conditioned physique into the ring to spar with the neighborhood boxing hero. It comes to light that the boxer is distraught because he had just learned that his last few fights were fixed. "All three of them dove into the tank like seals after sardines," he tells Bronson with a straight face. Kovac uses his photographic skills to get pictures for the boxer, who wants them as evidence to use to expose the scandal.[39]

In another episode, the crusading cameraman tracks a murderer who wants to settle their business with the gloves. The two men strip down to the waist and duke it out, with Kovac scoring the knockout.[40] Ironically, while Bronson acquitted himself admirably as a fighter, his skill as a photographer was suspect. Pulitzer Prize–winning photographer Nat Fein of the *New York Herald Tribune* noted that he handled a camera "like an M-1 Rifle," and that the only resemblance that he had to an actual cameraman was that he carried a camera.[41]

In a change of pace of sorts, Bronson appeared in "The Last Round," a 1961 episode of the science fiction program *One Step Beyond.* In a yarn that was a cut above the typical melodrama, Bronson portrays Yank Dawson, "an American scheduled to fight in the East End Arena during World War II. Many years earlier, a fighter named Paddy was killed in the Arena, and legend has it that his ghost visited other boxers before they met a similar fate in the same ring. The manager of Dawson's opponent exploits the ghost story to spook Dawson and hires an actor to portray Paddy. However, the real ghost appears to several remaining in the arena after the fight, including Dawson, who are then killed in a bombing raid, fulfilling the haunting."[42]

At least facially, the Western television series, depicting elements of nineteenth-century frontier life such as horses and the open range, did not provide a logical setting for boxing material. However, not unlike other seemingly incongruous pairings such as Tony Bennett and Lady Gaga, circumstance and timing would make their match an inevitability.

Televised boxing and the Western series peaked almost simultaneously. In 1958 and 1959, while boxing was still proliferating nationally, seven out of the ten top television programs were Westerns. And at one time, there were more than thirty primetime Westerns on the air in the same season.[43] Such an alignment of stars in television's constellation could not be ignored. A rough-and-tumble world featuring plenty of tough men prone to fisticuffs was a commonality that provided a basis for many a yarn. During the 1950s and early-1960s, many popular Westerns featured boxing-themed programming including *Annie Oakley*, *Have Gun Will Travel*, *Bat Masterson*, *Rawhide*, *Laramie*, *Yancey Derringer*, *Bonanza*, and *Gunsmoke.* Two programs, *The Westerner* and *Wagon Train*, even used boxing themes in their series debuts.

The major contribution of the Western series to the sport of boxing was its depiction of bare-knuckle boxing. It introduced nongloved fighting to generations born long after its demise in the late nineteenth century with the adoption of the Marquis of Queensberry rules.

Television writers did their best to create an air of legitimacy to these fictitious boxing legends by bolstering them with stout résumés peppered with known bare-knuckle heroes as their former opponents. Early in the episodes, the name-dropping would begin. In an episode of *Rawhide*, Victor McLaglen plays the delusional ex-champion of England and Ireland and waxes poetic about his bouts against Tom Hyer.[44] In *Bat Masterson*, "The Fighter," a nod to John L. Sullivan's nemesis Jake Kilrain is given,[45] and in the series opener of *The Westerner*, the ex-champion boasts of his feats against Victorian era standouts Charley Mitchell, Tommy Ryan, and Peter Jackson.[46]

Realism for these stories was further fortified by the re-creation of the landscape of bare- knuckle fighting. Barnstorming and the touring fighter were staples of the bare-knuckle era that was capitalized upon in such programs as *Laramie*'s 1959 entry "Bare Knuckles" and *Bonanza*'s "The Duke," which aired two years later. A common Western scenario featured a touring ex-world champion or other fighter of considerable pedigree roaming the vast plains or expansive prairies into the world of the television Western venue such as the Ponderosa or Dodge City. Also widespread during the bare-knuckle era was the "fight to the finish" and the "winner-take all" match, both of which were depicted in the 1959 episode of *Yancy Derringer*, "The Wayward Warrior."

Western series also utilized other indicia of the bare-knuckle era. In the same episode of *Yancy Derringer*, the contest takes place on a barge near New Orleans. Staging fights on barges was a practice commonly used to evade local fight laws prohibiting boxing whose jurisdiction did not extend into surrounding waters. We are also given a glimpse of training common to nineteenth-century America's rural society in an episode of *Bonanza* titled "The Duke," where the fighter goes through his paces in a barn. Similarly, we find the open brush of the West as the setting for the training camps in the 1958 *Have Gun, Will Travel* episode, "The Prize Fight Story." And in a 1964 episode of *Gunsmoke*, "The Promoter," as well as in other programs, we see evidence of the common practice of fighters "wearing their colors"—a bandana neatly tied just above the fighter's hip.

The quality of the choreography of the bare-knuckle matches presented varied. At their best, the fighters adopted realistic bare-knuckle stances and fought with a measured restraint commensurate with a long, grueling battle, as featured in "The Promoter." Even with the better productions, there was a tendency to exaggerate a knockdown or knockout blow. Producers seemed enamored with the long arching uppercut, a difficult punch to execute that landed on the button with uncanny regularity in television's boxing rings. The shot was purposefully staged with the back of the victim facing the TV audience. When the punch landed, the fighter's head violently snapped back, creating the illusion that the blow landed perfectly, although the audience never really sees it. At the very least, it made entertaining theater.

Television producers also took a liberal approach to the rules of bare-knuckle fighting in their stories. They often mixed and matched elements of the bare-knuckle fighting under the London Prize Ring rules with that of the gloved fighting under the Marquis of Queensberry rules. For example, in the aforementioned episode of *Laramie*, the contest is waged under the Marquis of Queensberry rules, except that the bout is contested with no gloves. In *Bonanza*'s "A Woman Lost," set in the Civil War era, the use of scheduled rounds and the ten-count are integrated into a bout that otherwise appears to be a bare-knuckle scrap under the London Prize Ring rules.[47]At least one television episode was true to the rules of bare-knuckle boxing. In *Bonanza*'s, "The Duke," Ben Cartwright takes to the ring and advises the ringside audience—and the television audience—of the London

Prize Ring rules under which the bout was to be contested: fighters fight until a man is down; when a boxer is downed, his seconds may help the fighter back to his corner for the rest period; after thirty seconds, the referee will call time, and both fighters have eight seconds to toe the mark or be deemed defeated.

The theme of boxing in the Western television program was utilized on a number of different levels. Some episodes were complete boxing stories in which the television audience was offered actual boxing contested in the ring. This type included the aforementioned episodes of *Have Gun, Will Travel, Bat Masterson, Laramie, Yancy Derringer, Bonanza,* and *Gunsmoke.*

Other entries failed to provide an actual boxing match but featured a fighter or ex-fighter duking it out in a bar fight, on a dusty street in town, or on the open range. In *Rawhide*'s "Incident of the Shambling Man," television audiences are treated to a brawl on the range between an ex-fighter portrayed by an aging Victor McLaglen and a young Clint Eastwood, a regular on the program.

Whether fighting in the ring or out, the star of the program often found himself thrust by circumstance into the fisticuffs. The expected results followed. In *Bonanza*'s "The Duke," a brawny but out-of-shape Hoss Cartwright demonstrates that he has the mettle to defeat the champion of the British Empire in a boxing ring. In *Have Gun, Will Travel*'s "The Prize Fight Story," Richard Boone proves a worthy last-minute substitute for a fighter. In *Gunsmoke*'s "Big Tom," a 1960 offering, James Arness, still wearing his marshal outfit, takes on a bare-knuckle fighter in a one-on-one bar fight. The marshal launches his opponent through a window and onto the street. Kitty then hands him a cold beer in victory.

Central to many of the boxing-themed stories was the use of a boxing background as a vehicle to tell a human interest story. Often these stories concerned an ex-fighter. A favorite twist to this theme was that the fighter was either an alcoholic or punch-drunk or otherwise had a diminished mental capacity. In *Wagon Train*'s "The Willy Moran Story," Ernest Borgnine guest stars as an ex-bare knuckle fighter who reached the apex of his profession fighting in France,

England, and Australia. Now a drunkard, he battles the bottle, ultimately proving his worth by spearheading the defeat of a group of raiders on the trail.[48]

In "The Incident of the Shambling Man," Victor McLaglen's character has moments of clarity such as having a clear recollection of having "broke Tom Hayer's jaw in the thirtieth round, Boston, 1846." However, he is unable to shake his dual handicap of delusional behavior and tendency toward extreme violence.[49] In "Big Tom," the fighter is hampered by both alcoholism and physical illness, which leads to his ultimate demise.

While most Westerns created fictitious fighters to insert into their stories, leaving the real boxers for name-dropping and to serve as props, in *Annie Oakley*'s 1956 episode, "Annie Rings the Bell," Bob Fitzsimmons, Peter Mayer, and James J. Corbett all figure in the ring action. The program begins with Fitzsimmons doing battle with Mayer in Mexico. Fitzsimmons comes off the canvas to knock out Mayer in the first round, with Corbett in attendance. When bandits steal the fight's gate receipts, Annie is pressed into action with her fabled six-shooters. Later, Corbett's stagecoach is robbed, along with his championship belt. Annie captures the belt from the robbers, and as a token of his appreciation, Corbett enters the ring to raise money in a charity bout. Implausibly, the town sheriff boxes like a complete amateur with wild swinging and no defense but lasts seventeen rounds with "Gentleman Jim." It is an irksome detraction from an otherwise enjoyable piece of light entertainment for the boxing fan.

In "Annie Rings the Bell," real-life events such as the Corbett-Mayer contest are mixed with fictionalized events such as the stage coach robbery of Corbett's championship belt. Other television programming featured historical re-creations that, while also subject to some puffery, were essentially historical re-creations. Boxing history received its just due through episodes on programs such as *You Were There*, which offered documentary-style programming regarding the fabled Sullivan-Corbett bout in which Corbett became the first heavyweight champion to win the title under the Marquis of Queensberry rules.[50]

Just as boxing would give ground to football and other entertainment during the early-'60s, television's Western hero would retreat in the wake of the space age and its related themes of science and fantasy. Although an unlikely counterpart for boxing, the use of science fiction programs to tell a boxing story was surprisingly effective, as two episodes of *The Twilight Zone* illustrated. In the 1960 program titled "The Big Tall Wish," Bolie Jackson is an African American fighter on the comeback trail scheduled to fight at St. Nick's Arena. A small boy who idolizes the fighter makes a wish for the aging boxer's safety. In the bout, Bolie is downed for a nine-count, but the boy's additional "big wish" freezes time. When it resumes, it is Bolie's opponent who is on the canvas and counted out. The boy reveals the power of the wish, to Bolie, but he refuses to believe in it. His lack of faith undoes the wish, and Bolie is back on the canvas and a knockout victim.

In the engaging and thought-provoking 1963 episode titled "Steel," starring Lee Marvin, boxing is brought into the future—1974. Prizefighters are now robots and Marvin's charge "Battling Maxo" is an aging model in mechanical disrepair. When the robot is unable to answer the bell, Marvin steps into the ring as his clandestine surrogate. [51]

As early as the days of Charlie Chaplin and the short silent film, boxing proved to be a successful comedic vehicle. Elements of early movie comedy such as slapstick and single-scene scenarios translated well to television's early sketch shows and variety programs. In 1950, Sid Caesar was one of television's early performers in this subgenre in his program *Your Show of Shows*'s "The Punching Bag Skit."

However, it was Caesar's contemporary, Red Skelton, who utilized the comedic sketch to its maximum by the repetitive performances of his fight character Cauliflower McPugg. Skelton, the son of a clown, developed the character for his radio program that had a ten-year run prior to moving to television. McPugg would appear in numerous episodes of *The Red Skelton Show* during a twenty-year run on television that began in 1951. He would become the quintessential punch-drunk fighter.

Red Skelton as Cauliflower McPugg, the quintessential punch-drunk fighter. Skelton portrayed the dim-witted boxer on *The Red Skelton Show* on radio and television throughout the '40s, '50s, and '60s. *By CBS Television via Wikimedia Commons.*

McPugg, decked out in baggy pants, wore his checkered cap sideways, with his name emblazoned in large bold letter across his sweatshirt. Skelton adorned McPugg with a perpetually dimwitted face with a punchy, quizzical look. Skelton often used the laconic McPugg in skits that were topical. In the 1954 episode in which Ed Sullivan introduces McPugg, Betty Furness, the star of her own television program at the time, is offered up as McPugg's next opponent. McPugg's clownish appearance also allowed him to navigate around the taboo hot topic of the day—ring fatalities—boasting of his next purse: "Fifteen dollars plus funeral expenses."[52]

In addition to skit and variety programs, the situation comedy stood at the forefront of comedic efforts featuring boxing. Situation comedies also borrowed from film utilizing slapstick ring antics to entertain their audiences. These programs were the progeny of skits worked out by comedic greats such as Chaplin and Buster Keaton. While one might find it sacrosanct to even mention these greats in the same breath as *The Many Loves of Dobie Gillis* and *I Married Joan*, these later television programs clearly attempted to model their efforts on the preceding works of these comedic geniuses.

Both *Gillis* and *Joan* feature the perfunctory gags of having a fighter become helplessly entangled within the ropes and the misguided bucket of water dosing an unintended target. Other standard boxing slapstick such as hitting the ref, chasing each other around the ring, and hiding directly behind the opponent are also utilized. However, to their credit, both programs added some creative variations of their own. In *Gillis,* we find Bob Denver standing on his head in his corner between rounds. When his manager asks him to get into a crouch, he adopts the stance of a sprinter. In *Joan,* when Joan Davis escorts her charge into the ring, she can't resist taking off her shoes and rubbing her feet in the rosin. After being bumped by the ring's retractable microphone, Joan finds herself hanging from it as it climbs back toward the ceiling. When her charge Wally is launched out of the ring onto the lap of the timekeeper, he tells him, "I'd like to leave a call for seven, please."[53]

While slapstick was occasionally featured in the boxing-themed situation comedy, undoubtedly its most popular subject was that of the "fighting son." It is hard to find a popular situation comedy of that period with a male child in the cast that did not feature this type of storyline. Even the son of the upstanding Stone family of *The Donna Reed Show* had a foray into fisticuffs in "Pardon My Gloves."[54]

The underlying theme of these programs was that while it was unacceptable to be a bully, it was also taboo not to fight. Mores of the 1950s did not embrace contemporary notions of diverse models of masculinity. If a male was not willing to fight, he was branded a coward. In *Leave It to Beaver*'s "The Black Eye," the father is rather ambivalent to the appearance of his son at the dinner table with a bruised face. However, he becomes noticeably perturbed when he learns of the fight's details. "You mean you didn't fight back?" he asks incredulously.[55]

In *My Three Sons*'s "The Bully," Fred MacMurray as Steve Douglas explains the masculine code to his youngest boy, Chip: "I certainly don't believe in starting a fight, but there are times when a man must defend himself."[56] *In Father Knows Best*'s "Bud, The Boxer," even the reserved and gentle Robert Young, playing Jim Anderson, embraced the societal norm: "Remember what I told you, never start a fight but never run away from them."[57]

In a 1950 entry of *The Life of Riley*, "Junior and the Bully," Riley is both ashamed and panicked when he is given a report on his son's fisticuffs. "I've seen the whole fight," Riley's friend tells him. "The other kid took one smack at him and your Junior took off like a flash. If he had a tail and two more legs I would swear he was Citation."[58]

Today, these comedic efforts can still bring a smile to one's face. In an episode of *Dennis the Menace* titled "The Bully," Mr. Wilson assumes his usual role, surrogating for Dennis's father, and attempts to teach a black-eyed Dennis the manly art of self-defense. "In my younger years I was sheer poetry in motion," Mr. Wilson tells Dennis before the boy gives him a shiner to match his own.[59] While some of these comedic moments still deliver, when examined retrospectively, these "fighting son" episodes are equally valuable as social commentary on mid-twentieth-century notions of masculinity of the American male and the importance of boxing during the period.

The handling of boxing subject matter by talented writers and performers in comedy shows illustrated that boxing programs of the era could be as humorous as any other subgenre. In *The Dick Van Dyke Show*'s "Who Owes Who What?" boxing was afforded only a brief minute of the program but offers some of the best comedy on the subject. The program opens with Van Dyke's character, Rob, watching a fight. Rob tries in vain to keep his wife, Laura, at bay as the fight comes to a conclusion, pleading to her, "Not now, honey, it's the fifteenth round, this is it." When Laura obscures the television, a dramatic knockout is scored, with the announcer heralding the blow as the punch of the century. "Are you angry with me?" a contrite Laura asks Rob. "Why should I be angry just because you made me miss the punch of the century?" a deflated Rob replies, like a little boy feigning bravery in the face of an empty cookie jar.[60]

In another classic program, *The Honeymooners,* Jackie Gleason and Art Carney bring their superlative talents to boxing, in "The Bensonhurst Bomber." Loud-mouthed Ralph (Gleason), assisted by a bumbling Norton (Carney), is backed into a fight with a neighborhood tough. As a bewildered Ralph contemplates his fight strategy and the certain beating he has coming, the ever-happy-go-lucky Norton strikes a pose with feigned microphone in hand: "This is 'Smilin' Ed Norton talking to you direct from the training quarters of the Bensonhurst Bomber. Would you like to say a few words to your fans out there, Bomber?" "Aw, Shut Up," a disgusted Ralph thunders in his typical manner. When Norton seeks to tutor Ralph on the finer points of the game, Ralph strike a comical bare-knuckle pose. Norton urges Ralph to cover up his face and then delivers a blow to Ralph's solar plexus. Ralph turns bug-eyed, contorting his facial features, and complements them with an equally expressive physicality, creating a hysterical image that only Gleason could realize.[61]

As with many televised programs featuring boxing, television's comedy writers could not resist fistic allusions. In an episode of *My*

Three Sons titled "Chip's Last Fight," grandpa Bub justifies his ability to school Chip about fighting: "I used to pal around with Jack Dempsey, the old Manassa Mauler, guys like Jack Dempsey, Jess Willard, Jack Johnson, Luis Firpo."[62] In *Father Knows Best,* after Bud is defeated in the ring, his dad observes his son looking at a picture of Jack Dempsey. "I remember when he was beaten by Gene Tunney," he comments.[63] In *The Many Loves of Dobie Gillis*'s "Requiem For an Underweight Heavyweight," a sarcastic boxer takes one look at Dobie and says, "What did you look like *before* you fought Sonny Liston?"[64] Because many of these programs used canned laugh soundtracks, no one will ever know for sure whether audiences of the day found these lines to be funny or had an appreciation for them. Today, they simply leave the boxing fan warm and fuzzy.

Epilogue

KINESCOPE AND VIDEO RECORDINGS FROM BOXING'S GOLDEN AGE OF TELEVISION: A PERSPECTIVE

What marks the beginning of the "Golden Age" of boxing on television is a matter of opinion. Most would agree that experimental and non-commercial broadcasts from the late-1920s through 1940 were merely preliminary and that the earliest start date possible would be the first American commercial boxing broadcasts beginning in July 1941.

Others might reasonably claim that the era did not truly begin until 1946 with the vastly more technologically proficient presentation of the Conn-Louis rematch. That fight also coincided with the recent proliferation of television receivers, allowing for audiences in significant numbers.

The end date of the Golden Age is also speculative. However, a fair argument can be made that it concluded in 1964 with the demise of Gillette's Friday Night/Saturday Night fights and the subsequent passing of the heavyweight scepter to Muhammad Ali (then known as Cassius Clay), who launched TV's rebirth and a second era.

As with radio, boxing historians are concerned with two fundamental questions regarding early television: Which boxing matches were televised, and of those, which ones survive today in some viewable format? Also similar to radio, there is no comprehensive catalog of the boxing matches broadcast on early television.

Regarding the second litmus question—What TV video has survived?—the answer is similar to the first. The telecasts that still exist are dispersed throughout corporate and private collections. They collectively fail to make available to the general public a composite picture of what had endured. In sum, the boxing public is largely ignorant to the actual facts regarding the body of work that has been preserved.

There are clearly dozens of early television broadcasts, with perhaps as many as a couple of hundred bouts circulating in the collectors' market (made available from more recent television replays that were recorded by collectors, many of which have been posted by personal YouTube contributors). However, the probability is that there are many more in existence that the average fan does not have knowledge of or access to.

Many times when watching boxing from the 1950s, the viewer is actually watching the *film* of a fight. These films have great historical value and superior audio and video quality. However, they are not something that was shown on a television set live. One is not experiencing a piece of television history.

In order to diagnostically analyze what is being viewed, one must understand kinescope and distinguish it from film. The term *kinescope* has various meanings, but in the context of this discussion, a kinescope is a recording of a television program made by filming the picture from a video monitor. Kinescopes were usually recorded on 16mm film. What distinguishes film from kinescope is that film records its subject matter directly.

On September 13, 1947, Eastman Kodak introduced the Eastman Television Recording Camera, in cooperation with DuMont Laboratories and NBC. The camera, which was trademarked under the name "Kinephoto," had the capability of recording images from a television screen and made the kinescope process available to the television industry at large. CBS and ABC would eventually utilize similar technology, as well.[1]

Prior to 1956, when videotape was introduced, kinescope was the only way in which to record television broadcasts. The downside of kinescope was that it had neither the audio nor visual quality of something shot directly on film, and it took time to develop a print. Still, it was the only viable means at the time of preserving the broadcast.

Therefore, when watching a boxing contest of a fight prior to 1956 (and some broadcasts for at least several years thereafter, if video had not been utilized for that particular program), it is either a kinescope copy of the original TV broadcast—a bona fide piece of television history—or you are watching a film of the fight that was not a part of television broadcasting.

There might be an announcer on the film version giving a blow-by-blow or narrative. However, this audio was taken from a radio broadcast or otherwise added in later in a studio and is not a reproduction of the original aired on television.

Actually, it is rather easy to identify kinescope broadcasts and distinguish them from film. The picture quality is noticeably degraded in comparison to film, and the picture will appear somewhat stretched or grainy, often with a "halo effect" or "ghosting" caused by a poor contrast of light and darkness. Video also has superior sound quality. Additionally, in the film version of fights, one can sometimes see long shots of the entire ring featuring the above hanging lights with a glimpse of the darkened surrounding seats, a view that TV did not typically offer.

Further, as mentioned above, the soundtrack of the film is added subsequent to the fight, and sometimes the announcer is speaking of the action in the past tense. In the worst versions, the broadcaster feigns that he is announcing the match live, but it is patently obvious he already knows what is coming next and what the result of the match is.

Finally, a caveat about creative editors on YouTube. They will often edit a kinescope by adding in a new soundtrack, cleaning up the existing audio and video images, and providing slow motion action. Like the colorization of films, one can argue the benefits and detriments of recasting kinescopes in this fashion, but what remains certain is that these versions are not a part of television history.

Interestingly, today no one knows exactly how clear the reception of those original broadcasts were, because the kinescopes viewed today are an imperfect filmed representation of whatever went out directly on the original airwaves. Additionally, contemporary copies of kinescope films are of a degraded quality resulting from the transfer of the kinescope itself.

Kinescopes were sometimes made and then shipped out to affiliated stations of a network that might not have aired a fight live. The viewers of those versions were not watching a live television signal but were actually watching the kinescope itself in what would essentially be referred to now as a taped replay.

In 1951, halfway between the advent of the kinescope and the arrival of video, a network of coaxial cable and microwave relays carrying programs to the West Coast was completed.[2] In 1952, this led to the "hot kinescope" process in which a live broadcast by NBC or ABC would be aired in New York, and then transmitted west. Next, the program would be filmed onto a kinescope machine, with film processing completed just in time for the show to be aired in Los Angeles three hours later in the Pacific time zone. Here too, the "original" TV broadcast was that of a kinescope.[3]

Understanding the history of kinescope allows for some basic parameters. Since the commercial use of kinescope did not begin until September 1947, there can be no historical record of live television boxing prior to that time. That includes everything from Lee de Forest's TV experiments at the beginning of the Depression, to the latter-day ring escapades of Max Baer, to Billy Conn's much-heralded but disappointing return against Louis.[4,5,6] Fortunately, the commercial use of kinescope began at the same time as the proliferation of television and televised boxing. However, equally unfortunate was the fact that kinescopes were intended for immediate broadcast or for occasional reuse as a prerecorded program. They were not produced to be retained. Consequently, only a small fraction of kinescope recordings still exist.[7] Boxing kinescopes most likely have the same scant survival rate.

The UCLA Film and Television Archive lists amongst its holdings an entry for *Boxing with Dennis James* (three episodes from 1949–50), episodes of *Boxing from Jamaica Arena* (1949–50), *Amateur Boxing Fight Club* (1949–50), and *Boxing From Sunnyside Gardens* (1949–55). All of these programs were carried by the DuMont Television Network.

Several other early boxing kinescopes are known to exist and can readily be found including the first Charles-Walcott fight held at Comiskey Park on June 22, 1949. The fight was presented by the *Gillette Cavalcade of Sports*, with Bob Stanton providing the blow-by-blow, assisted by Jimmy Powers. Additionally, readily available are the Louis-Charles encounter of September 27, 1950, and the Pabst Blue Ribbon broadcasts of May 24, 1950, between Cesar Brion and Charley Norkus, and of November 8, 1950, between Sugar Ray Robinson and Bobby Dykes, both which were announced by Ted Husing. Collectors have referenced their possession of kinescopes of the Rocky Graziano-Gene Burton, Charley Fusari-Tony Pellone, and Jimmy Flood-Artie Diamond matches from the same period. This list is more comprehensive than illustrative, and surviving boxing matches captured during the seminal period of kinescope's commercial use (September 1947 to December 1949) can be considered rare.

Although kinescope was the standard in the industry through 1955, videotape rapidly became the prominent means of recording telecasts after its arrival in late 1956. Early videotape was manufactured as a two-inch-wide plastic ribbon usually wound onto spools of 4,800 feet, with sixty-four minutes of playing time. One side of the ribbon was coated with iron oxide particles that recorded both picture and sound through electric signals.

One of the primary advantages of videotape was that it could be magnetically erased and reused. This factor, coupled with its "long-wear" durability and low handling cost, made it 50–90 percent cheaper than film. Another significant advantage was its diversity. Videotape, unlike film or the kinescopes made from film, had the ability to record something live and play it back immediately without time-consuming processing or development.[8]

The first videotaped network broadcast was made by CBS on November 30, 1956, of the *Doug Edwards and the News* program.[9] The oldest surviving videotaped television broadcast is that of *The Edsel Show,* featuring Frank Sinatra, Bing Crosby, and Rosemary Clooney, which was recorded live at CBS Television City in Hollywood on October 13, 1957, for a delayed broadcast on the West Coast.

The technology was still in its infancy stage, and wary producers made a kinescope recording as a backup. The approach left an excellent historical comparison proving videotape's superior sound and picture. It also serves as a signpost regarding the sport of boxing captured on video tape. Presumably, videotape was not in any sort of regular use for boxing broadcasts until at least 1958.[10]

An early application of videotape in the boxing world was demonstrated in 1958 during the first Archie Moore-Yvon Durelle fight. The telecast included what is now referred to as an "instant replay" of the final two rounds of the bout. As described by the *Chicago Daily Tribune,* "every motion of the fighters during the 10th and 11th rounds was reviewed with startling clarity. It was, one viewer said, as if time had been turned back seven minutes."[11]

Kinescopes were still used in the recording of television after the invention of videotape in the mid-'50s, with common usage still seen throughout the 1960s and into the early-1970s.[12] Consequently, there is no clear line of demarcation that can be drawn between the two forms of recording. However, an informal survey of boxing recordings reveals that the majority of the fights after the late-1950s were preserved on video, which has greater picture and sound quality than its kinescope predecessors. Videotape was often erased, so the healthy survival rate of these Golden Age boxing video telecasts is also suspect. As with kinescopes, what remains has yet to be defined.

There are many gaps in the record of the broadcast history of boxing on television. All who have a passion for the sport must be committed to serve as boxing archeologists. They need to continue to locate and preserve these fights and better catalog and share the glorious days of boxing history that still exist on kinescope and video. The willing and enthusiastic assistance of the owners of these properties will be instrumental in the success of this endeavor. Anyone with any relevant information whatsoever is urged to contact the author at Romanofrederick@gmail.com.

ENDNOTES

PROLOGUE A

1 Erik Barnouw, *A Tower of Babel, A History of Broadcasting in the United States Vol. I to 1933* (New York: Oxford University Press,1966), 4.

2 Nat Loubet and John Ort, eds. *The 1979 Ring Boxing Encyclopedia and Record Book* (New York: The Ring Book Shop, 1979), 146.

3 *The Ring*, November 1940, 27.

4 *The Ring*, November 1940, 44.

5 *New York Globe*, August, 1921.

6 *New York Sun*, August, 1921.

7 *New York Evening Mail*, August, 1921.

8 Sean Dennis Cashman, *America in the Twenties and Thirties—The Olympian Age of Franklin Delano Roosevelt* (New York: New York University Press, 1989), 447.

9 Cashman, *America in the Twenties*, 398.

10 Michael Emery and Edwin Emery, *The Press and America: An Interpretive History of Mass Media*, 6th Edition (Englewood Cliffs, New Jersey: Prentice-Hall, 1988), 312.

PROLOGUE B

1 Frank S. Nugent, "The Schmeling-Louis Fight Film and 'Border Flight,' at the Rialto—'Red Wagon' at the Globe," *New York Times*, 22 June 1936, p. 22.

2 "Screen Notes," *New York Times*, 15 February 1935, p. 23.

3 "Rickard is Fined $7,000 in Film Plot," *New York Times*, 31 May 1925, p. 23.

4 "Bars Censorship of Prizefight Films: Ottinger Rules Berlenbach-Stribling Bout in Current Event Class," *New York Times*, 17 June 1926, p. 2.

5 "Aim To Lift Fight Ban: Barbour Proposes a Bill to Legalize Telecast of Bouts Across State Lines," *New York Times*, 11 June 1939, p. X10.

6 Orlin Dunlap, Jr., "Watching a Battle," *New York Times*, 4 June 1939, p. X10.

CHAPTER 1

1 Robert Campbell, *The Golden Years of Broadcasting—A Celebration of the First 50 Years of Radio and TV on NBC* (New York: Charles Scribner's Sons, 1976), 18.
2 Ibid; Irving Settel, *A Pictorial History of Radio* (New York: Grosset & Dunlap, 1967), 17.
3 Campbell, *The Golden Years of Broadcasting,* 20.
4 Barnouw, *A Tower of Babel,* 4.
5 *The Wireless Age* 10 (February 1923): 20.
6 *The Wireless Age,* 9 (June 1922): 21.
7 *The Wireless Age* 10 (February 1923): 20.
8 "Gala Radio Program To Go To All Lands: Station KDKA, in New Studios, Will Celebrate Nine Years of Broadcasting," *New York Times,* 30 October 1929, p. 35.
9 Ed Salamon, *Pittsburgh's Golden Age of Radio* (Charleston, South Carolina: Arcadia Publishing, 2010) 15.
10 Today in Old Radio History, April, 11, 2012, OLDRADIO.org. Another source credits *Pittsburgh Post* sports editor Florent Gibson as providing commentary on the bout from Pittsburgh's Motor City Square.
11 "Gala Radio Program," p. 35. When radio station KDKA celebrated its ninth anniversary, it presented a recreation of the first ringside description of a boxing match.
12 Loubet and Ort, *The 1979 Ring Boxing Encyclopedia and Record Book,* 120.
13 Campbell, *The Golden Years of Broadcasting,* 22.
14 Barnouw, *A Tower of Babel,* 80.
15 For a comprehensive analysis of this notion, see the article by Thomas H. White, "Battle of the Century: The WJY Story," January 1, 2000, earlyradiohistory.us.
16 "Hopp Would Keep Rickard from Putting Bouts on Air," *New York Herald Tribune,* 1 May 1927, p.6. In 1927, Hopp would seek an injunction enjoining Rickard and J. Andrew White from broadcasting boxing contests on WMSG. Hopp argued that in 1921, the three men formed the Wireless Telephone and Telegraph Bureau for the purpose of establishing radio stations and to broadcast boxing. Despite this agreement, White made a similar agreement with RCA that excluded Hopp.
17 "Voice-Broadcasting the Stirring Progress of the "Battle of the Century," *The Wireless Age,* 8 (August 1921): 11–12.
18 Barnouw, *A Tower of Babel,* 80.
19 "Battle of the Century: The WJY Story."
20 Ibid.
21 Barnouw, *A Tower of Babel,* 80.
22 Settel, *A Pictorial History of Radio,* 53.
23 Barnouw, *A Tower of Babel,* 80.
24 *The Wireless Age,* 8 (August 1921): 20.
25 "Battle of the Century: The WJY Story." AT&T allowed a direct telephone wire connection to the transmitter for the Dundee-Ray bout. The motivation for their refusal just two months later was unclear. A fair speculation is that it was

the beginning of a dispute involving AT&T over the right to use telephone lines in conjunction with radio.

26 Nat Fleischer, *Jack Dempsey* (New Rochelle, New York: Arlington House, 1972), 15. Famed boxing publisher Nat Fleischer also claims to have been White's "assistant."

27 "Battle of the Century: The WJY Story."

28 "The First Big Broadcast," *Reader's Digest*, December, 1955, pp. 81–85.

29 *The Wireless Age*, 8 (August 1921): 14–15.

30 *The Wireless Age*, 8 (August 1921): 12.

31 "Joe Humphries Familiar Voice Saved For Boxing," *Chicago Daily Tribune*, 17 June 1933, 23.

32 Campbell, *The Golden Years of Broadcasting*, 24.

33 *The Wireless Age*, 8 (August 1921): 11.

34 Loubet and Ort, *The 1979 Ring Boxing Encyclopedia and Record Book*, 93.

35 Barnouw, *A Tower of Babel*, 81.

36 Ibid.

37 Ibid., 4.

38 Michael Emery and Edwin Emery, *The Press and America: An Interpretive History of Mass Media* (Englewood Cliffs, New Jersey: Prentice Hall, 1994), 378.

39 "Welterweight Battle To Be Described in Detail by Radio," *New York Tribune*, 25 June 1922, p. A7.

40 Maurice Henle, "Radio Telephone Gives Public Video Description of Leonard-Britton Bout," *The Wireless Age* 9 (August 1922): 30.

41 "To Broadcast Fight News: Story of Leonard-Tendler Bout Will Be Sent Out From Newark," *New York Times*, 25 July 1922, p. 24.

42 "Third Triumph Assures Practicability of Radio on Broadcasting Sport," *The Wireless Age* 9 (September 1922): 39–40.

43 "Story of Leonard-Tendler," p. 40

44 "Today's Radio Programs," *Washington Post*, 5 September 1923, p. 9. Leonard would rival Dempsey as the principal subject of early radio broadcasts, and WJZ would broadcast other Leonard bouts, including his match with Johnny Dundee from Yankee Stadium.

45 "Story of Leonard-Tendler," p. 40.

46 "Visiting in the Radio Home," *The Wireless Age* 10 (March 1923): 22.

47 "Paris Interested In Bout," *New York Times*, 30 May 1923, p. 12.

48 "Scientist Says Radio Waves Travel under the Land and Sea," *New York Times*, 3 May 1925, p. XX17.

49 "Relayed to South America: Ringside Account Distinctly Heard on Radio 6,000 Miles Away," *New York Times*, 7 May 1925, p. 15.

50 "Fight Returns at Emporium by Radio and Telegraph," *New York Amsterdam News*, 24 June 1925, p. 5.

51 "Distribute Fight Tickets By Plane: Promoters Use Novel Method to Facilitate Delivery for Dempsey-Gibbons Bout," *New York Times*, 2 June 1923, p. 8.

52 "Dempsey-Gibbons Fight To Be Broadcast By WGY," *Boston Daily Globe,* 4 July 1923, p. 15.
53 Jack Lawrence, "Advance of Weighing-In Hour Fools Some of Crowd," *New York Herald Tribune,* 15 September 1923, p. 11.
54 Grantland Rice, "Firpo Knocked Out in 2d Round After Flooring Dempsey," *New York Herald Tribune,* 15 September 1923, p. 1.
55 Capt. Robert Scofield Wood, "The Thrill That Left Millions Breathless," *The Wireless Age* 11 (October 1923): 22–23.
56 Raymond Francis Yates, "Radio Making Sport Interest Nationwide," *The Wireless Age* XI (December 1923): 31.
57 Special Cable to the *Tribune,* "Argentine Republic Awaits Outcome of Championship Fight With Confidence Born of Hope," *New York Herald Tribune,* 14 September 1923, p. 14.
58 "How the Fight Results Were Flashed to Argentina," *The Wireless Age* 11 (October 1923): 24.
59 *The Wireless Age* 9 (October 1921): 55.
60 Don Dunphy, *Don Dunphy at Ringside* (New York: Henry Holt and Company, 1988), 135.
61 "Today's Radio Program," *New York Times,* 29 January 1924, p. 17.
62 "Coming on the Radio," *Boston Daily Globe,* 7 September 1935, p. 14.
63 Stuart Hawkins, "On the Radio," *New York Herald Tribune,* 12 March 1927, p. 11.
64 "Today's Radio Program," *New York Times,* 23 February 1924, p. 13.
65 Notes from Radio Broadcasting Stations, *New York Times,* 30 November 1924: p. XX15.
66 Pioneer, "Last Night on the Radio," *New York Herald Tribune,* 18 May 1926, p. 17.
67 "Rickard Bans Radio In Garden; Says It Has Hurt Attendance," *New York Times,* 26 November 1924, p. 14.
68 "Radio Show Draws 165,000 Visitors," *New York Times,* 28 September 1924, p. S6.
69 R. A. Bradley, "To Reanimate a Dead Receiver," *The Wireless Age,* X1 (July, 1924): 63.
70 "Rickard Bans Radio," p.14.
71 Despite the radio ban, Garden fights with lesser financial importance found their way to the airwaves such as the Cathedral Fund boxing bouts, which aired on WJY-405, New York, several months later on March 10, 1925.
72 "St. Gaudens's Diana Homeless on May 1: Plans for Huge Office Building to Replace Madison Square Garden Almost Ready," *New York Times,* 26 November 1924, p. 22.
73 "Gibbons and Tunney Will Clash Tonight: 60,000 Expected to See Heavyweight Contenders in 15-Round Bout at Polo Grounds," *New York Times,* 5 June 1925, p. 13.
74 "Rickard to Ban Radio Events at Garden," *New York Times,* 16 January 1926, p. 16.
75 "Naval Boxing Bouts on the Air Tonight: Joe Humphries Will Describe Christmas Carnival of Sailors at Navy Yard," *New York Times,* 14 December 1927, p. 32.
76 "Rickard Joins With Group In Praise of Broadcasting: He Says Radio Is Killing Idea That Boxing Is Brutal," *New York Times,* 22 May 1927, p. XX18.

77 "Speaking of Radio," *Baltimore Sun,* 16 May 1927, p. 14.
78 "New York Stations Broadcast Fights," *Baltimore Sun,* 9 September 1928, p. MO9.
79 "Radio Fan's Likes and Dislikes Revealed By Questionnaires," *New York Times,* 21 February 1926, p. XX17.
80 "Weak Hands Failed To Dismay Delaney," *New York Times,* 17 July 1926, p. 8.
81 Pioneer, "Last Night on the Radio," *New York Herald Tribune,* 3 July 1925, p. 7
82 Walter Trumbull, "Loughran Wins, Retains Crown," *Daily Boston Globe,* 29 March 1929, p. 1.

CHAPTER 2

1 "Radio Rights Let To Business Firm: Royal Typewriter Company Will Broadcast Bout from the Philadelphia Stadium," *New York Times,* 21 September 1926, p. 24.
2 "Royal Typewriter Company," p. 24.
3 "How Radio Carried News of Big Bout: Broadcasting at the Ringside By White and McNamee as It Was Taken By Stenographers," *New York Times,* 24 September 1926 p. 4.
4 Lloyd Greene, "5,000,000 Of These Sets Will Be Sold This Year," *Daily Boston Globe,* 30 September 1928, p. B26.
5 "News of Big Bout," p. 4.
6 Ibid.
7 Ibid.
8 Ibid.
9 "England Stays Up To Learn Outcome: Radio Reports Heard With Greater Interest Than Any Fight In Recent Years," *New York Times,* 24 September 1926, p. 5.
10 "Radio Aided South African Newspaper Get Fight Results," *New York Herald Tribune,* 14 November 1926, p. 30.
11 "Tunney Calls Himself Sensitive Type: Admitting Nervousness in Radio Talk by The Associated Press," *New York Times,* 3 December 1927, p. 12.
12 "Prizefight Series Renewed at WGN," *New York Times,* 10 April 1927, p. XX17.
13 "Here To Consider New Wave Lengths, Commissioner Caldwell Sees Nationwide Shift Needed for Best Reception In City," *New York Times,* 3 May 1927, p. 23.
14 "Devise New System of Broadcasting: Experts Say It Should Enable 1,900 Stations to Operate Simultaneously, *New York Times,* 14 May 1927, p. 24.
15 "Story of The Fight as Told by Radio: Round-by-Round Description of the Contest Goes to Audience Estimated at 50,000," *New York Times,* 22 July 1927, p. 9.
16 "Ladies Aid Society to Feature Returns from Sharkey Fight," *Boston Daily Globe,* 20 July 1927, p.12.
17 "Pickups from the Ringside," *Boston Daily Globe,* 22 July 1927, p. 12.
18 "Story of The Fight," p. 9.
19 "Silence Of Radio On Foul Explained: Announcers Could Not Call Blow Low Unless Referee and Judge So Declared," *New York Times,* 23 July 1927, p. 6.
20 Cable to the *Herald Tribune,* "Fight Arouses Mexican Interest In Broadcasting," *New York Herald Tribune,* 7 August 1927, p. F1.

21 "Story of The Fight," p. 9.
22 "Silence Of Radio On Foul Explained p. 6.
23 FAV, Speaking of Radio, *Baltimore Sun*, 2 August 1927, p. 14.
24 "Boxing Body Curbs Radio Fight Detail: Commissioner Muldoon Rules Descriptions Must Be Minus Brutal Aspects," *New York Times*, 24 July 1927, p. S6.
25 John W. Desbecker, "Ruling for Expurgated Fight Descriptions Arouses Protest: Gory Details Wanted," *New York Times*, 27 July 1929, p. 22.
26 FAV, Speaking of Radio, *Baltimore Sun*, 7 June 1927, p. 20.
27 FAV, Speaking of Radio, *Baltimore Sun*, 4 June 1927, p. 11; "Speaking of Radio," *Baltimore Sun*, 2 June 1927, p. 15.
28 Stuart Hawkins, On the Radio, *New York Herald Tribune*, 18 February 1927, p. 8.
29 "Boxing Commission Ruling on Fight Broadcasts Disputed," *New York Herald Tribune*, 7 November 1926, p. 30.
30 Stuart Hawkins, "On the Radio: Guignol Gasps for WEAF and Goldman Band Returns; Mrs. McPherson Gets on Air," *New York Herald Tribune*, 19 February 1927, p. 11.
31 Station WMSG to Question Ruling, *Boston Daily Globe*, 10 November 1926, p. 27.
32 "Broadcasting; Mr. M.H. Aylesworth President of the NBC Co. Inc, Outlines Its Purpose and Plans," *The Wireless Age*, (October 1926): 8–9.
33 "Tries To Block Wire For Radio At Bout: Rickard Asks Telephone Company Not to Serve Columbia Chain at Chicago Contest," *New York Times*, 17 September 1927, p. 20.
34 "NBC Asks Writ On Fight: Transradio Fights Move to Bar It from Broadcasting," *New York Times*, 27 August 1937, p. 22; "Loses Broadcast Plea: Transradio Press's Plan to Cover Fight Is Barred," *New York Times*, 31 August 1937, p. 26. From time to time, disputes over broadcast rights would flare up. For example, ten years later, Rickard protégé Mike Jacobs and his partner NBC had to obtain an injunction to prevent Transamerica from attempting to broadcast the Joe Louis-Tommy Farr contest.
35 Radio broadcast of the Jack Dempsey-Gene Tunney II fight, September 23, 1926.
36 Mel Heimer, *The Long Count, The Legendary Battle for the World Heavyweight Championship When Prizefighting was a National Sport and Jack Dempsey and Gene Tunney its Heroes* (Kingsport, Tennessee: Kingsport Press, Inc., 1969), 234.
37 "W-G-N To Give Fight Broadcast From Ringside," *Chicago Daily Tribune*, 9 September 1927, p. 21.
38 "Trib Announcers to Put Dempsey Battle on Air," *Chicago Daily Tribune*, 11 September 1927, Part 8, p. J8.
39 "Dempsey's Life and Battles on Air From W-G-N," *Chicago Daily Tribune*, 28 August 1927, Part 7, p. 1.
40 "Dempsey Battle on Air," p. J8.
41 "58 Stations To Radiate Boxing Bout: Tunney-Dempsey Fight on the Air From Coast to Coast Thursday Night," *New York Times*, 18 September 1927, p. R13; Heimer, *The Long Count*, 235.
42 Heimer, *The Long Count*, 234.

43 Heimer, *The Long Count*, 235; "Nine Fall Dead Hearing Fight News by Radio," *New York Herald Tribune*, 24 September 1927, p. 1.

44 Heimer, *The Long Count*, 254.

45 "Dies After Fight News: Prof. C. L. Owen, Heart Disease Victim, Had Listened in at Seattle," *New York Times*, 26 September 1927, p. 25.

46 Grover Theis, "Boy Leaves Home for Heeney Camp: Elizabeth Lad, 15, Hikes 40 Miles in Rain in Quest of Brother, 10," *New York Times*, 14 July 1928, p. 13.

47 "Plans To Test The Effect Of Radio On Boxing: Rickard Says Tunney-Heeney Bout Will Show Whether Ticket Sales Suffer," *New York Times*, 19 July 1928, p. 24.

48 "Dempsey Called to Act as Second for Heeney to Aid Fight Ballyhoo," *Baltimore Sun*, 26 July 1928, p. 11.

49 "Rickard To Prohibit Fight Broadcasts: Will Ban Them Until A Way Is Found to Compensate the Promoter For Losses," *New York Times*, 28 July 1928, p. 8.

50 "Tunney-Heeney Fight Puzzles Children," *Daily Boston Globe*, 28 July 1928, p. 6.

51 "Rickard To Prohibit," p. 8.

52 "Rickard Returns $7 Sent by Radio Fan as Fight Fee," *New York Herald Tribune*, 3 August 1928, p. 32.

53 "Yonkers 'Fan' Flashes Fight to New Zealand," *New York Herald Tribune*, 17 April 1927, p. G1.

54 "Broadcast of Fight to Cover the World: Tunney-Heeney Bout to Be Sent Over Short Waves Thursday-New Zealand To Listen In," *New York Times*, 24 July 1928, p. 14.

55 Special Cable to the *New York Times*, "British See End of Big Ring Purses: Tunney Appearance Not Worth 21 Times Prime Minister's Salary, Says Expert," *New York Times*, 28 July, 1928 p. 8.

56 "Listener In The Alps Hears A Prize Bout In New York: Tunney-Heeney Contest Found Its Way to Switzerland —"Yodeller" Tells How He "Sat" at the Ringside and Tuned-In the Gong Across the Sea—Value of Short Waves Is Seen," *New York Times*, 19 August 1928, p. 127.

57 "British See End of Big Ring Purses."

58 "England Looks-In: Television Starts Quest For a New Word to Replace 'Listener,'" *New York Times*, 24 February 1935, p. X13.

CHAPTER 3

1 Allan Reagan, "15,000 File by Rickard's Bier at His Garden," *New York Herald Tribune*, 9 January 1929, p. 1.

2 James P. Dawson, "Sharkey-Stribling Clash Wednesday: Stage Set for First Series of Important Bouts calculated to Produce Champion," *New York Times*, 24 February 1929, p. 157.

3 "Radio Ban Booms Sale for Milk Fund: But $50 Section Lags, So Carey Decides to Reduce Number in This Group," *New York Times*, 20 June 1929, p. 28; "Loughran Defends Ring Title Tonight: Will Risk Light Heavyweight Crown Against Braddock at Yankee Stadium," *New York Times*, 18 July 1929, p. 15.

4 "Mandell To Meet Canzoneri Tonight: Lightweight Champion Ruled 2–1 Favorite to Retain Title in Chicago Bout," *New York Times*, 2 August 1929, p. 20.

5 "Passes and Radio Banned by Harmon," *Hartford Courant*, 26 May 1929, p. C6.

6 "Finds Broadcasting Cuts Ring Attendance," *Baltimore Sun*, 15 April 1928, p. MR11.

7 "Radio Hopes To Reinstate Microphone At Ringside. Broadcasters Plan To Campaign to Put Prizefighters on the Air—They Contend Box-Office Receipts Are Not Decreased—Promoter Carey Explains the Situation," *New York Times*, 6 October 1929, p. XX14.

8 Joseph C. Nichols, "Louis and Levinsky Meet in Chicago Ring Tonight: Detroiter Favored at 3–1 to Get the Decision in 10 Round Bout at Comiskey Park—Crowd of 50,000 Expected to Attend," *New York Times*, 7 August 1935, p. 24.

9 "Lewis, Marek Fight at Sox Park Tonight," *Chicago Daily Tribune*, 10 July 1936, p. 25.

10 "Fight Not To Go On Radio: Original Plans to Broadcast Sharkey-Scott Bout Are Changed," *New York Times*, 20 February 1930, p. 33.

11 "Radio Advisory Council Plans For The Future: Owen D. Young Sees Unlimited Possibilities With the Ultimate Effect Beyond The Realm of Prediction," *New York Times*, 17 March 1929, p. X18.

12 "Images Dance in Space, Heralding New Radio Era: Convincing Demonstration at Dr. Goldsmith's Home Shows Television is at Hand," *New York Times*, 14 April 1929, p. 159.

13 Ibid.

14 James P. Dawson, "Chocolate Forced to Postpone Bout: Cuban's Injuries in Auto Accident Cause Calling Off of La Barba Match May 28," *New York Times*, 20 May 1930, p. 42.

15 Sportswriters Damon Runyon, Ed Frayne, and Bill Farnsworth of the Hearst newspaper chain in conjunction with promoter Mike Jacobs sponsored boxing benefits commonly referred to as "Milk Fund Bouts." A portion of the proceeds went to purchase milk for babies from families that needed financial assistance.

16 "Radio Transcript of Fourth Round Describes Scene at Time of Foul," *Washington Post*, 13 June 1930, p. 11. As with a few of the latest heavyweight championship matches, a verbatim transcript of the radio broadcast was made and published in the newspaper.

17 "Schmeling-Sharkey Bout Will Be Heard on Nation-Wide Net," *New York Herald Tribune*, 8 June 1930, p. C5.

18 "Radio Transcript of Fourth Round."

19 Wireless to the *New York Times*, "Germany Jubilant; Schmeling Hailed: Press and Public Also Commend Fairness Here," *New York Times*, 14 June 1930, p. 18.

20 "Red Special In After 10,000 Mile Trip Showing Centralized Radio," *RCA News* XI (August 1930):14–15, 43.

21 "70,000 Are Expected at Polo Grounds Thursday Night for Berg-Chocolate Bout," *New York Times*, 3 August 1930, p. 131.

22 "Fight Broadcast Heard By Millions: Radio Account Goes Over Nation-Wide Network and to Germany and South America," *New York Times,* 22 June 1932, p. 29.

23 "Wide Radio Hook-Up to Carry The Fight: Canada, Germany, and South America Will Get Details, As Well As US," *New York Times,* 21 June 1932, p. 26.

24 "Germany Foresees Schmeling Victory: Experts Point to Fact That He is Younger Than Sharkey and is at Peak," *New York Times,* 21 June 1932, p. 26.

25 A favorite human interest story of newspapers focused on the mother or wife of a fighter and how she intended to "take in" the fight. Joe Louis's wife, Marva, was unwilling to travel the few miles from Harlem to Yankee Stadium and listened to the Tommy Farr bout on the radio. Harry Greb's wife had Westinghouse install a receiver in their home to listen to one of his bouts against Gene Tunney. Jersey Joe Walcott's wife listened to the first Louis bout on the radio but paced throughout. The wives of "Phantin" Phil Scott, Sammy Mandell, and Jack Sharkey could not bring themselves to listen to major bouts fought by their spouses carried on the radio. They waited until the matches were over to hear the results.

26 John Kieran, "Sidelights of the Fight," *New York Times,* 22 June 1932, p. 29.

27 "Board to Control Ring Broadcasts: Commission Adopts Resolution That Only Experts Are Assigned," *New York Times,* 6 July 1932, p. 24; "Radio Fight Fans Won't Get in on Schmeling Bout," *Chicago Daily Tribune,* 23 September 1932, p. 24.

28 *New York Times,* 6 July 1932, p. 24.

29 "Germany Puts Ban on Jews in Boxing: New Move towards Complete Ostracism of Athletes Also Bans Managers," *New York Times,* 26 April 1933, p. 20.

30 "Germany Puts Ban on Jews in Boxing." On April 25, 1933 the Union of German Professional Boxers issued the following statement: "All Jews, including those baptized, are ruled off the list of members; all honorary members of Jewish blood are asked to hand in their cards; every German boxer is ordered to tear up his contract with a Jewish manager; Jews are barred from the club rooms; Jewish capital is barred from participation in the financing of boxing shows."

31 "Baer Bout Here June 8th: Schmeling Match Set for Yankee Stadium, No Sharkey Date," *New York Times,* 8 April 1933, p. 22.

32 "Boxing Board Fixes Ring Dates. Dempsey and Mara Get Wednesdays for Polo Grounds and Yankee Stadium," *New York Times,* 5 April 1933, p. 26.

33 Tim Mara is better known as the founder of the New York Giants of the National Football League. Joseph Carr, NFL president, offered boxing promoter Bill Gibson ownership of the franchise first. Gibson, the owner of New York's last team, the New York Brickley Giants, refused the offer. However, he referred Carr to his friend Mara, who purchased the new franchise for $500.

34 Joseph C. Nichols, "Sharkey, Carnera End All Training," *New York Times,* 28 June 1933, p. 28.

35 Joseph C. Nichols, "Ross, Canzoneri to Box Tonight: New Yorker to Strive to Regain Lightweight Title at Polo Grounds," *New York Times,* 12 September 1932, p. 32.

36 James P. Dawson, "Schmeling Fight on Coast Planned: Bout With Baer, Who Stopped Ex-Champion Last Summer, Proposed for March 17th," *New York Times*, 12 January 1934, p. 34.
37 Radio broadcast of the Max Baer-Primo Carnera fight, originally aired June 14, 1934.
38 "Jack Dempsey to Try Restaurant Business: He Will Erect $250,000 Store and Café Building at Once Opposite the Garden," *New York Times*, 11 October 1934, p. 25; "Cornerstone Laid For Dempsey Café. Mayor Officiates as Former Champion Tosses in Gloves That Won Title," *New York Times*, 11 December 1934, p. 26.
39 John V. Grombach, *The Saga of the Fist: The 9,000 Year Story of Boxing in Text and Pictures* (South Brunswick and New York: A.S. Barnes and Company, Inc.,1977), 138.
40 "Baer-Braddock Contest for Title Set For June 13th in Garden Bowl: Commission Allots May 10 for Ambers-Canzoneri Lightweight Championship Bout," *New York Times*, 17 April 1935, p. 30.
41 "Betting Is Light Despite 6–1 Odds: Baer Money Goes Begging With Little Support Offered," *New York Times*, 14 June 1935, p. 30.
42 "Dispute at Garden is put to a Vote: Row between Hammond and Kilpatrick Factions is Fully Aired as Stockholders Meet," *New York Times*, 25 September 1935, p. 19.
43 "Betting Is Light," p. 30.
44 "Dispute at Garden," p. 19.
45 Grombach, *The Saga of the Fist*, 134.
46 Fred Van Ness, "Day of Relaxation Enjoyed by Louis: Joe is Ruffled Only When his "Managers Reuse to Let Him Play a Round of Golf," *New York Times*, 18 June 1936, p. 27.
47 "Today on Radio," *New York Times*, 17 June 1936, p. 21.
48 "Fight Will Be Broadcast: NBC Will Carry Description All Over Country and Abroad," *New York Times*, 18 June 1936, p. 27.
49 *The Fleischmann's Yeast Hour* a.k.a. Rudy Vallee Show, broadcast June 18, 1936 by NBC.
50 Radio broadcast of the Louis-Schmeling I fight, originally aired June 19, 1936.
51 "Goebbels Hails Victor. Cables Congratulations to Max-Fighter's Wife at Radio," *New York Times*, 20 June 1936, p. 10.
52 "Germany Acclaims Schmeling as National Hero for His Victory Over Louis: Campaign is Begun for Bout in Reich," *New York Times*, 21 June 1936, p. S11.
53 "Fight Excitement Causes 12 Deaths: 11 Succumb in United States and Canada While Listening to Radio Description," *New York Times*, 21 June 1936, p. S11.
54 Chris Mead, *Champion: Joe Louis, Black Hero in White America* (New York: Charles Scribner's Sons, 1985), 113.
55 "Contracts Closed For Chicago Fight: Braddock to Get $500,000 or 50% of Gate," *New York Times*, 20 February 1937, p. 11.
56 "Schmeling Makes $250,000 Offer To Braddock for Fight in Berlin: German Also Would Give Champion Film and Radio Rights, Which he Values at More than $100,000," *New York Times*, 11 March 1937, p. 27.

57 "Germans Incensed At Fight Decision: Phelan Target of Editorial Fury for Ruling Regarding Braddock, Schmeling," *New York Times*, 5 June 1937, p. 11.

58 Joseph C. Nichols, "Braddock Fined and Banned but Is Allowed to Keep Title: Schmeling Assails 'Lenient' Penalty Charges," *New York Times*, 4 June 1937, p. 29.

CHAPTER 4

1 James P. Dawson, "Louis Overwhelming Favorite to Keep Title in First Defense on Thursday: Farr Seen Doomed To Quick Knockout," *New York Times*, 22 August 1937, p. S8.

2 *Time* 30 (6 September 1937): 99.

3 "All-Night Celebration in Berlin Marks Victory," *New York Times*, 14 December 1947, p. 34.

4 Albion Ross, Schmeling Choice to Win Bout Today: Favored Though Outweighed 15 Pounds by Foord for Battle in Hamburg," *New York Times*, 30 January 1938, p. 67.

5 *Radio Guide* 7 (25 June 1938): 2.

6 James P. Dawson, "Schmeling Flies Here to Fight Louis for Heavyweight Championship Tonight: Louis Is 2–5 Choice to Retain Crown," *New York Times*, 22 June 1938, p. 28.

7 Radio broadcast of the Joe Louis- Max Schmeling II fight, originally aired June 22, 1938.

8 James P. Dawson, "Schmeling, in Hospital, Plans to Sail for Germany July 2," *New York Times*, 24 June 1938, p. 22.

9 James P. Dawson, "60,000 Expected to See Heavyweight Title Fight Tonight: Contestants in Heavyweight Title Bout at Stadium Tonight," *New York Times*, 28 June 1939, p. 28.

10 "Fans' Emotions Shift Speedily in Orange: Crowd at Galento Tavern Wildly Excited, Then Silent," *New York Times*, 29 June 1939, p. 26.

11 James P. Dawson, "Louis 1–7 Favorite to Defeat Pastor in Detroit Tonight: Principals in Bout for Heavyweight Title," *New York Times*, 20 September 1939, p. 40.

12 James P. Dawson, "Louis Favored to Knock Out Godoy Tonight in 9th Title Defense: Heavyweights Who Will Meet Tonight in Title Bout," *New York Times*, 9 February 1940, p. 28.

13 "Chile Is Disappointed: But Crowds at Radios Calmly Accept Godoy Defeat as Fair," *New York Times*, 10 February 1940, p. 16.

14 Orlo Robertson, "Mike Jacobs Not Likely To Give Godoy Another Shot At Louis," *Hartford Courant*, 11 February 1940, p. C4.

15 Joe Louis: America's Hero . . . Betrayed," first broadcast February 23, 2008, by HBO.

16 Ibid.

17 "Joy, Tragedy in Wake of Joe's Victory," *The Chicago Defender*, 2 July 1938, p. 6; "Harlem Celebrants Toss Varied Missiles," New York Times, 23 June, 1938. Meanwhile, in the German section of Yorkville, German-American "beer

dispensaries" and restaurants were crowded with "eager radio listeners." However, when the fight ended "there was an almost universal silence and then bursts of laughter that sounded sheepish to some observers."

18 "103-Year-Old Ex-Slave Is Ardent Joe Louis Fan," *Cleveland Call and Post*, 24 March 1945, p. 13.

19 Former champions also contributed to the war effort. Jack Dempsey, labeled as a slacker after World War I, redeemed his reputation by achieving the high rank of Lieutenant Commander in the Coast Guard. The "Fighting Marine," Gene Tunney made his second round as a leatherneck, this time as a Captain. Barney Ross joined Tunney in the elite corps and went on to become a decorated hero at Guadalcanal. Former middleweight champion Fred Apostoli was a swabbie, stationed at the Norfolk Naval Station. Former bantam claimant Georgie Pace served in the Army.

20 James P. Dawson, "Louis 1–7 Favorite Over Buddy Baer in Charily Contest at Garden Tonight: Gate Of $200,000 Is Jacobs's Hope," *New York Times*, 9 January 1942, p. 26.

21 Chris Mead, *Champion: Joe Louis, Black Hero in White America* (New York: Charles Scribner's Son, 1985), 212.

22 Ibid., 213.

23 "Louis-Simon Contest on Shortwave: Mutual System to Broadcast For Soldiers Abroad," *New York Times*, 19 March 1942, p. 30.

24 Mead, *Champion: Joe Louis, Black Hero in White America*, 219.

25 "Louis-Simon Contest," p. 30.

26 Mead, *Champion: Joe Louis, Black Hero in White America*, 219.

27 Ibid, 217–218.

28 James Edmund Boyack, "It Took Joe Louis to Give War A Name with A 'Punch,'" *Pittsburgh Courier*, City Edition, 16, May 1942, p. 17; "God on Our Side," *New York Amsterdam Star-News*, 21 March 1942, p. 6.

29 Mead, *Champion, Joe Louis, Black Hero in White America*, 217–218.

30 "Sergeant Louis to Take Part in 'This Is The Army," *New York Amsterdam Star-News*, 27 February 1943, p. 14. The following year, Sergeant Joe Louis continued his war efforts on the silver screen. He was assigned to appear in the Warner Brothers movie version of Irving Berlin's "This Is the Army," an American propaganda film.

31 John K. Hutchens, "Microphone Showshop: Notes on the Animal Kingdom as Visited by the Wireless, a Word About Accuracy, and Pugilistic Guest Stars," *New York Times*, 18 January 1942, p. X12.

32 Wireless to the *New York Times*, "Schmeling Drops to Crete With First of Air Troops, *New York Times*, 27 May 1941, p. 5.

33 "Schmeling Reported Captured, *New York Times*, 14 April 1943, p. 29.

34 "Schmeling Killed by British in Crete," *Los Angeles Times*, 29 May 1941, p. 1; By telephone to the *New York Times*, "Crete Battle 'Tough,' Schmeling Declares: He Says His Unit Lost Heavily After Parachute Landing," *New York Times*, 31 May 1941, p. 4.

35 "Schmeling Reported Captured," p. 29.
36 "Schmeling Getting Treatment," *New York Times*, 16 April 1943, p. 27.
37 "Joe Louis Whipped Max Schmeling On Foul, Says The Nazis—Now You Know They Are Nuts!," *Philadelphia* Tribune, 19 September 1942, p. 13.
38 "Prison Term For Schmeling," *Los Angeles Times*, 14, May 1946, p. 1.
39 "Schmeling to Fight Again," *New York Times*, 1 April 1944, p. X5.
40 Joe Louis Honored As Model Soldier: Legion of Merit Presented for His Exhibitions in Camps Here and Overseas," *New York Times*, 24 September 1945, p. 32.
41 *Time* 45 (16 April 1945): 52.
42 *The Bill Stern Sports Reel*, December 7, 1945.
43 "American Style Radio Reaches Troops Abroad," *Chicago Daily Tribune*, 7 May 1944, p. N7.
44 "Barney Ross Depicts Marine Corps Spirit," *Los Angeles Times*, 27 February 1943, p. 3.
45 "Silver Star Awarded to Barney Ross," *Washington Post*, 5 July 1943, p. 10.
46 "Red Cross Rally to Hear First Lady: Barney Ross, Guadalcanal Hero, also to Speak in Garden on March 15," *New York Times*, 7 March 1943, p. 35.
47 T. R. Kennedy Jr., "Little Touch of Home," *New York Times*, 28 May 1944, p. X5.
48 "Some Notes at Random," *New York Times*, 25 January 1942, p. X10.
49 John De La Vega, "KMPC Slates Golden Gloves War Bond Rally," *Los Angeles Times*, 9 February 1944, p. A7.
50 John De La Vega, "They'll Warble but Listeners Supply Notes," *Los Angeles Times*, 11 February 1944, p. A7.

CHAPTER 5

1 "Maj. White Out of Radio May 1, To Master Polo," *New York Herald Tribune*, 25 April 1930, p. 21.
2 Ibid.
3 "2 Veteran Radio Announcers Are Convention 'Ears' of Millions," *New York Herald, New York Tribune*, 4 July 1924, p. 5.
4 "Pioneer," The News on the Radio, *New York Herald Tribune*, 15 June 1924, p. SM19.
5 Roger N. Batchelder, "Curiosity Led McNamee, Singer To Radio Announcing And Fame," *Boston Globe*, 29 March 1925, p. B7.
6 Charles Roland, "Announcers You Have Heard," *New York Herald Tribune*, 17 July 1927, p. F2.
7 "Knockout Reilly," *The Hartford Courant*, 16 April 1927, p. 6.
8 Radio broadcast of the Max Baer-Primo Carnera fight, originally aired June 14, 1934.
9 Batchelder, "Curiosity Led McNamee," p. B7.
10 Radio broadcast of the Max Baer-Primo Carnera fight.
11 Stuart Hawkins, "On the Radio: Graham McNamee Describes Fight; Hanson Gould To-night," *New York Herald Tribune*, 2 March 1928, p. 20.

12 Albert A. Keane, "Calling 'Em Right," *Hartford Courant,* 4 July 1931, p. 13.
13 Pioneer, "Last Night On Radio," *New York Herald, New York Tribune,* 21 May 1926, p. 25; Stuart Hawkins, "On the Radio," *New York Herald Tribune,* 21 August 1926, p. 10.
14 Pioneer, "Last Night on the Radio," *New York Herald, New York Tribune,* 8 May 1926, p. 9.
15 Pioneer, "Last Night on the Radio," *New York Herald, Herald Tribune,* 11 May 1926, p. 19.
16 Pioneer, "Last Night on the Radio," *New York Herald, New York Tribune,* 8 May 1926, p. 9.
17 Don Dunphy, *Don Dunphy at Ringside,* 110–111.
18 Irving Settel, *A Pictorial History of Radio* (New York: Grosset & Dunlap,1967), 59.
19 "Maj. White Out of Radio," p. 21.
20 "First College Course in Broadcasting has NBC Man as Lecturer," *RCA News* XI (October, 1930): 22.
21 Stuart Hawkins, "On the Radio," *New York Herald Tribune,* 21 November 1927, p. 14.
22 "Ted Husing, Radio Announcer, Praises Godfrey's Ring Work," *The New York Amsterdam News,* 23 April 1930, p. 16.
23 Jack Saunders, "Hooks and Jabs," *Philadelphia Tribune,* 25 August 1938, p. 8. For example, Clem McCarthy was criticized by another African American newspaper, *The Philadelphia Tribune,* for misleading listeners by creating the impression that Lou Ambers defeated Henry Armstrong in their memorable bout.
24 "Ted Husing, Sports Announcer and Disk Jockey, Dead at 60," *New York Times,* 11 August 1962, p. 12.
25 Radio broadcast of the Joe Louis-Jack Sharkey fight. originally aired August 18, 1936.
26 Ibid.
27 Donald W. Smith, "All Gangsters Are Cowards, Declares Charles Noted Writer of Crime Stories Exposes His Outlaw Models," *Hartford Courant,* 2 June 1935, p. D1.
28 Joe Williams, *TV Boxing Book* (New York: D. Van Nostrand Company, Inc., 1954), 116.
29 Edgar T. Bouzeau, "Third Man In Ring Analyzes Fight For The Courier," *Pittsburgh Courier,* 11 September 1937, p. 1.
30 The Results of the Carnival of Champions: Harry Jeffra Dec.15 rds. Sixto Escobar, won bantam title; Lou Ambers Dec.15 rds. Pedro Montanez, retained lightweight title; Barney Ross, Dec.15 rds. Ceferino Garcia, retained welterweight title; Fred Apostoli K.O. 10 Marcel Thil, retained middleweight title as recognized by the New York State Athletic Commission.
31 Radio broadcast of the Joe Louis-Al Ettore fight. originally aired September 22, 1936.
32 Ibid.
33 Ibid.
34 Ibid.
35 Radio broadcast of the Joe Louis-Max Schmeling I fight. originally aired June 19, 1936.

36 "Calm During Fistic Storm: Tenseness Is Lacking London Fight Announcer Maintains Decorum but Crowd Cheers," *New York Times*, 25 April 1937, p. 174.

37 Ibid.

38 Kermit Holt, "Radio Superior to Ringside Seat at Boxing in Britain," *Chicago Daily Tribune*, 23 March 1947, Part 2, a3.

CHAPTER 6

1 Radio broadcast of the Max Baer-Primo Carnera fight, originally aired June 14, 1934.

2 During this era, it was commonplace for the referee to be announced just prior to a fight held in New York.

3 Radio broadcast of the Max Baer-Primo Carnera fight.

4 Ibid.

5 Don Dunphy, *Don Dunphy at Ringside*, 130; "The Merry-Go-Round of Broadcasting: Inquisitive 'Mike' Will Roam New York—Summer Plans of Performers," *New York Times*, 9 June 1935, p. X11.

6 Radio broadcast of the Billy Conn-Fred Apostoli II fight, originally aired February 10, 1939.

7 "A.B.C. Hires Stern for Fights On TV," *New York Times*, 6 January 1953, p. 32. Though primarily a radio announcer who had a career almost exclusively with NBC, Stern became a boxing commentator for ABC Television for their Saturday weekly series. The program debuted on January 24, 1953, with the Paddy DeMarco-Johnny Gonsalves match in Boston.

8 Radio broadcast of the Billy Conn-Fred Apostoli II fight.

9 Ibid.

10 Ibid.

11 Ibid.

12 Ibid.

13 Ibid.

14 Ibid.

15 Loubet and Ort, *The 1979 Ring Boxing Encyclopedia and Record Book*, 120.

16 Dunphy, *Don Dunphy at Ringside*, 130.

17 Ibid., 23–43.

18 Ibid., 53.

19 Ibid., 55.

20 Ibid., 55–57.

21 "Bill Corum Dead; Sports Writer, 64," *New York Times*, 17 December 1958, p. F2.

22 Radio broadcast of the Beau Jack-Tippy Larkin fight, originally aired December 18, 1942.

23 Ibid.

24 "They're in There Swinging for You: Mr. Barber at the Plate—Mr. Dunphy at the Ringside," *New York Times*, 28 September 1941 p. X10.

25 Gerald Eskenazi, "Don Dunphy, 90, Distinctive Fight Broadcaster," *New York Times*, 24 July 1998, p. B12.
26 "They're in There Swinging," p. X10.
27 Eskenazi, "Distinctive Fight Broadcaster," p. B12.
28 Donald Freeman, "TV Vital to Fight Game: Dunphy," *Chicago Daily Tribune*, 23 December 1962, p. n6.
29 Doug Miles interview of Don Dunphy on WBAU 90.3 FM, April 27, 1985, Don Dunphy Interview.wmv - YouTube.
30 Ibid.
31 Radio broadcast of the Rocky Marciano-Archie Moore fight, originally aired September 21, 1955.

CHAPTER 7

1 "Today's Radio Program," *New York Times*, 29 October 1923, p. 19.
2 "Today's Radio Program," *New York Times*, 14 November 1923, p. 22.
3 "De Forest to Talk on Physical Culture For the Radio Fans," *New York Herald Tribune*, 5 August 1923, p. B5.
4 "Radio Programs Scheduled For the Coming Week," *New York Times*, 23 March 1924, p. XX15.
5 "Radio Programs Scheduled For the Current Week," *New York Times*, 12 July 1925 p. XX15.
6 H. I. Phillips, "The Once Over," *Boston Daily Globe*, 25 March 1925, p. 16.
7 "Heard on the Radio Last Night," *Hartford Courant*, 2 May 1925, p. 12.
8 "Radio Programs Scheduled For the Current Week," *New York Times*, 19 July 1925, p. XX13.
9 Lawrence Sweeney, "Thrilling Ring Contest Should Result When Suggs and Herman Clash Tomorrow," *Boston Daily Globe*, 7 June 1926, p. A10.
10 John S. Daggett, "Our Gang Heads Kids Broadcast," *Los Angeles Times*, 26 August 1931, p. 17; "La Barba and Blake Go on Radio Today," *Los Angeles Times*, 13 June 1932, p. 11; "McLarnin May Go East For Title Battles," *Los Angeles Times*, 1 August 1933, p. A9.
11 Jack Saunders, "Bob Is 'Uncrowned Champion," *Philadelphia Tribune*, 22 November 1941, p. 14.
12 James P. Dawson, "Terris and Vinez to Box in Garden: Will Top Card of Lightweight and 130-Pound Title Contenders Next Friday," *New York Times*, 3 January 1926, p. S8.
13 "Testimonial to Tunney," *New York Times*, 24 October 1926, p. XX17.
14 "Tunney Elevated By Distilling Unit: Former Ring Champion Heads Board of American, Part of Commercial Alcohol," *New York Times*, 7 January 1938, p. 27.
15 "'Pro-American' Group Supported by Tunney: Former Boxer Announces New National Youth Foundation," *New York Times*, 14 August 1940, p. 23.
16 "Tunney Hits at Lindbergh: Calls Part of Radio Appeal on the War 'Impertinence,'" *New York Times*, 20 October 1939, p. 10.

17 "Radio and Television: Gene Tunney, Branch Rickey and Other Notables to Sub for Tunney In Broadcast," *New York Times*, 26 November 1930, p. 19.

18 "Rockne Eulogized By Radio Speakers: Tribute Paid to the Late Coach In Nation-Wide Pre-Game Broadcast," *New York Times*, 29 November 1931, p. S5.

19 Lowell Thomas, *New York Times*, 19 August 1949, p. 34. Tunney always seemed to have a nose for radio. When Lowell Thomas took a hiatus from his CBS radio commentary program in 1949 to take a trip to the Far East, Gene seized the opportunity to act as one of his replacements.

20 "Corbett Will Read New Boxing Rules," *Hartford Courant*, 6 January 1923, p. 5.

21 "7 New Series Premier on C.B.S. Net," *New York Herald Tribune*, 14 September 1930, p. C9.

22 "Corbett Envies Ruth's Appetite at 'Ad' Lunch," *New York Herald Tribune*, 28 October 1932, p. 28.

23 *Shell Chateau*, first broadcast July 13, 1935, by NBC.

24 "Little Bits 'Bout Boxers," *Philadelphia Tribune*, 28 May 1931, p. 11.

25 "Jack Johnson on Sports Quiz Show," *Philadelphia Tribune*, 23 January 1941, p. 12.

26 "Hear That Small Voice on Radio ? It's Jack Johnson's," *The Chicago Defender*, 10 October 1936, p. 14.

27 "Dempsey to Speak Upon Air Tonight," *Washington Post*, 4 May 1929, p. 10.

28 "Fight Bout of Dempsey Over WRC," *Washington Post*, 2 October 1929, p. 12.

29 "Tribute to Rogers Darkens Theatres: Film Houses Here Dim Their Screens as 18,000 in the Country Mark Funeral," *New York Times*, 23 August 1935, p. 16.

30 "Kid Galahad," *Lux Radio Theater*, first broadcast December 19, 1938, by CBS.

31 Special Cable to the *New York Times*, "Schmeling Acclaimed After Making Flight: German Admirers Welcome Him in Tempelhof Flying Field, Where He Talks Over Radio," *New York Times*, 6 September 1939, p. 29.

32 "Dies Suddenly," *Chicago Daily Tribune*, 22 November 1959, Part 2, p. b1.

33 Grombach, *The Saga of the Fist*, 137.

34 "Accidental Pistol Shot Burns Baer," *Los Angeles Times*, 10 May 1935, p. 1; Special to the *New York Times*, "Baer Burned in Chest by Blank Cartridge Wad: Champion is Treated at Hospital for Wound Received in Accident While Rehearsing for Radio Skit—Fight Not to Be Delayed," *New York Times*, 10 May 1935, p. 27.

35 Grombach, *The Saga of the Fist*, 138.

36 "Hoover to Talk to Byrd: Max Baer also to Broadcast to Little America Sunday," *New York Times*, 4 October 1934, p. 12.

37 Grombach, *The Saga of the Fist*, 140.

38 "The Inside Case of the Jersey Butcher Bandits," *Gangbusters*, November 18, 1947 by NBC.

39 John K. Hutchens, "Microphone Showshop: Notes on the Animal Kingdom as Visited by the Wireless, a Word About Accuracy, and Pugilistic Guest Stars," *New York Times*, 18 January 1942, p. X12.

40 John K. Hutchens, "Voice of the Devil: And Some Notes on an Actor Named Louis and J. Pearl's New Entertainment," *New York Times*, 18 October 1942, p. X12.

41 Caswell Adams, "Introducing the New Joe Louis," *Saturday Evening Post* 213 (10 May 1941): 26–111.
42 Robert Edgren, "Sharkey Puts Pep in the Heavyweight Situation," *Baltimore Sun*, 5 June 1927, p. SS3.
43 "Big Athletic Carnival at K. C. Hall Tonight," *Baltimore Sun*, 23 November 1926, p. 18.
44 E. B. Henderson, "Race Segregation," *Washington Post*, 18 July 1937, p. B9.
45 "Mountain Justice," *Fred Allen Show*, first broadcast January 31, 1940, by CBS.
46 "Perennial Comic," *Time* 36 (7 October 1940): 46.
47 "Zivic Becomes Glib Listening to Allen: Trades Left-Hook Lore for Lessons From Stage Wit in Training for Beau Jack," *New York Times*, 2 February 1943, p. 26.
48 "Jack Goes Into Training for Fight with Fred," *The Jack Benny Show*, first broadcast January 29, 1939, by NBC.
49 "Joe Louis Acts as Jack's Body Guard," *The Jack Benny Show*, first broadcast November 11, 1945, by NBC.
50 "Levinsky Sees Harm In Big Ring Pursues: Veteran Says American Heavyweights Are Being Ruined-Praises Loughran's Ability," *New York Times*, 23 January 1929, p. 23.
51 "The Microphone Will Present," *New York Times*, 28 August 1932, p. X7.
52 Sports Hero Held Model for Youth: Inspires the Underprivileged With Sportsmanship," *New York Times*, 12 May 1937, p. 12.
53 Richard L. Coe, "Radio: Ken Overlin KO's Dat Ole Debbil 'Mike,'" *Washington Post*, 17 August 1941, p. L15.
54 Val Adams, "News and Notes from the TV-Radio World: Shopkeeper and His Spouse," *New York Times*, 26 August 1956, p. X11.
55 *The Colgate Sports Reel*, first broadcast April 23, 1948 by NBC.
56 *The Colgate Sports Reel*, first broadcast April 2, 1948 by NBC.
57 *The Colgate Sports Reel*, first broadcast December 23, 1949 by NBC.

CHAPTER 8

1 "The Passionate Palooka," *The Adventures of the Thin Man*, first broadcast June 7, 1948, by CBS.
2 "Slow Burn," *Suspense*, first broadcast February 23, 1950, by CBS.
3 "The Gladiator," *Escape*, first broadcast August 1, 1951, by CBS.
4 "Slow Burn."
5 "Gunner's Last Fight," *Night Beat*, first broadcast August 14, 1950, by NBC.
6 "The Case of the Deadly Sell-Out," *The New Adventures of Nero Wolfe*, first broadcast January 5, 1951, by NBC.
7 "Angry Eagle," *The Adventure of Philip Marlowe*, first broadcast April 18, 1950, by CBS.
8 Ibid.
9 "Maestro and Man," *Suspense*, first broadcast July 20, 1944, by CBS.
10 "Heavyweight Murder Case," *Philo Vance*, first broadcast June 19, 1948, by NBC.
11 "The Case of the Deadly Sell-Out."

12 "Fourth Round Knockout," *The Adventures of Frank Race*, first broadcast September 11, 1949.

13 "The Prizefight Set-Up" *Rocky Fortune*, first broadcast December 29, 1953, by NBC.

14 "The Case of the Bellicose Boxer," *The Falcon*, first broadcast January 28, 1951, by NBC.

15 "Angry Eagle."

16 *The Screen Guild Theater* aired as a radio program from 1939 to 1952. It was created in 1924 to raise money for the Motion Picture Relief Fund, which maintained the Motion Picture Country Home. The radio program also operated under several other titles including *The Gulf Screen Guild Show*, *The Gulf Screen Guild Theater*, and *The Camel Screen Guild Theater*.

17 "Champion," *Screen Directors Playhouse*, first broadcast March 17, 1950, by NBC; "Body and Soul," *Screen Directors Playhouse*, first broadcast November 11, 1949, by NBC; "The Champ," *Lux Radio Theater*, first broadcast January 13, 1939, by CBS; "The Champ," *Lux Radio Theater*, first broadcast June 29, 1942, by CBS.

18 "Kid Galahad," *Theater of Romance*, first broadcast December 2, 1946, by CBS; "City For Conquest," *Lux Radio Theater*, first broadcast February 9, 1942, by CBS.

19 "Gentleman Jim," *The Gulf Screen Guild Show*, first broadcast February 14, 1944, by CBS.

20 "Champion."

21 "Body and Soul."

22 "Kid Galahad."

23 "Champion."

24 "Body and Soul."

25 "The Case of The Tell-Tale Tie," *Mystery Theater*, first broadcast October 8, 1952, by CBS.

26 "The Saga of Melody Jackson," *Destination Freedom*, first broadcast May 29, 1949.

27 Ibid.

28 "Little David," *Destination Freedom*, first broadcast October 10, 1948.

29 "Premonition of the Panther," *Destination Freedom*, first broadcast March 12, 1950.

30 "The Carolina Kid," *Lest We Forget: The American Dream*, first broadcast 1947.

31 Frederick V. Romano, *The Boxing Filmography: American Features, 1920–2003* (Jefferson, North Carolina: McFarland & Company, 2004), p.103; "The 15th Round," *Joe Palooka*, first broadcast November 12, 1945.

32 *The Ford Show* hosted by Tennessee Ernie Ford, starring William Bendix, 1956–1961, NBC.

33 "I Bought A Fighter," *The Red Skelton Show*, first broadcast June 11, 1952, by CBS.

34 *Lou Holtz Laugh Club*.

35 "I Bought A Fighter."

36 Ibid.

37 "The Champion-Set-Up," *The Jack Benny Program*, first broadcast May 22, 1949, by CBS.

38 Ibid.
39 "Champion," *The Jack Benny Program,* first broadcast March 19, 1950, by CBS.
40 "Irma Gives Rent Money to Al," *My Friend Irma,* first broadcast April 18, 1947, by CBS.
41 "Small Town Newspaper," *The Adventures of Maisie,* first broadcast October 12, 1950.

CHAPTER 9

1 "Servo Listens to Battle as He Fights It," *Chicago Daily Tribune,* 3 February 1946, Sec. Two, p. A7.
2 Ibid.
3 George Hicks "A Radio Man Remembers," in *The Fireside Book of Boxing,* ed. W. C. Heinz (New York: Simon and Shuster, 1961), 200–201.
4 Ibid.
5 Not to be cheated of his memorable moment, Hicks went on to give an historic radio broadcast of the "D-Day" invasion of Normandy, France.
6 James P. Dawson, "Chicago Bout Crowd Riots as Seats Fall: 18 Injured, One Perhaps Fatally When Temporary Stand Collapses in Coliseum," *New York Times,* 26 March 1929, p. 42.
7 "Pushed From Balcony, May Die," *New York Times,* 26 March 1929, p. 42.
8 Dawson, "Chicago Bout Crowd Riots," p.42.
9 "Pushed From Balcony," p. 42.
10 Ibid.
11 Barry Howard, "Chicago Boxers Fight New York Tonight," *Chicago Daily Tribune,* 30 March 1942, p. 19.
12 "W-G-N to Cover Chicago-European Bouts," *Chicago Daily Tribune,* 10 April 1940, p. 29.
13 Heinz Reichmann, "Germans Tackle Anything—Even Radio—And Win," *Chicago Daily Tribune,* 23 July 1932, p. 11.
14 Frank Mastro, "West Siders Pay Tribute to Hawaiian Boxers," *Chicago Daily Tribune,* 6 July 1940, p. 13
15 Maurice Shevlin, "New York, Chicago Square Off Tonight!" *Chicago Daily Tribune,* 20 March 1957, Part 4, p. d1.
16 Ibid.

EPILOGUE—RADIO RECORDINGS

1 J. David Goldin, *The Golden Age of Radio,* 13.
2 Goldin, *The Golden Age of Radio,* 20.
3 "Phonograph Takes Radio. Part of Proceedings at Convention Transferred to Wax Disks," *New York Times,* 28 June 1924, p. 4.
4 Goldin, *The Golden Age of Radio,* 13.

CHAPTER 10

1 Albert Abramson, "The Invention of Television," in *Television: An International History*, ed. 2. Anthony Smith (New York: Oxford University Press, 1995), 13.

2 Abramson, "The Invention of Television," 15.

3 Ibid, 16

4 Ibid, 29

5 "Radio Men Regard Television as an Ally," *New York Times*, 15 January 1928, p. 5.

6 "Radio Images Win Battle with Storm," *New York Times*, 3 May 1931, p. XX10.

7 Orrin E. Dunlap, Jr., "Listening-In," *New York Times*, 27 December 1931, p. 19.

8 Abramson, "The Invention of Television," 24. W2XBS was the pioneering television station of RCA. It was initially operated by their Research and Test Department at Van Cortlandt Park, Bronx, New York, under the direction of Dr. Alfred N. Goldsmith. The station would become WNBT Channel 1 on July 1, 1941, when it was granted a commercial license.

9 Orrin E. Dunlap Jr., "Television's Mail," *New York Times*, 7 August 1932, p. X7.

10 Orrin E. Dunlap Jr., "Faces That Lurk In Space: Television Observes in Indiana and Maine Look in on New York—But a Cat Looks Like a Scotty," *New York Times*, 15 May 1933, p. X10.

11 "Television Gains Lap," *Los Angeles Times*, 13 July 1928, p. 1.

12 "Compact Drum Scanner Advances Home Television," *New York Herald Tribune*, 7 July 1929, p. G5.

13 "Television Make-Up Is an Art," *New York Times*, 23 August 1931, p. X9.

14 "First Boxing Exhibition Broadcast by Television," *New York Herald Tribune*, 14 August 1931, p. 14.

15 Ibid.

16 "Store Shows Television," *New York Times*, 6 February 1932, p. 13.

17 Lawrence E. Davies, "Ring Fight Shown in Television Test," *New York Times*, 12 August 1936, p. 21.

18 "Slow-Motion Television Features Boxing Lesson," *New York Times*, 8 November 1936, p. X12.

19 "Television Broadcast of Leonard Ring Go," *Los Angeles Times*, 13 August 1931, p. A11.

20 "Television Eyes Is Focused On Miniature Football Field," *New York Times*, 11 October 1932, p. XX11.

21 Abramson, "The Invention of Television," 28–29.

22 Loubet and Ort, *The 1979 Ring Boxing Encyclopedia and Record Book*, 120.

23 While the first Baer-Nova encounter is sometimes cited as the first professional boxing match televised in the United States, the *1979 Ring Record Book and Boxing Encyclopedia* cites these earlier bouts.

24 "Today on the Radio," *New York Times*, 1 June 1949, p. 41.

25 Sam Taub served as the television announcer.

26 Orrin E. Dunlap Jr., "Watching A Battle," *New York Times*, 4 June 1939, p. X10.

27 "Television Brings Nova Fight Clearly To Theater Fans," *New York Herald Tribune*, 2 June 1939, p. 27.

28 Dunlap, Jr., "Watching a Battle," p. X10.

29 Loubet and Ort, *The 1979 Ring Boxing Encyclopedia and Record Book*, 120.

30 "Horse That Wouldn't Be Televised," *Daily Mail Atlantic Edition* (London), 15 June 1929, Issue 990, p. 14.

31 "Televisions Debut in London," *The Christian Science Monitor*, 11 October 1930, p. 7.

32 "Home and Foreign Radio," *Daily Mail* (London), 1 October 1931, Issue 11056, p. 16.

33 Loubet and Ort, *The 1979 Ring Boxing Encyclopedia and Record Book*, 120; "Boxing By Television," *Daily Mail* (London), 23 August 1933, Issue 11647, p. 10.

34 Collie Knox, "B.B.C. Enforces Its Ban On Song-Plugging," *Daily Mail* (London), 22 August 1933, Issue 11646, p. 3.

35 Forums.digitalspy.co.uk. Accessed June 18, 2015.

36 The *Daily Mail* (London) and Nat Fleischer give the date of August 22, while the *Times* (London) indicates August 23.

37 Loubet and Ort, *The 1979 Ring Boxing Encyclopedia and Record Book*, 120; *Times* (London), 4 April 1938, Issue 47964, p. 10.

38 *Times* (London), 23 August 1933, Issue 46530, p. 10; Loubet and Ort, *The 1979 Ring Boxing Encyclopedia and Record Book*, 120.

39 It is unclear why the Baxter-Lewis bout is not generally recognized as the first televised, nonexhibition professional bout in England. The contemporaneous television listing did not list the bout as an exhibition.

40 Grombach, *The Saga of the Fist*, 134. At least one other source cites an earlier bout as the first professional telecast—Max Baer's encounter with Englishman Tommy Farr on April 15, 1937, also described as a noncommercial broadcast not made for public viewers.

41 *Times* (London), 21 June 1938, Issue 48026, p. 5; *Times* (London), 3 October 1938, Issue 4811, p. 3. Other early English broadcasts of professional bouts included Ben Foord vs. Eddie Phillips from Harringay Arena on June 21, 1938; and two separate bouts held on October 3, 1938, headlined by Arthur Danahar and Benny Lynch, who opened the season at Empress Hall, Earls Court.

42 C. A. Lejeune, "All London Toys with Television," *New York Times*, 19 March 1939, p. 137.

43 Ibid.

44 Les Brown, "The American Networks," in *Television: An International History*, ed. Anthony Smith (New York: Oxford University Press, 1995), 267. DuMont Laboratories was the other major player along with NBC in early boxing broadcasts through the DuMont Network. Founded by Allen B. DuMont, an inventor and manufacturer of television sets and pictured tubes, the network also exhibited at the World's Fair but was overshadowed by its larger competitor.

45 "Dedication of RCA Seen on Television: *New York Times*, 21 April 1939, p. 16.

46 Ibid.

47 Sarnoff's speech and the boxing exhibition predated Roosevelt's iconic speech at the Fair made ten days later on April 30, 1939.

48 Ibid.

49 T. R. Kennedy Jr., "An Auspicious Beginning: First Month of Commercial Television Pleases Radio Men and Audience," *New York Times*, 3 August 1941, p. X10.

50 Ibid.

51 T. R. Kennedy Jr., "Engineers Send Theater Size Images," *New York Times*, 6 April 1941, p. X12.

52 "Watcher Miles Away To Broadcast Fight," *New York Herald Tribune*, 22 July 1941, p. 24; Loubet and Ort, *The 1979 Ring Boxing Encyclopedia and Record Book*, 121.

53 R. W. Stewart, "One Thing And Another," *New York Times*, 19 October 1941, p. X12.

54 Kennedy Jr., "Engineers Send Theater Size Images," p. X12.

55 wikipedia.org/wiki/WTMJ-TV.

56 Les Brown, The American Networks," 265.

57 "More Programs," *New York Times*, 18 January 1942, p. X10.

58 "Radio Today," *New York Times*, 1 February 1942, p. 31.

59 "Radio Today," *New York Times*, 8 May 1942, p. 41.

60 T. R. Kennedy Jr., "News of Television," *New York Times*, 17 October 1943, p. X11.

61 Ibid. W2XWV, for example, required the use of 1,028 vacuum tubes of all types including 28 cathode tubes necessary to monitor the video signal. The station, which normally put out 2,000 watts, would need to continually produce 50,000–60,000 watts of electrical power during a telecast.

62 "Radio Today," *New York Times*, 29 December 1943, p. 33.

63 "Radio Today," *New York Times*, 14 January 1944, p. 33.

64 "Radio Today," *New York Times*, 29 September 1944, p. 35.

65 "Radio Today," *New York Times*, 27 March 1944, p. 35.

66 "NBC Will Televise Events in the Garden, Chiefly for Wounded in Service Hospitals. *New York Times*," 12 October 1943, p. 29.

67 "50 Bouts to be Televised to Wounded Serviceman," *New York Times*, 29 September 1944, p. 26.

68 Fred Hawthorne, "Pep vs. Wright Fight Friday to Be Televised," *New York Herald Tribune*, 27 September 1944, p. 25a.

69 https://en.wikipedia.org/wiki/Gillette_Cavalcade_of_Sports

70 T. R. Kennedy Jr., "Hindsight In Television," *New York Times*, 19 March 1944, p. X5.

71 "New Plans Show Television Gains," *New York Times*, 7 April 1944, p. 21.

72 Larry Wolters, "W-G-N Ordering Equipment for Television Era," *Chicago Daily Tribune*, 30 January 1944, p. 3.

73 Ibid.

74 Larry Wolters, "Plan Intercity Show Telecast," *Chicago Daily Tribune*, 22 March 1944, p. 21.

CHAPTER 11

1 T. R. Kennedy Jr., "Television Covers A Prize Fight," *New York Times*, 23 June 1946, p. X7.

2 "Television Sets at U.N. Quarters Removed for Louis-Conn Fight and Other Events," *New York Times*, 16 May 1946, p. 11.

3 John Crosby, "Radio in Review," *New York Herald Tribune*, 21 June 1946, p. 36.

4 Kennedy Jr., "Television Covers A Prize Fight," p. X7.

5 Robert Shagawat, Television Recording—The Origins and Earliest Surviving Live TV Broadcast Recordings, earlytelevision.org, p. 15.

6 Kennedy Jr., "Television Covers A Prize Fight," p. X7.

7 Loubet and Ort, *The 1979 Ring Boxing Encyclopedia and Record Book*, 83.

8 James P. Dawson, "Louis 5–14 Choice Over Conn Tonight," *New York Times*, 19 June 1946, p. 23.

9 Larry Wolters, "End Sport Show Television as Glare Irks Fans," *Chicago Daily Tribune*, 6 August 1946, p. 23.

10 "Telecasts in Fall of Garden Sports Events," *New York Times*, 2 August 1946, p. 28.

11 Larry Wolters, "Basketball Is Fine Subject for Television," *Chicago Daily Tribune*, 8 December 1946, Section Two, p. 3.

12 T. R. Kennedy, Jr., "'Live' Color Show Televised By CBS: Fast Boxing Contest Yields Good Visual Results in Test Conducted Here," *New York Times*, 16 September 1946, p. 7.

13 Jesse Abramson, "Cerdan Knockouts Out Green in Second Round of Middleweight Bout Before 18,116," *New York Herald Tribune*, 29 March 1947, p. 15A.

14 "Radio Programs of the Week," *New York Times*, 21 December 1947, p. X12; William Boddy, "The Beginnings of American Television," in *Television: An International History*, ed. Anthony Smith (New York: The Oxford Press, 1995), 41.

15 Larry Wolters, "Tavern Video Sets Are 27% Of Total in City," *Chicago Daily Tribune*, 14 October 1947, p. 25.

16 Larry Wolters, "Stays at Home, And Goes Places Via Television," *Chicago Daily Tribune*, 10 February 1947; "Television Programs," *Chicago Daily Tribune*, 12 December 1947, p. 20.

17 Larry Wolters, "Coast To Coast Cable Planned For Television," *Chicago Daily Tribune*, 12 February 1947, p. 42

18 Larry Wolters, "Golden Gloves to Be Telecast for First Time," *Chicago Daily Tribune*, February 1947, p. 19.

19 Marguerite Ratty, "Women Cheer Michigan City Boxing Relays," *Chicago Daily Tribune*, 29 February 1948, p. N12.

20 Ibid.

21 Larry Wolters, "Crane to Hoist WBKB Pictures of Boxing Bouts," *Chicago Daily Tribune*, 27 March 1948, Part Two, p. a5.

22 Boddy, "The Beginnings of American Television," 41.

23 Tim Brooks and Earle Marsh, *The Complete Directory to Prime Time Network TV Shows: 1946-Present* (New York: Ballantine Books, 1988), xi.

24 Les Brown, "The American Networks," 266.

25 Wolters, "Coast to Coast," p. 42.

26 "Television," *Time* 27 (March 16 1936): 90. Quality television transmissions made through the air required ultrashortwave lengths, one to nine meters,

which only had a range of 25 to 50 miles. Coaxial cable, although designed for telephone and telegraph messages, could also handle a radio frequency band of 1,000,000 cycles wide—enough to carry the fluctuating light and shadow of television. The cable could be run city-to-city underground.

27 Troy Rondinone, *Friday Night Fighter: Gaspar "Indio" Ortega and the Golden Age of Television Boxing* (Illinois: University of Illinois Press, 2013), 33.

28 Jack Gould, "Television Builds for a Future of Boundless Promise: Its Present Audience of 1,750,000 Is Expected to Number Between Four and Five Million by the End of This Year," *New York Times*, 13 June 1948, p. XX1.

29 "WGN-TV Starts Telecasting Tomorrow," *Chicago Daily Tribune*, 8 April 1948, Part Five, Section 1, p. F1.

30 Jack Gould, "The News of Radio: Rochester Radio City to Open Next Friday—Golden Gloves Will Be Televised," *New York Times*, 7 February 1948, p. 26.

31 https://en.wikipedia.org/wiki/Boxing_from_Sunnyside_Gardens

32 Brooks and Marsh, *The Complete Directory*, 892.

33 Gould, "Gloves Will Be Televised," p. 26.

34 "Radio and Television: Food Costs to Be Analyzed on Air Show From Average Housewife's Viewpoint," *New York Times*, 18 August 1948, p. 50.

35 "Radio and Television: NBC Will Broadcast and Televise the Cotton Bowl Football Game New Years Day," *New York Times*, 21 May 1949, p. 28.

36 Brooks and Marsh, *The Complete Directory*, 890.

37 "Radio and Television: Zero Mostel and Joey Faye Sign for New Video Program on DuMont Network," *New York Times*, 17 September 1948, p. 50.

38 "Radio and Television: Ralph Bellamy to Star in New York Detective Series for CBS Video, Starting Oct. 7," *New York Times*, 29 September 1949, p. 58.

39 "Radio and Television; WMCA's 'Inside New York' Ends on April 15—'Report From Israel Moving," *New York Times*, 8 April 1949, p. 48; "Sports Today," *New York Times*, 15 August 1949, p. 23.

40 "Radio and Television: WABD Adding "Programming Playhouse' and Fight Shows to Video List Next Week," *New York Times*, 6 June 1949, p. 28.

41 "Radio and Television: Variety, Music and Quiz Show to Replace Jo Stafford Show on ABC May 12," *New York Times*, 7 May 1949, p. 28.

42 Brooks and Marsh, *The Complete Directory*, 891.

43 Sidney Lohman, "News of TV: Programming Innovation—Other Items," *New York Times*, 23 March 1952, p. X11.

44 Jack Gould, "Television in Review: WOR-TV Opens Seventh Metropolitan Station—'Band of America,'" *New York Times*, 23 October 1949, p. X11.

45 James P. Dawson, "Louis-Walcott Set for Title Contest," *New York Times*, 22 June 1948, p. 32.

46 "Radio and Television: WNBC and WCBS Each to Discontinue a 15-Minute News Program Next Week," *New York Times*, 2 September 1949, p. 34.

47 "Radio and Television: Opening of Coaxial Cable Link Brings Many New Programs to Video Audience," *New York Times*, 12 January 1949, p. 54.

48 "Radio and Television: DuMont Video to Broadcast Boxing Mondays From Philadelphia-Godfrey Extends Respite," *New York Times,* 22 February 1949, p. 43.
49 Sidney Lohman, "News of Television: Jobs in Video Will Be Scarce—Other Items," *New York Times,* 19 June 1949, p. X9.
50 "Radio and Television: WPIX and Madison Square Garden in Accord on 118 Dates, but Sponsor Must Be Signed," *New York Times,* 21 March 1950, p. 54.
51 "Radio and Television: Engineers Continue Strike at C.B.S. as Mediator Strives for Settlement," *New York Times,* 14 June 1950, p. 62.
52 "70 Shows Planned For Indoor Boxing: Norris Lists 24 at the Garden, 11 at St. Nicks, Others in Chicago, Detroit, St. Louis," *New York Times,* 27 July 1950, p. 40.
53 "WMAR TV Telecasts First Associated Press Newsreel," *Baltimore Sun,* 17 November 1947, p. 28; "Sunlight on Sports," *Baltimore Sun,* 23 April 1952, p. 20.
54 "Walcott's Son to Box On 'Kid Gloves,'" *Philadelphia Tribune,* 10 March 1951, p. 10.
55 "Cambria Television Bouts 'Break' For Negro Fighters," *Philadelphia Tribune,* 10 January 1956, p. 11.
56 "D.C.'s Video Infant Tackles Mobile Pick-Up," *Washington Post,* 29 June 1947, p. L4.
57 Dave Brady, "Official Asks TV Holiday for Boxing," *Washington Post,* 30 March 1953, p. 8.
58 "Television Today," *Washington Post,* 31 January 1949, p. B2; "Television Today," *Washington Post,* 1 February 1949, p. B11.
59 "New York Boxing Matches Televised to Boston," *Daily Boston Globe,* 24 January 1948, p. 5.
60 "U.S. Television Brings N.Y. Boxing Bouts Here," *Daily Boston Globe,* 21 February 1948, p. 12.
61 "WBZ-TV to bring N.B.C. Shows Here," *Daily Boston Globe,* 6 June 1948, p. B11.
62 *Daily Boston Globe,* 31 January 1949, p.7; *Daily Boston Globe,* 28 January 1949, p.28; "WNAC-TV Presents Video Magic," *Daily Boston Globe,* 10 October 1948, p. A29.
63 Jim Friedman, *Cincinnati Television (Images of America: Ohio)* (Arcadia Publishing, 2007), 14.
64 Gertrude Fletcher, Erie News, *Pittsburgh Courier,* 10 May 1952, p. 16.
65 Lindy Lindell, *Metro Detroit Boxing* (Chicago: Arcadia Publishing, 2001), 53.
66 "Pontiac Figures in Pioneer Development of Television," *Los Angeles Times,* 25 May 1941, p. F5.
67 Don Page, "Sportslook: Garden Boxing Finale End of Colorful Era," *Los Angeles Times,* 21 May 1960, p. B5.
68 Carmen McCormack, "Marathon, in the Keys, is Friendly," *New York Herald Tribune,* 26 July 1953, p. D9.
69 https://en.wikipedia.org/wiki/Saturday_Night_at_the_Garden.
70 "The Full Life," *Time,* 58 (26 November 1951): 75.

71 Jesse Abramson, "Walcott to Demand 45 percent As Share of Second Title Bout," *New York Herald Tribune*, 7 June 1952, p. 16. Shortly after the sport began broadcasting nationally, audiences were irked by the transmission of the fourth Walcott-Charles bout. The signal failed just prior to the decision being announced!

72 Loubet and Ort, *The 1979 Ring Boxing Encyclopedia and Record Book*, 21.

73 "Carter to Battle Aragon On Coast," *New York Times*, 14 November 1951, p. 52.

74 "Title Bout To Bring $175,000," *Chicago Daily Tribune*, 22 May 1952, Part 6, p. d1.

75 Sidney Lohman, "News of TV and Radio," *New York Times*, 24 August 1952, p. X9.

76 Sidney Lohman, "News and Notes from the Studios," *New York Times*, 1 June 1952, p. X9.

77 "Radio-TV Notes," *New York Times*, 2 December 1952, p. 44.

78 "C.B.S. To Televise Bouts by Kinescope," *New York Times*, 8 June 1951, p. 41.

79 https://en.wikipedia.org/wiki/Famous_Fights_from_Madison_Square_Garden.

80 "Brooklyn Club to Put Monday Fights On TV," *Chicago Daily Tribune*, 14 April 1952, Part 6, p. e2.

81 Brooks and Marsh, *The Complete Directory*, 896.

82 "Brooklyn Club," p. e2.

83 "School's Out," *Time* 58 (10 September 1951): 84.

84 "Bouts at Rainbow to be Put on TV for 26 Weeks," *Chicago Daily Tribune*, 29 April 1952, Part 3, p. b3.

85 Frank Mastro, "Announce T.V. Schedule of 10 Rainbow Bouts," *Chicago Daily Tribune*, 11 March, 1953, Part 3, p. b5.

86 Frank Mastro, "Fight Telecast Plans to be Drawn Today," *Chicago Daily Tribune*, 11 October 1954, Part 4, p. c2.

87 Anton Remenih, "Where to Dial Today," *Chicago Daily Tribune*, 30 March 1954, Part 2, p .a7.

88 Larry Wolters, "Thousands See TV Colorcast; Show Praised," *Chicago Daily Tribune*, 2 January 1954, Special Television Section, p. b1. A recent broadcast of the Tournament of Roses Parade from Pasadena, California, had similarly compromised results with reds morphing into burgundy or violet and colors disappearing altogether into monochrome.

89 Brown, "The American Networks," 267.

CHAPTER 12

1 "British Films Near Deal On Television: BBC Services Reported Being Made Available to Owners of Motion Picture Houses," *New York Times*, 9 November 1948, p. 54.

2 "Closed-Circuit TV Finds Picture Good as Industries use of Medium Increases," *New York Times*, 12 January 1959, p. 63.

3 Early Television Museum, Pre-1945 Electronic Television, RCA Pre-1945 Television Systems, earlytelevision.org.

4 Everett M. Walker, "Television Entertainment Gains as New Developments Are Made," *New York Herald Tribune*, 25 October 1931, p. C3. As early as 1931, a successful American experiment projected large-size images onto a New York theater screen. At that time, Edgar Wallace, chief visual engineer of W2XAB, also devised a system for "superimposing scenic effects that merge with the images of the performer before the television scanner." It was believed that the system could be used together with boxers in a studio to superimpose them "on a film showing a real ring with its surrounding crowd and general atmosphere."

5 Early Television Museum, Pre-1945 Electronic Television, RCA Pre-1945 Television Systems, earlytelevision.org.

6 "Big Image Television Demonstrated," *Radio and Television*, July 1941, 140.

7 Russ Ratchet, "1,000,000 Ringside Seats," *Mechanix Illustrated*, August 1941, p. 44.

8 Caswell Adams, "Soose Outpoints Overlin in 15 Rounds at Garden and Captures World Middleweight Title," *New York Herald Tribune*, 10 May 1941, p. 15.

9 "Big Image Television Demonstrated," 140.

10 "Theater Audience Attends Fight by Television," *Popular Mechanics*, September 1941, p. 6.

11 "1,000,000 Ringside Seats," p. 45.

12 Jack Gould, "Television Shown on Theatre Screen: 'Sneak Preview' at Paramount Sees 15 Minutes of Boxing Run into the Newsreel," *New York Times*, 15 April 1948, p. 27.

13 *Time* 51 (April 26 1948): 53. When the telecast of the boxing match began, the mere mention of Brooklyn brought cheers from the crowd. Many in the audience missed the explanation of the significance of what they were seeing and thought it was a typical newsreel.

14 Dan Streible, *Fight Pictures: A History of Boxing and Early Cinema* (Berkeley: University of California Press, 2008), 288.

15 "GE-Rauland-Fox Test Theater Video at WRGB," *Billboard* (April 13 1946). In 1946, a GE-Rauland-Fox test had already proven "that a passable picture could be projected direct from a receiving tube."

16 "Television Shown on Theatre Screen," p. 27.

17 Jack Gould, "Free Home TV Challenged: Only Theatres to Get Bout," *New York Times*, 6 June 1951, p. 1.

18 Ibid.

19 Ibid.

20 James P. Dawson, "Video In Theatres Seen Sports Boon: 'Fantastic' Success of Plan With Louis-Savold Fight to Lead to Expansion," *New York Times*, 17 June 1951, p. S9.

21 Ibid.

22 "Stock Market Closes Lower After Upturn," *Chicago Daily Tribune*, 19 June 1951, p. B7.

23 Dawson, "Video In Theatres," p. S9; "C.B.S. - T.V. To Offer Film Of Louis Bout," *New York Times,* 19 June 1951, p. 40.

24 "Louis-Savold Fight to Lead to Expansion," *New York Times,* 17 June 1951, p. S9.

25 "Local TV Viewers to Miss Title Bout: Robinson-Turpin Fight at Polo Grounds Sept. 12 to Be Shown in Theatres Outside City," *New York Times,* 14 August 1951, p. 31.

26 Ibid.

27 Jack Gould, "TV Dispute Rages On Fight Coverage: Protests Reaches Congress as the Movies Take First Step to Protect Box Office," *New York Times,* 14 September 1951, p. 35.

28 "New York: Sellout and Knockout," *New York Times,* 16 September 1951, p. E2.

29 Frank Mastro, "New York Fight Fans Make Vain Trip To Philly," *Chicago Daily Tribune,* 13 September 1951, Part 6, p. d2.

30 "Sellout and Knockout," p. E2.

31 Louis Effrat, "Loser's Followers: Visiting Press Demur, but Most Praise Goldstein," *New York Times,* 13 September 1951, p. 40.

32 "Telecast List Increased," *New York Times,* 18 August 1951, p. 17; "Saddler, Pep to Meet Wednesday in Title Bout at Polo Grounds: Fourth Installment of the Featherweight Rivalry to Draw $150,000 Gate—Champion Counts on Speed," *New York Times,* 23 September 1951, p. 167.

33 "TV Makers Gird for Battle for Sports in Home," *Chicago Daily Tribune,* 19 July 1951, p. D1.

34 Larry Wolters, "Home Viewers Get Thrill, Walcott A Title," *Chicago Daily Tribune,* 19 July 1951, p. W6.

35 "TV Set Makers to Bid for More Boxing Events," *Chicago Daily Tribune,* 20 July 1951, Part 3, p. b3.

36 Larry Wolters, "Video Industry and Jersey Joe Hit Theater T.V.," *Chicago Daily Tribune,* 19 July 1951, p. n6.

37 "TV Set Makers To Bid," p. b3.

38 "TV Makers Get Louis-Marciano Bout for Homes: Join with Razor Firm to Foot Bill," *Chicago Daily Tribune,* 18 October 1951, p. F2.

39 Joseph C. Nichols, "Ex-Champion Set for Unbeaten Foe: 10 Years Older and 23 Pounds Heavier, Louis Aims to End Marciano Streak at 37," *New York Times,* 26 October 1951, p. 29.

40 "$80,000 For Broadcast: Fighters to Share in TV and Radio Revenue at Chicago," *New York Times,* 11 April 1952, p. 27.

41 Larry Wolters, "Fred Allen Set for Quiet Life, Stage, Radio, TV: His Doctor Won't Stand for Steady Grind," *Chicago Daily Tribune,* 22 July 1951, p. 23.

42 "No TV for Marciano Bout: Blackout for Matthews Clash Will Include Theatres," *New York Times,* 16 July 1952, p. 30.

43 "Facts on Title Fight," *New York Times,* 23 June 1952, p. 24.

44 "Four Theaters To Show Title Battle On TV," *Chicago Tribune,* 22 June 1952, p. a5.

45 "Facts on Title Fight," *New York Times,* 23 June 1952, p. 24.

46 "Theatre TV to Get Bout in 30 Cities. Marciano-Walcott Fight Will Be On Screen In 49 Movie Houses, 8 of Them Here," *New York Times*, 19 September 1952, p. 29.

47 "Title Fight On TV Screen in Orpheum," *Los Angeles Times*, 23 September 1952, p. C3.

48 "Radio Injunction Sought: Asks Restraint on Broadcast of Running Account of Bout," *New York Times*, 22 September 1953, p. 41.

49 Theater Television of Fight Proves Successful Locally," *Washington Post and Times Herald*, 19 June 1954, p. 15.

50 "'Fight Fans' Calls Jam Switchboard at Times," *New York Times*, 24 September 1952, p. 41.

51 Jack Gould, "Radio and Television: 'Eavesdroppers' Hear Maxim-Robinson Title Bout by Listening to Canadian Broadcast," *New York Times*, 27 June 1952, p. 30.

52 "Radio Curb Is Flouted: Some Stations Defy the I.B.C. With Blow-By-Blow Broadcasts," *New York Times*, 25 September 1953, p. 24; "Weigh Decision In I.B.C. Title Bout Suit," *Chicago Daily Tribune*, 23, September 1953, p. C5.

53 William R. Conklin, "500,000 Expected to See Bout on TV," *New York Times*, 20 September 1957, p. 31. Women comprised as much as 40 percent of the audience for a typical theater showing.

54 Jesse Abramson, "Marciano and Walcott Meet for Heavyweight Title Friday," *New York Herald Tribune*, 10 May 1953, p. B3.The 3-D theater showing of Marciano-Walcott II was held three days after the fight, which was telecast live by NBC on commercial television.

55 William R. Conklin, "500,000 Expected to See Bout on TV," *New York Times*, 20 September 1957, p. 31.

56 Ibid.

57 Dan Hafner, "Ending Expected," *Los Angeles Times*, 23 July 1963, p. C2.

58 Sam Andre, Nat Fleischer, *A Pictorial History of Boxing*, (Bonanza Books: New York 1975), 170. Almost a decade later during a closed-circuit broadcast of the first Ali-Frazier fight in 1971, the equipment malfunctioned in the Chicago Coliseum. A riot ensued with the fans wrecking the arena.

59 Deane McGowen, "140 Cities Will Get Basilio Bout on Closed-Circuit TV Tuesday," *New York Times*, 20 March 1958, p. 37.

60 Sidney Lohman, "News of Radio and Television: 'Studio Audience,'" *New York Times*, 13 June 1954, p. X11.

61 "Ban Television, Radio for Matthews, Marciano Bout," *Chicago Daily Tribune*, 16 July 1952, Part 3, p. b3; Val Adams, "Small Disposes of TV Interests," *New York Times*, 7 August 1957, p. 39; Val Adams, "'Telephone Time' Will End April 1," *New York Times*, 24 January 1958, p. 47; Robert L. Teague, "Liston-Patterson Fight Is Expected To Bring In More Than $5,000,000," *New York Times*, 23 September 1962, p. 200.

62 Radio broadcast of the Rocky Marciano-Archie Moore fight, originally aired September 21, 1955.

63 Joseph C. Nichols, "Marciano to Defend Heavyweight Crown Against La Starza Here on Thursday," *New York Times*, 20 September 1953, p. S7; "Title Bout Off Home TV," *New York Times*, 21 April, 1954, p. 38.

64 William J. Briordy, "Ray Robinson Calls Off Fight After TV Dispute: Champion Claims Pack Is Violated," *New York Times*, 21 August 1957, p. 35.

65 "Before Shouting Began: Fight Basilio or Lose Title, Robinson Told," *Los Angeles Times*, 27 August 1957, p. B1.

66 Gordon S. White Jr., "Robinson to Ask Govenor's Help," *New York Times*, 22 August 1957, p. 34.

67 "Robinson Would Bar TV," *New York Times*, 26 August 1957, p. 27.

68 Gay Talese, "Robinson Agrees to the Theatre-TV Guarantee for Basilio Title Fight," *New York Times*, 30 August 1957, p. 14.

69 Ibid.

70 Conklin, "500,000 Expected," p. 31.

71 "Pooled Closed-Circuit TV Urged for Robinson Fight," *New York Herald Tribune*, 24 August 1957, p. B3. By 1957, approximately one in three theaters could be outfitted to telecast in color.

72 "Boxing Crowds Will Go to See and Stay to View," *New York Times*, 1 February 1958, p. 16.

73 McGowen, "140 Cities," p. 37.

74 "Closed Circuit TV Fights Due Here Oct. 16," *Boston Globe*, 12 September 1962, p. 41. The practice proved to be a success. It was utilized at the promoter's discretion provided it was within the rules and regulations of the governing state athletic commission. In 1962, promoter Sam Silverman gave a closed-circuit/live card presentation from the Boston Arena that featured Gene Fullmer versus Dick Tiger from Candlestick Park, San Francisco. Almost a quarter-of-a-century later, the practice was still being used with the closed-circuit broadcast of the Marvelous Marvin Hagler-Thomas Hearns title clash, which followed a live card at the Boston Garden.

75 Ibid.

76 Ibid.

77 John De La Vega, "TelePrompTer Draws Blast from Pilot as Boxing's New Monopoly," *Los Angeles Times*, 2 May 1961, p. C3.

78 "Head of N.B.A. Warns Boxing on TV Control," *New York Herald Tribune*, 2 September 1959, p. B2.

79 "Court Decree Breaks Kahn TV Fight Grip," *Los Angeles Times*, 6 February 1960, p. A3.

80 "TV Money Across the Nation Is Tied Up by Revenue Agents," *New York Times*, 27 September 1962, p. 60.

81 Joe Nichols, "Fight Looks Good At 144 Box Offices," *New York Times*, 18 July 1963, p. 20.

82 John Hall "Liston Hypnotizes SRO TV Crowds Here," *Los Angeles Times*, 26 September 1962, p. C2.

83 "Floyd-Sonny TV Rights Sold; Biggest Ever," *New York Herald Tribune,* 25 June 1962, p. 20.
84 "Title Fight Seen By 192,762 on TV," *New York Times,* 3 September 1958, p. 44.
85 "$5,000,000 Gate Seen For Patterson-Ingo Bout," *Boston Globe,* 20 January 1961, p. 35.
86 Ibid. While Patterson is not known for being a civil rights activist, he took a stance in the third Johansson match, requiring there be no segregated seating at the Convention Hall in Miami. Mayor D. Lee Powell of Miami Beach gave his assurances, and the promoter Feature Sports headed by Roy Cohn posted a $10,000 bond as a guarantee.
87 William R. Conklin, "Garden to Show Patterson Bout on Closed-Circuit TV March 13," *New York Times,* 11 January 1961, p. 11.
88 Val Adams, "News of T.V. and Radio," *New York Times,* 15 May 1960, p. X15.
89 Joseph C. Nichols, "2,000,000 Gross Looms For Fight," *New York Times,* 20 June 1960, p. 36.
90 "TV Boxing at Pilgrim," *Daily Boston Globe,* 29 March 1950, p. 28.
91 Special to the *New York Times,* "New Process Puts TV in Movie Theaters," *New York Times,* 21 November 1963, p. 43.
92 Larry Wolters, "Plan To Test Ownership of Video Shows," *Chicago Daily Tribune,* 13 February 1948, p. 19.
93 "Use of Present Tense Barred In Radio Reports of Title Fight," *New York Times,* 19 August 1958, p. 55.
94 William Boddy, "The Beginnings of American Television," in *Television: An International History* (New York: Oxford University, Press, 1995), 50.
95 Jack Gould, "The Experiment," *New York Times,* 18 March 1962, p. 131.
96 "Box-Office TV Foes to Petition F.C.C.," *New York Times,* 20 June 1951, p. 35.
97 Boddy, "The Beginnings of American Television," 51–52.
98 Ibid.
99 Gould, "The Experiment," p. 131.
100 Nitin Bhandari, "Top 10 Highest-Grossing Pay-Per-View Boxing Matches," therichest.com, November 21, 2013.
101 Brian Steinberg, "Mayweather-Pacquiao Boxing Match Shatters Pay-Per View Records," variety.com, May 12, 2015.

CHAPTER 13

1 James P. Dawson, "Boxing, Wrestling, Net State $469,248: Tax Yield for 1946 on Nearly $8,000,000 Cross Almost Doubles That for 1945," *New York Times,* 16 January 1947, p. 36.
2 Jesse Abramson, "Janiro to Battle Roach Jan.16 in Garden Bout," *New York Herald Tribune,* 24 December 1947, p. 21.
3 "Garden Must Televise Bouts; Managers Moan," *Chicago Daily Tribune,* 9 August 1947, p. 17.
4 Paul Zimmerman, "Sportscripts," *Los Angeles Times,* 22, September 1947, p. 8.

5 Ibid.
6 Ibid; Cal Whorton, "Enrique Bolanos Tabbed Outstanding Local Boxer," *Los Angeles Times*, 28 December 1947, p. A8.
7 "'Times' Dinner Fetes Sports' Best Of '47," *Los Angeles Times*, 30 December 1947, p. 11.
8 Cal Whorton, "Legion Fight Television Parley Fails," *Los Angeles Times*, 31 December 1947, p. 8.
9 "Hollywood May Be Dark Friday," *Los Angeles Times*, 6 January 1948, p. 12.
10 "Legion, Pilots Declare Truce; Fights Tonight," *Los Angeles Times*, 9 January 1948, p. A9.
11 "Managers Give Decision Today," *Los Angeles Times*, 7 January 1948, p. A9.
12 "Legion, Pilots Declare Truce," p. A9.
13 Jesse Abramson, "Boxing Guild to Boycott Garden Unless Cut In On Video Receipts," *New York Herald Tribune*, 28 March 1948, p. B2.
14 "St. Nick Bills Bouts In Defiance of Strike," *New York Herald Tribune*, 20 April 1948, p. 33.
15 "Garden Threatens to Drop Pro Boxing," *New York Times*, 29 April 1948, p. 27.
16 Ibid.
17 "Managers Guild Rejects Strauss Television Offer," *New York Herald Tribune*, 10 April, 1948, p. 15
18 "Garden Threatens To Drop Pro Boxing," p. 27.
19 "Boxers Guild to Meet," *New York Times*, 30 April 1948, p. 32.
20 "Video Share of 25% For Boxers Is Seen," *New York Times*, 7 May 1948, p. 30.
21 Michael Strauss, "Boxing Battle over Television Receipts Here Is Settled," *New York Times*, 11 May 1948, p. 32.
22 "Eagan Advocates Clinics for Boxing," *New York Times*, 13 January 1949, p. 29.
23 William J. Briordy, "Garden Bid Fails; Graham Fight Off," *New York Times*, 26 May 1949, p. 41; "All Summer Fights By Garden Group in New York Cancelled," *Chicago Daily Tribune*, 27 May 1949, p. B1.
24 Jesse Abramson, "Managers' Video Dispute with Garden Stalls Robinson-Gavilan Signing," *New York Herald Tribune*, 27 May 1949, p. 23; Jesse Abramson, "Bolanos-Graham Fight Off as Managers Fail to Accept Garden's Television Offer," *New York Herald Tribune*, 26 May 1949, p. 30.
25 "Boxing Battle Settled, Managers Guild, Garden Agree on Television Split to Fighters," *New York Times*, 14 June 1949, p. 39.
26 "2 Clubs Agree on Video Split with Fighters," *New York Herald Tribune*, 3 June 1949, p. 23. Other independent venues in New York faced the same television issue as the Garden. Just prior to the Garden settling its dispute, management of the Queensboro Arena and the Coney Island Velodrome settled with the boxing Managers, with main-event fighters splitting evenly 50 percent of the television receipts.
27 "Dove of Peace Coos at Legion Mitt Gathering," *Los Angeles Times*, 28 June 1948, p. C3.

28 Frank Finch, "Managers Boycott Legion Stadium," *Los Angeles Times*, 23 January 1949, p. 23.
29 "Ring Managers Ask for 50% Radio-Video Cut," *New York Times*, 6 April 1950, p. 47.
30 "Boxing Guild Ultimatum: Managers Demand 50 Percent of Video, Radio From I.B.C.," *New York Times*, 22 April 1950, p. 28.
31 William J. Briordy, "Graziano's Signing Cut Off By Dispute," *New York Times*, 16 May 1950, p. 45.
32 "New Issue in Boxing Row, Pilots, Trainers, Split Over Title-Bout Spar Mates," *New York Times*, 31 May 1950, p. 44.
33 Briordy, "Graziano's Signing Cut Off," p. 45.
34 "Managers Guild Rejects Norris TV Money Offer," *Chicago Daily Tribune*, 29 June 1950, p. D2.
35 "Ring Managers Accept Offer," *Baltimore Sun*, 15 July 1950, p. 12.
36 "N.Y. Boxing Boycott Ends," *Los Angeles Times*, 15 July 1950, p. B3.
37 "The News of Radio: Work on Washington Cable Halts Telecasts of Events From National Capital," *New York Times*, 12 November 1947, p. 54.
38 Barney Nagler, *James Norris and the Decline of Boxing* (Indianapolis, New York: The Bobbs-Merrill Company, Inc., 1964), pp. 89–92, 109–111.
39 Ibid., p. 90, pp. 110–111.
40 Frank Mastro, "Salas-Carter Fight Moved for T.V. Cash," *Chicago Daily Tribune*, 8 October 1952, Part 4, p. c4.
41 Sidney Lohman, "News and Notes Garnered From The Studios," *New York Times*, 7, November, 1948, p. X 11.
42 *New York Times*, 10 June 1948, p. 31.
43 "Philly Boxing War Brews," *Baltimore Sun*, 6 August 1948, p. ES20.
44 "Radio and Television: Video Barred for Robinson-Belloise Bout Aug. 24—CBS Will Carry Broadcast," *New York Times*, 15 August 1949, p. 32; Joseph C. Nichols, "Eagan Denies Bout World Title Claim: State Commissioner Suggests Charles-Lesnevich Be Part of Elimination Series," *New York Times*, 30 July 1949, p. 11.
45 "Radio and Television: Walcott and Charles Heavyweight Match, June 22 to Be Seen on NBC Video," *New York Times*, 15 June 1949, p. 58.
46 Frank Mastro, "Louis Respects Robinson's Punch, Picks Robinson. Ex-Champion Recalls His Knockout by Schmeling," *Chicago Daily Tribune*, 16 April 1952, p. C2.
47 Frank Mastro, "TV Fights Help Maintain Boxing Interest During '53," *Chicago Daily Tribune*, 20 December 1953, Part 2, p. a3.
48 "Boston Promoter Blacks Out I.B.C.," *Chicago Daily Tribune*, 14 January 1956, Part 3, p. b1.
49 Frank Mastro, "Eight Bouts at Stadium Draw 14,521," *Chicago Daily Tribune*, 31 August 1956, Part 4, p. C5.
50 "New York to be Blacked Out on Monday Fight TV," *Chicago Daily Tribune*, 20 January 1955, Part 6, p. d3.

51 "I.B.C. Backing TV Talent Show for Young Boxers," *Philadelphia Tribune,* 6 January 1953, p. 11.

52 Arthur Daley, "Is Boxing on the Ropes?: Yes, Says a Veteran Critic of the Manly Art Who Can Remember Tony Canzoneri as a Preliminary Boy—And He Blames It All On TV," *New York Times,* 31 January 1954, p. SM19.

53 Jesse A. Linthicum, "Sunlight on Sports," *Baltimore Sun,* 28 June 1953, p. 2D.

54 "Boxer Stages Fight Card Exclusively for TV Fans," *Daily Boston Globe,* 19 July 1950, p. 20.

55 Loubet and Ort, *The 1979 Ring Boxing Encyclopedia and Record Book,* 120.

56 "Costa Triumphs in Chestnut Bout," *New York Times,* 17 February 1954, p. 38.

57 https://en.wikipedia.org/wiki/DuMont_Television_Network

58 "Fight Television Approved," *New York Times,* 6 May 1954, p. 48.

59 Val Adams, "N.B.C.- TV To Drop Detective Series," *New York Times,* 31 October 1960, p. 54. As the oldest fight club in America, St. Nick's would continue to operate, regardless of the loss of their television network and other financial and industry woes. Although they were without the network coverage they enjoyed on television courtesy of NBC and DuMont, they reemerged locally in New York on WPIX with veteran announcer Jimmy Powers. calling the action. The arena would eventually close its doors in 1962.

60 Mike Gray, "What's Wrong with TV Boxing?" *Chicago Daily Tribune,* 7 July 1956, TV Week section, p. c8.

61 Ibid.

62 Ibid.

63 Frank M. Blunk, "Boxing Monopoly Charges Are Denied: Member of Guild Testify at Inquiry," *New York Times,* 13 November 1954, p. 20.

64 Ibid.

65 Frank M. Blunk, "Boxing Board Suspends Six Pending Official Hearing of Monopoly Charges. Commission Acts Against 4 Pilots," *New York Times,* 20 November 1954, p. 14; "N.Y. Ring Body Suspends Six," *Baltimore Sun,* 20 November 1954, p. 15.

66 "Boxers Gifts Lead To Fine, Suspension," *Chicago Daily Tribune,* 24 November 1954, p. B5.

67 William J. Briordy, "Helfand Moves To Abolish Boxing Managers' Guild: Athletic Group Moves to Be Disbanded by Jan.15—Members Regard Action as Threat to Bouts in State," *New York Times,* 13 December 1955, p. 1; "Sports of the Times: Witness For the Prosecution," *New York Times,* 14 December 1955, p. 55.

68 Undoubtedly, this reference was addressing the guild's relationship with smaller promoters and copromoters with the IBC, but not the IBC itself. The IBC controlled television and had great sway over the guild.

69 Briordy, "Helfand Moves To Abolish," p. 1.

70 Anthony Lewis, "Boxing Guild, Managers Johnston and Daly Indicted By Federal Grand Jury," *New York Times,* 11 January 1956, p. 38.

71 "N.Y. Will Ban Boxing Guild," *Baltimore Sun,* 13 December 1955, p. 21.

72 Joseph C. Nichols, "Norris Fears TV Tangle After Move to Bar Boxing Managers Guild: Ring Pilots Ready To Challenge Ban," *New York Times*, 14 December 1955, p. 57.

73 Joseph C. Nichols, "Norris Assures Helfand of Cooperation and Continuation of Boxing Here," *New York Times*, 7 January 1956, p. 12.

74 Nichols, "Norris Fears TV Tangle," p. 57.

75 Joseph C. Nichols, "New York Boxing Managers Vote to Ignore Helfand's Order to Quit Guild," *New York Times*, 6 January 1956, p. 27.

76 Ibid.

77 "New York Loses Monday Night Television Fights," *Washington Post and Times Herald*, 4 January 1956, p. 17.

78 Julius Helfand, "My Battle With The Fight Mob," *Saturday Evening Post* 228 (9 June 1956): 36–146.

79 Ibid.

80 "Helfand's Partner Owns Coliseum," *Washington Post and Times Herald*, 5 January 1956, p. 29. Nahum Bernstein, one of Helfand's law partners, owned the Baltimore Coliseum. Bernstein claimed that he didn't think that Helfand knew he owned the Coliseum, nor did he know that Sullivan and Gilzenberg wanted to rent the arena in response to the Helfand edict. Bernstein did admit, "I knew Julie had some of the boys on the run."

81 Nichols, "Norris Assures Helfand," p. 12.

82 Joseph C. Nichols, "Marciano's Pilot Resigns, Dooming Local Ring Guild," *New York Times*, 8 January, 1956, p. S1.

CHAPTER 14

1 1. "New Ring Group Moves in on Jacobs," *Los Angeles Times*, 9 April 1948, p. A9; Nagler, *James Norris and the Decline Of Boxing*, 38.

2 Ibid.

3 "Fusari Knocks Out Larkin In the 6th Round," *New York Times*, 22 October 1948, p. 34; "Fusari Stops Tippy Larkin in 6th Round," *Baltimore Sun*, 22 October 1948, p. 19.

4 Nagler, *James Norris and the Decline of Boxing*, 38.

5 Jesse Abramson, "C.B.S. Becomes Partner in Tournament of Champions," *New York Herald Tribune*, 2 December 1948, p. 31.

6 "Tournament of Champions Makes Huge Sports Television Plans," *Los Angeles Times*, 2 December 1948, p. C3.

7 James P. Dawson, "Set-Up for T of C Formally Revised; Group Now Allied With Entertainment Firms to Develop Sports for Television," *New York Times*, 2 December 1948, p. 44.

8 "Niederreiter Quits As T.C. Matchmaker," *New York Times*, 11 December 1948, p. 19.

9 "T. of C. Leases 34th Street Arena as Boxing Club," *New York Herald Tribune*, 6 January1949, p. 22; "March Bout Planned For Villemain Here," *New York Times*, 6 January 1949, p. 31.
10 "Payne-Sheppard Top Gotham Card," *Los Angeles Times*, 19 January 1949, p. C4.
11 Frank Mastro, "I.B.C. Gets Sole Right to Hold Stadium Bouts," *Chicago Daily Tribune*, 11 August 1949, Part 3, p. a2.
12 "$300,000 Receipts Forecast By Louis: Television, Radio Rights Not Included in Estimate on Walcott-Charles Bout," *New York Times*, 11 May 1949, p. 42.
13 "Deal in Making for Sale of the T. of C. to Garden Combine," *New York Times*, 12 May 1949, p. 38; Edward Prell, "I.B.C. Men Confer with Garden Head," *Chicago Daily Tribune*, 14 May 1949, p. A3.
14 "Radio and Television: Garden Arranges for Boxing Bouts to Be Aired—Networks Will Split Coverage," *New York Times*, 8 July 1949, p. 36.
15 "Cerdan Returns to Fight La Motta, Arrangements Being Made for Champion to Defend Title in Detroit Ring June 15," *New York Times*, 21 May 1949, p. 16.
16 "Purchasing of the T of C by N.Y. Garden Sets Up Greatest Boxing Monopoly," *Daily Boston Globe*, 12 May 1949, p. 15.
17 "Cerdan, La Motta Sign Articles For Detroit Title Bout June 15: Frenchman to Defend for First Time World Crown He Won From Zale Last September," *New York Times*, 24 May 1949, p. 36.
18 Frank Mastro, "N.B.A. Chiefs Arrive Today for Meeting," *Chicago Daily Tribune*, 8 September, 1951, p. A4.
19 "Pro Football Sued By U.S. On TV Curb. Violation of Trust Law Charged to National League in a Test Aimed at All Sports on Air," *New York Times*, 10 October 1951, p. 1.
20 "Suit Urged To End Boxing Monopoly. Federal Jury Advises Trust Action—Athletic Body Rules on Contracts Next Week," *New York Times*, 8 March 1952, p. 18.
21 "U.S. Opens Monopoly Probe: Federal Jury Questions 3; Calls Robinson," *Chicago Daily Tribune*, 9 October 1951, p. B1.
22 "Suit Urged To End Boxing Monopoly," p. 18.
23 "U.S. Opens Monopoly Probe," p. B1.
24 Edward Ranzal, Government Files Anti-Trust Suit Here Against International Boxing Club," *New York Times*, 18 March, 1952, p. 30; "IBC, Garden and Norris Sued By Government as Boxing Monopoly," *New York Herald Tribune*, 3 March 1952, p. 26.
25 Ibid.
26 June Hearing Set to Determine If I.B.C. Should Lose Licenses. State Commission Delays Consideration of Charges of Practices Detrimental to Boxing—Expose Threat Fizzles, *New York Times*, 10 May 1952, p. 25.
27 Luther A. Huston, "Oil Latest Target of Fight On Trusts. Fewer Actions Started This Year, But Importance of Interests Involved Strikes New Note," *New York Times*, 5 January 1953, p. 80.

28 Arthur Krock, "In The Nation: The Supreme Court, 'Pro' Sports Section," *New York Times*, 1 February 1955, p. 28; "Supreme Court to Hear Governmental Appeal on Suit on Boxing: Case Against The International Club and Others Accused of Anti-Trust Act Violation, to be Argued in October," *New York Times*, 25 May 1954, p. 30.

29 "'Ring Promoters Win Bout in Court: Anti-Trust Suit Dismissed—Noonan Puts Sports in the Same Realm as Baseball," *New York Times*, 5 February 1954, p. 27.

30 "Boxing Anti-Trust Suit Goes To Supreme Court Today," *Chicago Daily Tribune*, 10 November 1954, p. C2.

31 "Rules Boxing Bound By Anti-Trust Laws: High Court Labels Sport As Business," *Chicago Daily Tribune*, 1 February 1955, p. B1.

32 "High Court Labels Sport," *Chicago Daily Tribune*, p. B1; "Theaters and Championship Fights Are Subject to Antitrust Laws," *New York Herald Tribune*, 1 February 1955, p. 1.

33 "Boxing Officials Forecast Victory: But They Expect Long Legal Fight with U.S.—Dowling Hails Theatre Ruling," *New York Times*, 1 February 1955, p. 20.

34 Arch Ward, "In the Wake of the News," *Chicago Daily Tribune*, 3 February 1955, p. D1.

35 Nagler, *James Norris and the Decline of Boxing*, 125.

36 Ibid. p. 142, citing Plaintiff's brief United States v. International Boxing Club of New York, Inc., et al.

37 Nagler, *James Norris and the Decline of Boxing*, 162.

38 Ibid, 163.

39 Ibid.

40 "TV Boxing Contract is Extended," *Chicago Daily Tribune*, 28 February 1957, Part 6, p. d2.

41 "Norris Resigns, Gibson Will Head I.B.C.," *Chicago Daily Tribune*, 19 April 1958, p. e1.

42 Frank Mastro, "Jones Battles Crawford in Stadium Ring," *Chicago Daily Tribune*, 10 September 1958, Part 4, p.c3; J.P. Shanley, "Televised Fights Shifted to A.B.C: Wednesday Night Bouts on C.B.S. Transfer June 1—Sponsor Cities Schedule," *New York Times*, 11 March 1955, p. 33.

43 Jack Hand, "International Boxing Club Told To Dissolve By Federal Judge," *Washington Post*, 25 June 1957, p. A17; Nagler, *James Norris and the Decline of Boxing*, 165.

44 Will Grimsley, "Boxing Boss Ruled Guilty of Monopoly," *Washington Post*, 9 March 1957, p. A10. Just two weeks prior, on February 25, the US Supreme Court ruled that professional football was subject to federal antitrust laws. At that time, both the majority and the dissenting opinion questioned whether baseball should also be placed in the same class.

45 "Silverman Sues I.B.C. For $9 Million in N.Y.," *Daily Boston Globe*, 18 May 1957, p. 6.

46 "Hockey Players Charge NHL with Monopoly," *Daily Boston Globe*, 11 October 1957, p. 1.

47 "Akins and Jordan Sign," *New York Times,* 30 October 1958, p. 39.

48 Frank Mastro, "I.B.C Ends its 10 Year Rule Over Boxing in Illinois," *Chicago Daily Tribune,* 27 January 1959, Part 3, p. b2.

49 "TV Plan Set by Stadium and Skiatron," *Chicago Daily Tribune,* 7 April 1959, Part 4, p.c2. Their commercial television empire dismantled, Norris and Wirtz, who still headed the Chicago Stadium Corporation, soon signed an agreement with Skiatron, Inc., to televise events for home subscription and large screen television; Frank Mastro, "Award N.B.E. 5 Stadium TV Boxing Dates," *Chicago Daily Tribune,* 9 December 1959, Part 4, p.c3. The IBC's Truman Gibson also reconstituted himself in a venture with Norris, grabbing his pro-rata share of the independently promoted commercial television world as vice president of National Boxing Enterprises, Inc., securing five network television fights with Chicago Stadium to be broadcast in early 1960.

50 "Norris Sees End of Weekly Fights on TV," *Chicago Daily Tribune,* 13 January 1959, Part 3, p. b2.

51 Ibid.

52 Richard F. Shepard, "NBC May Drop Fights on Friday," *New York Times,* 9 January 1960, p. 43.

53 William R. Conklin, "Sponsor Shifts to New Network," *New York Times,* 17 March 1960, p. 40; Jesse Abramson, "ABC Replaced NBC in Multi-Million TV Deal," *New York Herald Tribune,* 17 March 1960, p. 27.

54 Conklin, "Sponsor Shifts to New Network," p. 40. The cost for the rights was $24,500 per broadcast. "Blackouts" were intended to be kept to a minimum. The number of championship bouts would be consistent with previous years.

55 Loubet and Ort, *The 1979 Ring Boxing Encyclopedia and Record Book,* 120.

56 Jack Gould, "Television Network Will Drop Boxing From Weekly Programming in 1964," *New York Times,* 23 December 1963 p. 39.

57 Loubet and Ort, *The 1979 Ring Boxing Encyclopedia and Record Book,* 120.

58 Gould, "Television Network Will Drop Boxing," p. 39.

59 Randy Roberts, "The Wide World of Muhammad Ali: The Politics and Economics of Televised Boxing," in *Muhammad Ali, The People's Champ,* ed. Elliott J. Gorn (Chicago: University of Illinois Press, 1995), 38.

60 Robert Lipsyte, "Boxing Blackout Regarded As Bane and Benefit," *New York Times,* 23 December 1963, p. 39.

61 Ibid.

CHAPTER 15

1 The Horton Law had no limit to the number of rounds a match could be scheduled, allowed for a decision by the referee, and was not regulated by the New York State Athletic Commission.

2 J. J. Johnston and Sean Curtin, *Chicago Boxing* (Charleston, S.C.: Arcadia Publishing, 2005), 20. Before his death in 1910 from tuberculosis, Gans admitted he took a dive. McGovern was unaware of the fraud.
3 Red Smith, "Octopus, Inc.," *New York Herald Tribune,* 30 September 1960, p. 18.
4 Nagler, *James Norris and the Decline of Boxing,* 69.
5 "Frankie Carbo, Underworld Figure Once Known as the 'Czar' of Boxing," *New York Times,* 11 November 1976, p. 46.
6 The United States Treasury Department Bureau of Narcotics, *Mafia: The Government's Secret File on Organized Crime* (New York: Skyhorse Publishing, 2009), 399.
7 Tom Wicker, "Basilio, Kearns Also Take Stand," *New York Times,* 8 December 1960, p. 49.
8 Special to the *New York Times,* "Palermo Called His Intermediary," *New York Times,* 16 June 1960, p. 42.
9 Nagler, *James Norris and the Decline of Boxing,* 22.
10 Ibid, 25–26.
11 Ibid., 29.
12 Ibid., 32–33.
13 Tom Wicker, "Boxer Describes Rise from Prison," *New York Times,* 14 December 1960, p. 54.
14 Ibid.
15 David Condon, "What Happened to Boxing?" *Chicago Daily Tribune,* 15 December 1957, Part 8, p. 24.
16 Nagler, *James Norris and the Decline of Boxing,* 96–98.
17 Ibid.
18 Ibid., 107–108.
19 Ibid., 99–100.
20 Tom Wicker, "Wallman Links I.B.C. And Convict: Manager Calls His Chances of Getting Garden Fights 'Zero' Without Carbo," *New York Times,* 7 December 1960, p. 61.
21 Red Smith, "View of Sport, Innocents at Home," *New York Herald Tribune,* 21 May 1955, p. 13.With Carbo in his corner, Wallman would become the vice president of the International Boxing Guild. Carbo was a regular guest at Wallman family weddings. Like Norris, Wallman denied a relationship with Carbo until the Carbo empire began to unravel.
22 Nagler, *James Norris and the Decline of Boxing,* 82–83.
23 Ibid., 91–92.
24 Ibid., 26.
25 Paul Zimmerman, "Palermo Linked To Ring Scandal," *Los Angeles Times,* 17 May 1959, p. C1.
26 Nagler, *James Norris and the Decline of Boxing,* 26.
27 https://en.wikipedia.org/wiki/Frank_Palermo
28 Malcom Poindexter Jr., "Sports I View: TV Bouts Here Forestalled By 'Ironman' of Boxing," *Philadelphia Tribune,* 13 January 1953, p. 10.

29 "Near Murder Laid To Boxing Thugs," *Philadelphia Tribune*, 12 January 1954, p. 11; "Arcel Slugged; Critical Condition," *New York Herald Tribune*, 20 September 1953, p. B1.

30 "Arcel Slugged; Critical Condition," p. B1. Arcel was returning from Yom Kippur Services at a Boston synagogue. He was slugged outside a hotel and taken inside, where he received eight stiches. He was then whisked by ambulance to the hospital where he was adjudged to be in critical condition.

31 "Ike Williams Tells of Spurning 4 Bribe Bids," *Los Angeles Times*, 13 December 1960, p .C1.

32 Malcom Poindexter Jr., "Sports I View: Shenanigans In Saxton-Bratton Fight (?) Came As No Big Surprise," *Philadelphia Tribune*, 2 March 1954, p. 10.

33 Ibid.

34 Wendell Smith, "Commissioner Saw Fight on Vacation," *Pittsburgh Courier*, 20 March 1954, p. 24.

35 Jack Saunders, "Gavilan May Have Finished Bratton," *Pittsburgh Courier*, 6 March 1954, p. 24

36 Carlos Acevado, "Strange Days, The Johnny Saxton Story," thecruelestsport.com, October 27, 2009.

37 Julius Helfand as told to Barney Nagler, "My Battle with the Fight Mob," in *The Saturday Evening Post*, 228 (2 June 1956): 19–80.

38 Acevado, "Strange Days, The Johnny Saxton Story," thecruelestsport.com.

39 Helfand, "My Battle With The Fight Mob," 36–146.

40 Nagler, *James Norris and the Decline of Boxing*, 122,130.

41 Rondinone, *Friday Night Fighter*, 129.

42 "Genovese Surrenders: Denies Indictment's Charge of Undercover Fight Role," *New York Times*, 30 July 1958, p. 14. Nevertheless, top members of organized crime were not necessarily disconnected from boxing's illegal activities. Vito Genovese's cousin Gabriel Genovese, "a chief lieutenant of Frankie Carbo," was indicted for operating as an unlicensed boxing manager. It is not unreasonable to argue that a portion of Gabriel's money from these activities and money from others might have been "kicked up" to Vito.

43 Wicker, "Wallman Links I.B.C.," p. 61.

44 Helfand, "My Battle With The Fight Mob," 36–146. As late as June 1956, crusading New York State Athletic Commissioner Helfand was publicly acknowledging that investigations of Carbo had established "no undercover relationships."

45 Emanuel Perlmutter, "Hogan Will Seek Racketeer Link to Boxing In City," *New York Times*, 23 March 1958, p. 1.

46 "Carbo, Boxing King, Is Seized In Hideout: Carbo Arrested; Long Hunt Ended," *New York Times*, 30 May 1959, p. 1.

47 David Lyle, "Carbo Tells N.J. Police: 'Thought It Was Rubout,'" *New York Herald Tribune*, 31 May 1959, p. 1.

48 Jim Brady, *Boxing Confidential, Power Corruption and the Richest Prize in Sport* (Lytham, UK: Milo Books, 2002). p. 96. One theory suggests that Vito Genovese's recent assassination attempt of Frank Costello and his murder of Albert

Anastasia left Carbo without his underworld protectors and vulnerable to more emboldened law enforcement officials.

49 Jack Roth, "Carbo Ends Trial With Guilty Plea," *New York Times*, 31 October 1959, p. 1.

50 Nagler, *James Norris and the Decline Of Boxing*, 226–227.

51 "Pressure Is Charged: Promoter Says Carbo Tried to Dictate Boxing Cards," *New York Times*, 15 March 1961, p. 50.

52 "Gibson Admits Telling Blinky to Leave State," *Los Angeles Times*, 27 April 1961, p. C6.

53 "Pressure Is Charged," p. 50.

54 "Leonard Tells Fears of Mob's Vengeance," *Los Angeles Times*, 28 July 1959, p. 1.

55 Tom Wicker, "Licensing Power Is Core of Plan," *New York Times*, 15 December 1960, p. 65.

56 Wicker, "Wallman Links I.B.C.," p. 61.

57 Wicker, "Licensing Power Is Core," p.65.

58 Ibid.

59 "Carbo Loses Plea: Is Given 25 Years," *New York Times*, 3 December 1961, p. 50.

60 Red Smith, "Blinky Is More Sad Than Angry," *New York Times*, 15 March 1978, p. B6. Palermo served seven and a half years of his fifteen-year sentence. "Blinky" never could get boxing out of his blood. As late as 1978, he was applying for a manager's license in Pennsylvania. He withdrew his application due to what he described as an unforgiving press that harped on his past transgressions. "I paid my debt to society," he said, "so what do they want?"

CHAPTER 16

1 Larry Wolters, "Video Stations Grow From 17 to 50 In Year: Some Vital Questions Are Raised," *Chicago Daily Tribune*, 30 December 1948, p. 12.

2 "Television Vital Factor in Divorce of Briton," *New York Times*, 13 October 1954, p. 10.

3 By The Way . . . with Bill Henry, *Los Angeles Times*, 14 March 1951, p. A1.

4 William Boddy, "The Beginnings of American Television," in *Television: An International History* (New York: Oxford University, Press, 1995), 40–41.

5 Larry Wolters, "Survey Shows How TV Alters Use of Leisure," *Chicago Tribune*, 1 August 1949, p. B6.

6 "New Gadgets Help Television Party: Serving Devices of Plastics Ease Hostesses, Task in Entertaining Guests," *New York Times*, 26 March 1949, p. M19.

7 Sidney Lohman, "News and Notes of Television," *New York Times*, 19 February 1950, p. X11.

8 John Crosby, "Radio and Television: Speechlessness at Great Length," *New York Herald Tribune*, 23 July 1951, p. 13.

9 "Judge Rules Boxer's Rights Do Not Include Television," *Baltimore Sun*, 6 December 1947, p. 13.

10 "Turner Took Fight With Cardell to Get on TV, Says Pilot," *New York Herald Tribune*, 25 December 1951, p. 24.

11 Jim Boyack, "Gil Turner Ready to Try Gavilan After Cardell Win," *Pittsburgh Courier*, 5 January 1952, p. 15.

12 "Rocky Offered Television Bouts," *Washington Post*, 14 March 1947, p. 13.

13 Francis Sugrue, "TV Reunites Boxer, 26, Here, Mother on Coast," *New York Herald Tribune*, 23 November 1952, p. 1.

14 "Television Betrays Boxer Mims; Spotted on Screen as Deserter," *Washington Post*, 20 January 1950, p. 1.

15 "Ring Managers Who Break Rules Face Life Suspension by N.B.A.," *New York Times*, 22 May 1948, p. 28.

16 "Seconds Must 'Dress Up' For Telecasts in Jersey," *New York Times*, 29 October 1948, p. 34.

17 Ibid.

18 James P. Dawson, "Last Rites Given Boxer In Hospital: Doyle, Halted by Robinson in Cleveland Fight," *New York Times*, 25 June 1947, p. 33.

19 "West, 29 Year Old Boxer, Dies From Injuries Received In Ring," *Chicago Daily Tribune*, 22 December 1950, p. B1.

20 Jerry Nason, "Boxing Faces Protests from TV Witnesses of Sonny Boy's Death," *Daily Boston Globe*, 22 September 1950, p. 19.

21 "29 Year Old Boxer,"p. B1.

22 Ric Roberts, "See $25,000 Fund for West Family," *Pittsburgh Courier*, 6 January 1951, p. 16.

23 "CBS Bans Reissue Video Films of Bout Fatal to West," *Washington Post*, 23 December 1950, p. 12.

24 "29 Year Old Boxer," p. B1.

25 Rondinone, *Friday Night Fighter*, 179.

26 "Rebroadcasts of 'Death Bout Cancelled By CBS'" *Los Angeles Times*, 23 December 1950, p. B3.

27 Jesse Abramson, "Boxer, 24, Dies of Brain Injury After Knockout on His Birthday," *New York Herald Tribune*, 24 February 1950, p. 1.

28 "Television Obscurities, Television's First Act of Censorship?" tvobscurities.com, July 25, 2009. Television censors of the period had no problem cutting the audio or adjusting video shots if warranted. The first act of television censorship occurred on the first regularly scheduled commercial television relay between WNBT in New York and WPTZ in Philadelphia on May 24, 1944. Censors objected to the sexual nature of Eddie Cantor and Nora Martin's performance of "We're Having a Baby, My Baby and Me."

29 "One of Most Brutal Fights Ever, Say Nation's Sports Writers," *Daily Boston Globe*, 26 April 1953, p. D52.

30 "US Fans Disgusted Over Hub 'Slaughter,'" *Daily Boston Globe*, 25 April 1953, p. 1.

31 "Collins to Answer Christenberry Blast on Television Tonight," *Daily Boston Globe*, 21 February 1953, p. 4. After the bout, New York State Boxing Commis-

sioner Robert K. Christenberry described Collins as not being a legitimate candidate for the lightweight title. Collins was given an opportunity for a rebuttal during the national broadcast of the Johnny Gonsalves-Henry Davis bout sponsored by Phillies Cigars.

32 Harold Kaese, "UP Front: TV May Help Refine Brutal Sport of Boxing," *Daily Boston Globe*, 28 April 1953, p. 1.

33 James P. Dawson, "Durando's Knockout of Castellani Precipitates Disorderly Scene," *New York Times*, 12 January 1952, p. 18.

34 Ibid.

35 Ibid.

36 James P. Dawson, "Boxing Fans Praise Commission for Decision Reversal to Graham," *New York Times*, 21 December 1952, p. S1.

37 Ibid.

38 "Victim in Ring Reversal on Way to Court," *Chicago Daily Tribune*, 24 December 1952, p. A1.

39 Loubet and Ort, *The 1979 Ring Boxing Encyclopedia and Record Book*, 164.

40 Bob Cooke, "Another Viewpoint," *New York Herald Tribune*, 2 March 1953, p.18. The protracted affair was ripe for the jibe of boxing journalists. "Why not save time and invite Justice Botein to preside on Friday?" one writer quipped while discussing an upcoming match. "Then everyone will know who won, including the television audience, and we won't have to wait the customary fifty-nine days."

41 "TV Boxing Show Raided: Indianapolis Teen-Age Bouts Declared Long Under Inquiry," *New York Times*, 20 December 1954, p. 40; "Johnson Acts 'Dopey' As He Sags To Canvas," *Washington Post and Times.*

42 *Herald*, 7 May 1955, p. 13.

43 "Dope Charge Laid To Mederos Pilot: Pennsylvania Inquiry Learns Cuban Boxer's Ex-Manager Was Arrested 10 Times," *New York Times*, 25 May 1955, p. 45.

44 "Hospital Firebug's Story," *Chicago Daily Tribune*, 31 March 1950, p. 1.

45 "Man Ousted at Bar Kills 1 and Wounds 2," *New York Times*, 28 May 1947, p. 28.

46 "Child Slain by Hang and Young Father Held," *Los Angeles Times*, 11 February 1952, p. 5.

47 "Two Admit Slaying Weiner: Gangster, Ex-Convicts Make Detailed Confession, Differing Only on Motive, Prosecutor Says," *New York Times*, 17 March 1948, p. 52.

48 Television Broadcast of Emile Griffith-Benny Paret III, originally aired March 24, 1962.

49 Rondinone, *Friday Night Fighter*, 197.

50 Gordon S. White, Jr., "Paret, Hurt in Ring, Given Little Chance," *New York Times*, 26 March 1962, p. 1.

51 Layhmond Robinson, "State Legislature Creates Committee for Boxing Inquiry," *New York Times*, 31 March 1962, p. 19.

52 Deane McGowen, "Clamor Grows Here and Abroad For End of Professional Boxing," *New York Times*, 5 April 1962, p. 52.

53 Jack Gould, "TV: 'Last Round' Examines Boxing, *New York Times,* 29 April 1964, p. 83.

54 Anton Remenih, "Television News and Views," *Chicago Tribune,* 16 December 1952, Part 2, p. a5.

55 Rondinone, *Friday Night Fighter,* 44.

56 "Ricky and Fred Are TV Fans," *I Love Lucy,* first broadcast June 22, 1953, by CBS.

57 Rondinone, *Friday Night Fighter,* 19.

58 James P. Dawson, "Famechon Takes Unanimous Decision Over Flanagan in Garden 10-Rounder," *New York Times,* 16 December 1950, p. 23.

59 "Sunlight-On-Sports," *Baltimore Sun,* 24 February 1951, p. 11.

60 James A. Hagerty, "A 'Serenade to Ike' Is Theme At Rally Of 15,000 In Garden," *New York Times,* 9 February 1952, p. 1.

61 "Boxing Off At Ridgewood Grove," *New York Times,* 2 June 1953, p.40; "Fight Fans Bow to the Queen," *New York Herald Tribune,* 23 May 1953, p. 15.

62 "Television and Radio Show Canceled as Networks Cover President's Talk," *New York Times,* 1 March 1956, p. 14.

63 Jane Gardner, "Here's A Twist: The Dog Goes to Television," *Chicago Daily Tribune,* 13 July 1952, p. NW5.

64 Bob Becker, "Tribune Readers Intriguing Dog Stories Show Intelligence of Man's Best Friend: Davenport, Ia., Pooch TV Addict, but Sniffs at Mat Shows," *Chicago Daily Tribune,* 7 September 1952, p. A3.

65 "A Bird Brain Tale: All Talk," *Chicago Daily Tribune,* 26 July 1954, p. 1.

66 "Animals Are Living In the Lap of Luxury, Thanks to TV," *Daily Boston Globe,* 3 December 1950, p. A56.

67 Robert Daley, "France Cries Over A New Cerdan," *New York Times,* 24 November 1959, p. 47.

68 Ibid.

69 Val Adams, "The Girl Who's Heard but Never Seen," *New York Times,* 27 April 1952, p. X11.

70 Ibid.

71 Moe Berger, "Lawyer Sings for Fans at Fights," *New York Times,* 3 December 1955, p. 22.

72 "Life Hands 2 Low Blows to Girl Fight Fan," *Chicago Daily Tribune,* 13 February 1953, p. 1.

73 David Condon, "In the Wake of News," *Chicago Daily Tribune,* 8 December 1955, p. E1.

74 "Boxing Fan Wins $64,000 Decision: Woman Psychologist, on TV Show, Answers Questions on History of the Ring," *New York Times,* 7 December 1955, p. 79.

75 Jesse A. Linthicum, "Sunlight on Sports," *The Baltimore Sun,* 15 November 1955, p. 23. In an earlier appearance on the show, Dr. Brothers tackled a series of questions that ranged from easy—Joe Louis's real name and the number of his title defenses (Joseph Louis Barrow, 25) to fairly difficult—How many Baltimoreans won world ring titles? (Five: Joe Gans, Joe Dundee, Vince Dundee, Harry Jeffra, and Kid Williams.)

76 "Boxing Fan Wins," p. 79; "$64,000 TV Quiz Won by Blonde Boxing Expert," *Daily Boston Globe*, 7 December 1955, p. 1.
77 Condon, "In the Wake of News," p. E1; "Boxing Fan Wins $64,000 Decision," p. 79.
78 Marie Torre, "A New Life for Dr. Brothers," *New York Herald Tribune*, 12 June 1956, p. A1.
79 Val Adams, "Quiz Expert Wins Commentator Job," *New York Times*, 18 May 1956, p. 51.
80 "Joyce Brothers and Pat Rooney Deny Quiz Aid," *New York Herald Tribune*, 9 October 1958, p. A5; "All Big $64,000 Stars Were Helped, Probe Told," *New York Herald Tribune*, 4 November 1959, p. 1. In 1958, when questioned by Joseph Stone, the assistant district attorney in charge of the investigation of alleged irregularities on television quiz shows, Dr. Brothers asserted that she had not received any answers or even "hints" as a contestant on *The $64,000 Question*. However, the following year, others connected with the program claimed that Nat Fleischer, editor of *The Ring* magazine and a consultant to the program, "was helping prepare" Dr. Brothers.
81 "Bloomgarden Is Beaten," *New York Times*, 9 July 1957, p. 59.

CHAPTER 17

1 Loubet and Ort, *The 1979 Ring Boxing Encyclopedia and Record Book*, 120.
2 Shagawat, "Television Recording," p. 63.
3 For a rare glimpse of Stanton's style, one can listen to the 1:46 clip of Louis-Conn II or Charles-Walcott I from June 22, 1949. The last two rounds are available in the collectors market.
4 "Dedication of RCA Seen on Television: Ceremonies of the Fair Are Depicted To Spectators," *New York Times*, 21 April 1939, p. 16.
5 Early Television Museum, Pre-1945 TV, Early Electronic Television, RCA Pre-1945 Television Systems, earlytelevision.org.
6 https://en.wikipedia.org/wiki/Gillette_Cavalcade_of_Sports.
7 https://en.wikipedia.org/wiki/Dennis_James.
8 Shagawat, "Television Recording," p. 27.
9 Wayne Oliver, "Star Era Doomed," *Baltimore Sun*, 25 April 1954, p. L12.
10 Chris Schenkel, "'I Worked in a House of Upsets," in *Television Boxing Guide*, ed. Ed Pazdur (Chicago: Windsor Press, 1954), 26.
11 Ibid.
12 NBC television broadcast of the Lahouari Godih-Don Jordan fight, originally aired August 29, 1958.
13 Jimmy Powers, "From John L. to Rocky, The Cavalcade of Boxing," in *Television Boxing Guide*, 12.
14 Val Adams, "A Commentator's View on Boxing: Jimmy Powers Discourses on the Tribulations of Fight Announcers," *New York Times*, 8 June 1952, p. X9.
15 Ibid.
16 Ibid.

17 Don Page, "Sportslook: TV's Armchair Fans Revolutionize Boxing," *Los Angeles Times*, 24 January1959, p. B5.

18 Ibid.

19 Don Dunphy, *Don Dunphy at Ringside*, 101. His first telecast with an announcing partner was the 1965 Patterson-Chuvalo bout with closed-circuit producer Lester Malitz.

20 Donald Freeman, "TV Vital to Fight Game: Dunphy," *Chicago Daily Tribune*, 23 December 1962, p .n6.

21 Jack Gregson, "'TV Can be Deceiving,'" in *Television Boxing Guide*, 22.

22 Closed-circuit TV broadcast of the Rocky Marciano-Jersey Joe Walcott I fight, originally aired September 23, 1952.

23 Ibid. Corum also detailed the controversial incident concerning a foreign substance in Marciano's eye. In between the eighth and ninth rounds: "They're trying to get that, whatever it is—chemical—or something, that they put on the cut I assume, out of Marciano's eye; he was squinting badly at the end of that round . . . apparently he is saying that something is being done, that something has got in Marciano's eyes possibly from the patch on Walcott's eye." At the beginning of Round 9: "Weill talking to referee Charley Daggert off camera . . . now, Weill says to the referee do you see that stuff on his eye, meaning on Walcott's eye." Later in that round: "Rocky's eyes are open again this round."

24 Television broadcast of the Charley Norkus-Cesar Brion fight, originally aired May 5, 1950.

25 CBS television broadcast of the Joe Louis-Ezzard Charles fight originally aired September 27, 1950.

26 https://alchetron.com/Ted-Husing-1325095-W; https://en.wikipedia.org/wiki/DuMont_Television_Network.

27 CBS television broadcast of the Joe Louis-Ezzard Charles fight.

28 Television broadcast of the Charley Norkus-Cesar Brion fight, originally aired May, 5, 1950.

29 CBS television broadcast of the Joe Louis-Ezzard Charles fight.

30 https://en.wikipedia.org/wiki/Ted_Husing.

31 "Why Did Husing Resign? Because He Was Fired," *Chicago Daily Tribune*, 10 March 1951, Special TV and Radio Section, p. a4.

32 Dunphy, *Don Dunphy at Ringside*,143.

33 Hodges used the same greeting, but it did not convey the same feeling.

34 CBS television broadcast of the Chuck Davey-Rocky Graziano fight, originally aired September 17, 1952.

35 CBS television broadcast of the Chuck Davey-Chico Vejar fight, originally aired May 7, 1952.

36 Ibid.

37 Ibid.

38 Jack Drees, "'My TV Champion,'" in *Television Boxing Guide*, 16.

39 Television broadcast of the Carmen Basilio-Tony DeMarco II fight, originally aired November 30, 1955.

40 Jack Drees, "How to Score A Fight on TV," *New York Herald Tribune*, 24 June 1956, p. F17.

41 Drees, "My TV Champion," 16.

42 Television broadcast of the Ray Robinson-Ralph Jones fight, originally aired January 19, 1955.

43 Television broadcast of the Ray Robinson-Ralph Jones fight, originally aired January 19, 1955. Perhaps at times, Hodges was a bit too complacent in his approach. During the eighth round of Tiger Jones's upset of Sugar Ray Robinson, when the tension was building and there were less than three rounds to go with Robbie trailing, Hodges left an incredible one minute and twenty seconds of dead air space!

44 Hugh Beach, "Fight of the Week—a Producer's Headache," *Chicago Daily Tribune*, 18 August 1963, p. s5.

45 Ibid.

46 Beach, "Fight of the Week," p. s5; Dunphy, *Don Dunphy at Ringside*, 164.

47 Beach, "Fight of the Week," p. s5. In another *Fight of the Week* telecast, the timekeeper's hammer broke, preventing the bell from being sounded at the three-minute mark. The din of the crowd prevented the timekeeper from catching the attention of the referee, forcing him to venture into the television production area, where he swiped a spare microphone stand. The timekeeper then proceeded to smash the implement across the bell, bending it in half, mercifully ending his personal ordeal and the round at the four-minute mark.

CHAPTER 18

1 "Jack Dempsey and Abe Roth Appear On Station KTTV," *Los Angeles Times*, 19 July 1949, p. C1.

2 "Jake La Motta Scores Knockout in Fourth Round over Tex McCrary on Television," *Washington Post*, 21 August 1949, p. C3.

3 Elizabeth L. Sullivan, Radio and Television, *Daily Boston Globe*, 21 August 1949, p. A15.

4 "Tony Zale to Appear On WGN-TV Sports Interview Tonight," *Chicago Daily Tribune*, 26 January 1949, p. B3, 63.

5 James P. Dawson, "Wrestling Bouts Return to Garden, Promoter Johnston Will Hold First Mat Program There Since 1937 on Feb. 22," *New York Times*, 20 January 1949, p. 38.

6 Hedda Hopper, "'Kiss Them For Me' Looms For Widmark," *Los Angeles Times*, 11 December 1956, p. B8.

7 "Radio and Television: N.B.C. Signs Guest Conductors and Soloists for Symphony's Summer Programs," *New York Times*, 2 June 1950, p. 31.

8 "Rocky, Braddock Assisting Louis on TV Quiz Test," *Daily Boston Globe*, 3 September 1956, p. 51.

9 Val Adams, "'Can Do' Won't Do On NBC Network," *New York Times*, 12 December 1956, p. 63.

10 Don Page, "Sportslook," *Los Angeles Times,* 26 January 1963, p. B2; John Hall, "Louis Boxing Shows to Run Weekly on TV," *Los Angeles Times,* 22 January 1963, p. B1; John Hall, "Louis TV Pact Ends in 2 Weeks," *Los Angeles Times,* 18 May 1963, A4.

11 Will Robinson, "Nation's Top Golfers Set for Joe Louis Tournament," *Pittsburgh Courier,* 20 August 1949, p. 24.

12 *The Colgate Comedy Hour,* first broadcast June 22, 1951, by NBC.

13 Val Adams, "C.B.S. Switches 3 T.V. Producers: Says Move Involving 'Best of Broadway', 'Climax', and a New Show Is Not Unusual," *New York Times,* 4 February, 1955, p. 28.

14 *I've Got A Secret,* first broadcast September 23, 1959, by CBS.

15 *This Is Your Life,* first broadcast October 23, 1960, by NBC.

16 Romano, *The Boxing Filmography,* 5.

17 "Killer's Wife," *The Abbott and Costello Show,* first broadcast in 1953.

18 Ibid.

19 Walter Ames, "Max Baer Plays White Hunter in Series; Wyman Inks Edward for Role," *Los Angeles Times,* 26 September 1955, p. 30.

20 Mellowed Max Baer Loves Everybody on Own Flourishing Television Show, Page, Don, *Los Angeles Times,* 14 September 1958, p. G6.

21 "Dies Suddenly," *Chicago Daily Tribune,* 22 November 1959, Part 2, p.b1.

22 Val Adams, "The Marriage May Be Resumed. N.B.C. and Sponsor Seek To Resolve Time Period for Cronyn-Tandy Show," *New York Times,* 8 December 1954, p. 51.

23 Val Adams, "Rocky Graziano: TV Actor and Ex-Fighter," *New York Times,* 29 November 1953, p. X11.

24 Ibid.

25 http://www.tv.com/people/rocky-graziano/

26 "Puncher and Judy," *Car 54, Where Are You?,* first broadcast April 7, 1963, by NBC.

27 Ibid.

28 *I've Got a Secret,* first broadcast February 11, 1959, by CBS.

29 Ibid.

30 Gay Talese, "Marciano Seeks Career as Actor," *New York Times,* 12 January 1957, p. 28.

31 Television broadcast of the Fritz Von Erich-"Whipper" Billy Watson wrestling match, originally aired January 12, 1961.

32 *The Colgate Comedy Hour,* first broadcast September, 19, 1954, by NBC.

33 http://www.tv.com/search?q=rocky+marciano.

34 Talese, "Marciano Seeks Career as Actor," p. 28.

35 "Masquerade," *Combat,* first broadcast October 1, 1963, by ABC.

36 *You Bet Your Life,* first broadcast April 28, 1960, by NBC. Marciano's mother, Pasqualena, appeared on the program a week before. "Did you ever hear anybody say he fought a lot of stumble bums on his way to the top?" Groucho

queried his guest about her son. "Grouch," mama Marciano begins, cocking her head slightly, "now you makin' a big mistake," she warned.

37 *You Bet Your Life*, first broadcast May 5, 1960, by NBC.
38 *Main Event*, first broadcast 1961 (episode 2).
39 *Main Event*, first broadcast 1961 (episode 3).
40 Robert Goldsborough, "Ex-Fighter La Starza Sees Action on TV," *Chicago Daily Tribune*, 10 September 1962, Part 4, p. c9.
41 Ibid.
42 *Dinah Shore Chevy Show*, first broadcast October 4, 1959, by NBC.
43 "TV: Hour-Long Variety Show With Dinah Shore," *New York Times*, 5 October 1959, p. 63.
44 Val Adams, "Johansson to Act Ex-Fighter's Role," *New York Times*, 13 October 1959, p. 78.
45 "Johansson Acts Like a Fighter, Fights Like an Actor—for TV," *New York Times*, 16 November 1959, p. 47.
46 Ibid.
47 John P. Shanley, "TV Review," *New York Times*, 20 November 1959, p. 63.
48 *What's My Line?*, first broadcast February 1, 1959, by CBS.
49 *What's My Line?*, first broadcast June 19, 1960, by CBS.
50 Robert Daley, "Nonringside View of I. Johansson," *New York Times*, 22 May 1960, p. SM30.
51 *What's My Line?*, first broadcast December 16, 1956, by CBS.
52 John P. Shanley, "Olivier and Bergman Win Emmys," *New York Times*, 21 June 1960, p. 67.
53 Dave Anderson, *Sugar Ray, The Sugar Ray Robinson Story* (New York: Da Capo Press, 1994), 238–245.
54 "Sugar Ray," first broadcast July 9, 1989, by CBS.
55 "Robinson to Get $5,600 For Singing Before Bout," *New York Times*, 8 September 1962, p. 22.
56 "Dancing, A Man's Game," *Omnibus*, first broadcast on December 21, 1958, by NBC.
57 Val Adams, "Money Is Found In TV Education," *New York Times*, 26 September 1957, p. 37; Val Adams, "'Green Pastures' Turns To Fighter," *New York Times*, 16 September 1957, p. 55.
58 Adams, "Green Pastures," p. 55.
59 *What's My Line?*, first broadcast July 1, 1956, by CBS.
60 Lu Riles, "They Belted Their Way Into TV," *Chicago Daily Tribune*, 31 August 1957, Part 4, p. c7; Don Page, "Exposure He Gets as TV's U.S. Marshal, Is Amazing Thing to Johnny Bromfield," *Los Angeles Times*, 14 December 1958, p. G5.
61 Ibid.
62 Priscilla Campbell, "No Changes Wanted: Barbi's Face Is His Video Fortune," *New York Times*, 4 July 1954, p. X9.
63 Bob Cooke, "Vince Barbi, Preliminary Fighter," *New York Herald Tribune*, 9 November 1957, p. A1.

64 Campbell, "No Changes Wanted," p. X9.

CHAPTER 19

1 "The Giant Jack Rabbit," *The Beverly Hillbillies,* first broadcast January 8, 1964, by CBS.

2 "Jack Goes to a Concert," *The Jack Benny Program,* first broadcast December 11, 1960, by CBS.

3 "The Kleebob Card Game," *The George Burns and Gracie Allen Show,* first broadcast October 12, 1950, by CBS.

4 "Bub's Sacrifice," *My Three Sons,* first broadcast June 13,1963, by CBS.

5 "The Doreen Maney Story," *The Untouchables,* first broadcast March 31, 1960, by ABC.

6 "The Bridge Group," *The Adventures of Ozzie and Harriet,* first broadcast June 4, 1958, by ABC.

7 "The Seventh Vote," *The Untouchables,* first broadcast May, 18, 1961, by ABC.

8 "Ring of Terror," *The Untouchables,* first broadcast April 13, 1961, by ABC.

9 "The Money Fight," *Tightrope,* first broadcast November 17, 1959, by CBS.

10 "The Prizefighter Story," *The Public Defender,* first broadcast April 8, 1954, by CBS.

11 "The Knockout," *Racket Squad,* first broadcast December 27, 1951, by CBS.

12 "Head of Fire, Feat of Clay," *Untouchables,* first broadcast April, 21 1960, by ABC.

13 "Head of Fire, Feat of Clay," "The Prizefighter Story," "The Knockout," "The Money Fight."

14 "Decision in the Ring," *The Fugitive,* first broadcast October 22, 1963, by ABC.

15 "The Opponent," *Route 66,* first broadcast June 2, 1961, by CBS.

16 "The Ganyika Kid," *Sheena, Queen of the Jungle,* first broadcast November 2, 1955.

17 "The Fighter," *Lassie,* first broadcast December 19, 1954, by CBS.

18 "Young Osceola," *Everglades,* first broadcast January 8, 1962, by CBS.

19 "Once Around the Circuit," *Adventures in Paradise,* October 17, 1960, by ABC.

20 "The Long Count," *Stage 7,* first broadcast March 27, 1955, by CBS.

21 "Knockout," *Four Star Playhouse,* first broadcast January, 1, 1953, by CBS.

22 "No Skin Off Me," *General Electric Theater,* first broadcast February 3, 1957, by CBS.

23 "Winner by Decision," *General Electric Theater,* first broadcast November 6, 1955, by CBS.

24 Ibid.

25 Special to the *New York Times,* "Palance To Star In A Boxing Story," *New York Times,* 5 September 1956, p. 55.

26 "Slapsie Maxie" Rosenbloom was also effectively used in a small role, appearing in several scenes portraying a punchy fighter reliving his past glories with other ex-pugs in a bar.

27 M. A. Schmidt, "Palance From 'Panic To Pagan,'" *New York Times,* 14 March 1954, p. X5.

28 Ibid.
29 "Requiem for a Heavyweight," *Playhouse 90,* first broadcast October 11, 1956, by CBS.
30 A few years later, director Ralph Nelson would lead a new cast in Columbia Pictures' equally memorable film production starring Anthony Quinn, Jackie Gleason, and Mickey Rooney.
31 "The Return of Gentleman Jim," *General Electric Theater,* first broadcast February 6, 1955, by CBS.
32 "The Week in Review," *Time,* 66 (August, 1955): 40; "Packing the Studio, When TV Show Calls for a Boxing Ring—Producers Come Up With Just That!," *Daily Boston Globe,* 12 February, 1950, p. A20.
33 "Fight For the Title," *Telephone Time,* first broadcast March 17, 1957, by ABC.
34 *The Red Skelton Show,* first broadcast January 6, 1952, by NBC.
35 "The Knockout," *The Roy Rogers Show,* first broadcast December 28, 1952, by NBC.
36 "Two Rings For Eddie," *The Joe Palooka Story,* first broadcast 1954.
37 "Cornered," *The Public Defender,* first broadcast March 24, 1954, by CBS.
38 "No Time At All," *Playhouse 90,* first broadcast February 13, 1958, by CBS.
39 "Second Avenue Assassin," *Man with a Camera,* first broadcast October 10, 1958, by ABC.
40 "The Picture War," *Man with a Camera,* January 4, 1960, by ABC.
41 "Man with a Camera," *New York Herald Tribune,* 16 November 1958, p. G58.
42 Romano, *The Boxing Filmography,* 80.
43 Brooks and Marsh, *The Complete Directory to Prime Time Network TV Shows,* 317.
44 "Incident of the Shambling Man," *Rawhide,* first broadcast October 9, 1959, by CBS.
45 "The Fighter," *Bat Masterson,* first broadcast November 5, 1958, by NBC.
46 "Jeff," *The Westerner,* first broadcast September 30, 1960, by NBC.
47 "A Woman Lost," *Bonanza,* first broadcast March 17, 1963, by NBC.
48 "The Willy Moran Story," *Wagon Train,* first broadcast September 18, 1957, by NBC.
49 "Incident of the Shambling Man."
50 "On Television, Sullivan, Jim Corbett Fight Today," *Washington Post and Times Herald,* 12 June 1955, p. C4.
51 "The Big Tall Wish," *The Twilight Zone,* first broadcast April 8, 1960, by CBS; "Steel," *The Twilight Zone,* first broadcast October 4, 1963, by CBS.
52 Brooks and Marsh, *The Complete Directory to Prime Time Network TV Shows,* 655–656; *The Red Skelton Show,* first broadcast February 9, 1954.
53 "The Lady and the Prizefighter," *I Married Joan,* first broadcast March 2, 1955, by NBC; "Requiem for an Underweight Heavyweight," *The Many Loves of Dobie Gillis,* first broadcast May 1, 1963, by CBS.
54 "Pardon My Gloves," *The Donna Reed Show,* first broadcast October 1, 1958, by ABC.
55 "The Black Eye," *Leave It to Beaver,* first broadcast 1957, by CBS.
56 "The Bully," *My Three Sons,* broadcast January 26, 1961, by ABC.

57 "Bud, the Boxer," *Father Knows Best*, first broadcast April 4, 1956, by NBC.

58 "Junior and the Bully," *The Life of Riley*, first broadcast March 14, 1950, by NBC.

59 "The Bully," *Dennis the Menace*, first broadcast June 10, 1962, by CBS.

60 "Who Owes Who What?" *The Dick Van Dyke Show*, first broadcast January 24, 1962, by CBS.

61 "The Bensonhurst Bomber," *The Honeymooners*, first broadcast September 8, 1956, by CBS.

62 "Chip's Last Fight," *My Three Sons*, first broadcast November 15, 1962, by ABC.

63 "Bud, the Boxer"

64 "Requiem for an Underweight Heavyweight."

EPILOGUE

1 Wesley S. Griswold, "Why TV is Going Movie-Mad," *Popular Science*, February 1955, 18; Shagawat, Television Recording, p.8,

2 "Radio & TV Coast to Coast," *Time*, August 13, 1951.

3 Arthur Schneider, *Jump Cut! Memoirs of a Pioneer Television Editor* (Jefferson, North Carolina: McFarland & Company, Inc. Publishers, 1997).

4 Ron Simon, "The Dead Sea Scroll of TV History," Paleycenter.org, August 25, 2009, There are a few rare exceptions. Possibly the earliest surviving significant footage of the medium of television is an eleven-minute clip of the August 31, 1939, live television adaptation of the melodrama *The Streets of New York or Poverty Is No Crime.*

5 Shagawat, Television Recording, p.15, There is also a very brief clip of the Louis-Conn bout running one minute and forty-six seconds that has been proffered as footage of the original television broadcast—a prekinescope recording that was made as an experiment before kinescope was commercially used. One commentator claims that the pedigree of the footage is debatable and it may in fact be 16mm film, but a visual inspection of the footage would tend to favor a claim of television broadcast originality.

6 Shagawat, p. 63. At least an "audio only" version of the original television broadcast made by the *Gillette Cavalcade of Sports* has survived. Bob Haymes, brother of actor Dick Haymes, announced the bout under his broadcasting alias Bob Stanton.

7 Albert Abramson, *The History of Television* (Jefferson, North Carolina: McFarland & Company, Inc. Publishers 2003), 48.

8 Robert Anderson, "Tape Is Revolutionizing TV!," *Chicago Daily Tribune*, 5 April 1959, p. nw16.

9 Albert Abramson, "The Invention of Television," in *Television: An International History*, ed. Anthony Smith (New York: Oxford University Press, 1995), 33.

10 Richard Wirth, "From Kinescopes to Digital Camera," provideocoalition.com, September 14, 2014.

11 Anderson, "Tape Is Revolutionizing TV!," nw 16.

12 Shagawat, p. 73.

INDEX

Note: Photographs and illustrations are indicated by page numbers in *italics*.